THE TERRITORIAL IMPERATIVE

Robert Ardrey

THE TERRITORIAL IMPERATIVE

A Personal Inquiry into the
Animal Origins of
Property and Nations

ILLUSTRATED BY
BERDINE ARDREY

COLLINS
St James's Place, London

First published in Great Britain 1967
Reprinted 1969
Reprinted 1971

ISBN 0 00 211819 X
Portions of this book have previously been published in *Life*
Copyright © 1966 by Robert Ardrey
Set in the United States of America
Printed in Great Britain by
William Clowes & Sons, Limited, London, Beccles and Colchester

TO THE MEMORY OF

Henry Eliot Howard

A Preliminary Meditation

Some years ago—it was February, 1955, late in the southern summer—I was introduced by Professor Raymond A. Dart to a room filled with fossil bones in the basement of Johannesburg's Medical School. In that room I met more than bones, for I encountered a variety of things that I had never heard of. I had never heard of man's origin on the continent of Africa. I had never heard of our probable ancestors, the australopithecines, a zoological group of small-brained erect-running creatures, hesitating between the roles of ape and man, who haunted the high African savannahs a million or two years ago. Neither had I heard that man's last animal ancestors were hunters and for unknown ages had been killing other species for a living before we started killing each other for fun.

I had heard of none of these things. In the early 1930's I had lectured in anthropology for a season or two at Chicago's World's Fair. But after that I wrote a play, and so I became a playwright. For twenty years I divided my life between theater and films, and I naturally lost touch with the sciences. It was in these twenty years that all had happened. When I entered Dart's basement room I was anthropology's Rip Van Winkle, encountering the most enormous of alarm clocks.

Normal human beings, jarred into consciousness of their own ignorance, tend to keep the information to themselves. Authors, being shameless, tend to rush into print. So fathomless was my ignorance, however, and so oceanic were the dimensions of scientific accomplishment while my back had been turned, that the rush consumed six years of my life, and even then I learned only to float. For it was not just a matter of *Australopithecus* and the predatory transition; there were alpha fish and pecking orders, gene pools and displacement activities, exploratory behavior and ritualized aggression, and all had bearing on the human condition. Above all, there was territory.

There is a virtue, I must presume, in shamelessness, since by placing on parade the things one does not know, one discovers that no one else knows either. The publication of *African Genesis* in 1961 dropped a clue as to how many people in how many lands shared the shock of my discovery in Dart's basement room, and could share as well the excitements of a six-year safari through unknown scientific lands. An intellectual excursion which a generation earlier could have concerned but an educated few now concerned an educated many. We forget, all of us, that not all the explosions in our reverberating era are those of population and nuclear devices. There is a literacy explosion, too.

This perhaps was the most shining emblem to decorate my ignorance. I had not guessed how many people would care about what I was doing. Out of personal obsession I took my long detour through the new biology's beckoning yet forbidding fields. A playwright is a specialist in human nature, and as a playwright I sheltered a conviction that these specialists in animals extant and extinct had something to say about man. But it was a personal enlightenment I sought. As a playwright I had my normal nostalgia for fields more familiar than fossil beds and tanks filled with fish. I had no least intention of pursuing my investigations beyond those broad conclusions recorded in my book.

I had not reckoned, however, on my fellow man. With the book's publication my last alarm clock went off. Not only had the new anthropology in the time when I slept produced a revolutionary interpretation of man's emergence from the animal world; not only had the new biology begun a revolutionary interpretation of the behavior of animals in that world from which we came: also, as I was now to discover, our time of high stress was producing a revolutionary class of human being. A new human force—a force anonymous and unrecognized, informed and inquisitive, with allegiance to neither wealth nor poverty, to neither privilege nor petulance—was silently appearing on earth. And the class was massive.

There is nothing so moving—not even acts of love or hate— as the discovery that one is not alone. It is part of our evolutionary heritage that this should be so, and the ancient chemistry worked on me. Theater and films need not be totally abjured but might on occasion be the object of a sentimental journey like a visit to the town where one was born. But what could not be denied—what could be denied no more than the future itself—was this land of high adventure which science was exploring. And since somebody cared, I went back to work.

The Territorial Imperative is a volume comparable to *African Genesis*. Like the first book, it is a personal investigation into the contemporary, little-known accomplishments of the natural sciences, and a personal interpretation of what these revolutionary studies may bring to our knowledge of man. Unlike the first book, however, which attempted to gather in long perspective our increasing evidence for man's evolutionary nature, the present investigation resembles what we should call in films a close shot. It brings into focus a single aspect of human behavior which I believe to be characteristic of our species as a whole, to be shaped but not determined by environment and experience, and to be a consequence not of human choice but of evolutionary inheritance.

In a way it is a pity that we must isolate from all that rich carpet of human impulse a single pattern for contemplation. No man or other animal lives as other than a whole being. If I am a dominant male lion with a vast impressive mane, then at once I am a predator seeking candidates for my next meal, or I shall grow unbearably hungry; I am also prey, and I must keep a wary nostril for men carrying guns, or I shall end up decorating somebody's wall; I am a proprietor, and I must keep rival lions out of my hunting territory, or game will grow scarce; I am a husband, and when one of my wives comes into heat then I must entertain her; I am a father, and with due regard to future lion generations I must brook no nonsense from my cubs while teaching them all I can; and I am also a social being for, sad to confess, I am deathly slow on my feet and an appallingly bad hunter except at close quarters, so I am dependent on the assistance of my wives and my friends, and whether I like them or not I must somehow get along with them.

If I am a lion I am many things at once, and if I am a man I am even more. And so it may seem a temptation toward unreal simplification to select a single aspect of the human condition with which to absorb ourselves. And indeed it is most surely a temptation and an almighty hazard. In precisely such fashion some have reduced men to a sexual symbol, and others have excavated him like a kitchen midden, as if he were nothing but a cultural accumulation, and still others have embalmed him in economic determinism, like many of our friends on both sides of the iron curtain. Shall we not when we are done have reduced him to a walking territorial principle? Well, I can only say that I find myself dedicated to man's elevation, not his reduction; to his desimplification and not his distillation to a pale white definitive liquid. I shall do what I can.

Focus our attention, however, we must. Territorial behavior in animals, over the past few decades, has attracted the attention of hundreds of competent specialists who have recorded their observations and their reasoned conclusions in obscure professional publications. The subject is very nearly as well known to the student of animal behavior as is the relation of mother and infant to the student of human behavior. Furthermore, many of the concerned scientists, as we shall see, believe as do I that man is a territorial species, and that the behavior so widely observed in animal species is equally characteristic of our own. And yet—it is astonishing—there exists in all the scientific literature but one book devoted exclusively to the subject. That book was written in 1920 and it concerned only bird life, and it established the concept of territory, and I have dedicated my book to its author. Since then no attempt has been made to publish in any language, for the benefit of either the layman, the scholar, or the scientist himself, a single volume exploring a subject which could be vital to our understanding of men.

This book, then, must in the manner of a combined operation do several things at once: It must collect and organize a fair sample of science's observations of territorial behavior in animals. It must record all that is salient concerning the history, the interpretations, and the scientific controversies bearing on the concept. And it must attempt to derive from biology's conclusions whatever illumination may exist concerning ourselves. This will be about all that I can handle in one volume, and we must defer to some future date inquiry into other aspects of comparative behavior of equal importance to our daily affairs.

The Territorial Imperative, in other words, is but a single forward step toward an understanding of man's evolutionary nature, an understanding compatible on the one hand with the revolutionary findings of biology, and on the other with our age-old human experience. Author and reader alike, however, must keep in mind that we are entering *terra incognita,* and that the crossing of an all-but-unknown intellectual continent may have its fascinations, but it has also its casualties. Many a conclusion which I recorded in *African Genesis,* only five years ago, today lies a victim of biology's ruthless, incessant raids. I shall acknowledge my losses. And with equal truth, many of contemporary thought's most sacred convictions are being pressed toward oblivion by the biological onslaught. I shall point to their corpses along our way, if I do not in all mercy shoot them down myself.

Finally, before I close these preliminary meditations, there are motions of gratitude which I should like to offer. Many scientists have helped me in measure far beyond the line of duty; for one, my friend and counselor and drinking companion, the late Professor K. R. L. Hall of the University of Bristol, I have neither words nor means to express my gratitude, since his death occurred before the book was finished. To the others I must extend the hope that by treating their work with the discipline expected of me I have repaid their generosity. And for two longtime friends, Dr. Kenneth P. Oakley, of the British Museum of Natural History, and Professor Raymond A. Dart, until his retirement head of the anatomy department of the University of the Witwatersrand, I extend most special thanks: they got me into all this in the first place, ten long years ago.

This work—this combined operation—could not be possible except for the collaborative assistance of many minds. I shall not neglect my wife, who has furnished me with far more than the illustrations which grace my pages. Nor shall I neglect a Middle Western American businessman, a manufacturer of machine tools and a man of many parts. It was Leighton A. Wilkie who in a critical hour of Dart's career rode to the rescue like a regiment of U.S. Cavalry in an old-time western film: And it was Leighton Wilkie, with his Wilkie Brothers Foundation of Des Plaines, Illinois, who rode to my rescue in a comparably critical hour and underwrote the formidable costs of field research involved in the present volume. Just where we should all be without him, I cannot say.

Robert Ardrey

Rome, 1966

Contents

Bibliographical Key

To avoid the use of footnotes or reference numbers within the text, the key, which follows the text, is provided as a guide to the numbered references in the Bibliography. For each section of each chapter the reader will find appropriate identification of material in the text, along with a number to indicate the source from which it is drawn. Wherever possible I have used the original source material; when this has not been possible, and I have used a secondary source in which the original material has been cited, then the reader will find that the key number is italicized.

THE TERRITORIAL IMPERATIVE

1. Of Men and Mockingbirds

A territory is an area of space, whether of water or earth or air, which an animal or group of animals defends as an exclusive preserve. The word is also used to describe the inward compulsion in animate beings to possess and defend such a space. A territorial species of animals, therefore, is one in which all males, and sometimes females too, bear an inherent drive to gain and defend an exclusive property.

In most but not all territorial species, defense is directed only against fellow members of the kind. A squirrel does not regard a mouse as a trespasser. In most but not all territorial species—not in chameleons, for example—the female is sexually unresponsive to an unpropertied male. As a general pattern of behavior, in territorial species the competition between males which we formerly believed was one for the possession of females is in truth for possession of property.

We may also say that in all territorial species, without exception, possession of a territory lends enhanced energy to the proprietor. Students of animal behavior cannot agree as to why this should be, but the challenger is almost invariably defeated, the intruder expelled. In part, there seems some mysterious flow of energy and resolve which invests a proprietor on his home grounds. But likewise, so marked is the inhibition lying on the intruder, so evident his sense of trespass, we may be permitted to wonder if in all territorial species there does not exist, more profound than simple learning, some universal recognition of territorial rights.

The concept of territory as a genetically determined form of behavior in many species is today accepted beyond question in the biological sciences. But so recently have our observations been made and our conclusions formed that we have yet to

3

explore the implications of territory in our estimates of man. Is *Homo sapiens* a territorial species? Do we stake out property, chase off trespassers, defend our countries because we are sapient, or because we are animals? Because we choose, or because we must? Do certain laws of territorial behavior apply as rigorously in the affairs of men as in the affairs of chipmunks? That is the principal concern of this inquiry, and it is a matter of considerable concern, I believe, to any valid understanding of our nature. But it is a problem to be weighed in terms of present knowledge, not past.

How recently our information about animal territory has come to us is very well illustrated by reflections recorded only thirty years ago by the anthropologist Julian H. Steward, now of the University of Illinois. "Why are human beings the only animals having land-owning groups?" he wondered. And he brought together observations of twenty-four different hunting peoples so primitive that their ways differ little, in all probability, from the ways of paleolithic man. Their homes were isolated and far-spread—in Philippine and Congo forests, in Tasmania and Tierra del Fuego, in Canada's Mackenzie basin, in the Indian Ocean's Andaman Islands, in southwestern Africa's Kalahari Desert. So remote were they from each other that there seemed small likelihood that any one could have learned its ways from others. Yet all formed social bands occupying exclusive, permanent domains.

How could it be that such a number of peoples in such varying environments so remote from each other should all form similar social groups based on what would seem to be a human invention, the ownership of land? Steward came to a variety of conclusions, but one line of speculation was denied him. Even in 1936 he could not know that his assumption was false, since many animals form land-owning groups. Lions, eagles, wolves, great-horned owls are all hunters, and all guard exclusive hunting territories. The lions and wolves, besides, hunt in cooperative prides and packs differing little from the bands of primitive man. Ownership of land is scarcely a human invention, as our territorial propensity is something less than a human distinction.

4

Man, I shall attempt to demonstrate in this inquiry, is as much a territorial animal as is a mockingbird singing in the clear California night. We act as we do for reasons of our evolutionary past, not our cultural present, and our behavior is as much a mark of our species as is the shape of a human thigh bone or the configuration of nerves in a corner of the human brain. If we defend the title to our land or the sovereignty of our country, we do it for reasons no different, no less innate, no less ineradicable, than do lower animals. The dog barking at you from behind his master's fence acts for a motive indistinguishable from that of his master when the fence was built.

Neither are men and dogs and mockingbirds uncommon creatures in the natural world. Ring-tailed lemurs and great-crested grebes, prairie dogs, robins, tigers, muskrats, meadow warblers and Atlantic salmon, fence lizards, flat lizards, three-spined sticklebacks, nightingales and Norway rats, herring gulls and callicebus monkeys—all of us will give everything we are for a place of our own. Territory, in the evolving world of animals, is a force perhaps older than sex.

The survival value that territory brings to a species varies as widely as do the opportunities of species themselves. In some it offers security from the predator, in others security of food supply. In some its chief value seems the selection of worthy males for reproduction, in some the welding together of a group, and in many, like sea birds, the prime value seems simply the excitement and stimulation of border quarrels. And there are many species, of course, for which the territorial tie would be a handicap to survival. Grazing animals for the most part must move with the season's grass. Elephant herds acknowledge no territorial bond, but move like fleets of old gray galleons across the measureless African space. The gorilla, too, is a wanderer within a limited range who every night must build a new nest wherever his search for food may take him.

In those countless species, however, which through long evolutionary trial and error have come to incorporate a territorial pattern into their whole behavior complex, we shall find a remarkable uniformity. Widely unrelated though the species may be, a few distinct patterns are endlessly repeated. In the next chapter, for example, we shall examine arena behavior, in which solitary males defend mating stations to which females come solely for copulation. It makes little difference whether the species be antelope or sage grouse, the pattern will be almost the same. And in the chapter after that we shall consider the pair territory, that portion of space occupied and defended by a breeding couple, as in robins and beavers and men. So we shall move along, surveying the territorial experience in the world of the animal as it has been observed by science in our generation.

It is information, all of it, which failed to enter your education and mine because it had not yet come to light. It is information, all of it, which yet fails to enter our children's textbooks or the processes of our own thought, through nothing but neglect. To me, this neglect seems a luxury which we cannot afford. Were we in a position to regard our knowledge of man as adequate in our negotiations with the human circumstance, and to look with satisfaction on our successful treatment of such human maladies as crime and war, racial antagonisms and social loneliness, then we might embrace the world of the animal simply to enjoy its intrinsic fascinations. But I find no evidence to support such self-satisfaction. And so this wealth of information concerning animal ways, placed before us by the new biology, must be regarded as a windfall in a time of human need.

If, as I believe, man's innumerable territorial expressions are human responses to an imperative lying with equal force on mockingbirds and men, then human self-estimate is due for radical revision. We acknowledge a few such almighty forces, but very few: the will to survive, the sexual impulse, the tie, perhaps, between mother and infant. It has been our inadequate knowledge of the natural world, I suggest, that has led us to look no further. And it may come to us as the strangest of thoughts that the bond between a man and the soil he walks on should be more powerful than his bond with the woman he sleeps with. Even so, in a rough, preliminary way we may test the supposition with a single question: How many men have you known of, in your lifetime, who died for their country?

And how many for a woman?

Any force which may command us to act in opposition to the will to survive is a force to be inspected, at such a moment of history as ours, with the benefit of other than obsolete information. That I believe this force to be a portion of our evolutionary nature, a behavior pattern of such survival value to the emerging human being that it became fixed in our genetic endowment, just as the shape of our feet and the musculature of our buttocks became fixed, is the premise of this inquiry. Even as that behavior pattern called sex evolved in many organisms as nature's most effective answer to the problem of reproduction, so that behavior pattern called territory evolved in many organisms as a kind of defense mechanism, as nature's most effective answer to a variety of problems of survival.

I regard the territorial imperative as no less essential to the existence of contemporary man than it was to those bands of small-brained proto-men on the high African savannah millions of years ago. I see it as a force shaping our lives in countless unexpected ways, threatening our existence only to the degree that we fail to understand it. We can neither accept nor reject my premise, however, or even begin to explore its consequence, on any basis other than science's new knowledge of the animal in a state of nature. And since that knowledge has been acquired at the same time that radical changes have come to our understanding of evolution itself, we shall do well to defer until the next chapter our entrance to the field and our first specific inspection of territory. Before we inspect the behavior of the animal, let us inspect the behavior of that equally intriguing being, the scientist.

2

A bird does not fly because it has wings; it has wings because it flies.

Such a statement may seem, from a variety of viewpoints, to be a triumph of obviousness, of absurdity, or of unimportance.

But reflect on it for a moment and something in the statement will begin to nag at you. It will take on the aspect of one of those psychologist's cubes that at a quick glance present one face to the observer and then, in the most puzzling fashion,

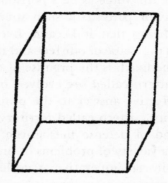

turn themselves over and present another. Just what is the relationship of body to behavior? Do we think because we have brains, or do we have brains because we think? It may not matter too much if you are late for an appointment and trying to catch a taxi on a rainy afternoon in Piccadilly or the Piazza di Spagna. But it has mattered mightily to evolutionary thought in the past thirty years, and it must matter to us.

In this period during which most of us have had our minds on other things, three questions have disturbed not a few scientific disciplines. What is the relationship of behavior to body, of how we act to what we act with? What is the relationship of learning to instinct, of what we acquire in the experience of a lifetime to what we were born with, assuming that we were born with anything? And, finally, what is the dominant influence in our daily lives, the compulsions of our immediate environment or the inner dictates of our evolutionary past? The last two might be considered rephrasings of the same question, but they do not come out quite that way. In any event, each of these three questions concerning the roles of behavior, of instinct, and of heredity on the evolutionary stage has received a giant body of inquiry in our time, each has induced giant cases of apoplexy in its more dedicated partisans,

8

and each not only is central to our newer concepts of evolution but is essential to any approach to our story of territory. And while it is true that the question of instinct and learning is most sharply related to conclusions which we may draw concerning man, let us turn first to the question of body and behavior as more nearly settled and withdrawn from the field of controversy.

Should you have access to any of the older zoology textbooks, you will find either little reference to behavior, or none. Discussion is confined to those animal attributes which zoologists call morphological and physiological—that is, dealing with physical structures and processes. Such a preoccupation with body—what an animal is and how he looks—as opposed to concern about behavior—how he acts and why—dominated our thoughts about evolution until about 1930. Should your curiosity lead you on to wonder about what is being taught in the field today, you will find available slim paperback volumes called the College Outline Series, used widely in English-speaking schools, which will give you at a glance a fair summary of what your children are being taught in any subject. I have before me those volumes treating biology and zoology, both in editions published in 1962. You will find the bulk of both devoted to the anatomical classification of animals into species and genera and families and so on, a subject of immense fascination to zoologists in the later decades of the nineteenth century. Ecology has crept in to the extent of a chapter in each volume: ecology is the relationship of an animal to his environment. But you will find no mention of behavior at all. And yet biology is in general agreement today that it is behavior—such behavior as territory, or the manner in which an animal evades predators—that determines whether bodily characters have selective advantage or not. It is behavior, in other words, that evolves and is central to the evolutionary process. Your children are being taught an interpretation of evolution discarded by modern biologists for quite some time.

Let us look at the matter more closely. I have mentioned the wolf. A group of Arctic wolves has a hunting territory of about one hundred square miles. The boundaries are fairly precise, and periodically the adults will make the rounds, refreshing their markers as a warning against intrusion. Like the dog, the wolf marks his property with a squirt of urine the fragrance of which is reinforced by the output of a special scent gland. Since the dog is promiscuous, we might interpret his marking as an attraction for females. But the wolf is monogamous. He mates for life, is intractably faithful, and if widowered will probably not re-mate but will remain a bachelor to the end of his days. To spread that much sexually attractive scent over that much mileage would seem in a beast of such temperament an impressive waste of time. The gland has evolved, of course, as a bodily character of selective value to territorial behavior. By the marking of boundaries wolves reduce the likelihood of lethal conflict over property rights.

The howling monkey, another passionately propertied creature, has likewise evolved an anatomical specialty of no earthly use but to his behavioral preoccupations. Since monkeys have lived for tens of millions of years almost entirely in trees, the sense of smell, useful if you live on the ground, has suffered reduction. Stereoscopic vision and depth perception have become of prime arboreal importance, faces have flattened, snouts have retreated, scent glands have for the most part vanished. Thus the howler possesses no wolflike equipment for marking the boundaries of his preserve. But he has something else. As his name implies, he has come into possession of a voice box to humiliate an air-raid siren. At dawn the howler will deafen the awakening forest in a cry raised in unison with the fellows of his clan. Every other clan for a mile or so about is put on warning as to the home clan's whereabouts. Should two such groups in the course of the day's wanderings meet at some point where unmarkable boundaries are vague, then all argument will be settled by out-howling. Again, a body structure has evolved through its selective advantage to a form of behavior.

As a last territorial example, I may recall a group of captive ring-tailed lemurs that I encountered a few years ago in Tananarive, in the laboratories of the *Institut de Recherche Scientifique de Madagascar*. Lemurs are among the most primitive of primates, from an evolutionary horizon so much earlier

than monkeys that they have not renounced loyalty to the sniffing way of life. The combination of foxy snout, delicate hands, and long striped tail makes the ring-tail one of nature's most beguiling creatures. I knew little about them at the time of our first encounter, and when at the sight of me one began running its tail through its arms and another backed its rear against the edge of the cage and started rubbing, I put it all down to captive nervousness. It did not occur to me that, as warning, they were preparing to mark out their territory, the cage.

Some time later I ran into a full explanation by Heini Hediger, world-famous director of the Zurich zoo and professor of animal psychology at the University of Zurich. The ring-tail has glands on the inside of his arms which he rubs with his tail when disturbed; I had been correct that far. But also the ring-tail has a perineal gland near the anus, used for border marking. At Zurich, Hediger had a group in a large cage, and for years he would take his students to watch the demonstration. As they approached, the dominant animal would invariably go to a position at the lower left corner of the cage, do a hand stand, and with tail upraised squeeze the perineal gland against the wire mesh. The leader would then go on to eight more predictable spots, including one on either side of the door, to place warning marks. That the warnings were serious found testimony on an occasion when a volunteer entered the cage with the regular keeper. The little lemurs were accustomed to the keeper. The volunteer, however, was hospitalized for some weeks with a severed artery in the leg.

It is of passing interest that the captive lemur will defend a territory against species other than his own. It is of more immediate interest that the leader of this group was a female. Both male and female ring-tails possess the same gland, which despite its position has no sexual relevance. Like the urinary gland of the wolf, it has evolved as an anatomical character with a single value: to warn away trespassers.

Let me wind this up with an example of body as a function of another sort of behavior. Konrad Z. Lorenz, the Austrian naturalist, is the father of ethology, the modern study of animal behavior. Among the many creatures which have fallen under his imaginative yet critical eye has been the night heron. Three different genera of night herons all have a behavior trait in common. As a dog wags its tail to indicate friendly intentions, so the night herons bob their heads. To emphasize the head bob, all three genera have crests which they raise like flags for the amiable occasion. But the flags differ in pattern. Does the night heron bob his head to display the crest he possesses? Or does he possess a crest because he would bob his head anyway? Lorenz reasoned that since the three crests differ whereas the gesture is the same, some ancestor of the family must have found such a gesture of value in keeping down disputes, and that the bodily structures had evolved in descendant species to enhance the value. His reasoning is confirmed by herons so young that they have not yet grown crests; they too bow.

As any Lorenz devotee comes to know, he has run into some of his most charming experiences through accident. Such an accident revealed the importance of the head bob in the life of the night heron. One of the objects of his study was a family nesting in a tree near his house. When the father heron would return to the nest, he always bowed to the young inside with what might seem the most remarkable paternal courtesy. But there was more to it than manners. One afternoon when the father was absent Lorenz climbed the tree to check up on the young and see how they were coming along. They were accustomed to him and raised no fuss. But in the midst of Lorenz' examination the father returned unexpectedly and, outraged by the intrusion, made threatening displays at the naturalist. Unhappily, however, the distracted father forgot to make his bow of friendly intentions, and was promptly attacked by his own young.

Harvard University's Ernst Mayr is biology's unrivaled authority in the field of systematics—that is, the evolutionary classification of species. At a symposium in 1958 he said, "On the whole it seems correct to state, as Lorenz has emphasized, that behavior movements often precede phylogenetically the special structures that make these movements particularly conspicuous." In other words, as in the case of the night herons, it would be a normal situation for some ancestor to start bobbing a crestless head as a form of behavior of survival value, and for natural selection in descendant species to favor incidental but effective ornaments. Five years later, in his definitive *Animal Species and Evolution,* Mayr went even further: "A shift into a new niche or adaptive zone is, almost without exception, initiated by a change in behavior. The other adaptations to the new niche, particularly the structural ones, are acquired secondarily."

What truly leads the evolutionary procession, in other words, is behavior. Let us say that some tiny rodent species has lived for a million years deep in the shelter and the succulence of a prevailing grassland. Then comes a change of climate. For decade after decade and for century after century remorseless drought burns away the grasses and reduces the land to unending desert. The little rodent must change his entire way of life or perish. He must eat new foods and discover perhaps a means of hoarding and storing what in his meadows had never suffered scarcity. Through hundreds of generations of selection those who hoard tend to raise offspring successfully, those who live for today tend to fail. A hoarding behavior pattern becomes established, and with it arises a necessity for storage places. The little rodent must dig. And with his new burrowing way comes selective pressure to favor those who by chance have paws best adapted to digging, coats best adapted to underground life. The dainty-footed, soft-coated meadow dweller becomes a brand-new species, rough-coated, heavy of paw and claw.

But the burrowing way of life in the desert has brought survival challenges of other sorts. From the beginning of his new career the rodent has been exposed to the hawk, with no sheltering grasses to hide in. And so for many a generation now the darker members of the meadowland species have become morsels in the diet of hawks, and the new desert species has become cryptic in color and difficult to spot from the air. But hawks are clever, and menace still remains. The burrow becomes a haven. It is a haven also against the terrifying, desiccating summer heat that scorches animals and their food alike. And so more and more the little rodent tends to stay in the cool of his burrow through the merciless summer, to sleep, to accommodate physiological changes that permit him, as a bear hibernates in winter, to estivate.

Rodent and burrow have become one. A way of life impossible in the meadow's tightly rooted land has encouraged such changes of body and bodily process that he can never return to his former way. The burrow is his castle, his exclusive domain, and he will permit none of his kind to come near it. Even at the risk of exposing himself to the hawk, he will chase away any intruder who either through designs on his burrow or by simple accident comes near. This new territorial pattern of behavior may have bodily consequences, too, one day. Through the infinite span of generations, chance will present one little rodent or another with a special pungency of urine or fecal matter, or a gland with a particularly lasting secretion. Within the species a differential rate of survival will be set up. Those old-fashioned members who lack means of warning and who must chase away every intruder will have one set of odds with the watchful hawk. But for the new sort, the smelly sort, the sort who on their territorial boundaries may substitute warning signals for their vulnerable selves, a more favorable mathematics will invest the desert. And a more invulnerable species will assemble its genes.

Birds do not fly because they have wings; they have wings because they fly. The newer concept of evolution, and of the relation of behavior and body, might seem an interesting mental exercise, a parlor game of no pressing significance to our understanding of territory in relation to man, had it not been for a flip of the psychologist's cube that occurred in 1953. In that year Oxford's J. S. Weiner and Sir Wilfrid Le Gros Clark together with the British Museum's Kenneth P. Oakley combined their gifts to prove that the world's most famous fossil of early man, the Piltdown skull, was a fraud. And out of the logic of birds and wings an enormous question was placed before us: Do we think because we have brains, or do we have brains because we think? The new biology's logic dictates the answer, but there have so far been few members of either the biological or social sciences who have chosen to pursue the never-ending implications.

Let us recall that Piltdown man was found early in the century in some river gravels in Sussex. The skull combined a large, relatively modern human brain-case with a distinctly ape-like jaw. With the fossil were associated certain remains of extinct animals indicating a date earlier than that of any other human remains known at the time. A few skeptics muttered to themselves in their scientific cellars, but the body of science, including almost all of the world's most influential anthropologists, accepted Piltdown as a true representative of primal man.

Now, had Piltdown truly represented primal man, then its huge brain would have confirmed all that we should like to believe about ourselves: that in our progression from the simian background we received, whether by divine or muta-tional intervention, the great human brain freeing us from animal necessity. So it was interpreted by one of the most respected authorities of the time, Sir Grafton Elliot Smith, who referred to "this wonderful skull" and stated things quite clearly: "The outstanding interest of the Piltdown skull is the confirmation it affords of the view that in the evolution of Man the brain led the way. It is the veriest truism that Man has emerged from the simian state in virtue of the enrichment of the structure of his mind."

We think because we have brains. There matters stood for some decades until Oakley revealed with his fluorine tests that skull and jaw bore no relation to each other. Some unknown joker with a most superb grasp not only of human paleontology but of human gullibility had assembled the whole bone collection and planted it in the Sussex gravels. Not a thimbleful of evidence remained to indicate that we behave as we do because we have brains. Piltdown man expired in the acid of Oakley's tests; but Piltdown thinking thrives today—as it will thrive tomorrow, without doubt—unaffected by the most acidulous solvents which history so abundantly provides.

The effect of Oakley's tests, so far as our understanding of human evolution was concerned, was immediate and uproarious. I pursued in detail those effects in *African Genesis,* since they made possible the acceptance of Raymond Dart's theories concerning the evolution of his small-brained australopithecines, pressed by the selective necessities of the hunting life, into the large-brained *Homo* anatomically equipped to deal with the complex necessities of that life. In the years since my book was published in 1961, the spectacular discoveries of L. S. B. Leakey and his family in East Africa have gone so far to prove Dart's thesis that I can conceive of no informed body of scientific thought which today actively opposes it. But the effects of Oakley's tests on a broader assessment of man have been a story less than uproarious; one might think, indeed, that nothing had occurred.

It has been demonstrated that the human brain came into existence like any other evolving structure—like the night heron's lovely bluish crest or the wolf's less lovely scent glands —the more adequately to deal with pre-existing behavioral demands or opportunities. Are we then to conclude that those earlier modes of proto-human behavior have had no hand in shaping our brain's form and structure? That the behavioral patterns which were so essential to survival half a million or so years ago, and which forced the enlargement of our brains to their present dimension and complexity, left no mark upon them? Without doubt the enlarged human brain, with its capacities for memory, for foresight, for self-awareness, for conceptual thought, brought something new to the natural world which had existed previously merely as hints. But if our brain exists as something new in an old, old world, it remains likewise something quite old in a new one.

The anatomical arrangements of the human brain recall its behavioral necessities at the time of the brain's final enlargement some hundreds of thousands of years ago. If we are to believe otherwise, then we must deny that the form of a hummingbird's wing has been adjusted, through selective pressure, to other than its function in flight. Our brain, through its enlargement, may have achieved a qualitative breakthrough into spheres of activity which neither the australopithecine nor his Miocene ancestor, the Proconsul family, could have within their limitations foreseen. But to deny the formative influences of an animal past on our human mentality is to deny all present understanding of the evolutionary process. We may, with or without happiness, accept such a denial as a portion of our children's education. We cannot, however, in such an adult inquiry as this, accept the probability that those animal patterns of behavior which have shaped our minds have entirely vanished from our being.

3

I have so far avoided any use of the word "instinct" for what seems to me a sound enough reason: because no one, apparently, has a glimmer as to what an instinct is. In *African Genesis* I used the word blithely, chopping off behavioral heads with it in a manner to have delighted Alice's Red Queen. Such use was justified in an inquiry so broad. But if we are to inquire with any depth or definition into innate patterns of behavior, then we can neither avoid the word, in the manner of many psychologists, nor can we use it like a two-handed axe in the hands of an absent-minded dentist.

What in the actions of any individual, man or other animal, can be attributed to instinct? What to learning? The question, stated or unstated, lies at the heart of some of our most heated controversies. It is difficult to discuss any contemporary issue—crime or race, techniques of education, aid to underdeveloped countries or ways to bring up baby—without finding oneself in the presence, sooner or later, of this ambiguous monster which seems always proceeding in two opposite directions at once. In many a parlor of contemporary discussion the word "instinct" is banned more severely than some of its fellows boasting only four letters. To such subjective depths has an essentially objective problem been reduced that Abraham Maslow, the astute chairman of Brandeis University's psychology department, has suggested a political explanation. To refer to human instincts is to damn oneself as a reactionary, probably of the most fascist-minded sort. Total devotion to learning, on the other hand, is to label oneself as liberal, progressive, securely democratic.

Our troubles with instinct began, I suspect, with those studies of insects that initiated a modern fascination with the animal world. There is something about a butterfly called *Hoplitis milhauseri* which can be neither dismissed nor forgotten. Its soft little pupae lie in cocoons as hard as nutshells. How do they get out? Well, each pupa has a built-in can-opener on top of its head and, when the moment comes, cuts a circular hole in the shell so that its metamorphosed self may emerge as a butterfly. Instinct most obviously has something to do with this, as well as a natural tool kit. To examine the instinct with precision, an experimenter in Zurich once carefully removed two pupae from their nutshells a day or two before their time had come and laid them on the floor of a little breeding cage. They remained there quietly. Then, however, nature commanded. The pupae moved. They scrambled, in fact, to the

wall of the breeding cage, where for an hour they made thrusts and circular turning movements with their heads. Only then, the instinct satisfied, did they go about the developing of wings.

When the work of the French entomologist Jean Henri Fabre was collected and published as *The Wonders of Instinct* early in this century, the wonders were so astounding that we never quite got over them. A fair example is the Capricorn beetle, whose helpful offspring any parent must envy, and whose instincts make the pupae with the can-openers seem crude.

The larva of the Capricorn beetle is a tiny wormlike being who starts out life no thicker of body than a straw. He burrows into an oak tree, ingesting wood at the front end and leaving a tunnel behind. You may have seen the same traces in old furniture. For three years he wanders around in the heart of the oak, very much on his own without parental guidance, increasing in size until he is as thick as your finger. About then he is ready to turn into a beetle, and this he will do inside the oak. The problem confronting Fabre was how the beetle gets out. Only the larva has the capacity to dine off oak. The beetle would be helpless.

Fabre gave long attention to the matter and found that while in the whole three years of wandering the larva would never approach the bark, at the end of his journey he headed directly to it, leaving his tunnel behind him and stopping only when the thinnest film of bark separated the tunnel from the outdoors. Then the larva backs up. Having moved an appropriate distance from the exit, he proceeds to hollow out a chamber not his size but large enough to accommodate the beetle who does not yet exist. The larva's brush with destiny, however, is not yet done. He seals the chamber at either end with a natural cement produced in his stomach. Now, with doors neatly closed, he rasps down the walls of his sealed chamber to cover the floor with a soft down. Using the same wood-wool, he completes the decor by felting all walls a millimeter thick. Now at last his preparations for the accouchement are finished and he lies down and sheds his skin, becoming a pupa which in turn will become a beetle. But the wonders of instinct have not yet been finally recorded. He lies down always with his head toward the exit. Were he to lie down the wrong way, the beetle would be unable to turn around.

The instincts of the larva of the Capricorn beetle may be compared, perhaps, to the programming of a computer. And perhaps someday, when we have become a bit more relaxed in the presence of these modern beasts with all their mechanical wonders, we shall better understand, through analogy, such natural wonders as Fabre presented to the world. But we have no such understanding today. Biology, whether old or new, has no more to say about the Capricorn beetle than it had half a century ago.

Did we reject instinct because we could not understand it? The human mind is capable of its own wonders, and this may in some cases have been true. On the whole, however, I believe that the rejection came about through more reasonable processes. The kind of instinct observed in the insect world—a total programming in which learning plays no part—occurs rarely in the world of the vertebrate, and never in the world of man. If one's understanding of the word is limited to insect example, then one is apt to reject instinct as a factor in human motivation.

The great rejection took place in the 1920's, headed in America by a scientific cult, brief of glory, called behaviorism.

J. B. Watson, treading hard on the heels of Pavlov's salivating dog, demonstrated that the human being consists of nothing but a few striped muscles and some conditioned reflexes. Today, like Jean-Jacques Rousseau and his earlier but equally extreme views concerning the natural goodness of man, Watson musters few defenders. Both, nevertheless, left deep scars on the face of human thought. The primacy of the conditioned reflex contributed lasting damage to American psychology and, like some great wave which gathers fury and greater destructive power the farther it moves from the storm center, brought to other departments of American learning devastation typical of a disaster area. We do not know—we Americans—how unquestioning is our devotion to the conditioned reflex as we search for human explanations. In but one other nation, the Soviet Union, can one witness a dedication so profound and so unanimous.

It was in the 1920's, then, that we rejected instinct and the demands of the past as of any great relevance to human behavior and turned to the immediate present and that conditioned reflex called experience for all final answers as to why men today are the way they are, or as to what they will be tomorrow. Our premature conclusions concerning animal instinct had been drawn from the termitary, the beehive, the anthill. Not until the following decade would biology's focus shift to the vertebrate.

Ethology is a new science, pioneered by Austria's Konrad Lorenz and Holland's Niko Tinbergen in the 1930's. Some of its leading contributors today are Americans, but its work is best known in Europe. In a way, the science has been badly named, for the word is easily lost in the scientific jumble of ethnology, entomology, and etymology. Furthermore, ethology suggests ethics to the ear, whereas its major concern is with the precise study of innate behavior patterns in animals. In the long run, however, the significance of the word will probably surmount its temporary handicaps, for ethology is most certainly revealing universal patterns of behavior and may someday uncover by most objective means an *ethos* in the nature of all living beings.

The existence of innate, genetically determined behavior patterns was first discussed, I believe, by an American, C. O. Whitman, in a series of lectures delivered at Woods Hole, Massachusetts, in 1898. Ten years or so later Oskar Heinroth in Berlin independently explored the possibility of patterns to which learning makes a contribution but which are in themselves genetically controlled. Serious study of genetically determined behavior had to wait, however, until in the 1930's biologists and comparative psychologists at last turned their attention from the zoo and the laboratory to the way of the animal in a state of nature. And in field and forest, on seashore and desert, these adventurers found a world that no man had guessed before.

That the actions of an animal in captivity bear remote resemblance to his actions in the wild proceeds from the simplest of logic: only in the wild does he face those pressures and opportunities which give expression to his total nature. We tend to feel sorry for the captive animal, as indeed we frequently should. But we tend also to forget that captivity shelters him from that most conspicuous fact of natural existence, the empty stomach, whether his own or that of the predator who seeks to devour him. Much of his natural energy has been organized to deal with this daily, hourly problem of the natural way: to eat without being eaten. Captivity has subtracted fear from his life, and substituted boredom. And it is for this reason that we should feel sorry for him.

Only when a new generation of scientists went out into the field could we begin to apprehend, for example, the subtlety of organization in those natural animal societies which cannot exist in the zoo. Only when we watched the whole range of behavior exhibited by the animal as he meets the whole range of life contingencies could we begin to guess at those processes by which evolution has so ably perfected his remarkable capacities. The laboratory would retain its worthy place for experimental purposes, but only as measured against the new observations in the field could indoor conclusions be accepted as meaningful.

New hypotheses, new theories, sprang up to take account of

the new, revolutionary evidences. Konrad Lorenz in 1937 published in English his landmark paper, *The Companion in the Bird's World,* breaking the news that in the life of our backboned comrade, the vertebrate, problems of instinct could not be reduced to the programmed specifics of insect life. In 1951 Tinbergen published his *The Study of Instinct,* a work so glacial in its objectivity that no scientist, whatever his emotional allegiances, could ignore it entirely. (That some succeeded, of course, may be deduced from the fact that the book is today out of print and unavailable in both Britain and America.) Then in 1955 Tinbergen's rival and fellow Dutchman, Adriaan Kortlandt of the University of Amsterdam published his *Aspects and Prospects of the Concept of Instinct,* demonstrating in a single, erudite, bristling document that ethology was going to be other than the polite preserve of a Pall Mall club of like-minded students, but more fun than a barrel of argumentative monkeys.

In its short career ethology has touched many a facet of the central problem of instinct. The one to engage us at this moment, however, is the reality of inherited, genetically determined behavior based on open as well as closed programs. The larva of the Capricorn beetle may execute his entire life cycle instructed by none but his inward computer. The weaver bird may build his most complex of nests after four generations of removal from nest-building materials or opportunities. These are closed patterns to which nothing need be added by experience to serve perfectly the needs of the species. But let us take an excursion into bird song.

Every species of singing bird has a song specific to its kind. Throughout the nineteenth century it was generally accepted that a bird learns its song from the parent. Then in 1926 Heinroth questioned this. At last, a quarter of a century later, a Dane named Holger Poulsen concluded a series of observations and experiments demonstrating just how widely instinctual patterns may range.

By raising birds either in isolation or in contact only with other species, Poulsen found, for example, that the linnet must learn. Raised with other birds, it will sing almost anything but a linnet's proper song. The skylark must learn too, but it is a little different from the linnet. Reared only with other birds, the skylark will learn the complete songs of the chaffinch, the goldfinch, or the yellow bunting. But there will always be a few skylark notes and phrases, learned from none. Then at the opposite end of the range there is the reed bunting, who will remain quite indifferent to the songs of other species and when the time comes will make his perfect reed-bunting song. Poulsen wondered if such innate capacity might be a character of birds with simple calls, but he found that the tree pipit, with one of the most complex of songs, sang as innately as the reed bunting.

It is the chaffinch, however, that provides an illuminating example of the open instinct. In Denmark the chaffinch begins to sing about February 15. Poulsen raised males in isolation. By the middle of January they were beginning to twitter and in two weeks were producing an abbreviated chaffinch song, imperfect of pitch, imperfect of rhythm. When Chaffinch Day came in the middle of February, he freed them but allowed them at first to mix only with linnets. They imitated the linnet and succeeded in producing some of its notes. But then they heard a chaffinch. Immediately they perfected their chaffinch song, nor did they imitate the linnet ever again.

Instinct may vary from the closed program of the tree pipit, in which nothing is learned, through the moderately open program of the chaffinch, in which there exists a design and a general disposition to learn only from one's own species but in which much must be filled in by experience; then on to the skylark, who derives from his genetic heritage only a few disorganized hints as to how a skylark should sing, and finally to the linnet, in which instinct directs only that he sing at a certain season, but in which all else must be learned.

When we discuss behavior patterns, such as the territorial, we deal with these open programs of instinct. The disposition to possess a territory is innate. The command to defend it is likewise innate. But its position and borders will be learned. And if one shares it with a mate or a group, one learns likewise whom to tolerate, whom to expel. To the human eye all herring gulls look alike. The male herring gull, however, will allow none on his little territory but his mate, and he will recognize her coming fifty yards away in a crowded colony of thousands.

This capacity to fill out with learning a behavioral pattern of innate design seems in itself somehow to be related to instinct. It is not simple experience, for example, that teaches an animal territorial boundaries which he will cross at his peril. Eskimo dogs in East Greenland live in packs, each pack defending rigorously a social territory. At an early stage of his career Tinbergen observed that immature males wander about, violating boundaries and continually taking severe punishment in consequence. Yet they seem unable to learn, despite the most bitter experience, where to go and where not to. Then, however, they mature sexually and immediately learn all boundaries. Tinbergen recorded two cases in which first copulation, first territorial defense, and first avoidance of the next pack's territory all occurred in the course of one week.

Even in insects not all instincts are closed, by any means. The honey bee learns the location and variety of many kinds of nectar. But there is a digger wasp called *Philanthus triangulum,* with no such capacity. She preys on hive bees, and no conditioning, no most formidable scarcity of edible bees, will induce her to prey on anything else. One would not expect in a creature with a mind so closed any extraordinary capacity for learning. Yet in another of Tinbergen's experiments he placed a ring of pine cones around a nest hole while the wasp was still inside. She emerged, circled the area for precisely six seconds, and made off on a bee hunt. He then moved the circle of pine cones a few feet. An hour and a half later she returned and settled without hesitation at the middle of the circle. Helplessly she looked for her nest and was entirely incapable of finding it until the pine cones were returned to their proper position. *Philanthus triangulum* may be unable to learn to hunt anything excepting bees, but she can learn the landmarks around her home in just six seconds.

The open instinct, a combination in varying portion of genetic design and relevant experience, is the common sort in all higher animal forms. As beginning with the digger wasp we proceed higher and higher in the animal orders, the closed instinct all but vanishes, the open instinct incorporates more and more a learned portion. In man it reaches a maximum of learning, a minimum of design. The same pattern, filled out by a thousand different tracks of experience by a thousand different men, yields a richness which has made man, in a famous phrase, the most variable of all wild species. And we may understand why natural selection has permitted man, at least temporarily, to come out on top: in human behavior those patterns common to the animate world have been permitted the widest latitude of adaptation to circumstance. We retain genetic resolve while obtaining the diversity of experience. But what the sophisticated man in our time tends to ignore is that, no matter how open the instinct, no matter how much learning is incorporated into the completed pattern, the total influence on individual behavior will proceed with very nearly the form of a closed program directing an insect in the heart of an oak. It remains an instinct.

We tend, in our contemporary vocabulary of human motivation, to refer to "drives." This word is a bastard child of a common-law marriage between our rejection of the concept of instinct and a necessary acceptance of certain facts of life. It is a euphemism, as were those Victorian words and phrases referring in most genteel terms to a variety of undeniable human activities revolving about sexual intercourse. But euphemism has no lasting place in the sciences. As a psychological cynic, Professor Cyril Burt, once commented, a drive is an instinct under a new name. "Flung out at the front door, the old instincts are allowed in at the back after assuming an alias and a slight disguise." It is no help to the student of man, groping for an understanding of his fellow being, that psychology has arrayed the open instinct, a form of innate behavior exhibited by man and all higher animals, in a crêpe beard and well-placed rouge, has termed it a drive, and has expected of its objective study any superbly significant conclusions.

But there remains the undeniable problem that we have no information as to how an instinct operates. Ethologists have assumed that there must be a neurological foundation in the central nervous system providing an anatomical switchboard for handling messages. Yet no neurologist has been able to isolate the switchboard. One of our most distinguished authorities in the field, T. H. Bullock, gave a recent symposium this desperate conclusion: "At the bottom we do not have a decent inkling of the neuronal mechanism of learning or the physiological substratum of instinctive patterns. . . . Indeed if one considers the other great problems in natural science it seems clear that the gulf between our knowledge of neurophysiology and our knowledge of behavior is at least as wide as any other that confronts us."

That, then, is in general where things stand today. There are many American psychologists, like Harry Harlow, J. B. Calhoun and Jay Boyd Best, deeply engaged with laboratory study of the relation of instinct to learning. In England, Cambridge's W. H. Thorpe has published *Learning and Instinct in Animals,* the most comprehensive single volume on the subject. Many others, in America and elsewhere, have turned their experiments and meditations from the problem of genetically determined behavior to that of genetically determined needs, a rich subject to which we shall turn our own attentions at a much later moment in this inquiry. In general, however, American psychologists pursue their studies of learning almost as if instinct did not exist, while on the Continent ethology observes the behavior patterns of animals in the wild, with rare excursions into the problems of learning. Beyond some shining exceptions, neither side is well informed as to what the other side is up to. And without exception whatsoever, none has found the secret link between organism and organization, between body and behavior. It is a widely held hope, however, that the infant science of molecular biology will bring us suggestions that both learning and instinct, like the genetic code itself, may be based on the molecule within the cell. Then at least we shall have some fresh hypotheses to work with, whereas now we have only spooks.

Under the conditions of present scientific ignorance, one cannot blame too severely the student of man who tends to place instinct somewhere between the angels of medieval schoolmen and the heads of the pins they danced on. Nevertheless, instinct exists and we cannot dismiss it from our doorstep just because we do not know where it lives. Instinct exists and it makes use of learning the way a furnace sucks in air. One may consider the scientist himself as an example. Many a physicist or chemist, deficient not at all in the humanitarian virtues, has in our time placed at the disposal of the machinery of war the most sophisticated attainments of his discipline. All apparent conscience, all cultural instruction and religious teaching concerning the immorality of killing vanish before the higher command to defend his country, and the scientist makes available to the art of murder the most intricate secrets of his trade. In the language of this inquiry we should say that he fills out from the particularity of his learning the generality of that open instinct, the territorial imperative; and, having done so, he will act according to the finished pattern with the predictability of a Capricorn beetle.

4

Briefly we skip like a water bug across the surface of the new biology's still, deep pools.

We may say that behavior—the frame of possibilities available to any animal's actions—is as characteristic of species and subspecies as is length of claw or shape of shoulder bone. Body and behavior form an organic unit, subject within a species to normal variation in individuals and populations, which will be tested in the field of worth by natural selection.

We have seen that instinct—the genetically determined pattern which informs an animal as to how to act in a given situation—has tended in the evolution of vertebrates to become increasingly of an open sort. As ways of life have become more complex, it has become of selective value to support instincts which make use of experience and learning. One can no more say that the *kind* of instinct motivating man is qualitatively different from the *kind* of instinct motivating higher animals than one can inspect the fossil record of the gradual human emergence and say: Here, here at this anatomical moment, animals ended and men began.

Now finally we come to the general problem of heredity and environment. And my best advice is to refresh one's drink, sit deep in one's chair, and hold fast. It is at this dangerous corner that the natural and social sciences collide.

In America, and to a lesser degree elsewhere, the dominant school of thought in the study of man for the last thirty years has been cultural anthropology. It was founded by Franz Boas and a brilliant group of students at Columbia University. One of those students was Margaret Mead, today our most distinguished anthropologist, and in a recent work she has described her field more concisely and more persuasively than can I:

> In the central concept of culture as it was developed by Boas and his students, human beings were viewed as dependent neither on instinct nor on genetically transmitted specific capabilities but on learned ways of life that

accumulated slowly through endless borrowing, readaptation, and innovation. . . . The vast panorama which Boas sketched out in 1932 in his discussion of the aims of anthropological research is still the heritage of American anthropology.

At this particular point in my narrative, I prefer to allow authorities to speak for themselves. M. F. Ashley Montagu is another eloquent onetime student of Boas, a geneticist as well as anthropologist. In 1962 he wrote in his introduction to *Culture and the Evolution of Man:*

> It is principally through cultural pressures that primate nature, in the case of man, has been changed into human nature. It must be emphasized that this change has been brought about not—among other things—by the suppression of primate instinctual drives, but by their gradual supplantation by an adaptively more effective means of meeting the challenges of the environment, namely, by enhancing the development of intelligence. . . . In the course of human evolution the power of instinctual drives has gradually withered away, until man has virtually lost all his instincts. If there remain any residues of instincts in man, they are, possibly, the automatic reaction to a sudden loud noise, and in the remaining instance to a sudden withdrawal of support; for the rest, man has no instincts.

I mentioned in the last section that Watson and his striped muscles did not last long in psychology and would find, like Rousseau, few defenders today, but that the work of the behaviorists brought lasting effects on other areas of thought. It was Watson who reduced the human endowment to two instinctive fears: of falling and of loud noises. Perhaps we should regard it as less than surprising that cultural anthropology leans with various degrees of frankness on the work of the other rejected master and tends at least implicitly to accept Rousseau's concept of original goodness. In another book published in 1962, *The Humanization of Man*, Montagu is both frank and explicit: "Evil is not inherent in human nature, it is learned. . . . Aggressiveness is taught, as are all forms of violence which human beings exhibit."

In fairness to anthropology, it should be recorded that not all of its authorities have remained so aloof to contemporary developments in evolutionary thought. A. Irving Hallowell is professor emeritus of anthropology at the University of Pennsylvania. He comments:

> Whereas opponents of human evolution in the nineteenth century were those who naturally stressed evidence that implied discontinuity between man and his primate precursors, anthropologists of the twentieth century, while giving lip service to morphological evolution, have by the special emphasis laid upon culture as the prime human differential, implied what is in effect an unbridged behavioral gap between ourselves and our closest relatives.

As divine intervention, in other words, was the last century's means of disavowing evolution's relationship to man, so the primacy of culture is this century's. In further fairness to anthropology as well as to my fellow Americans, I feel the need to include one more quotation, this from the broader field of sociology and from a Briton. The quotation carries extraordinary authority. A few years ago there was published in London a volume called *A Century of Darwin* in which fifteen world-famous specialists were invited to sum up the present influence of *Origin of Species* on their various scientific fields. Donald G. McRae, reader in sociology at the University of London, discussed with admirable candor the present influence of evolutionary theory on the social sciences:

> The tendency of the social scientist to whore after theories drawn from natural science—physical or biological—has a long history. Something has been gained, but the mass of consequent error suggests that the price may well have been too high. It is certainly the case that the place of both specifically Darwinian and more broadly evolutionary ideas is smaller in modern social science than has been true at any time in the past century. . . . It used to be said that the last word of biology was the first word

4

of sociology. Logically it ought to be the case, but for it to become so biology will have to offer the social sciences something other than Darwinism—or at least something additional.

I myself have nothing but gratitude for McRae's intellectual courage in stating the truth with such clarity in the midst of such a volume. That for thirty-five years a revolution in evolutionary thought has been holding sway in biology, and that almost every page of *A Century of Darwin* offers the sociologist the additional something he demands and at once ignores, is beside the point. What McRae does is to expose cleanly the break to which Hallowell referred: Evolution is all right for animals, but it has nothing to do with men. And the layman must ask, How in the world did the sciences—in which if nowhere else reason must be presumed to rule—ever develop such a split personality?

It is the influence of heredity, of course, which is denied just as the influence of environment is exalted. But the denial is impossible, since the two are in balance. Through the shufflings and sortings of heredity, through normal variation of individuals and populations, through sexual combination and recombination, through novel mutation and sleeping with strangers, an infinite variety of living possibilities is and always has been continually created, just as worth is being eternally tested on the field of environment.

Such fields are many. Environment exists within your body, where physiological combinations will face germs and parasites from the outside world; some combinations will succeed and others will fail, and the survivors in a population after sufficient generations will perfect a heritable genetic arrangement to provide a degree of immunity for descendants. This is what happened in Europe in the Middle Ages when developing communications with Asia brought us strange diseases for which we had no immunities. Epidemics like the Black Death decimated our populations. But the plagues lost their virulence long before the advent of modern medicine. We developed immunities. Had they not been heritable, we might possess today no generation of sociologists to decry the significance of heredity.

Or environment may be social. If you are an adolescent chacma baboon of overly bellicose nature and your aggressions lead you to pick quarrels again and again with fellow members of your troop, then the chances are that someday you will get hurt. And you will not be able to keep up with your troop as it moves about its range seeking food. And you will fall behind and the leopard will eat you. Your troop will be the better for it, since baboons simply cannot survive without their highly organized co-operative societies. This capacity to form disciplined societies is the baboon's most valuable genetic endowment. You were a variant, but happily you will leave no offspring since the leopard has eaten you.

Cultural traditions are also a part of our environment. If there is a tradition, as in almost all African tribes, to kill twins as soon as they are born, then you will not find many twins around, and if you pursue the tradition through a sufficient number of generations the genetic potentiality to twin should be considerably reduced. In this sense the cultural anthropologist is correct: Variations between the cultural traditions of human populations must, if pursued for a sufficient number of generations, have a selective effect on the quality of a population's gene pool. The capacity for a human population to form cultural traditions which become a significant selective force in a particular environment has probably contributed to the rapid rate of human evolution. To underrate the long-term genetic consequences of a cultural tradition is as dangerous as to overrate the short-term conclusiveness of cultural determination.

Environment tests us in many ways, and time itself may be a factor. There have been epochs like the Pliocene, when times were so changeless that time itself seemed scarcely to move. Such periods test the conservatism of beings, since the probability is high that if one acts today as one acted yesterday, one will survive. But there have also been epochs of an opposite nature. Such has been the Pleistocene in which we yet live, when climates changed, and changed again, and the great cold would come to consume a continent or rains would change desert to forest and then drought would return it to sand. Through such unending panoramas of shifting, changing times there passed like figures in a fragmented dream those little bands of struggling beings who someday would be men. They survived by courage in the face of adversity, endurance in the face of extremity; they survived, like baboons, through recognition of a need, one for another; they survived through enormous selective pressure encouraging the expansion of normal primate wit. Above all, however, they survived through plasticity, through a broadening power to incorporate experience into the iron of old behavioral patterns, through a growing capacity to recognize, in changing times, that today is different from yesterday, and tomorrow from today.

Many—most without doubt—were conservative creatures. These died by dry, unanticipated stream beds, or numbed and froze in unanticipated storms. These quite obviously were not your ancestors. It was the others—the witty, the sensitive, the flexible, the ones who could recognize a changing environment when they saw one and incorporate new information into the program of their instincts—these were the ones to assemble, ever so slowly, a new and most remarkable genetic package: ourselves.

As a layman I can understand an academic position which accepts my description but says, "You have forgotten two things. First, that a time came when these open instincts, under selective pressure, vanished entirely, to be supplanted by unencumbered intelligence. And, second, you have forgotten that man came at last so thoroughly to control his environment that it ceased to have selective force."

To the first reminder I can only reply, "Am I truly expected to believe that the history of man, to this date, has been written by unencumbered intelligence? And even if, for the sake of argument, I were to accept a proposition so outrageous, there is this matter of how we came to be. Every living creature, man or mosquito, has an unbroken ancestry going back at least two billion years to the first chemical stirrings of life. No responsible authority would dare to maintain that longer ago than at

34

the most ten thousand years, when man first secured control of his food supply through domestication of grains and animals, our human ancestors were exempt from the natural processes that I have described. Are we seriously to believe that in ten thousand years, without divine intervention, we have repealed those natural laws that prevailed for the previous one billion, nine hundred and ninety-nine million, nine hundred and ninety thousand years, and that brought us into being?"

I am entirely willing to grant that anything is possible, but to me the statistics seem against it. And to the second reminder concerning the control we exert over our environment, I must reply, "You are thinking of environment in terms of physical arrangements. You are thinking of drainage ditches and antibiotics and slum clearance and hybrid corn. *You* are forgetting something—that the most important element in the human environment is man himself. And so long as we live in a time when a few human beings, by pressing an arrangement of buttons, can in a few hours so alter our physical environment as to make life all but insupportable on this planet, then I am unimpressed by the argument that we have gained control of any part of it."

One must brood. For a man in the street to be compelled to present such childlike logic to the professional thinker is little less than embarrassing. What ails us? What is this inhibition afflicting so many of our finest minds which renders them incapable of adding two and two? I believe that I know, although it will require a subjective digression to explore it. And it will be useful, also, if we recall Maslow's hint that to refer to instinct or heredity in our time is to expose oneself as a political reactionary. I believe that it goes beyond that, however, into an area as much moral as political.

Many established leaders of contemporary thought today spent all or most of their formative years, as did I, in the 1930's. It was a decade, as any of us old enough will recall, at once splendid in its creativity and all but annihilating in environmental hardship. Poverty was the normal condition. As the decade opened I emerged from the University of Chicago with a Phi Beta Kappa key and a degree with honors, of which neither raised my wages as a lecturer in anthropology above fifty cents an hour. After seven or eight years I managed somehow to achieve an income of eighteen hundred dollars a year, but since I received it as a Fellow of the Guggenheim Foundation, even this might be regarded as less than honest money. I must hasten to confess, of course, that I cannot blame all on the depression. I might perhaps have done better financially had I not been imbued with such unforgettable standards of literary excellence as flowed from the immaterial soul of Thornton Wilder, my mentor for five unforgettable years.

In any event, the 1930's were impressive times. If you were an American, there was unending unemployment at home and Adolf Hitler across the seas. If you were a European, there was unending unemployment at home and Adolf Hitler next door. This was our environment. So encompassing was it, so whole-heartedly inimical to human hopes, so wonderfully varied in its gambits of disaster, that if you were young and impressionable there was no conclusion which you were likely to reach other than that environment is responsible for human fault.

I was one of a handful of young playwrights who established as fashionable what might be called the Theater of Social Protest. There was Sidney Kingsley, and *Dead End,* and an audience that fell in love with the Dead End Kids. The play said that poverty is responsible for crime. There was Lillian Hellman, and *The Little Foxes,* and we thrilled to her match-less panoply of villains. The play said that money is the source of all evil. There was Clifford Odets, and *Golden Boy,* and the tragedy of commercialism vs. art. We all envied Clifford, for he found himself with the biggest commercial hit on Broadway. And there was Irwin Shaw, and the terrifying *Bury the Dead,* which convinced us that but for propaganda there would be no wars. (Irwin, a few years later, became the best soldier that the Dramatists Guild would produce. By that time he had taken *Bury the Dead* off the market, refusing to allow its further public presentation.)

My own best contribution to the genre was a play called *Jeb.* It was about American Negroes, and it said that when a white man asks, "Would you want a Negro to marry your sister?" what he really means is, "Would you want a Negro to get your

36

job?" It was a good play, by general agreement, though perhaps in subject matter a bit ahead of its time. It did not last long. But it was typical of the way we looked at things through the window of the 1930's.

Now, what can one say of plays like these? That they were untrue? That economic motive does not enter into racial discrimination? That propaganda is not a factor in war? That the struggle for material gain does not spawn greed and cruelty? That poverty does not breed crime? They were true; but they were half-truths. And a half-truth presented as a whole truth becomes, in the end, a total lie. How could we know that in the end there would come a changed environment and a prosperity such as no man had ever seen? And that such an age of affluence and material security would witness a level and degree of juvenile delinquency that did not exist in the depression years; racial conflict and bitterness that we had never known; and a crime rate beyond our most monstrous imaginings? Crime could not even have been described as a major problem when poverty was king.

A changed environment demonstrated that our environmentalist conclusions were inadequate. Perhaps some of us sensed it at an early date. The Theater of Social Protest vanished in the 1940's, to be replaced by the Theater of Self-Pity, which yet commands. But we had done our mighty bit to make fashionable the Age of the Alibi, to make acceptable an attitude which seeks fault anywhere but in oneself, and damns it as immoral to do otherwise. In July, 1934, to have said to an unemployed British workingman "You have none but yourself to blame" would have been to commit an outrage both moral and intellectual. In July, 1964, when for the first time in Britain there existed more jobs than job-seekers, to make the same proposal would carry a reasonable degree of intellectual merit, at least as a hypothesis; yet it would meet the same moral rejection now as before.

Is it possible that the environmental severity of the 1930's induced—particularly in the most aware, alert, and compassionate of men—a morality which makes no sense today? Is it possible that some of us—like Konrad Lorenz' endearing ducks, to whom we shall return one day—were somehow imprinted with an attitude which was reasonable then, but which clings now as nothing but a moral posture? Is this the inhibition that prevents many of those who, while exalting intelligence and environment, are incapable of recognizing the nature of the new environment in which they themselves now live?

Should this be the case, then again we may witness scenes of natural selection resembling the immense panoramas of the Pleistocene. As in another fragmented dream we shall behold small bands of struggling beings against backgrounds of shifting climates. Again we watch while unsentimental forces select or reject, accept or discard, encouraging the plastic, the flexible, those with instincts open enough to accommodate today's information, those beings genetically capable of reading clues in the sky when clues appear and of recognizing a novel environment when they see one. And then again there must be, I suppose, those little bands of conservative creatures struggling with today as if it were yesterday, staggering across bewildering, unrecognized landscapes, chanting weary hymns to unencumbered intelligence while acting the closed programs of insects, lying down at last by some dry, unanticipated stream bed or vanishing, selected out, into some uncompromising, unanticipated storm. So works evolution.

The sciences, one must hope, will come in time to bury their dead.

5

Men, unlike mockingbirds, have the capacity for systematic self-delusion. We echo each other with equal precision, equal eloquence, equal assurance. But be it said for mockingbirds, hidden by the indigo of a California night, that they do not risk their species' future with the lush inflation of their song.

I have set down enough in these pages, I believe, to allow us to get started. I have permitted us an opportunist's glance at just those few of the new biology's interpretations which we need to begin with. I have tried to present a certain sense of that broadening conflict within the sciences, between evolutionist and anti-evolutionist, that one cannot gain as yet from the newspapers. Having myself been science's witness for many years, I am convinced that we shall all witness in the near future a resumption of those passionate controversies of almost a century ago, in the time of T. H. Huxley and Bishop Wilberforce, which followed the publication of *Origin of Species*. Biology had not the resources in Darwin's day to carry the logic of natural selection beyond the evolution of man's bodily being. It has the resources now. And I cannot see our appointment with the deferred debate as anything but inevitable. But there will be a difference in the character of the contestants. In the nineteenth century science as a whole spoke for the continuity of living beings, whereas religion spoke for the uniqueness of man. In our time the controversy must arise between two wings of science itself.

So far as my own position is concerned, I should like to believe that it can be found somewhere in the neighborhood of a statement by Harvard's beloved biologist George Gaylord Simpson which he wrote in the introduction to one of his books: "I am trying to pursue a science that is beginning to have a good many practitioners but that has no name: the science of four-dimensional biology or of time and life." That is about it. I do not believe that we are towns without histories, ships without compasses, moments without memories. We carry in that region known as the unconscious certain patterns inherited from ancient days. They are patterns of survival value, or we should not be here. And they are a legacy of all that life which has come before us, assuring us that we are not alone.

I believe, furthermore, that what we call the age of anxiety is in truth a transitional time, an uncertain moment in the adolescence of a species, when the superstitions and imaginary identifications of childhood are no longer enough but the larger comprehensions of maturity are yet unavailable. In such an awkward emotional age we lose faith in fathers, divine or domestic, and yearn for more suitable stars to steer by. We lose confidence. We feel ourselves children of inconspicuous circumstance, dry leaves tumbling before unimportant winds, victims of worlds not of our making, will-less trespassers on dubious pastures. Yet self-knowledge cannot be denied. Maturity must come.

It was only a generation or so ago that the physical sciences added the dimension of time to their three-dimensional calculations of matter and energy, and with a single mathematical leap plunged us into the world of the atom. It is a world as exhilarating as it is hazardous, a world to stir the most stagnant of imaginations even as it frightens the most dashing of souls. Above all, however, it was the feat of the physical sciences to present man with a confidence that he was the master of material things.

It is the turn now of biology, I believe, to extend our calculation of man by the addition of that same fourth dimension, time. It will be a leap, I believe, of not incomparable consequence. There will be terror of a sort in losing, once and for all, this comfortable, pupa-like, three-dimensional chamber of human uniqueness, the only world we have ever known. And there will be hazard, most particular hazard, in the chance that we may discover ourselves the pale prisoners of a determinate past, whereas before we were at worst the nervous victims of an indeterminate future. But it is a chance I believe worth taking: in part, because I have reason to suspect that this will not be biology's answer; in part, because I believe that the winning of self-knowledge is worth every risk; and in part, because I have no choice, for truth is peering in my window and I cannot ask him to go away.

One of the nineteenth-century thinkers most influenced by Darwin, most despised by fashionable thought today, was Herbert Spencer. And in a minor, forgotten work he once recorded a major, everlasting thought: "The profoundest of all infidelities is the fear that the truth will be bad." I may quake in my boots, I may shake in my bed. But I do not have the courage to live a life so dangerous as that of a gambler against the truth.

The protozoa (or is it the egg that once I was?) has his eye on me. And he knows all about me, all my secrets, for he was there when I began, and he knows when I am lying, and he is watching me, right now, just as he watches you.

2. Arena Behavior

The Uganda kob is among the supreme beauties of the antelope world, a photographic delicacy for antelope connoisseurs. Less graceful than the impala, less majestic than the kudu with its corkscrew horns, the kob has a sturdy elegance unlike either. His coat is a golden brown, like proper toast. There are black-and-white markings about his face, and they vary considerably, so that two kob, like two people, seldom look quite alike. He stands about three feet high at the shoulder, but his neck is so long, his curved, lyrate horns are so sweeping, his dark eyes regard his fellow kob so imperiously, that he seems much larger. He is a superb beast, and in 1960 I thought I knew all about him.

I spent the month of June of that year in the eastern Congo and western Uganda, home base for the kob. It was the last month of Belgian rule, and while things were still quiet in the Congo, it required the assistance of no witch-doctor's bones to inform me as to what would happen next. Tourists vanished. My wife and I were the last two guests at the Congo's magnificent game reserve, the Parc Albert. We had it to ourselves. My heroic qualities, however, are less than notable, so when independence day came we too cleared out of the area, managing to reach Uganda's capital before the Congo blew up behind us.

There were many occasions in that depopulated month when we could not put aside the sensation of being either the last two people in the world or the first. We shared the African sky, the yellow, unending savannah, the choked, narrow strips of forest along swirling streams, the hazy, gray-blue central African lakes with our hosts, the elephant, the buffalo, the hippo, the lion and topi and waterbuck and kob. We were their only guests. A sense of extraordinary intimacy pervaded our arrangements. The kob must have water every day, and so he favors this area around Lakes Edward and Albert. For hour upon hour we watched herds grazing on some long yellow slope, impala-like family parties with a dozen or fifteen does and a master ram, or perhaps, again like the impala, all-male bachelor parties. And the does watched us, raising their long-necked, delicate, hornless heads out of the deep grass, ears raised like signs of V-for-Victory; as did the males, with their challenging eyes and S-curved, swept-back horns. My sense of intimacy came to include a sense of authority. On the way out of kob country I discussed them with the director of the Uganda National Parks. When many months later I returned to my writing table in Rome, the conclusion was inescapable that, so far as the kob was concerned, I knew everything.

It was three years before I had the opportunity to return to Uganda. Rome, as we left, broiled like a chicken on a midsummer grill. We de-planed on the high, cool equator with the joy of escaped prisoners who have somehow eluded the hot seat. The air of Kampala, most adorable of African capitals, was that of a shaded garden, newly watered. Dizzily I embraced the Kampala panorama: the temples and churches topping its hills, the blossoms and bank buildings, Indian merchants, African politicians in black jackets and black silk ties, Baganda students, the university's green lawns. On the veranda of the Grand Hotel (it had been the Imperial on my last visit, but that, of course, had been before Uganda's independence) I met an old friend, an anthropologist, who could scarcely wait to get past proper greetings so that he might pull at his beard and inform me that for over a year there had been an American scientist around who had been looking for me, who claimed he had a bone to pick with me, and who said that everything I had written in *African Genesis* about the Uganda kob was wrong.

I was outraged. Professionally I was outraged, and I quoted my observations and my authorities while my friend just shook his head and nursed his happy secrets. Personally I was outraged that friends could prove so faithless, and I condemned his soul to dust. But spiritually I was worse than outraged, for I had been back in Africa for only two hours and already I had been ambushed, my euphoria was gone, and there was nothing I could do about it. I inquired gloomily as to what it was that I had got so wrong about the Uganda kob. "Territorial behavior," said Merrick Posnansky joyfully. I demanded the name of the American scientist who knew so much. "Buechner," he said, with regret. "A pity. He had to go back to the United States two weeks ago." He beamed evilly. "But his Swiss assistant's in town."

That afternoon I met Walter Leuthold, the assistant from Zurich. He was pink-faced, young, amiable, apparently harmless. But when tea and his story were finished my vanity was finished too. The family parties that I had watched for so long were the most casual social relationships. Not in a thousand kob years would one of those imperious rams have sexual relations with a member of his seeming harem. Copulation, by general species agreement, is left exclusively to a dozen or fifteen males, out of every population of eight hundred or a thousand, who discharge their massive obligations on something called a stamping ground. It was this stamping ground that Buechner had discovered. That I had been fooled no more thoroughly than several generations of game wardens, hunters, naturalists, and explorers was a poor sort of salve for my injuries. Since I was leaving for western Uganda within a few days in any event, I put the stamping ground on my itinerary. I had to see it before I could believe it.

Helmut K. Buechner is professor of zoology at Washington State University. It had not truly been Buechner but Mrs. Buechner who had for the first time looked at the kob with eyes unglazed by preconception. At about the time when I was coming to my staid conclusions, Buechner was working on a project in the Semliki Flats, a broad remote area partly in Uganda, partly in the Congo, separating Lakes Albert and Edward in the hot, flat bottom of the Rift Valley. There, one day, his wife came home and announced that something went on with the Uganda kob. Since the Semliki Flats contain some twelve thousand members of the species, it was not too bad a place to look into the matter. In consequence, ethology was presented with a study as elegant as the discovery itself was spectacular; an author was presented with one more hard lesson on taking nothing for granted; and this inquiry is presented with an example of territorial behavior which, while of a most special sort, still makes an excellent jumping-off place.

A stamping ground, the breeding arena of a single population of kob, looks like nothing so much as a series of putting greens conveniently arranged for the benefit of idle guests behind a luxurious resort hotel. With a little help I found one among the most southerly foothills of the Mountains of the Moon. Without help I stumbled on still another several hundred miles to the north, on the bank of the Albert Nile. As Buechner's long research demonstrated, members of the two populations could have had no possible contact. The complicated sexual game as played at my two widely separated arenas —and Buechner's arenas in the Semliki Flats as well—followed precisely the same formal pattern. Yet it could not have been learned one from another.

We deal here with an open instinct in which final behavior is regulated by a genetically determined pattern filled out by social tradition and individual experience. The pattern, governing motivation and what might be called the rules of the game, is common to the species and is instinctual. It never varies. The location of the stamping ground is traditional within each population. Probably accident and environmental assets combined originally to determine the location. Just as champion cricketers in London converge on Lord's, so champion males in a kob population converge on their stamping ground, because generations before them have done it and it is simply the place to go. Finally, the individual competitor must learn his territories and his opponents, those whom he can beat and those he can't, out of his own experience whether glorious or painful. So it is, then, that the open instinct of the kob, with all its authority and startling complexity, absorbs the traditions of a society and the learning of the individual to perfect its final, inviolable determination.

A stamping ground is not large, a quality of great appeal for animal observers such as myself who look with distaste on all forms of violent exercise. Each little putting green with its close-cropped grass is about fifty feet in diameter and is a territory occupied and defended by a single male. A closely bunched cluster of a dozen or fifteen or eighteen such territories in a main arena may occupy an area no more than two hundred yards across. Here the champion males out of a population of almost a thousand—a kind of sexual Olympic team—fight, display, and jockey for position. Here needy females come seeking consolation.

Certain necessities of the gladiators' daily life dictate an aesthetic appeal for the human observer. To begin with, a single kob is beautiful, and fifteen kob commanding their putting greens are fifteen times as beautiful. Also, the site must stand in the midst of wide, rich grasslands with ample forage, water, and preferably a salt lick not too far away. It is best if it stands on a slight rise with an open view for a mile or so around. The lion, a beast with a dislike for wasted effort as pragmatic as my own, is discouraged by fast prey in a position to see him first. That the fabled Ruwenzoris, with their ice and their clouds, loomed up behind my first stamping ground must be regarded as a pleasant accident, not as a sexual necessity in the life of the kob.

There is, however, a vital ecological necessity for such an institution as the kob's. It is an equatorial species found only in areas of Africa where seasonal changes of weather and pasture are slight. The place may be permanent since herds need not migrate with the rains and the grass. And there is a vital physiological factor lending character to the institution. The female adheres to no season of heat. Unlike the females of most mammal species, she will come into her sexual season whenever she weans her latest offspring, in whatever part of the year that may be, and will promptly seek the entertainments of the arena. But from the male's point of view, this female peculiarity commands a towering obligation. Gladiators must be on duty 365 days a year. Buechner studied fifteen stamping grounds in the Semliki Flats and was able to demonstrate that at least seven of them had been in continuous operation at their present locations for at least thirty years. Realizing that a stamping ground was not going out of business just because he was around, Buechner built a wooden stand beside one for the convenience of himself, his cameras, his notebooks, and his guests.

When from car or grandstand one watches the sexual shenanigans of the Uganda kob, one watches evidence that an open instinct, once perfected, can provide a natural performance as rigorously regulated as any to be found in nature. The female, for one thing, is sexually unresponsive to any male who has not succeeded in gaining one of the putting greens. She may linger for protection near one of those males whom we saw in the deep yellow grasses; she is incapable of copulation with him. But he, likewise, is incapable of copulation with her. The male who has not gained a territory on the stamping ground is sexually unmotivated. Such males gather as a rule in all-male bachelor herds, as careless of the ladies as male patrons in a Portuguese café.

The sexual action of a population is therefore concentrated on this little assembly of putting greens before us. But while it may seem that the action is simple—that males fight for territories and females flirt with winners—it is not simple, for there are still more regulations. Within the arena, for example, some properties have greater sexual values than others. In a normal city, real-estate values increase block by block to the city's core; so on the stamping ground sexual values increase from the suburban market of the periphery to the flashing excitements of Times Square. Young ambitious maturing males fight for a foothold on the periphery, to gain a property even in the suburbs; the peripheral males challenge, fight, wait for an opening to gain better locations in the main arena; and on a few central territories—perhaps only three or four—stand the champions of the moment, challenged by all, envied by all, desired by every female heart.

The female wants her affection, but she wants it at a good address. Whether or not our human sensibilities are offended or intrigued, it is a harsh truth that the doe is attracted and excited by the qualities of the property, not the qualities of the proprietor. George Bartholomew once puzzled over comparable behavior on the part of Alaska fur seals in rookeries on lonely St. Paul's Island. Cows might congregate in harems passing a hundred on one bull's territory, in twos or threes on those of others. Yet they exhibited the most disdainful indifference to the bull himself. What attracted them to this territory, repelled them from that? Bartholomew concluded that they were attracted by the presence of other cows, somewhat in the manner of the nylon rushes of World War II.

We need not puzzle over the selective value in the Uganda kob of the female's addiction to high-value property. Since it coincides with the male's sense of value, it results in a scheme of natural selection of a remarkable order. Only a super-kob lasts long on a central territory. If he leaves his property for water and forage, he will return to find it occupied and must fight to regain it. On his putting green he will be continually challenged by the ambitious. One afternoon I watched a champion resist five such challenges in an hour and a half, one a twenty-minute horn-locked pushing contest that left him scarcely able to stand. Yet the doe, despite her apparent fragility, may in full sweep of estrus demand copulation ten times in a day. In a busy season the proprietor of one of the central territories must somehow sandwich between invasion problems presented by his colleagues perhaps twenty emotional problems presented by his admirers.

The human male, encountering a stamping ground for the first time, cannot fail to identify himself with the contestants before him. And despite his most secret dreams of sex and riot, he will thank a merciful evolutionary destiny that made him a man and not a Uganda kob; it is all just a bit too much trouble. The human female, on the other hand, will have a response quite different. Identifying herself with the doe, she will be embarrassed for all femininity.

One faces a grassy area of African space. Omnipotent males stand their posts, occasionally challenging another with a tussle, more often retreating before an imperious wave of the head. Then business arrives. Four or five slender, long-legged does come gamboling along like high-school girls on their way to an ice-cream soda. They may graze for a bit beyond the arena's perimeter in a preliminary display of how little such nonsense concerns them. Then one will break away, enter, and pass through the peripheral territories without a glance for the suburban opportunists. Arriving at a major territory, she will begin diligently to crop the proprietor's grass. Suddenly one understands that the putting greens are so conspicuous not because the beleaguered proprietors have eaten them down to their last caloric morsel but because the does, with all of western Uganda for a dining table, have a special appetite for their limited ration.

Our anthropomorphic sympathies for the male, however, are wasted. All that seems to matter to him as his grass is devoured is that somebody cares. He draws himself up, he puffs himself out. He puts his head far back, his nostrils to the sky, and with tiny, strutting steps the noble animal minces back and forth before his intended. One recalls: every posture and movement of his body is that of a drum-majorette leading a school band down the Main Street of a Middle Western town. Dignity vanishes. He holds his head high in this unseemly ritual so that he may exhibit to the grass-cropper his long, strong, sexually irresistible, gloriously buff-colored neck. She continues to crop his grass, but now the action takes a turn. The male,

evidently convinced that by now her heart is aflame, approaches her, nose to tail, sniffs her genitals. She gives up the grass and sniffs his. Slowly they circle, sniffing. To the uninitiated observer the game seems won, judgment vindicated. He approaches her rear and with a last ritualistic gesture raises his forelegs between her hind legs. Having done the proper, he mounts her. And she promptly goes back to eating grass.

The scientific voyeur watches in disbelief. She gives a flip of her slim haunches and he slides off. All around the stamping ground similar charades by now are in progress where other does have arrived. Males are mincing back and forth, noses to heaven, throats displayed, while voracious little females eat up their grass. On still other putting greens lone males ignore the shows, offer no interference, continue their games of challenge-and-defend, or simply stare into space. On our putting green the male is making another try. He mounts her. She moves. He tries to keep up on his hind legs, a maneuver adding little to his splendor. He falls off. Once again, however, he makes his try. And now comes the startling climax. She crosses the boundary into his neighbor's putting green.

It was as if a wand many millions of years old, borrowed for the occasion from some dusty collection of animal witchcraft, waved across the scene. All changed. Now his neighbor was marching back and forth with mincing step, exhibiting his glorious, buff-colored throat, while she clipped the neighbor's putting green. And our male?

Our male took all in good grace. When you are a member of an animal elite, then you are not only a proprietor but you also observe proprieties. When you are a member of a sexually privileged club with a charter going back into dim reaches of antelope beginnings, then you observe club rules. He forgot her in a moment. Noble, statuesque, he stood alone in the middle of his putting green, looking off at the distant, cloud-cloaked, immortal Mountains of the Moon. When she passed over his territorial boundary, she passed out of his world.

2

Buechner's observations of the Uganda kob furnish us with one of the most recent and sophisticated studies of territorial behavior. And since I intend to compare them with science's earliest reflections on the territorial principle, it will be useful to note a few of his conclusions for our future recollection.

1. Males compete for real estate, never for females. The kob's territorial and sexual appetites are so profoundly intermeshed that fights generate sexual stimulation. The champion whom we watched in a twenty-minute defense of his property had an erection through most of the combat. Nevertheless, when the female arrives on a territory, she becomes the sole if momentary property of the male whose grass she crops. No rival will interfere. A flourishing arena is a Breughel-like scene of scattered kob couples in various stages of intimate disposal amid a scattering of solitary males paying no regard whatsoever.

2. Despite the hazards of his profession, the proprietor almost

always bests the challenger. Selection throughout the herd has brought only top specimens to the arena, so all are quite equally matched. Possession of a territory offers some mysterious advantage usually sufficient to guarantee victory for the defender. In his first fifteen months of intensive observation, Buechner saw the challenger win on only a dozen or so occasions. Champions fall, of course, but usually from exhaustion. They fail to return from foraging or, returning, fail to regain their posts.

3. So powerful is the proprietor's psychological advantage that dangerous fighting is minimized. Simple ear-lowering, horn-waggling, or other stern display is frequently enough to discourage challenge. Leuthold reported to me a male with a broken leg who in a triumph of psychological warfare held onto his property for eight long days.

4. Off the stamping ground the gladiators display no antagonism. Should a hungry-enough lion appear, the first to spot it gives a stiff-legged hopping signal alerting his fellows. All retire by customary paths to wait amicably until the lion goes away.

5. The inspiration of ownership seems necessary to stimulate sexual desire in both males and females. Away from the stamping ground copulation is only rarely attempted, and apparently never consummated.

6. In the vast population of the Semliki Flats, each group of herds holds allegiance to a definite, traditional ground. Buechner marked many males, and reobserved them on two thousand occasions. Only seven of these reobservations were as far as five kilometers from home grounds.

7. Leuthold has given special attention to an aberrant design for living in kob country. Most males who fail to achieve the main event, or achieving it fail to hold on, join the contented bachelor herds. But there are lonely exceptions. Such a male stakes out a territory of his own somewhere. Near this jutting outcrop or that spreading tree he will always be found. A party of does may join him—a dozen, fifteen, twenty—for the companionship or the security of his august presence. There you will see them in the sleepy afternoon, as I had observed them in

1960, the does lying in the grass, the male standing alert beneath his swept-back horns, an apparently normal antelope family. In a week or so the party of does will drift on to farther pastures. And the male will remain beside this rock, beneath that tree.

"Attachment to a piece of ground," writes Buechner, "is stronger than to the female herd."

Such attachment to a piece of ground has been the subject of organized study in the natural sciences since 1920. In that year Eliot Howard published his memorable volume *Territory in Bird Life* and established the word and the concept in the language of science. But for many a century before Howard, observers had pondered, briefly or at length, on the notable attachment of a particular animal for a particular piece of earth.

Aristotle had puzzled over birds of prey: "A pair of eagles demands an extensive space for its maintenance, and consequently cannot allow other eagles to quarter themselves in close neighborhood." Pliny, in Rome, bothered too about eagles: "One pair of eagles needs a very considerable space of ground to forage over, in order to find enough food; for which reason they mark out by boundaries their respective allotments, and seek their prey in succession to one another." A thirteenth-century German emperor, Frederick II, like many another royal figure of the day, was a dedicated falconer, and recorded thoughts to be published some centuries later: "After fledgling falcons have learned to fly and hunt bird prey, the parent drives them away not only from the immediate neighborhood of the eyrie but from the entire nesting locality. Were the mother and her offspring to hunt in the same territory, their bird quarry would soon take fright and there soon would be not enough food to supply the needs of the whole family."

Aristotle, Pliny, and Frederick II, we should say today, all subscribed to the food theory of territory. They were not the last to ascribe attachment for a piece of ground to the economic motivation of securing a food supply—a type of motivation which the Uganda kob has so conspicuously never heard of.

Other early bird-watchers considered the robin. Zenodotus

seems the earliest, in the third century B.C., when he stated flatly and inarguably, "One bush does not shelter two robins." In 1622 G. P. Olina gave his attention to the robin in his *Uccelliera,* an attention concerned mostly with the bird's bad disposition: "It has a peculiarity that it cannot abide a companion in the place where it lives and will attack with all its strength any who dispute this claim." Not till 1772 did anyone, to my knowledge, bring sex into it. Then Gilbert White wrote: "During the amorous season, such a jealousy prevails among the male birds that they can scarcely bear to be together in the same hedge or field . . . and it is to this spirit of jealousy that I chiefly attribute the equal dispersion of birds in the spring over the face of the country." White's famous contemporary, the Count de Buffon, took exception and opted for economics in the life of the nightingale: "Nightingales select certain tracts and oppose the encroachment of others on their territory. But the conduct is not occasioned by rivalship, as some have supposed; it is suggested by the solicitude for the maintenance of their young, and regulated by the extent of ground necessary to afford sufficient food."

The naturalists of the late eighteenth century were staking out territories of controversy which descendant scientists still quarrel over today. But not until 1868, when the German ornithologist Bernard Altum published *Der Vogel und Sein Leben,* did anyone take the time to construct a theory out of it. Altum established two main hypotheses that have stood the erosion of time and research: first, that male birds fight for the possession of land, not of females; and, second, that birds sing not for the joy of life but to warn off any intruders who may be contemplating intrusion on their private domains. These were revolutionary thoughts that today have been validated in the notebooks of a thousand researchers. At the time, however, Altum's thoughts vanished. They had been recorded in but a few pages of a study of the life of the bird; and, besides, no one seemed to be listening.

Another pioneer even more emphatically neglected was an Irish ornithologist named C. B. Moffat. He recorded his odd notions in 1903 in a paper called "The Spring Rivalry of

Birds," published in the obscure *Irish Naturalist*. Only now are we beginning to know what he meant. Like Altum, he had observed that property-holding birds sing not so much to impress the female, nor even to express the sheer joy of being rich, so much as to scare the appropriate daylights out of anybody with designs on their property. In ornithology, this today is scripture. But Moffat went further. With daring opposition to Darwin's best thoughts, he suggested that the male's bright coloration exists for the same reason. "Have we not here some ground afforded us for suspecting that the bright plumage may have been originally evoked as war paint? In other words, as a sort of warning coloration to rival males, rather than attractive coloration to dazzle the females?"

Not even in our time have we caught up with the challenge that Moffat laid down. Whom does the male have on his mind? The male or the female? For many chapters in Darwin's second great work, *The Descent of Man,* he develops the proposition called sexual selection—that the focus of masculine life is the female, and that evolutionary dynamics rest on the male's success or failure at enchanting her. Moffat said no. What the male has on his mind is the male. The female will make her choice, well and good. What is eternally bothering the male is not female estimate, but how he is doing in the eyes of his fellows. Many a contemporary school of psychology would regard this as a homosexual tendency. Nature sighs.

Less articulately, Moffat explored in his little paper another grand notion (and a startling one to have originated in Ireland) : that territory acts as a natural mechanism of birth control. The interpretation cannot be valid in such arena species as the kob, but it operates rigorously in species basing social arrangements on the breeding pair. Through the defense and antagonism of territorial proprietors a given area is divided between a consequent number of breeding pairs; surplus population is condemned to sexual nonexistence, and the reproductive population is limited to the land that will support it. This seems a rough way to go about birth control, but the Scottish ecologist and ornithologist V. C. Wynne-Edwards, in his monumental *Animal Dispersion in Relation to Social*

Behavior, has demonstrated that it works.

When we have finished our inspection of arena species other than the kob, I shall come back to what I regard as the most revolutionary thought of this forgotten Irish ornithologist: that territory acts not so much in the interest of the individual as in restraint *against* the individual in the interest of the group, the population, and the species. It is enough now to wish that someone, someday, would record for us the life of C. B. Moffat. He was evidently a member of the Dublin Naturalists Field Club. He inscribed his paper "Ballyhyland, Wexford." Beyond that I know nothing about him other than that, like the stout Cortez upon a peak in Darien, he gazed upon a blue, unexplored philosophical sea that we have yet to traverse.

Altum died, his ideas neglected. Moffat died, his ideas unknown. Others made an observation here, put forth a speculation there. An American ornithologist named Brewster was impressed by the way one bird will honor the next bird's "rights." It was a profound impression, but it faded with the sunset. Another American named Herrick studied gull communities and speculated on the relation of territory to society. One more grand boulevard of inquiry was opened, then vanished. There is small likelihood that Eliot Howard, watching his warblers and his buntings among Worcestershire's hills, was conscious of Altum or Moffat or Brewster or Herrick. In the ruthless language of natural selection, the difference between Howard and his predecessors is that their ideas died without offspring, while his left progeny all over the map.

Henry Eliot Howard was a businessman who finished his career as director of Stewarts and Lloyds, one of Britain's two largest manufacturers of steel pipe. His place of business was near Birmingham, but his home was in the country, at a house called Clareland. He began all the days of his life by rising long before dawn, assembling his unprepossessing country costume, and hanging about his neck a pair of binoculars. Eliot Howard was a member of that extraordinary British breed, virtually a species in itself, the bird-watcher. At eight in the morning he would return from the fields and have breakfast. At eight thirty he departed for work, in the 1890's via bicycle and train, later

on in a motor car. At teatime he would return. He had five
children, a son and four daughters. He would play tennis or
chess, discuss Plato. After dinner the family would gather in
what the children called the smoking room, an interesting
name for it since no one smoked except Father. Mother sat on
one side of the fireplace, Father on the other, making his notes
of the morning or simply inspecting space. Mother occasionally
said to the children, "Shh! Father's thinking."

Father, as things turned out, was doing a fair job with his
thinking. Through a series of volumes published in this
century's early decades he became the acknowledged authority
within a limited field, that of the British warbler. Then in 1920
he produced the slim monument that will recall his name until
men cease to ponder, a book called *Territory in Bird Life*. It
was the first, and until this present volume, the only book
devoted solely to the innate relationship between property and
animate behavior.

He was a silent man, on the whole; handsome in a British
way, with narrow angular face and slender mustache. He had
several great friends in the sciences, Lloyd Morgan for example,
and the young Julian Huxley. One finds among his old bits and
pieces letters from another young scientist, Konrad Lorenz in
Austria. Howard was an amateur, and yet he practiced a
scientific discipline that any professional might envy. Never in
his book does he allow his conclusions to stray beyond the
species he knew so well, the world of birds. Not once does he

permit himself speculation concerning territory in the life of men. Rarely did he share his preoccupations with his family, for it was not his way. And yet I have spoken with a very old woman who today lives in the north of Wales and who was nanny at Clareland when the children were young. And she recalls a startling night when the silent man came into the nursery and sat down and stared at her. To judge by the age of the children then, it must have been in the year 1904 or 1905. And he said to her, out of nothing, "Nanny! It's territory. That's what everything's all about. Territory. Territory." It gave her quite a turn.

Eliot Howard died at Christmastime in 1940. The Battle of Britain had engaged his countrymen in one of history's most memorable demonstrations of the territorial imperative. Howard was an old man now, but to the end he went out every morning with his boots and his binoculars and his unbeguiling costume. By this date, of course, many another Englishman was out in the fields and on the hilltops with binoculars, spotting not birds but bombers, and keeping a wary eye out for Nazi parachutists. One morning Howard came in to breakfast. He was meditating and seemed to have something most puzzling on his mind. At last he inquired mildly, "Who do you suppose they think I am?" Days later he was dead.

I dedicated *African Genesis* to the memory of Eugène Marais, South Africa's pioneer naturalist. If it were the task of a dramatist to invent a character the precise antithesis of Marais, then one could only end up with Eliot Howard. The two were contemporaries. When Marais at the turn of the century was watching baboons in the Transvaal's Waterberg, Howard was watching warblers beside the River Severn. Marais was lonely, tortured, a morphine addict. Howard led one of the calmest lives of the twentieth century. Marais was a lawyer, doctor, journalist, poet, teacher. Howard went to the office. Marais was a genius, a Van Gogh of the natural sciences, whose career was written in waste and passion and demons and who died of his own hand. Howard had a clear eye and a clear mind and he died in bed, and there will be no man, someday, who is not his inheritor.

According to James Fisher and Sir Julian Huxley, who have written an introduction to a new edition of *Territory in Bird Life* now fortunately available in both Britain and America, the book caused small commotion when it was published. (I believe, indeed, that its only printing had to be remaindered.) *Ibis,* the journal of British ornithology, rated it "an attractive and thoughtful little work." It is entirely normal that when an astonishingly new idea comes off somebody's mental assembly line, it will take a while before other people's assembly lines tool up sufficiently to deal with it. By the close of the 1920's such tooling up had been accomplished, at least in ornithology. It would still be a while, of course, before the new concept would be recognized as applicable to animals other than birds.

In a way the territorial principle was not that revolutionary, since Howard presented few conclusions unanticipated by someone else. Also, one might say that what came off his intellectual assembly line arrived in unfinished condition; nowhere did he define territory. His failure to attempt it may have been just as well, however, since no one down to this date has been able to offer a definition unshadowed by doubt and unpunctured by exception. Howard's accomplishment was to prove that an instinct called territory exists, and he did it through example after example drawn from the lives of those birds he knew so well. Reed buntings and guillemots pass through his pages: ravens, moor hens, pied wagtails, cuckoos, wood pigeons, whitethroats, sedge warblers, tree pipits, ruffs and rooks, nightingales and skylarks, all pass in a testament of love, giving each his sworn statement that the author's word is true.

To wander through Eliot Howard's prose is to walk through budding woodlands under April skies. The quiet of the man commands us. Our hearts are stilled. We hear birds sing. And when theory comes to us, we inhale it through our nostrils like a pungent recollection of last autumn's leaves.

In such modest fashion was the word "territory" lastingly introduced to the vocabulary of science. Others might in later years discover its significance in the lives of lizards and lions, crickets and men. Howard made no such claims. The bird's world was the world he knew, and he made no claim beyond. We, however, may today compare a few of Howard's conclusions, drawn from the Worcestershire countryside in 1920, with a few of Buechner's, drawn forty years later in central Africa's Semliki Flats. By such a brief exercise in comparative ethology we shall begin to see territory both as a particular reality and as an underlying pattern in animal affairs. And we shall be wise to remember that we are comparing birds with antelopes, creatures as remotely related as are birds and ourselves.

I recorded seven of Buechner's conclusions to hold in our memories:

(1) That male kobs compete for territories, never for females.

It was Eliot Howard's principal conclusion that, contrary to Darwin's "law of battle" and to all of our most romantic tenets, male birds never compete for females.

(2) On a kob stamping ground, the territorial proprietor almost always wins.

Another of Howard's principal conclusions was that the invulnerability of the proprietor (in the quite different situation of breeding pairs) is a chief guarantee for the security of the nest and of the young.

(3) The psychological advantage of the proprietor reduces the incidence and severity of actual fighting.

Like Altum before him, Howard concluded that bird song is a territorial display and that, while an invitation to hostilities, it is associated with invulnerability and so discourages challenge.

(4) Antagonism between male kobs is confined to the stamping ground. Elsewhere their relations are amiable.

Eliot Howard had a gift for incisive observation. His mind swept away all irrelevant or obscuring detail that might detract from the purity of a conclusion. Perhaps the quality was no different from that of an artillery officer who carefully and intuitively clears away all obstruction from the range of his fire.

Howard watched moor hens. The moor hen is a water bird

living in and around marshy reed-fringed pools, feeding frequently in nearby fields. He (a moor hen can be a he) is an amiable enough citizen throughout most of the year, swimming or waddling about his damp little world. But then, about the middle of February, all changes. Pairs establish territories in what has been a peaceful pond, each territory including a bit of rushy shore. Intolerance rages, for the moor hen's new belligerence is not confined to the male. Pairs fight pairs, storming about the pond and its shores like little modern landing craft fighting by sea or land. Remarkable in territorial conflict, the antagonism is not confined to the species. The moor hen's intolerance for any intruder is such that a pair will attack harmless strangers who have simply dropped by for a sip of water—lapwings, thrushes, starlings, even a partridge covey if it comes too close to the pool. Yet in the fields where he goes to feed, or in any area beyond the reedy shore, the moor hen becomes again in an instant an amiable creature. Pairs feed beside pairs. Hostility vanishes. The thrush is ignored.

(5) Copulation occurs nowhere but on the stamping ground.

Another of Howard's fundamental conclusions was that in territorial species breeding pairs are limited in number to those who gain an exclusive property. A male with a mate and no territory is a natural impossibility. Even the puzzling, parasitic cuckoo must have her territory, even though she lays her egg elsewhere in somebody else's nest.

(6) Populations of kob do not really mix, though to the eye they may seem to. Each breeding population retains an identity with its own stamping ground, making interbreeding unlikely. Genetic isolation is thus achieved.

Warblers are mostly migratory species, returning each spring from winter quarters to northern breeding grounds. It was difficult for Howard to prove, but he became convinced that the same birds return, season after season, to the same breeding grounds. If it were true, then the same genetic isolation would be achieved as in the Semliki Flats. (Post-Howard research of a most exact sort would reveal that the Laysan albatross, for example, which breed on Midway Island in the north Pacific, build their nests in the same spot from year to year. Although all nests have been demolished by the winter's storms, and there seem few landmarks, 50 percent will succeed in building within four feet of last year's site.)

(7) "Attachment to a piece of ground is stronger than to the female herd."

Again and again and again Howard stresses the attachment of the male bird to a piece of ground or leafy space, and the attraction for the female of a male so attached. But never to my knowledge did he observe anything to resemble the solitary territory of the bachelor kob. Perhaps for once preconception clouded his eye. Howard regarded territory as invariably a portion of the reproductive process, something that broader investigation would show is usually but not always true. Perhaps there were propertied bachelor birds whom he failed to notice. It seems more likely to me, however, that it is something that just does not happen at the evolutionary level of the bird. In any case, we must record one aspect of territorial behavior in western Uganda which Eliot Howard, forty years earlier, failed to recognize in the fields and the pools, the heaths and water meadows and woodlands of a manicured English county.

There is a moral, somewhere, in the story of the quiet English businessman: perhaps that it is not a downright necessity to die of drink, wear your hair to your shoulders, beat your wife, and starve in a garret in order to enter the magical forests of human adventure and bring back in your pockets much remarkable fruit.

3

The force called territory as it affects a world of living beings bears at least one resemblance to a force called electricity as it affects a world of apparatus: the substance of each is as elusive as the effects are spectacular. Most of us will go to our graves still unable to describe with any precision what actually happened when we touched the little flipper in the wall and the lights went on. Similarly, though we may speak of open instincts and innate behavior patterns, no biologist alive can today tell you just what are the genetical arrangements that command a territorial animal to behave in the manner of his species. Someday, perhaps, we shall know. In the meantime, just as one way to find out about electricity is to keep turning on lights, one way to find out about territory is to keep turning on species.

It is a far leap from a stamping ground in central Africa to an athletic field in Brooklyn, and it is a farther leap, so far as evolution is concerned, between a species of antelope and a species of predatory wasp. Simpson has calculated that the mammal and the insect could have had a common ancestor not less than 500 million years ago, and probably closer to a billion. Yet any comparison between the two species will reveal how, despite such disparate inheritance and disparate environments, their arena behavior follows closely the same rules and regulations.

There are hundreds of genera of wasps and thousands of species, and Tinbergen's digger wasp who preyed only on bees was quite normal in her closed-mindedness. Only a few species will choose victims from more than a single sort of insect, and many will hunt their special victims only in a special situation. One species preying only on flies became known as "the horseguard" from hovering constantly over the flanks of horses. A *Bembix* species also preys on flies but hunts only at twilight, when they have first settled for a night's rest. A species of digger wasp, with a disposition somewhere between that of Karl Marx and that of the Marquis de Sade, preys only on queen ants, never on workers, and takes none but winged ones at the moment of nuptial flight. One might judge, therefore, that so far as wasps go there is nothing too extraordinary about one called the cicada-killer. And yet in his addiction to territory—so far as we know—he is unique among wasps and remarkable among insects.

In general, territory is a vertebrate expression, and I am aware of no other insect species which has evolved that highly specialized territorial pattern, arena behavior. But apparently anything can happen. Only a few years ago a man named Norman Lin, walking beside a high wire fence enclosing a Brooklyn baseball field, found the equivalent of the kob's stamping grounds being operated by cicada-killer wasps. With fence posts at nine-foot intervals, it was not too difficult for Lin to lay out a precise grid for observation. With a few dyes and a spray gun it was not too difficult to mark his contestants.

Cicada-killers are ground-nesting wasps who live in colonies of several hundred burrows from which the female emerges when she is mature. The males arrange themselves in territories not unlike the kob's putting greens, tightly adjacent and small. The properties on Lin's ground ranged from four feet square to longer areas up to six by sixteen. On each property a male has a perching place, such as a pebble, which he always returns to after a chase. It is generally accepted that a male bird has his favorite twig, his accustomed fence post, to advertise the fact that he is home and is prepared to take on all intruders. The cicada-killer wasp, on a remote evolutionary track, has evolved his trait through similar selective advantage.

The attachment for his territory is as profound as in any species. Having chased off an intruder, he will return in seconds to his perch. Lin experimented with marked wasps. He took one 1000 feet away, released it out of sight of the home grounds. It was back on its perch in twenty minutes. He took another almost half a mile away. It was back in fifteen. How did they get back? It is as fascinating a problem as any in science.

So far as defense is concerned, it is continual and inviolable. The wasp will repel an intruder by threat, or by a chase if threat is not enough, or by butting him in mid-air if chasing will not do, or, in the last resort, grappling with him, tumbling to earth and trying if possible to bite out his eyes. It is a rough game. Lin found that in five cases out of six the conflicts took place between adjacent proprietors, just as in colonies of sea gulls the real rows go on with the fellow next door. The loudly buzzing wasp, either because he is angrier by nature or more dim-witted by historical endowment, will defend his preserve against anything, a passing butterfly or bird. He will attack a pebble rolled across his border. Off the territorial ground, however, such conflicts never take place. Like the kob when the lion comes along, the wasp is a practical creature. When the afternoon grows unbearably hot, all retire for a siesta.

The complete exhibition of arena behavior is demonstrated only when the female comes along. Females are larger than males and easily recognized. He may attack a pebble, but he will never attack her. The female mates only once, and so as she comes flying across a territorial ground there is a question to be settled: is she not ready yet, is she ready, or is it too late? She answers it simply. If she is sexually unresponsive, she will always fly a zigzag course, and always slowly. Males may rise from their perches to investigate, and they may pursue her gently, but never across a territorial border. She will be escorted, as it were, by a succession of males, each crossing his territory with her. But if she is responsive, she always flies straight. And the first alert male whose property she crosses will rise and grasp her from behind, and they will fly off together in tandem to alight somewhere and copulate.

Lin has one story garnered from his jungle in Brooklyn which illustrates what instinctual bewilderment can come about when events take an unexpected turn. Normally a fevered couple vanish somewhere to perform their rites. One copulating pair, however, landed on another male's territory. Since it was his place he promptly landed on her, attempted copulation, and discovered of course that she was occupied. Then a third male intruded on his territory. The proprietor chased him, grappled with him, drove him off, returned to within a few inches of his coupled guests, quite obviously lacking a clear inward directive as to what to do about them. Two more males came over his territory, hovering, and he rose and drove them off, again returned. Still attracted, the two intruders returned and by now the proprietor was committed to defending his guests along with his rights. Until affections had been exhausted and they departed, he continued to protect their privacy.

Perhaps Lin's bewildered wasp suggests why insects so seldom indulge in the delights of the arena: its demands are too trying. For a creature whose instincts tend to be closed with less room for the final programming of tradition and learning, the arena becomes a complicated place. Should this be so, then the wonder remains that cicada-killer wasps have mastered its intricacies as well as they have. Or perhaps, on the other hand, Lin's wasps seem unique only because we do not know enough about insects. Certainly it is the long-studied world of birds that furnishes us with our richest arena examples.

Ruffs and reeves constitute a single species related to the sandpiper, but because male and female look so very unlike, custom has held separate christenings. This quality which zoologists call sexual dimorphism, a marked dissimilarity between sexes, is more common than not in arena species. I mentioned how unlike are the sturdy, splendid male kobs and the slender, delicate does. Although it is not true in the cicada-killer wasp, the chances are that in species where the male has no part in raising babies or protecting a nest, but devotes maximum energy to impressing his fellows in the local arena, natural selection speeds up the acquisition of finery. The process has gone to an extreme in the ruff. For eight months of the year the cock, although a bit larger, is no more conspicuous than the hen, and neither has an appearance more notable than that of any other sandpiper. Then with the first breath of almighty spring something happens to the cock, and he starts assembling his costume for the arena.

The ruff takes his name from the most impressive of his adornments, a circular shield of feathers which he sprouts about his neck and which he can raise or lower as occasion demands. Patterned in white, black, bay, chestnut, gray, blue, violet, even gold, no two cocks ever look exactly alike. Few living creatures acquire in a time so short an adornment combining such beauty and individuality, such pomposity and practicality. For the ruff's ruff is a shield so strong that it protects his chest from his rivals' bills.

Thus arrayed like a medieval knight in his loved one's colors, the ruff with the breath of awakening spring proceeds to the hilling ground. No parting tears, however, signal his departure. Aside from a moment's classic attention which he will pay the hen in the arena, the cock lives a cock's life in a cock's world, and throughout the year has no more to do with the reeve than if she indeed were of another species.

Along the Dutch coast the traditional hilling ground—as permanent as Buechner's stamping ground—lies adjacent to the traditional breeding ground of the reeve. Occupied as she is with nest-building and feminine sociality, the reeve ignores the arena except when the moment of desire arrives. In the meantime, from early April until June, the hilling ground is the ruff's ball park and social center. They are smallish birds, and their territories are smallish, and each has a little hill less than two feet in diameter kicked up by ruff feet over many a decade. On this hill he displays his glories, defends his real estate, and insults his neighbors.

Back in 1920, the year of *Territory in Bird Life,* a Miss E. L. Turner visited several hilling grounds in Holland and reported her bewilderment in the journal called *British Birds:* "The ruff is either as motionless as if he were carved in stone, or else he is vibrating like a toy on wires. . . . They rush around with the regularity of a clockwork mouse. When several are fighting

together they are an indistinguishable blur of feathers. . . .
They filled me with amazement. Why do they behave in this
ridiculous manner?"

The ridiculous activity about which Miss Turner com-
plained cannot compare, I should say, with the ridiculous
inactivity when a reeve at last appears. We are beginning to
note, I hope, how in these sporting events of the natural arena,
whatever the fierceness of the competition, there are always
rules and conventional restraints. As part of his display before
his competitors, the ruff has developed a dismaying capacity for
holding his breath. By such means he distends himself to his
anatomical maximum and spreads his ruff to its grandest
proportions. Now, as the reeve enters the ground, all on their
little hills bow low. Beaks almost to the ground, ruffs perpen-
dicular like hanging shields, they hold their breath while she
inspects the art show. None moves. That would be against the
rules. They have reminded many an observer of a bed of
flowers. She wanders here, she wanders there. At last she
chooses, pecking the neck feathers of the ruff of her choice. They

mate immediately. There will be no objection from the disappointed for the very good reason that they have all collapsed.

Ernst Mayr has defined arena behavior as a territorial pattern in which males defend mating stations unrelated to feeding or nesting. But V. C. Wynne-Edwards, in a description of the lek, the traditional dancing arena of the blackcock in Scotland, has recently introduced another point which we must not neglect: that these displays, directed by males toward one another, decide and maintain the social status of each.

On an early page I regretted the necessity of fixing the attention of this inquiry on the territorial principle. As important as territory to social animals—and we may find someday that it is more important—is the compulsion to achieve status within one's society. Territory is essentially defensive, an inward mechanism aiding us to defend what we have; status is essentially aggressive, an inward pressure to achieve dominance over our social partners. In the arena the two innate forces combine to bring about a single pattern. Through the holding of a territory, we defend what social status we have achieved; by challenging our neighbor, we attempt to better ourselves. In the kob, differential real-estate values prevailing on the stamping ground provide a neat territorial ladder: this rung offers security for status so far achieved, while the next beckons us to rise. We shall find something very much like it in Wyoming's sage grouse, an example even better for our purposes than Wynne-Edwards' more famous blackcock.

Until the early 1940's there was so little known about the mating of sage grouse that a rumor thrived on our high western plains that the cock drops sperm and the hen pecks it up. Since the sage cock is another elaborate bird with an appearance very nearly as vain as a turkey's, the rumor was of a most derogatory sort. Then J. W. Scott, of the University of Wyoming, discovered the first known strutting ground, and from then on no further reflections could be cast on the cock's reputation.

A seasonal creature like the ruff, the sage cock has an arena of a seasonal nature. In winter the flocks mingle in peace, both sexes together. Then in March the cocks go their way, descending on the strutting ground, where for the next three months they will display, browbeat, scramble for geographical position, and sort themselves out into a hierarchy. Like the kob, a population has from 800 to 1000 members; unlike the kob, however, all males will participate in the carnival and so the arena must be enormous. The first ground Scott studied was half a mile long and 200 yards wide. Nevertheless, it had the same permanence of site as all natural arenas; one that he later studied had a road built through it, but the birds refused to abandon their hallowed area of sagebrush and space. As in other arena species, too, the contestants had that intent preoccupation with matters at hand which allowed Buechner to build a wooden platform beside his field of glory; Scott put up a comfortable tent, with windows, in the middle of his.

There was plenty to view. Even on the first day of the season, toward the end of March, with ice still a half-inch thick on ponds, 175 cocks reported for assembly. It was not hen weather. One showed up, either by accident or because she was a mutant creature equipped with central heating. Her presence was unnecessary, since the male motive is to impress the next male. Claims were staked out. On a strutting ground every cock in the population gets a court, but, as Scott was to learn, only central courts have either social status or sex appeal.

The scramble continued virtually henless for some time. Normally the cocks scattered about the countryside, feeding most of the day, to assemble in the afternoon and to continue their exercises into the twilight. If a golden eagle soared into view, all fled, to resume their disputes when the eagle had passed. As a new moon came on, the performance carried on later and later, until it was possible for an hour-long riot to take place at three in the morning. But by this season the hens were arriving in numbers.

Action on a stamping ground in Uganda concerns a mannered elite who, like any elite, may seem preposterous but still retain an elegance. Action on a Wyoming strutting ground is an orgy organized in a rush hour. I seem to recall that in the early days of silent films Hollywood presented a few massive scenes of bacchanalian grandeur which might favorably be compared with the sexual entertainments of the sage grouse in Wyoming's open air. On one single occasion Scott counted 355 cocks and 141 hens. And yet it is an orgy organized to the last feather.

Only five courts at the most have sexual value. Each is no more than eight feet by twelve, and onto these jam the entire population of ready hens. On each court is a master cock, the survivor of the status struggle. Nature has wisely recognized that the arithmetic of such a system, while flattering to the master cock, may be one which neither the species nor the master cock will survive. And so each court is equipped with his chief rival, a subcock, who will spell him off when the situation becomes trying. Each court is also equipped with two or three guard cocks, whose duties, whether taking tickets or subduing the mob, have never been quite clear to me.

The hen, however, will as a rule have no part of any but Number One, and for an hour or so, if he is the worse for wear, then his admirers jammed closely together will simply wait for his recovery. How physiologically directed is the sage hen to those behavioral laws applicable to her species may be judged by some of Scott's figures: On one strutting ground which provided only four mating courts for a normal population, three-quarters of all matings were accomplished by the four master cocks. Over half the remainder were provided by the four strutting rivals, the subcocks. The guard cocks in moments when the traffic was heavy managed to get in on a few. And there is a very small indelicate remainder or reminder, the score of sage-grouse immorality chalked up in the anonymous sagebrush; the sage hen on occasion is only human.

4

For one who lives in Rome within walking distance of the Colosseum, of circuses, of amphitheaters—the very term "arena" is a Roman word—there is a temptation to ask, Is man at least in part an arena species? We have our prizes of property and status, our market places of male competition. We all of us shelter memories, comical or terrifying, poignant or absurd, of human behavior not unlike these animal exhibitions we have witnessed. And there are sound evolutionary reasons to inspire a moment's wonder, too.

Thomas Gilliard, of the American Museum of Natural History, has given many a fascinated year to contemplation of the bowerbird, of whom he writes: "A nineteenth-century naturalist once suggested that just as mammals are commonly divided into two groups, man and lower forms, all birds should be divided into two categories: bowerbirds and other birds." No creature in the animal world aside from man has gone quite so far in the creation of what must be called a culture, and Gilliard believes that arena behavior has been responsible for the bird's quite incredible accomplishments.

Arena behavior is rare. Of the world's million-odd animate species, not over a hundred so far known indulge in its patterned heroics. All authorities agree that the strenuous competition of the arena brings about a speed-up in the evolutionary process. Is it possible that arena selection has contributed not only to man's astonishing speed of development but also, as in his opposite number in the world of birds, to the evolution of culture as a substitute for sweeping horns, prestigious crests, and many-splendored tails?

The bowerbird is a zoological group with a few species in Australia but its greatest flowering in New Guinea, where Gilliard has done most of his work. Why New Guinea should be the home of the world's nonhuman cultural champions, while on that lavish island the human species has restrained its own cultural accomplishments to such unremarkable activities as the collection like postal issues of other people's heads, must be written down, I presume, as an embarrassing evolutionary joke. But that New Guinea has presented us with the animal Acropolis none can dispute. Nor are the cultural wonders confined to birds who build playhouses.

Alfred Russel Wallace, Darwin's great contemporary and co-originator of the theory of natural selection, was one of the first European naturalists to explore the East Indies. While he never came on the bowerbird, he discovered the bird of paradise, and brought back two lively specimens properly to astonish English zoology. This most gorgeous of creatures, likewise an arena being, gives us more than a hint as to how natural selection started encouraging the aesthetic improvement of real estate.

In 1857, on a little island called Aru just off the New Guinea coast, Wallace encountered the species known as the great bird of paradise. He described its display: "The head and neck is of pure straw yellow above, and rich metallic green below. The long plumey tufts of golden orange feathers spring from the sides beneath each wing and when the bird is in repose are partly concealed by them. At the time of excitement, however, the wings are raised vertically over the back, the head is bent down and stretched out, and the long plumes are raised and expanded till they form two golden fans, striped with red at the base. The whole bird is then overshadowed by them, the crouching body, yellow head, and emerald green throat forming but the foundation and setting for the golden glory that waves above."

Now, the temptation to regard such a display as a purposeful performance is very nearly irresistible. But had Wallace proceeded farther into the lowland rain forests of New Guinea proper, he might have encountered another species, the magnificent bird of paradise, which at the height of a comparable display opens wide its mouth to reveal the pale-green lining. And what we must keep firmly in mind is that *Diphyllodes magnificus* has never seen the green lining of his own throat. He performs the display by innate command. We may interpret —wrongly—all the remainder of the bird's complex performance as one of purpose motivated by a desire to show off his breathtaking finery. But when the pale-green lining of his mouth comes along, we must recognize that since the bird possesses no mirror he cannot know what he is showing off. The final action, like the entire display, is a form of innate behavior as much a part of the bird as is the finery itself. The bird of paradise comes in one evolutionary bundle.

Having reminded ourselves of this, we may move on to the magnificent's cultural accomplishment. And I recognize that if the natural selection of the arena can bring about a bird who opens his mouth to display a green lining he has never seen, then it is not too great a wonder that he has developed an innate concern for the arrangements of his court. Nevertheless, I am pleased not to be reporting an observation of my own. Let Austin Rand, of the Chicago Natural History Museum, be the Munchausen.

The trade winds deposit on some New Guinea lowlands a rainfall of ninety inches a year. The consequent rain forest is profoundly shadowed. Some species of the bird of paradise hold their courts in the treetops, others in the middle branches. But two, the magnificent and the Queen Carola's, have their courts either on the ground or very near to it in a dark tangle of vines and branches. And Rand has described how the magnificent will spend hour after patient hour in the branches high above, snipping away leaves, so that a shaft of light may penetrate the shadowed forest, reach his court, and illuminate to best advantage the iridescence of his colors.

Among the cultural wonders of New Guinea the next evolutionary step beyond arrangement of the stage lighting, as Gilliard analyzes it, is construction of the stage itself. These display stages are what early travelers in New Guinea found along forest paths and assumed were little houses built by native children. They were the bowers, of course, that have given the bowerbird its name. A dozen species build the little decorated houses, some complete with roof, as stages for display. They are never nests, but like nests the appearance and construction varies between species. Within a kind it is always the same.

Archbold's bowerbird, for example, is a relatively primitive species in cultural achievement. He clears a small stage in his high mountain forest and carefully carpets it with fern. Then he decorates it with snail shells, dead beetles, lumps of charcoal, and other attractive bric-a-brac. He waits, perched well above his sidewalk display. If a female comes by, he drops to the middle of his stage, crouches, makes begging sounds, crawls toward her. Should she be unimpressed, she will move on to another Archbold's bowerbird. The rejected one will rearrange his ornaments and resume his wait like a patient Arab.

At the other and more evolved extreme is the gardener bowerbird, frequently referred to as a maypole-builder. He leans sticks against a sapling in the shape of a teepee, adding more and more until the structure may be taller than a man. The most advanced species, the crestless gardener, will create internal chambers in his tower, then top it with a broad roof against the forest's heavy rains. In the cleared area around the tower he plants moss for his dancing stage. He will decorate his little lawn with shells, berries, and piles of cut flowers.

Lauterbach's bowerbird is another advanced member of the family, but he uses an entirely different construction scheme. He is classed as an avenue-builder. Instead of building a round house supported by a central sapling, he plants two sticks firmly for support and constructs a four-walled structure. Gilliard examined one of these bowers and found 1000 pale pebbles used to pave the stage, over 3000 sticks in the rigid, interlocking construction of the bower itself, and 1000 strands of grass used to line the interior walls. At least sixteen such parlors built in a spread-out area on the edge of New Guinea's grasslands were attended each by a member of a single clan waiting for susceptible females.

Gilliard waited too, and on three occasions he had the luck to be present when a female came by. The male danced with excitement on his pebbled pavement. She entered his bower.

Now enormously excited, the male picked up a bright red berry, and just as the ruff displays his intricate collar or the kob his glorious throat, the bowerbird displayed the berry for his intended's delight.

Now again, it is very difficult for the human mind, with all its preconceptions, to resist the conclusion that Lauterbach's bowerbird has done all this purposefully for the sake of getting the girl. But we must remember the magnificent bird of paradise who displays the green lining of his mouth without knowing he has one. This is innate behavior specific to the species. Lauterbach's bowerbird builds an elaborate house on the edge of the grasslands, paves it with pebbles, and displays his red berry because he has substituted culture for a green throat and a fancy crest. Like the male member of any arena species, he competes with other males, by inward compulsion, to achieve status. In his particular species to achieve that status he must gain and defend a piece of property and improve and display it in a particular fashion. As a key fits a lock, so his success in a demanding masculine competition turns something in the female heart. It attracts her. Those of the species who have failed in the basic competition, who are not one of the sixteen members of the club dancing before their sixteen houses, are somewhere off in the woods, sexually discarded. But even for this member of the exclusive club, the key may not turn all the way, the red berry may not do, her sexual desire will not be aroused, and she will go elsewhere. In that case he can do nothing, for to do anything now would be to violate club rules. As the kob looks off to the mountains, as the ruff collapses on his hill, he must go back to his bower.

Among all these species the satin bowerbird is the champion's champion, since he not only builds a house but paints it. I shall defer this ultimate animal, however, to a more appropriate place in the story: not because he is an Australian instead of a New Guinean, but because I believe my earlier question has been answered. Man is not, has never been, and can never be an arena species. We lack the biological morality.

There is probably a sound enough physiological reason why we cannot be creatures of the arena, whatever our playful indulgences, for it is unlikely that the human female, unassisted, can raise our long-maturing offspring to independence: the cock cannot be spared to lead a cock's life in a cock's flock. In no arena species which we have inspected or which has ever been studied do you find other than disposable males. But it is in the realm of comparative behavior that arena species reveal an evolutionary truth little known until today but salient to our inquiry into the territorial imperative.

For the century or so since *Origin of Species* you and I and our fathers have been taught that the animal's only motivational pole is self. It is what we have meant by the struggle for existence and the survival of the fittest. The animal struggles to survive: to eat, to avoid death, to mate, at the most to nourish and protect his offspring. He inhabits a world of self, and all of his instincts are organized to promote his success in that narrow corridor. We may call it Ego, or we may call it jungle law. What has seemed inconceivable is that evolution could encourage any physical or behavioral trait running contrary to the interest of the individual: such behavior could have no survival value.

It is this understanding of evolution which has brought such puzzlement, and sometimes despair, to human thought. No informed mind today denies that man is descended by slow but explicable process from the world of the fish and the frog, the bird and the lizard, the monkey and the ape. No mind, informed or otherwise, denies that man is capable of moral conduct, of choice between right and wrong, of action directed at goals taller and more luminous than self alone. How, then, did we get that way? If evolution with its struggle for existence can provide other animals with behavioral equipment necessary only for individual survival, then by what evolutionary bootstraps has man raised himself to the human condition?

No more impenetrable conundrum has faced human thought in the past century. We have come to a variety of answers. For excellent reasons, many of us have clung to divine intervention and the uniqueness of the human soul to explain the otherwise inexplicable. And, as I have already mentioned, there have been many of us who have denied that man has instincts to impede his conduct, or who have asserted man's new independence from the evolutionary process. Some have shrugged, skipped the problem, and simply described man as the moral or ethical animal, a description furnishing no explanation at all. And there have been those, of course, who have seized on our classical understanding of Darwinian evolution to justify, through its jungle law, man's every basest action.

I shall submit what I regard as the most pressing argument in these pages: that our earlier understanding of evolution is false. As I weigh the evidence gathered by the new biology in these remarkable years, I can discover no qualitative break between the moral nature of the animal and the moral nature of man. Evolution has been as ready to equip the animal with innate behavioral commands restraining the interests of the individual on behalf of larger or more immortal goals as it has been ready so to equip the human species. In the case of the arena species, indeed, evolution has gone further than with ourselves, and that is why I have begun our inquiry with a form of behavior so rare.

Whether we turn our regard to the formal antics of the kob's stamping ground, the sexual pandemonium of a sage-grouse strutting ground, or the quiet, preoccupied community of a bowerbird clan, we are watching the consequences of an order so moral—or a moral order so foreign—as to fall beyond human comprehension. Toward a single biological end, a high degree of selection of male genes within a population, individual interest is channeled or inhibited. The female, despite all sexual heat, is *not* free to mate with the first male she encounters, but must seek a proven member of the elite. The defeated male is *not* free to wander off and try his luck on another mating ground, but, tied by mysterious cords to his home community, must accept psychological castration and join the ranks of the discarded. Even the elite, the one in ten or twenty or thirty or forty, must obey the sexual rules and regulations and offer no interference with the final workings of female choice. Were any portion of the innate code governing the sexual activity of an arena species to be disobeyed or disregarded, then the arena itself would fall into genetic nonsense. Yet no part of that code corresponds to our conventional view of animal instinct.

The key to that code, I believe, is territory, and that is why I have called this book *The Territorial Imperative*. I cannot claim that these observations of a few highly specialized species can do more than suggest that our century-long interpretation of evolution may be wrong. But I believe that as we go along we shall see unfolding a mass of evidence that through natural selection evolution is capable of fostering inborn traits, as Moffat anticipated, restraining the individual to the ultimate benefit of his species. I see no reason to regard this as other than a biological morality. Nor do I find reason to believe that territory is other than the chief mechanism of natural morality, something more than a mere behavior pattern, more than an open instinct, more than a superb defensive instrument—in truth, a natural mediating device between the good of the one and the good of all.

So far as man is concerned, we have our territorial moralities, as I shall attempt to demonstrate. But they are not of an arena sort. Were we an arena species like the bowerbird, and our capacity for the rapid creation of cultures and assimilation of civilization a product of this form of evolutionary speed-up, then life would not be quite as it is. If a man failed to produce some minimum standard of culture or failed to behave according to some minimum standard of civilization, then he would find himself sexually impotent and sexually uncaring. Women, on the other hand, would find themselves incapable of intercourse with other than civilized men. And if not enough men succeeded in the competition to furnish numbers sufficient to service all our women, then we should be in a handsome pickle indeed. Most of our women, like surplus sage hens, would have no one to sleep with. And the population explosion, along with a good many other problems, would be removed from the list of contemporary concern.

I shall not deny that it might be an excellent idea for *Homo sapiens* to become an arena species, for then we should proceed like a genetic rocket toward our rendezvous with Utopia. But like so many comparably excellent ideas, it falls victim to a natural fact or two. We lack the particular biological morality.

7

We lack that innate command which shapes our sexual impulses to our whole selective good. And so we must press on with our search for natural advantages more a portion of the human resource. And if we remain convinced that the line between man and the animal is that we are capable of moral action, whereas the animal is not, then we must reflect on the mystery that a few arena species possess a sexual morality that man can by no means claim.

3. To Have and to Hold

The pair is a social arrangement with sexual conveniences of varying reward. The evolutionary value of the pair does not rest, however, on sexual necessity, for we have seen in natural arenas how flamboyantly sex can flourish without permanent arrangements. Natural selection's concern has been with offspring. Arena behavior is an evolutionary luxury permitted species in which the mother is fully capable of rearing young without masculine aid; there remain species beyond counting in which life is not so easy. The children may be too numerous, too complicated, or too long in their growing up. For these the pair, and what biologists call the pair bond, have been among evolution's most successful devices. But there has remained always a problem: how can nature ensure that the father will stay around and do his duty?

Julian Huxley made his first major contribution to biology in 1914, years before Eliot Howard wrote his book on territory. It was a study of the great crested grebe, an aquatic bird not uncommon in England. Like the penguin, the grebe is of a family so ancient that its origins may well go back to the later days of the dinosaur and pterodactyl. And since the young zoologist came of fairly ancient lineage himself, he evidently felt that a Huxley could not plead youth as an excuse for jobs half done. His study of the great crested grebe was comprehensive, detailed, penetrating. It anticipated conclusions that the new biology, then unborn, would not reach for decades, and it established its author as the biologist of rank which he remains to this day.

Two of Huxley's countless observations concern us here. The first was his basic observation that the male grebe does not wind up his courtship of the female when coitus has been accomplished and eggs properly laid, but continues his displays all summer. Why? Huxley tentatively concluded that in a species requiring both parents to maintain the young, something must ensure that the bond between them be not disrupted. The male therefore keeps to his gallant ways long after the sexual lure can inspire them.

It was a startling conclusion, coming at a time when the repressed Victorians still tended, as did Freud himself, to explain everything by sex. But Huxley's other observation was just as far ahead of its time. He pondered over the unquenchable antagonisms of pair against pair, and wrote: "There may be simple hostility between members of one pair and members of another, but the only reason I can discover is the trespassing of one or both birds on the territory of another."

In those pre-territory days it was enough for Huxley to perceive the law that Howard was to elaborate; he did not attempt to relate it to the pair bond. But as scientific thought developed in later decades, it became apparent that the private territory held by a pair is a prime reinforcement for the bond between the two. Sexual attraction may initiate the bond, as it does in man—or it may not, as we shall shortly see in the roebuck. Continued sexual activity may reinforce the bond, again as in man and to a degree in the gibbon; or it may offer little, as we shall see a bit farther along in the robin. But whatever the contribution that sex may make to the permanence of a parental arrangement, it is the private territory of a breeding couple that provides most reliably that the children will not be neglected. Through its strange enhancement of powers in the male proprietor, energy not otherwise available is placed at family disposal. And through isolation of the two in their little world, and their joint antagonism for all others of their kind, nature keeps the pair where they belong, at the service of the next generation.

Whether evolution for reasons of selective benefit has encouraged the pair territory in the human being, just as in other animals, must be the final question of this chapter. We may dismiss the possibility that man is an arena species with the sad conclusion that we lack a morality of the proper biological order. No such dismissal can be made of the pair territory. Nevertheless, as we shuffle through the species and the developing thoughts of science, we must keep skeptically in mind that mere analogy will not prove that human institutions are the product of animal law.

The discovery that roe deer defend territory gives us a good place to start. For almost thirty years—ever since the publication of *A Herd of Red Deer,* Frank Fraser Darling's contribution to the masterpieces of naturalists' prose—it had been assumed that no species of deer defend territory. Even the superbly organized studies of the relationship between tiger and deer in Deccan India, made by George Schaller so recently that they have not yet been published, reveal no species that may be described as territorial. It was with some shock, therefore, that in 1964 I came on a feature story written by Colin Willock, author of *The Enormous Zoo,* and published in one of London's Sunday papers, implying that roe deer in southern England not only defend territories but are being used as an instrument of forest conservation. I called Willock and found that my surmise was correct. At the first opportunity

I gathered together my safari equipment and set forth to penetrate the hazards of the Salisbury plain. In a village with the unlikely name of Six Penny Handley, fifteen miles north of Salisbury Cathedral's tall spire, I met the young forester who had wrested from Britain's manicured wilderness this secret previously unknown, and had put it to work.

The background for the discovery lay in the painful encounter between the British Forestry Commission and an animal who would not be dismayed. Soon after the 1914–18 war Britain determined to regrow its dilapidated forests in the hope of achieving at least partial self-sufficiency in lumber supply. Marginal farmland was retired from cultivation and planted in trees; old neglected forests were cleaned up and renewed. The effort was massive. And nothing, of course, could have pleased the roe deer more. They are a woodland species who enjoy nature's leafy corridors, browse on new growth, and in this and other fashions make of themselves an unholy nuisance to forestry commissions. Deer multiplied faster than new trees could come up. Not even wholesale slaughter discouraged them, for if you are not a herd species and you take naturally to hiding in woods, then you are difficult to wipe out.

By 1957 the Forestry Commission came to a policy decision that murder would not suffice, and turned ignominiously to science. Richard Prior was at this time a young London businessman, thoroughly successful, who had encountered an equally harsh fact of British life: that since a family owned his business he could advance no further. As thoroughly fed up, he accepted an appointment from the Forestry Commission at £10 a week and received custody of a 2000-acre forest called Cranborne Chase on the edge of the village of Six Penny Handley.

Prior received his assignment on a try-anything basis partly out of the commission's desperation, and partly—as he points out—because it is embarrassing to pay a man that little and then interfere with his work too. Untrained in the sciences, he came of a hunting family, had known deer since he was a boy, and was a first-rate shot. When he arrived at Cranborne Chase it was with a hunter's desire to save the deer as well as his employer's forest. That he lacked the ethologist's specialized knowledge was of no importance, as things turned out.

Roe deer are not large animals, and they never form herds. In winter they tend to gather in disorganized groups wherever there is young growth to browse on. They will eat almost anything except white cedar—beech, Norway spruce, even the Douglas fir which, transplanted to moist southern England, grows so well. The doe in this winter season is accompanied by her young of the previous year. Also, she is pregnant from last season's rut and will bear her new young in May. Despite her maternal preoccupations, however, she must fend for herself. Not until the middle of March, when the normally mild winter is lifting, will the does with their growing fawns and nearing accouchements start a dispersal through the forest, and will pairing begin.

Had Prior been trained in the sciences—particularly in the sciences of our schools—the error of an older biology might have fogged his view. Even ornithology until most recently has regarded pairing and territory as necessarily associated with the sexual impulse, and you and I have seen how in arena species sex and territory are woven in a tight, austere pattern. But when Prior began his systematic observations, he faced something quite different. The roebuck joins a doe who was probably *not* his mate last year, at a time when she is already pregnant. The rutting season is far away at summer's end. Nevertheless, the two will drift together through the budding forest to some congenial area probably of her choice. There he will establish a private territory of considerable size, sharing it with his doe and her last season's young. Not till May will she deliver her new fawns, sired almost surely by somebody else. He will protect the lot, and unless we are to regard it as a system for stepfathers, paternal impulses can be credited no more than can sexual.

I have suggested that natural selection's concern is with offspring, not sex, and the roebuck's territorial urge, seasonal in nature, seems to coincide with nothing else. When her time comes, she twins. Single births are normal in deer species. Roe, however, not only have twins but have them at a time when last year's fawn (as a rule only one has survived the winter) is not yet independent. Here is the biological situation of a mother with offspring too numerous to handle alone, and the biological answer of the pair, and a husband who though temporary will defend her and ensure both her privacy and an exclusive food supply. And to make sure that he will not wander, evolution has nailed him with a territorial instinct.

Roe territories may be seasonal, but within that season the roebuck is a sturdy defender who will tolerate no trespassers. The larger and stronger he is, the greater area will he control, and it is this quality in the male, I discovered, which makes possible the Prior system of forest conservation. Since the buck is monogamous and will tolerate none on his territory but his wife and stepchildren, the roe population in a forest has an inverse proportion to the quality of the bucks. If all are Grade A, each defending successfully perhaps one hundred acres, the population will be small; if all are Grade Q, each able to defend no more than ten, the population will be large. By careful culling of weaker bucks, Prior not only acts as an agent of natural selection in the improvement of the roe-deer breed, but also guarantees the Forestry Commission that Cranborne Chase with maximum territories will shelter a minimum roe-deer population and suffer a minimum of roe-deer damage.

I was delighted. Never before had I encountered anyone who had taken the territorial principle and put it on a paying basis. But my delight was merely getting started, for the young ex-businessman had unconsciously reached into one of the subtlest corners of Continental ethology to perfect his system. His recognition that a roe-deer "displacement activity" is the source of the most severe forest damage led him to the conclusion that territories must be large but not too large. And to comprehend his discovery, we must make an ethological detour.

An antelope like the kob or the kudu has horns which are a lifetime fixture; deer, as we know, grow an annual crop of antlers which they shed in the fall. The tender young bumps which replace last year's antlers are covered with the skin called velvet, and when the bony growth has reached full spread and hardness, the buck scrapes off the velvet against the trunks of trees. It is an action known as "fraying," and an early Prior discovery was that fraying does far more damage to the forest than winter browsing off new growth. The scraping back and forth of hard antlers against soft young tree trunks may de-velvet the antlers, but it also de-barks the trees and distorts their growth. But the most damaging of all fraying, because of its violence, has nothing to do with scraping off dead skin. It occurs when two wrought-up roebucks face each other across a mutual territorial boundary. Will they fight? Not likely. They will attack the neighboring trees.

Displacement activity, widely observed by students of animal behavior, is a concept which in its precise instinctual impli-cations has been carried over into human psychology. Just the same, what is bothering the embattled roebucks is something that not infrequently bothers you and me. When we are con-fronted by two opposite courses of action—to fight or to flee, for example, or to prolong our insults or apologize—we tend for the moment to take a predictable third course unrelated to the other two.

One of the more hilarious antics in the repertory of animal behavior is that of the herring gull, as described by Tinbergen, when one gets into the situation facing the roebucks. He too operates a pair territory—a small one surrounding his nest—and if he discovers a neighbor intruding on his property, then with beating wings and resounding screeches he will chase him back where he belongs. The indignant intruder, no longer an intruder but safe on his own property, will now face his antagonist at the boundary. There will be threats, and heads will be lifted high and wings readied for beating. Since they face each other not two feet apart yet both are still gripped by ferocity's storm, any observer will predict instant battle. But there will be no battle. Both gulls instead will suddenly, murderously, start pulling up grass.

It is nest-building; or rather, it is a third course of action, neither fighting nor fleeing, derived from an unrelated activity, building a nest. Tinbergen found the key to it by means of comparative behavior. The three-spined stickleback, a belliger-ent, highly territorial fish, has exactly the same displacement

87

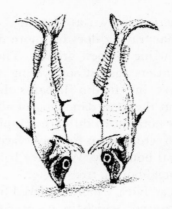

activity. The male stickleback digs a nest in the sandy bottom of those shallow waters which he frequents at breeding time. And when two male sticklebacks, proprietors of adjoining properties, get into a border uproar and pursue one another back and forth, now on one property, now on the other, to wind up facing each other at the invisible wall bubbling rage and frustrated fury, both will as suddenly as the herring gulls up-end to a vertical position and while goggling at each other in loathing stand on their heads and dig holes in the sand.

Displacement activity is species-specific, a zoologist's term meaning that all members of a species will have the same specific trait, whether color of feather or manner of behavior. The herring gull will always pull grass, the stickleback always dig a hole. When antagonists face each other over a boundary, each inhibited from further attack or further flight, their energy is still popping away. And so it "sparks over"—another ethologist's term—into a third instinctual channel which will cause no damage to either party but will give outlet to the energy. It is as if a built-in short circuit or safety valve is arranged in the switchboard of instinct. That outlet, of course, will not always be nest-building. Uncertain fighting cocks will peck at the ground as if for food. So will skylarks. Since great tits feed not on the ground but in trees, they find their outlet in tearing at leaves and buds.

Recognition of displacement activity as a fundamental process has been one of ethology's major achievements. Preening—

88

poking at one's feathers or licking one's fur—is a third course in so many species that Niko Tinbergen has been able to isolate an independent instinct which he calls "care of body surface." Were it not an instinct with a pattern of its own, then there would be no circuit into which frustrated energy could spark over. And however sincerely the cultural anthropologists may advise you concerning the insignificance of your instincts, a playwright who for many a season has made a profession of watching his fellow beings must necessarily wonder: is not man a "care of body surface" species?

Watch a prizefight on television, or small boys in a school-yard fight. Hesitant, uncertain as to whether to attack or back away, antagonists will dab at their noses. Care of the nose is an important human outlet in moments of indecision; women will powder it. Hair, however, is just as important. Whether I am a Filipino or a New York executive or a tribesman in Ruanda, when I do not know what to do, say, or think next, I shall probably rub my chin or scratch my head. It is a species-specific gesture which I cannot believe is a product of learning and which seems to be older than modern man, since it is interracial. But if I am a woman I shall almost never rub my beardless chin; I shall feel around instead in my back hair where it is longest. Yet there is something about attention to hair which seems associated with sexual maturity. Children rarely do it, tending instead to bite their fingernails. The adult is unlikely to bite his fingernails, but in moments of inner stress or distraction or embarrassment will carefully inspect them.

Whether man is or is not a "care of body surface" species must be a matter of fair significance to those who dismiss patterns of instinct from the human mechanism. Since no school of human psychology has ever, to my knowledge, pursued the question, we have no scientific evidence to go on and shall be well advised to abandon it to future and more competent authority. Of one thing, however, we may be sure: man may have learned to rub his chin at his mother's breast, but the roebuck did not learn to take apart trees at the same source.

In roe forests, when furious territorial neighbors face each other over their common boundary, daring neither to advance nor to retreat, their frustrated rage will spark over into that activity normal to scraping dried velvet from their antlers. It may be summer and the velvet long gone, the antlers bare and as hard as iron. Nevertheless, fraying will absorb their energies and, to the terror of the Forestry Commission, they will attack all convenient trees with a racket to be heard for hundreds of yards. And as a solution Prior is applying still another ethological principle.

There is a law of territorial behavior as true of the single roebuck defending his private estate as it is of a band of howling monkeys defending its domain held in common. Huxley long ago observed that any territory is like a rubber disc: the tighter it is compressed, the more powerful will be the pressure outward to spring it back into shape. A proprietor's confidence is at its peak in the heartland, as is an intruder's at its lowest. Here the proprietor will fight hardest, chase fastest. That confidence, however, will wane as the proprietor approaches his border, vanish as he crosses it. Having entered his neighbor's yard, an urge to flee will replace his urge to fight, just as his neighbor's confidence and fighting urge will be restored by the touch of his vested soil.

It is a subtle law, a profound one, and it is universal. Richard Prior made use of it in his adjustment of roebucks and lumber. He reasoned that if too many roebucks share the forest, then each will have a territory too small for its energy, rage at the border will be at a maximum, and fraying and damage to trees at its most disastrous. On the other hand, if there is underpopulation, then territories will be too large for proprietors to control and the spring of the rubber disc will be exhausted short of the boundary. In quantitative terms, there will be more space in the forest than the total of roebuck confidence, and younger bucks will infiltrate, establish new territories in weakly defended areas, and restore the old situation of tight borders, vast angers, and dilapidated trees.

Lack of training in the sciences did not prevent the former London businessman from pursuing his far-out exercises in behavioral mathematics. Season after season, through careful culling and continual observation, he has come closer and closer to that perfect balance of population and space which satisfies the territorial confidence of every male but gives him the least reason to rage at the border, and the least surplus energy for demolishing trees.

By the time of the rutting season, of course, the major threat to the forest fairly well ends. The rut starts as a rule in the last week of July when the doe has weaned her new fawns. Her time of physical vulnerability has ended, her time of romantic vulnerability has arrived. The buck turns his energies from chasing his neighbor to chasing his wife, from the ruination of young oak trees to the consummation of young affections. Next door his neighbor is similarly diverted. It is a strenuous season, since for satisfactions quite unknown the male pursues the female at high speed, frequently to the point where both are too exhausted for copulation. "Roe rings," beaten, circular paths, are a feature of English forests. Some may be quite ancient, a cultural modification of the landscape favored by generation after generation of does and bucks in the heat of their romantic pursuits.

Early in August the rut ends. The roebuck is in a state of collapse, and the territorial system collapses with him. He wanders off. Where he goes, no one can quite say, perhaps for a holiday in another forest. She may see him again in the late autumn when frosts sharpen and nights lengthen and the roe

drift through the bramble and hazel and red oak to their winter establishments. If she sees him she will not recognize him. She and he will be strangers. The bond between them, so close for a season, was defined in truth by nothing but real estate.

2

No natural arrangement in all the colorful departments of vertebrate life is quite so prevalent, and perhaps quite so primitive, as the pair on its territory. Gilliard has described the pair bond as the central fact in the lives of 99 percent of the world's bird species. Some, it is true, reinforce that bond through astonishing means. The jackdaw is nonterritorial, yet pairs for life, with a record of broken homes that is virtually nonexistent. The male jackdaw, however, is a husband more gallant than even the great-crested grebe, and he continually feeds his mate beakfuls of minced worm and saliva. In *African Genesis* I described that harried episode in the career of Konrad Lorenz when a misguided jackdaw fell in love with him and, finding no undefended orifice in which to place his affectionate tribute, finally dumped it in the naturalist's ear.

A still more original means of reinforcing the pair bond has recently come to light in the studies of Kenya's bou-bou shrike by Myles North and W. H. Thorpe. In heavy tropical foliage, it seems, a pair of birds may have difficulty keeping in contact. For such species territorial isolation and defense may be impractical and be discouraged by evolution as maladaptive. Yet there remains the eternal problem of keeping pairs unbroken. In the bou-bou shrike natural selection has perfected a startling capacity for antiphonal singing. The birds, though out of sight of each other, sing duets. Melodies are peculiar to the pair, and since either may sing any portion of the duet, the songs become means of identifying one's mate. Such a substitution of musical composition for territory, however, places a dismaying demand on bird creativity. One pair, recorded by

North, sang seventeen different melodies in the course of a single day. And such bird creativity places a dismaying demand on human capacity for explanation: pairs in the Kenya wild sing in the basic intervals of what we regard as our conventional, man-created, diatonic scale.

The bou-bou shrike's system of keeping father home because he can sing duets with none but his wife we may regard as exotic. The bread-and-butter system is the pair territory. One finds it dominating the life of one of our closest primate cousins, that small successful ape, the gibbon. C. R. Carpenter's study of the lar gibbon in Thailand, published in 1940, survived decades of skepticism to find confirmation in John Ellefson's 1965 report on the same species in Malaya.

Unlike any other ape and like few monkeys, the gibbon lives in a single-family group, paired on a territory usually for life. The male's great siren call, which one hears so frequently echoing through a zoo, is an announcement of his location to his neighbors, a warning to all that trespassers will not be tolerated, and when he is in a restless mood it is an invitation to any like-spirited gibbon to appear on the boundary and do battle. Small though he is, the quick acrobat of the

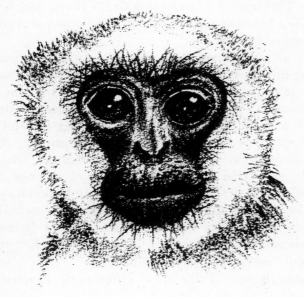

treetops can control a forest area as large as a quarter of a square mile. Though his mate will never join him in actual combat, she may accompany him to the embattled border, there to groom him and lend him moral support between forays.

The question of Why? has dominated territorial ponderings from the beginning. Why spend so much energy in the defense of a portion of land indistinguishable from the next portion? So far as the gibbon is concerned, both Carpenter and Ellefson see the principal function as protection of food supply. But up to a hundred acres of tropical forest is a lavish pantry for a mother and father gibbon, along with two or three growing gibbons. It was dissatisfaction with the food theory, among others then projected, that led the English ornithologist David Lack to relate territory to the pair bond.

Lack is at present director of the Earl Grey Institute of Field Ornithology at Oxford. In the mid-1930's he was a teacher at Devon's Dartington Hall. There for five years he kept one eye glued on children and the other eye, evidently, as firmly glued on robins. Out of this dedicated robin-watching came a book called *The Life of the Robin,* which must stand with Eliot Howard's classic, with Darling's tribute to a herd of red deer, with Niko Tinbergen's *The Herring Gull's World* and Konrad Lorenz' *King Solomon's Ring,* among the literary treasures of the new natural history.

As early as 1933 David Lack had expressed his uneasiness concerning interpretations of territory then current. What was the chief selective value that such behavior brought to a species' chances of survival? By then—as I reviewed in the last chapter—several interpretations had been suggested and were being argued: that territory protected food supply, that it dispersed population in relation to environmental resource, that it offered a criterion for the selection of superior males. Lack found so many exceptions to any single interpretation that he began to doubt territory as a general law in the behavior of birds. Then in that year he reported for work at Dartington Hall and began clambering out of bed in the early hours to watch robins busy at their daybreak deeds.

The robin is one of the most enthusiastic of territorial

creatures. (And as an American I must point out with territorial deflation that what we call a robin is a thrush with a red breast.) Besides his enthusiasm for exclusive property, the English robin has an equal enthusiasm for battle. Lack built a huge aviary thirty feet long with the plan of trapping birds and placing them in the aviary where he could watch them work out their social arrangements. But the plan developed complications. The aviary allowed a beaten bird no room for escape, and one male killed four other males in just four days. While it is possible that the murderer may have had a bad family background, suffered a deprived youth, or been a victim of propaganda, it seems on the surface more likely that he enjoyed nothing more than a good fight. Lack recorded that while sex may be the most fun that some animals get, in robins it is definitely fighting.

Trapping robins, in truth, was far easier than knowing what to do with them. A cock stakes out his borders on a lawn. From then on he has such an excessive curiosity concerning any foreign object lying about on his property that, should it be a trap, he will promptly find himself inside it. Lack had only to put out the most conspicuous trap available, and he would have a robin within two hours. One cock became a nuisance. He came to like traps. Trying to trap his mate, Lack had to let out the cock seven times on one particular day, eight times the next.

Like most birds, the robin sings only within his borders, where he pours out his defense and defiance. As in most species, the song is usually enough to keep away intruders. Should song fail, then the cock is ready for battle, but his opponent must be a robin. By experiment Lack discovered that it was an intruder's red breast that inflamed the proprietor's rage. He would ignore or merely investigate a variety of stuffed birds placed on his lawn; a mere tuft of red feathers was enough to bring on warfare. But since battle is preceded by one last attempt of the proprietor to discourage intrusion by peaceful means, Lack had to witness a scene of fair absurdity: his cock robins, red breasts puffed out like toy balloons, turning from side to side through an arc of 180 degrees while they displayed

8

their frightening frontside to a bunch of red feathers a few inches away.

Niko Tinbergen had a comparable experience with his three-spined sticklebacks, the same creatures who stand on their heads in the water and dig holes in the sand during border disputes. When the breeding season arrives, the male stickleback stakes out a territory and develops a red underside and a furious disposition. He too will attack anything red. In his laboratory Tinbergen had some twenty aquaria lined up along window sills facing the street, all loaded with three-spined sticklebacks shielded from each other's view but yearning for mortal enemies. One day, to the scientist's astonishment, every male dashed to the window side of his tank, dorsal spines raised for action. One of Britain's red postal vans had passed in the street outside.

There is a considerable difference, however, between robins and three-spined sticklebacks: robins do not confine either their red breasts or their fiery belligerence to the breeding season, and neither do they confine them to the male. The hen has a red breast too, and in the autumn may stake out a territory of her own, sing on it, and respond to any intrusion with energy equal to the cock's. One autumn morning David Lack put a stuffed robin on the end of a six-foot stake and planted it within the borders of a notably fierce hen. For forty minutes she postured and sang and flew at the insolent specimen, pecking it again and again. Then the breakfast gong rang and Lack's appetite overcame his scientific curiosity. He pulled up his stake and went into the house. Fortunately he looked back. The hen was still attacking the place in the air where the stuffed robin had been. And she continued her attacks, violently pecking the air but with each attack striking an imaginary target that sank lower until at last it was only three feet off the ground. I do not believe that any reputable scientist has ever attempted an explanation for this one.

It is almost as difficult to offer an explanation for how cock robins and hen robins, equally ferocious, equally stimulated by their identical red breasts, ever get together and have little robins. It is a fact of robin life that they do. She will appear on his territory one winter day. He will fly to her. He will become most excited for a few minutes, and then, we must assume, they will consider themselves paired. They will share the territory, defending it together, as from then on they share their daily life. When springtime comes they will mate and raise a brood. But why did he let her into the place to begin with? Lack's only explanation after five years of robin-watching is that the cock knows it must be a hen because if she were a cock she would have lost her courage and flown away. The answer may not sound very scientific, but since there seems no better one, it will have to do.

These were the long years of robin-watching, however, that put Lack to pondering the value of the pair territory to the pair bond. Robins on the lawns of Devon might pair with a little moment of display and excitement as early as December. Through three hard months until nesting time they will lead a most ordinary life, feeding, finding shelter from the cold, driving off intruders, largely ignoring each other. It is not too different from the life of roe deer before the rut. The roebuck, of course, has his specialized activity of territorial defense, while the doe must bear and care for her young. But it is a social relationship, isolated from all other members of the species by the privacy of the pair territory. So it is with robins. Unburdened by young, he and she in these early months lead a life alike. Isolated on a mutual territory, joined in its defense, they form a special relationship, a familiarity, which can be described by no word other than psychological. Rarely in this period of betrothal will one desert the other. The relationship —this bond—has become of such potency that neither can do without it.

With warming weather, sap will flow in the veins of trees and hormones in the veins of robins. One fine day she will hump over, giving the signal, and he will mount her and that will be just about that. It is difficult to think of a species that gets less fun out of sex. There will be a fine to-do of nest-building, for the hen is very fast. A gardener at Basingstroke hung up his coat in a toolshed at nine fifteen one morning and returned shortly after noon to discover an almost complete robin nest in a pocket. And confusion may confound the haste. The robin builds always in a hole. One hen built in a stack of pipes, got mixed up, and rounded out the experience building twenty-three nests. Another was attracted by the pigeonholes of an old-fashioned desk in a workshop. There were sixteen pigeonholes and she built twelve nests before mastering the situation. But she still raised her brood. Among the wonders of the natural world is determination, shared equally by animals and, at their best, by men.

When young robins hatch, one begins to understand why pair bonds are necessary. Robin-raising is not the kind of industry which the male can desert to visit an arena, a bower, or the saloon at the corner. For a few days the female will spend most of her time on the nest, and he will bring all the food, passing it to her to be stuffed into the four, five, or six gaping mouths. By the end of a week she will spend no time at all on the nest, since the collective appetite it shelters will have developed by then to proportions which two parents can scarcely keep up with. In England green caterpillars swarm during the robin's major breeding season. On a day in early May, Lack kept count on a nest containing five young. The parents paid it twenty-nine visits per hour, each time bringing two or three caterpillars. He reckoned that in the course of a full working day the pair harvested about one thousand caterpillars. There is also fecal matter to be hauled away. Baby robins deliver their feces in little gelatinous sacs which the parents carry at least twenty yards away from the nest. In the same day there will be forty or fifty such sacs to be disposed of.

After about two weeks the fledglings leave the nest, but they will pick up no food for themselves for another eight or ten days. The parents are relieved of the necessity of returning to the nest, since the young follow them about, or of carrying away fecal matter. But that is all they are relieved of, for through this time the young are growing bigger and bigger, their gullets more and more cavernous. Finally, three weeks after leaving the nest, they will be on their own. One would think that the pair, after all this, would take a holiday at some robin resort. But they will not. She will hump over a little, and he will get the signal and mount her, and then she will get busy building another nest in somebody's coat pocket, and they will have another brood.

For such heroic labors evolution must provide heroic tools. The pair bond, such a tool, holds in most species only for a season, since that is sufficient. In the life of the robin, a day will come when she will fly away, and that will be the end of it. He will remain on his territory, investigating foreign objects, singing, displaying his red breast to tiresome intruders, getting into brawls. Perhaps she will migrate; perhaps she will take up an autumn territory, sing, and attack stuffed robins on the ends of stakes. Perhaps—only perhaps—they will pair again some winter day, but it is most unlikely. If it occurs, it will be due to accident. She will have been drawn to the same old territory, and if a cat has not got him, he will still be there.

In many species, however, the bond holds for life. Wrens, like gibbons as we have seen, will pair and occupy the same territory all of their days. Mockingbirds will share a territory through the breeding season. She will grow a bit bored with him, though, when the young have flown away, and she will take up a property next door. Maybe it is for the sake of her career, since she cannot sing unless she has a place of her own. Through autumn and winter, if the weather is fine, they will sing to each other almost as do bou-bou shrikes in Kenya. Then a time will come, I suppose, when the bond will pull hard, or her career will seem not enough, and she will move back with him and give up singing for another season.

David Lack, thinking it over on shivery mornings in Devon, was willing to grant the economic advantages of a private domain. If you are going to have to harvest a thousand green caterpillars a day, then it is an advantage to draw many of them from a nearby, private stock. And yet if it were simply economics, as Altum had thought, then robin territories should be of a fairly standard size to supply a fairly standard larder. And they were not. They varied in Devon from two acres down to a quarter of an acre, and even on the smallest a pair could successfully raise their brood. Then there was that other answer of Eliot Howard's, the selection of males through territorial competition. In some species this might be of critical or even total importance. But four out of five cock robins succeed in gaining properties, and while the elimination of the fifth from breeding represents a selective value to the species, it did not seem to Lack a value that critical. The pair bond, however, was another matter. Without such a link between cock and hen, enduring so long as the young need them, there would be no more robins. And it is the mutual territory that forges the link.

One encounters again the moral implications of territorial behavior. That scientific thought, despite the Moffats and the Lacks, has remained for so long absorbed by territory as an expression of self-interest is entirely natural. The private territory represents a monopoly of a portion of the earth's land or water; as such, it tempts the most obvious question, what does the proprietor get out of it? But to take such a view is to see nothing but trees; the eternal forest escapes us. It is only when we brood, dissatisfied as was Lack with older views, that the evolutionary landscape emerges.

The pair territory is a restraint on the actions of the individual. The attachment of male and female to a single property is an attachment to each other more permanent than sexual opportunity. Freedom is denied, anarchy forestalled. A biological necessity for the male to be responsible for the welfare of his offspring is enforced through a biological attachment for the space they occupy. As the territorial imperative reaches into the lives of all members of an arena species, shaping and channeling the sexual instinct to the species' genetic good, so it reaches into the lives of all members of a pair species to shape and constrain their physical freedom according to the necessities of their demanding offspring.

The cock robin, displaying his puffed-up, pompous breast to a tuft of red feathers, may seem to possess an ego as large as all the countryside. But if it be so, then he has been trapped by that ego. Nature—brilliantly, subtly—has turned the tables on him and made of his little kingdom a moral prison from which he cannot escape his obligation to future robins.

3

The parallel between human marriage and animal pairing requires no lecturer with a long, pointed wand. The parallel between human desire for a place that is one's own and animal instinct to stake out such a private domain requires even less demonstration. Equally obvious must be the classification of the human species among those animal species facing the biological problem of offspring with demands of appalling proportions. And as obvious in our modern society as on a lawn in Devon is the necessity to reinforce the pair bond in the interest of normal development of our forever-demanding young. Are we then, confronted by parallels of such a conspicuous order, to dismiss the possibility that man is a territorial species and that evolution, with its territorial imperative, has perfected an innate behavioral mechanism commanding precisely the morality we seek? Yet we do so dismiss it as with our every righteous thought we denigrate the role of private property in human affairs.

That man is a territorial species has been the conclusion of many a scientist. Zurich's Heini Hediger has written: "It can be assumed that the natural history of territoriality in the animal kingdom represents the first chapter of the history of property in mankind." Harrison Matthews, of London's Zoological Society, was asked at a symposium if he regarded man as a territorial animal. He replied most simply, "Yes, certainly. You have only to notice the signboards dotted all over the countryside announcing that 'Trespassers will be prosecuted.' " Years ago the University of Michigan's respected zoologist W. H. Burt wrote: "Man considers it his inherent right to own property, either as an individual or as a member of a group or both. Further, he is ever ready to protect that property against aggressors, even to the extent at times of sacrificing his own life. That this behavioristic pattern is not peculiar to man, but is a fundamental characteristic of animals in general, has been shown for diverse animal groups." Even longer ago, in 1931, Walter Heape wrote in his *Emigration, Migration and Nomadism:* "It may be held that the recognition of territorial rights, one of the most significant attributes of civilization, was not evolved by man but has ever been an inherent factor in the life history of animals."

That man's territorial nature is inherent and of evolutionary origin is scarcely a new thought; it is merely an ignored one. It has been pressed aside by our political antipathies, by our sexual preoccupations, by our romantic fallacies concerning the uniqueness of man, by our contemporary dedication to the myth that man is without instinct and a creature solely of his culture. Yet it would seem to me a thought which we may ignore no longer. As our populations expand, as a world-wide movement from countryside to city embraces all peoples, as problems of housing, of broken homes and juvenile delinquency, of mass education and delayed independence of the young rise about us in our every human midst, as David Riesman's phrase "the lonely crowd" comes more and more aptly to describe all humankind, have we not the right to ask: Is what we are witnessing, in essence, not the first consequence of the deterritorializing of man? And if man is a territorial animal, then as we seek to repair his dignity and responsibility as a human being, should we not first search for means of restoring his dignity and responsibility as a proprietor?

Our first search, of course, must be for evidence that he is indeed a territorial animal. Though many a scientist will testify that he is, many another will disagree. And while we may pursue without end certain parallels between animal and human behavior, there will remain always the chance that what we observe in man is a kind of mirror held up to nature; our culture and our learning reflect the natural way without in a biological sense being beholden to it. I myself do not take such an outside chance very seriously, but still the argument must be answered. If we behave as we do in our attachment for property because we have been taught to, because our culture and our social mechanisms demand it of us, then we deal with nothing fundamental. What is learned may be unlearned, and we may assume that man will adjust himself to collective existence or to the lonely crowd. But if, in sharp contrast, we deal with an innate behavior pattern, an open instinct, an inward biological demand placed in our nature by the selective necessities of our evolutionary history, then we deal with the changeless. And we hold in our hand a secret key: if lost, it will leave locked and starved and frustrated a vital portion of our nature, but if used, it may open human potentials which today we cannot glimpse.

I believe that our century has presented us with a means to demonstrate that our attachment for property is of an ancient biological order. At the opening of this chapter I suggested that the value of the pair territory to the animal pair is twofold. Through isolation of the pair on the mutual property a guarantee is effected that neither will desert the family obligations. This we have inspected. But also I suggested that the mysterious enhancement of powers which a territory invariably summons in its male proprietor places energy otherwise unavailable at family disposal. If such enhancement of energy occurs in man, then one cannot explain it as a cultural lesson. And so let us now take another glance through the species and consider the beaver, a fish, a cricket, and a worm, before we return to man.

"As busy as a beaver" is a phrase that must have come to our tongue a very long time ago, and whoever first described the beaver as busy perhaps made further discussion of the animal superfluous. Some years ago, however, an American named Glenn W. Bradt—a man evidently unwilling to leave any cliché unturned—made a thorough study of about forty beaver colonies in Michigan. It was one of those solid, careful, thoughtful jobs on which this inquiry thrives. Bradt came to the conclusion that beavers are busy.

We may regard a pair of robins harvesting a thousand caterpillars a day, while between servings having to haul away fecal matter in countless small packages, as creatures whose beaks have been pressed rather heavily against the evolutionary grindstone. But between robins and beavers there is an eminent difference: robins work that hard through a few hysterical weeks in the breeding season; beavers do it the year around. And the beaver, not unlike man, seems to have got himself into this life of hard labor through dependence on a culture which may have seemed a bright evolutionary idea to begin with but developed into one of relentless demand.

To be fair to the beaver, it was not his cultural achievement that got him into trouble so much as his vulnerability to predators and his strange appetite for trees. The food supply for a beaver colony consists of a reserve of young saplings such as aspen, willow, or maple. And the beaver's cultural solution for problems of both food and security has been, as we all know, the dam in a wilderness stream, the backed-up pond, and island lodges protected by surrounding water. Since he builds his installation out of the same material from which he prepares his dinner, he has at all times a quick snack handy.

Just how hard he works to support all this may be judged from the records of one of Bradt's colonies. There were six beavers. In 353 days they cut down 1040 trees, hauled them to the pond, stripped them, cut them into segments, and used them either for construction, for the evening meal, or for storage in the pantry. If the beaver does not have four conditions in his life—permanence of site, an assured supply of wood, a limited population in a single colony, and a willingness to work hard—he cannot attain real success. He has solved all four through the pair territory.

We speak of a beaver colony, but the forty colonies studied

by Bradt were all in reality families, and there is reason to believe that no colony is ever larger than a family group. The male pairs for life. The pair establish a territory. It must be large enough to offer permanent food supply, but if it is too large they will be unable to defend it, and, more important, they will be unable to work it economically. The mother has one litter of kits in a year, usually four in number. And so the population consists of the kits of the season, the yearlings of the previous season, and the pair. Two-year-olds are never found in a colony. When next season's kits are born, this season's yearlings will leave or be driven out. The homeplace cannot support them. They must go forth into the wilderness, furnish food for the foxes, or happily found other dams on other streams.

Like the robin, the beaver is easily trapped. For bait one has only to cause some slight break in his dam and he will be there in moments to repair it. In the winter when the pond is frozen and the family sleeps securely within the lodge, the father frequently lives in a burrow on the bank. There is the risk of the predator, but it is a risk he must take. He must be free to keep an eye on his property. The energy to work at a tireless pace, the unflagging attention, the willingness to gamble individual survival, are all a portion of the beaver's territorial psychology.

Why the possession of a territory should be a source of extra energy in the proprietor is a mystery, as I have indicated, which science may never solve. Some of our best ethological thinkers have analyzed the phenomenon in terms of confidence in the familiar and fear of the strange. This would do if we dealt always with areas fairly large or complex or in one way and another offering surprises to the intruder, comforting secrets to the defender. But it cannot explain to me why a Uganda kob, standing on his putting green, is very nearly invulnerable. His little property with its close-clipped grass offers as few secrets as it does surprises. Nor can it explain to me why sea birds like the gannet or the guillemot or the herring gull should be all but unbeatable on territories measuring a few feet in diameter. Nor does it truly explain to me why two roebucks or two three-spined sticklebacks or two pine squirrels or two infuriated seals can face each other across an unseen line, each with perfect confidence that if he is attacked he will win, each with perfect lack of confidence in his survival prospects just a few feet across the border.

"Victory goes not to the strong but to the righteous—the righteous of course being the owners of property." This was how David Lack put it, concerning birds. But the law holds just as good for primates and defending groups, as C. R. Carpenter discovered over thirty years ago in his observations of the howling monkey. No matter what the circumstance of battle, Carpenter concluded, the home team wins. Later research would show that the increase of energy brought by property to its proprietor, while beyond explanation, is not beyond measurement.

The late W. C. Allee of the University of Chicago was one of the founders of the new biology. I shall enter little into his work in this book because his chief concern was with society and orders of dominance. But part of Allee's greatness was his capacity to turn out able students, and one of those students was a man named J. C. Braddock, who in 1949 performed with platys an experiment of unrivaled scientific elegance. It was the kind of laboratory experiment to remind us that not everything can be learned in the open air.

Platypoecilus maculatus is familiar to anyone who has ever tolerated a tankful of tropical fish in his home. The platy is tiny, and Braddock used over three hundred of them to demonstrate in precise, quantitive terms what the simple factor of residence can mean to the confidence of a living organism. The platy is not territorial. We deal here with some essential ingredient of life that becomes formalized by territory. To demonstrate it, Braddock put each of his platys into a small aquarium, half of the bowls with a little duckweed, half with none. Those with the duckweed he termed residents; those without, intruders. He allowed his residents a little time to become familiar with their duckweed-distinguished homes. Then to each tank of a resident he introduced an intruder.

When two or more fish are in the same tank, there will always be a struggle for dominance. When the struggle is resolved, a fairly stable relationship will be formed in which one fish usually or always gives way to the other, usually or always retreats when attacked, usually or always in the end will allow the other priority in feeding or females or favorite resting places. In *African Genesis* I described an experiment with male swordtails, another tropical fish, who when water has been cooled to a certain degree will lose all interest in a ready female but will continue their struggles to dominate one another. "Alpha fish" is the term used by the new biology to describe the winner of such a competition.

Braddock's experiment was designed to test what effect prior residence would have on the outcome of the competition for dominance. Half of his intruders were larger than the residents, half smaller. And he found that size and strength would have some effect on the determination of which would be the alpha fish, but not much. It was residence that counted. Even when the resident was the smaller fish, he would be the first to challenge four times as often as the larger intruder. And when the struggle was resolved, the intruder would be the loser four times as often if he was the smaller fish, three times as often even though he was the larger.

One would think that as time went by and both became familiar with the tank, the slim advantage of prior residence would cease to have meaning. And to a degree it was true. Even so, of those original residents who were smaller than the original intruders, half remained permanently the alpha fish. And such was the outcome, we must keep in mind, in a species which is not truly territorial. Comparable experiments by G. P. Baerends, a Dutch ethologist, with members of the cichlid group of fishes, all of whom defend true territories, have shown that for an intruder to oust a proprietor he must be very nearly twice as big.

I am choosing examples from fairly primitive creatures. I mentioned in connection with the cicada-killer wasp that territorial behavior has been observed in few insects. Several years ago, however, in the University of Michigan's zoology department Richard Alexander was experimenting with domi-

nant orders in crickets. They are renowned fighters, and in
some parts of the world people gamble on them as they do on
cocks. (A cricket match in the Orient has a rather different
meaning than in England.) Alexander had a batch of fighting
crickets which he matched again and again in varying combinations to determine the order of dominance. Two of the crickets
were quite even in size and strength and agility. Even so, one
dominated the other so thoroughly that in 200 bouts he
was the winner of all but one. Then both crickets found niches
where they would retire and sing. The niches were territories.
After that, domination was over and every bout was decided by
where it took place. The winning cricket was invariably the
cricket closest to his niche.

I am making no effort to explain this force, because obviously I cannot. But since in my opinion it is a force as
demonstrable, as predictable, yet just as inexplicable in men as
it is in crickets, I shall present one more example from the life
of a creature even more primitive than the insect.

For some years the planarian worm has been a riotous citizen
of a good many American laboratories. He has been shocked
by electricity, denied food and water, taught everything but
the ABC's, and even chopped up and fed to his less-educated
friends. There is little doubt that many of the experiments are
leading us toward a moment when we must form new principles
concerning life itself; but there is little doubt also that some of
the conclusions being formed are premature. Among the
experiments, however, there has been one so unspectacular in

its outline, so careful in its controls, so haunting in its implications that it bears inspection here. This was a study made by Jay Boyd Best and Irvin Rubinstein at the Walter Reed Army Institute in Washington.

The planarian worm is a small marine creature found, for example, in the bayous of Louisiana. He has no true central nervous system, but simply a pair of nerves running down his back, an arrangement fashionable half a billion years ago. What evolved as a brain in later ages consists in the planarian of nothing but a pair of enlarged ganglia furnishing connectives between the two nerves. The ganglia provide a semblance of a head sufficient to indicate which end of him is which, but it cannot be very important, for if you cut him in two he will grow a new head at the front of the old back section. Also, he has no circulatory system, and his origins go back so far as to antedate common biological developments in plumbing; he has no rectum, and rids himself of waste through special pores in his skin. So far as sex is concerned, the world of the planarian worm offers limited entertainment. He is capable on occasion of laying an egg, although normally he reproduces himself by division. Nature presented this creature to our ancient swamps somewhat before she completed her experiments with sex. It was a long time ago.

Now, it stretches imagination to the breaking point if we attribute to a creature lacking brain, blood, sex, and even rectum any elaborate emotional or intellectual life, or any notable capacity for nostalgia. And yet Best and Rubinstein in the course of their tests of the planarian's capacity to learn came up with hard evidence concerning his capacity to remember. He "prefers" to eat in places where he has been before, although what he prefers or remembers with, I cannot say.

The experiment was as simple as it was conclusive. The worms were kept in glass bowls. A batch, to ensure a hearty appetite, was allowed to fast for three days. It was then divided into two groups. One group of worms, to be familiarized, was placed in a plastic receptacle without food for an hour and a half, then returned to its home bowl to go on being hungry for another half-hour. In this interval the receptacle was scoured and rinsed with hot water to remove any traces of spoor or identifiable remains. Now both groups, equally hungry, were placed in feeding receptacles with a proper dinner of chopped liver floating in water. One group had never been in its receptacle before; the other, of course, had had its ninety minutes of residence but because of the scouring was presented with no clues—odors, tastes, landmarks—by which the receptacle could be identified. Nevertheless, the worms of prior residence began eating on the average in twenty minutes, while the worms encountering their receptacle for the first time took forty-two. And when the experiment was repeated with fresh batches of worms denied food for six long days, the results were precisely the same: those familiar with the dish took just half as long to start eating as those who had never been there before.

It is common knowledge that a dog enjoys eating in a customary place, and that many higher animals will eat better where they feel familiar. This is normally interpreted as anxiety and caution in a strange place, confidence and security in an accustomed one. But here we are dealing neither with long custom nor higher animals. What is the confidence that a planarian worm derives from a ninety-minute exposure to a plastic dish? And how does he know that he has been there before? And beyond all that, just what does he have to know with or feel confident with, beyond two bumps on his symmetrical nerves?

There are ghosts in evolution's attic. A shutter slams on a windless night. There is a scraping sound above our heads, and with a considerable palpitation we move about our room, inspect the ceiling. The sound stops. A single step on the stairs outside gives a soft creak; then there is silence. We rush out the door. There is no one. Who was it? Where did he go?

Man is as invested by the unknown but measurable forces of the natural world as is the planarian worm. We are as haunted by old voices, as driven by old dictations, as contained by old and sometimes inappropriate regulations as is the cricket near his niche. And while it may seem an unlikely leap to fling ourselves from plastic dishes and numbered fish bowls to the modern farm, I believe that we shall recognize on its familiar acres those same ghostly, unfamiliar, uninstructed forces animating ourselves even as they animate the least among us.

A riddle of our times—one far more agonizing to the Russians than to ourselves—has been the collapse of Soviet agriculture. That the world's second most powerful nation, one fully capable of exploring the moon, should be unable to feed itself is a truth finding testament in every grain market in the world. Why? We have answers by the dozen, but in all their collected urgency they cannot, in my opinion, explain the calamity that has come to the collective way. We and the Russians and the Chinese too will understand it, I maintain, only when we recognize that among the instruments of a successful modern farm —among the fertilizers, the insecticides, the proper seed, the proper machinery, the proper know-how—there stands an unseen tool. And that tool is the farmer's dedication to his work. No profit motive can command it, for there are easier ways to become a millionaire. No appeals to a sense of duty can summon it forth, for there are shorter roads to the patriot's pedestal. The dedication must spring from within the man.

If we think back, we shall recall that farm and farmer have been the central problem of civilization, even as they have been its central cause, ever since in neolithic times almost 10,000 years ago we began our domestication of plants and animals. Having gained control over an abundant food supply, we made possible populations of such number that the old hunting life could never again support us. We could not return. Like the beaver, we mastered a culture which in turn mastered us. Pasture and field, orchard and garden became like portions of our body, organs without which we could not exist. And like the beaver's dams and lodges and wooded acres, they commanded an intolerable lot of work.

Which of us from dawn to dark would bend in the rice paddies, cut hay in the fields? As the millennia progressed, we supplied many an ingenious answer. We tried at first to push the work off on our women, an answer favored in much of Africa even today. We tried human slavery, a solution respected throughout the civilized world until a century or so ago. We tried serfdom in many guises, chaining the worker to someone else's soil. But there was always a shortcoming: that the involuntary worker is inefficient.

Until the industrial revolution the inefficiency of our agriculture was of no alarming moment. So long as the slave in the field was pressed to feed only a handful of nobles and warriors and priests and artisans, involuntary labor was good enough. But with the rise of industry and the massive increase of a factory and office population, our old systems collapsed. Despite the most humane or brutal attentions of landlord and overseer, the involuntary worker in the field could not produce the surplus food which such populations required. Slavery and serfdom vanished. To whatever extent other forces, moral or political, may have caused the final dismissal of our ancient institutions, the first cause was that they no longer worked. And we turned, most of the world's peoples, to another old if less prevalent institution, the peasant family on its freehold.

It is an accident of history that in 1862 the American President, Abraham Lincoln, with his signature on the Homestead Act committed the American agricultural future to the principle of private ownership based on a one-family unit, and that two years later Karl Marx with his call for Communism's First International committed what would someday be the Soviet Union to public ownership and the collective way. A giant race, of which we are almost as unaware today as we were then, was set in motion. As in two enormous living laboratories, the two human populations that would someday dominate the world's affairs were placed on opposite courses to solve a common problem. And that problem, in an industrial age, became in time the problem of all peoples the world around.

How many workers can be released to the wheel by a single man at a plow? As nations came to compete for power and prestige under the single racing flag of industrial worth, a stubborn equation of human mathematics came to limit their most splendid ambitions. What fraction of a people's numbers must remain in the field to free the remainder for the ultimate competition? And by what means may the energies of that farming fraction be so enhanced as to reduce its number to a minimum?

No argument exists—certainly not in Moscow's Central Statistical Administration—concerning the current state of the competition. In the United States of America one worker on a farm produces food for himself and for almost twelve more in the city; 92 percent of all Americans are freed for industry by a rural 8 percent who not only feed them but produce a food surplus of politically embarrassing dimensions. In the Soviet Union one worker in the field, but only in good years, feeds one worker in the factory. A doubtful half of the Russian population is freed from the soil. And as if to confirm the Soviet calamity, its major partner in the collective way, China, pursuing more extreme communal policies, must combine the efforts of six in the field to free one man for the industrial adventure.

China's pretensions to power are young, enveloped in a cloak of secrets, and cannot be inspected here. But the Soviet Union has been with us for almost half a century and makes no effort to hide or dismiss its failure. We know that many a blight besides proscription of private property has fallen on the Russian farm. Stalin's liquidation of the kulaks eliminated at an early date the ablest Russian farmers. The reign of Lysenko and his Lamarckian nostalgias all but annihilated Russia's science of plant genetics. Permafrost, that layer of permanently frozen earth underlying so much of the broad Russian plain, has been less than helpful. Drought, combined with the blunder of putting to the plow so much virgin but marginal land, has enforced the disaster in recent years. And for decades there was the naive pressure to favor the factory over the field, to neglect fertilizers; farm machinery, irrigation.

Like Chekhov's man of two-and-twenty misfortunes, the Russian farmer has had his full share. But does the total misfortune explain in full the catastrophe which has come to Russian hopes? There, of course, lies the argument. And I submit that were the ratio between American and Russian effectiveness, as measured by this final yardstick, a matter of two to one or three to one, or even of four or five to one, then American wealth, soil, science, and luck might account for the difference. But that the American farmer can feed twelve men besides himself, whereas the Russian can feed only one, is a little too much. I submit that a final multiplication of natural American assets arises from the biological value of the pair territory.

The smallness of American farms is among the best-kept secrets in the arsenal of American power. The Soviet Union's collective farms, in which workers shared until 1966 nothing but surplus earnings, average 15,000 acres, each with about 400 families. The state farm, hiring all workers at a fixed wage, averages 70,000 acres and employs 800 workers. Yet of America's two and one half million commercial farms, only one in ten is over 500 acres. The average number of workers, including the farmer and his sons if he has any, is five. Despite those advances in farm machinery which permit a worker to cultivate an acreage far greater than in Lincoln's day, still half of our farms are no larger now than then. The factory-in-the-field exists, but it is of minor significance. The American agricultural miracle has been produced by a man and his wife with a helper or two on a pair territory.

Many years ago I visited an enormous corporation cotton farm in California's Central Valley. Water was drawn from wells 2000 feet deep, each costing $65,000. The resident manager shrugged off the entire giant enterprise. "It's all the cost of the wells," he said. "A normal water supply, and this place would be subdivided tomorrow. Nobody can compete with a farmer on his one hundred and sixty acres." I had never heard of territory in those days, and I did not believe him.

Much more recently I visited a kibbutz in Israel. The kibbutz is the only successful collective farm in the history of modern agriculture. I was skeptical: was it truly a success? Between Tel-Aviv and Haifa there is one of the oldest and most respected of Israeli kibbutzim, Gan Shmuel, the Garden of Samuel. Here 400 adults farm 1200 acres and in the year before my visit produced crops valued at about $1.5 million. The special circumstance of Israeli vision and dedication, and the special situation of their nation besieged, might account for the success; but that Gan Shmuel is a success is unarguable. Then, however, I visited a private farm on comparable land only a few miles away. Here a former Polish doctor and his son and their wives worked thirty acres. Productivity per acre was about the same as at the kibbutz, but I was struck by a difference. On the collective farm it would have required nine adults to work thirty acres; on the private farm it took only four. I inquired. The former Polish doctor stretched: "Well, *they* work eight hours a day."

One recalls the beaver and his saplings, and a vigilance concerning his dam that makes him so easily trapped. One recalls the parent robins gathering a thousand caterpillars a day. One recalls the platys and their duckweed, and the intruding cichlid fish who must be twice as big to challenge a proprietor. One recalls the planarian worm who will take twice as long to start feeding, despite all hunger, if his plate is unfamiliar. Are we to believe that a biological force, commanded by a sense of possession, which plays such a measurable role in the affairs of animals plays no part in the measurable discrepancies of man?

In any final inspection of the Soviet-American experiment with the territorial imperative one might thumb through statistics as dreary as they are endless to demonstrate the superior efficiency of the man who owns over that of the man who shares or works for wages. Some have their fascinations, such as that process called stock raising, in which availability of fertilizer and machinery and irrigation provide limited advantage. Yet to achieve a net gain of one hundred pounds in a walking unit of beef, the American farmer will expend three and one-half hours of labor, the wage worker on a Soviet state farm twenty-one, the sharing worker on a collective farm an impossible fifty-one. But it is a situation within the Soviet farm economy that provides the last garish touch.

From the days of Stalin's enforced collectivization of the land, the peasant has been permitted to retain a tiny private plot for family cultivation. It is the last bedraggled remnant of the pair territory in the Soviet Union, and in times of political crisis and ideological pressure its size has been reduced. Today the private plot averages half an acre in size, but there is little likelihood of further reduction. Without it Russia would starve.

Private plots occupy about 3 percent of all Russian cultivated land, yet they produce almost half of all vegetables consumed, almost half of all milk and meat, three-quarters of all eggs, and two-thirds of that staff of Russian life, potatoes. After almost half a century the experiment with scientific socialism, despite all threats and despite all massacres, despite education and propaganda and appeals to patriotism, despite a police power and a political power ample, one would presume, to effect the total social conditioning of any being within its grasp, finds itself today at the mercy of an evolutionary fact of life: that man is a territorial animal.

Natural selection deals ruthlessly with any population, bird or beaver, which fails to solve the problems of its environment with all those resources, learned or unlearned, which may be at its disposal. It deals as ruthlessly with men. And in a time when we should like to pretend that natural selection no longer pertains to the human being, the most cynical observer must be moved by compassion for all those hundreds of millions of his fellow beings, in this earthly setting or that, who are being subjected to selection's surgery to prove that man is a being more ancient than all man's theories. But the evolutionary process grinds on, whatever our hopes or compassions, undeterred by tyranny, undeterred by dogma, undeterred by our most soaring excursions or delicate perfections of human self-delusion.

The territorial nature of man is genetic and ineradicable. We shall see, farther along in our inquiry, a larger and older demonstration of its powers in our devotion to country above even home. But as we watch the farmer going out to his barn with the sun not risen above the wood lot's fringe, we witness the answer to civilization's central problem which none but our evolutionary nature could provide. Here is man, like any other territorial animal, acting against his own interest: in the city he would still be sleeping, and making more money too. What force other than territory's innate morality could so contain his dedications? But here also is the biological reward, that mysterious enhancement of energy and resolution—territory's prime law and prime enigma—which invests the proprietor on his own vested acres. We did not invent it. We cannot command it.

Nor can we, not with all our policemen, permanently deny it.

He who has will probably hold. We do not know why; it is simply so. It is a law that rings harshly in the contemporary ear, but this is a defect of the ear, not the law. I believe that we shall see, as this inquiry develops, that, harsh though the law may be, in this territorial species of which you and I are members it has been the source of all freedom, the curse on the despot, and the last desperate roadblock in the path of aggression's might.

4. *The Voyage of the Animals*

Green turtles are seagoing monsters weighing up to a quarter of a ton, who boast ancestors that swam, perhaps, in Permian seas 200 million years ago, who survived somehow the fall of the great reptiles nearly 100 million years ago, yet whose heroic qualities until about five years ago had been recognized by none but cooks. Then a few stubborn scientists, heroes themselves as we shall see, began to wonder how green turtles find their way home.

In my last chapter we inspected those mysterious commands of both energy and responsibility which the homeplace directs to the possessor. They are commands mediating with impartial calm the affairs of men and other animals. Now, however, we turn to a force equally mysterious, equally, it would seem, beyond our present powers of explanation, which so far as we know does not animate our kind. We human beings may have our nostalgias. My thoughts may wing like the sooty tern toward the place where I was born. But unlike so many of my animal fellows, I lack the innate power to find it. Man is one species brilliantly equipped by nature to get himself hopelessly lost.

We may lack the animal's navigational ingenuities and find consolation in our own ingenuities—maps, sextants, compasses. Nevertheless, from the moment we grant the possibility that man is a territorial species, then we must begin to wonder about this force called home. What is this thing that I shelter within me and share with citizens of most ancient seas? If I am to know and respect the dedication that is mine, then I must know and respect the green turtle's.

Here and there throughout the tropical world from Borneo to the Carribbean are beaches, usually remote, where the old monsters come out of the sea to lay eggs in sandy nests. Where do they come from? The mature green turtle, like a cow, is herbivorous and must have its pastures of turtle grass in shallow, coastal waters. But such feeding haunts are rarely to be found in the vicinity of those beaches where turtles come to mate in the surf and lay their eggs in the sand. Archie Carr, professor of zoology at the University of Florida, became so intrigued by the question that over a period of years he tagged thousands of turtles on a beach in Costa Rica, and found that when nesting time was over the turtles would reappear at feeding grounds from Venezuela to the Florida keys.

Was it by simple chance and random wanderings that turtles from all over the Caribbean gathered at a particular nesting beach on the Costa Rica shore? It seemed unlikely. No turtle tagged by Carr on Tortuguero Beach ever returned to another nesting beach in the area. For those turtles who came, this beach seemed home. But how did they find it when every two or three years the reproductive urge came their way? Carr's curiosity led him on to make the discovery which we shall inspect here. He published his findings in 1965, and they may be regarded as science's last word—or dying gasp—on the homing of animals.

Ascension Island is in mid-Atlantic between Africa and South America. On it is a famous green-turtle nesting colony spread over several beaches. But on Ascension Island there is no least pasture of turtle grass, nor do such water meadows exist closer than the lush Brazilian shore. By tagging, Carr and his student Harold Hirth found that female turtles laying eggs on Ascension's beaches had come from Brazilian pastures 1400 miles away.

We must look at this journey from the green turtle's point of view. It is all open sea without an island or reef or shallows or other landmark. The equatorial current comes from Africa and is of no assistance. Ascension Island is a target just five miles across, with its loftiest point about one mile high. Until the invention of modern navigational aids, the island was difficult for human mariners to find. Yet the green turtle, who can lift her head but a few inches above the water and cannot see the island until she is a few miles offshore, finds it after a voyage of 1400 miles. And she not only finds it, but apparently finds it again and again. Five of the turtles tagged in 1960 have returned to Ascension at a later breeding season, four to the same beaches.

How do they do it? And how did they ever start doing it? The green turtle, of course, is so ancient that its ways may have been determined before the continents assumed their present shape and relationship. But as to how the memory of home can direct innately the journeys of animals, we have no answer. It is a question with which science has struggled manfully. It is a question as profound as any which biology faces today, for within its unknown answer must lie qualities and properties and potentialities of which we have no least knowledge. Yet it is· a question which scientists, with the sublime exception of a few like Carr, have largely abandoned.

When I was a young fellow in and out of the New York theater, a giant musical comedy opened at the old New York Hippodrome. It was a circus spectacle, and its name was *Jumbo,* and its two most spectacular stars were an elephant and that ageless miniature of a demented man, Jimmy Durante. And there came a moment in the show when Durante had a line worth recalling now, as we think of the green turtle, the Alaska fur seal, the sciences, and even of ourselves. The moment came—a moment which a playwright might be tempted to describe, technically, as the obligatory scene—when Durante stole the elephant. He entered from the shadows upstage, tiptoeing, making shushing noises at his vast companion. And when all seemed well, he encountered a policeman. Durante shrank. The policeman glowered.

"Where did you get that elephant?" growled the policeman.

Durante looked all about, blank, disturbed.

"What elephant?" he said.

What elephant? is the harried, half-demented reply of the sciences these days, when you ask them how animals find their way home.

2

The "homing problem," as it is discreetly referred to, did not truly exist fifteen or so years ago. No one had yet related it to territory, and there was a prevailing assumption that those animals, like pigeons, demonstrating a remarkable capacity for finding their way home were guided by nothing more inexplicable than a remarkable memory for landscape. Terms like "homing instinct" and "migrating instinct" were used, but loosely, and were intended to identify creatures relentlessly determined to return to familiar places, rather than to explain how they did it. It was assumed, for example, that in flocks of birds migrating over intercontinental distances to specific breeding grounds, there must be always those experienced older birds who showed the way. The young ones, next year, would be the wise ones.

A few disturbing experiments, it is true, haunted the blue scientific sky like little black distant clouds refusing to abandon a happy, well-organized picnic. As far back as 1931 O. J. and A. Murie, able naturalists, had come back from Wyoming's Grand Teton Mountains with some observations not easily explained. They had spent a summer in the high forests of fir and lodgepole pine trapping and retrapping deer mice. It is a standard technique for determining the range of small mammals. Live traps are set every so far apart, according to a pattern, over a fair-sized area. When a mouse or vole is trapped, he is marked and released. After the same individual has been retrapped enough times, and each location of his forced detention recorded on a chart, the observer gains a reliable notion concerning the limits of his range. The Muries' investigations led to some questions about homing for which there could be no sound answer except, What elephant?

Trapping and retrapping demonstrated that the tiny deer mouse rarely leaves a range fifty yards in diameter, and that one hundred yards is just about his lifetime limit of wandering. This area might be described as the world view of *Peromyscus maniculatus*. Yet when the Muries turned their attention to homing, some wonders showed up. Five deer mice were able to find their way home from a distance of one mile. Knowledge of the terrain was impossible; nor does the deer-mouse way of life, any more than the green turtle's, make attainable a bird's-eye view of a problem. Also, if you are the size of a deer mouse, then returning one mile is a little like returning from the other side of the world.

The Muries noticed that the best travelers in their collection were usually sub-adult, those with the least experience. And so they selected a young female, one about five weeks old. A deer mouse that age never leaves the immediate vicinity of the nest. This one, transported two miles, reappeared contentedly in her home trap in exactly two days.

Several other early if less spectacular studies went into the literature. C. M. Breder, Jr., later to become director of the New York Aquarium, as far back as 1927 was puzzling over the navigational capacities of frogs and toads. A German investigator demonstrated that when a dog returned eight or ten kilometers to his home, over largely unknown terrain at a certain recorded speed, he could only have come on a beeline without time for scouting around. One student confirmed a general fish rumor by marking steelhead trout. Of 238 caught when they returned to spawn, 233 were in their home stream, only five in a stream four miles away.

Little black clouds definitely hovered about the horizons of the scientific picnic. Besides deer mice and frogs and steelhead trout there was always, of course, the Eel Story. But the Eel Story was a little like Hitler's Big Lie. Nobody could possibly take it seriously. I have checked into every corner of the Eel Story, and I know that it is true. Nevertheless, were I to be sitting down to eat smoked eel tomorrow, I should still not believe that what I was eating had spent its youth in the Sargasso Sea. I do not even believe that there is such a place as the Sargasso Sea. When I was a boy I saw a film called *The Isle of Lost Ships,* and its scene was the Sargasso Sea, where all the seaweed in the Atlantic winds up in a warm, enormous eddy. According to the movie, all the lost ships wound up there, too, and there were Spanish galleons and wrecked clipper ships and old Roman galleys, and people lived forever, and there was Lewis Stone in some kind of costume. You went home afterward and could not sleep and lay in bed and listened to switch engines, somewhere, shunting freight cars around in Chicago yards, and you thought what a wonderful, wonderful world it was and how could you ever wait to grow up? But you did not honestly take the Sargasso Sea seriously, just as no sane scientist could ever take the Eel Story seriously. And I do not wonder.

It was a man named Johannes Schmidt who discovered that every eel in the Western World gets hatched in the Sargasso Sea. Eels are an important business in Denmark, and it was the Danish eel industry that supported his work over a period of some sixteen years, until he published it in 1922. What was known about the eel was that in the autumn all make their way down the rivers of Europe to the Baltic or the North Sea or the Atlantic, and never come back. The following spring a myriad of baby eels—called elvers, about two or three inches long—appear off the coast and make their way to fresh water. It was also known that the American eel, a different species with a few less vertebrae in its back, did the same thing. What happened to the old eels? And where did the elvers come from? Nobody knew. A mild puzzler for the biologist, too, was that from Iceland to Cyprus there are no local races of eel. All of the European species are a single variety, and all of the American the same. The biologists would have done well to stay mildly puzzled, and to have stayed away from Schmidt. Because he discovered that a very small, transparent, marine creature, *Leptocephalus brevirostris,* known from the Sargasso Sea, was in fact the eel larva.

It was, of course, impossible. It meant that all the mature eels in Europe, and America too, set out for the Sargasso Sea in the autumn, breed there in the spring, and die. The European larva takes two years to reach full size, and a third year to metamorphose into an elver, by which time they have sorted themselves out, and all the European elvers have migrated to Europe, where they have never been, and all the American elvers have migrated to America, where they have never been either. But how do they know where they are going? And how does an eel with 115 vertebrae know that he should report off the Dutch coast, and one with 107 vertebrae know that he should go up a river in North Carolina?

No bigger cock-and-bull story had ever hit science. The only trouble was that the Danes even provided Schmidt with a research vessel, and he proved it, and published the results in the *Philosophical Transactions* of the Royal Society of London, one of the staidest scientific publications in the world. Once in a while as the years went by, attempts would be made to disprove Schmidt's story, but they always failed. Only recently someone published in *Nature* a good, solid, environmentalist solution showing that in truth there is only one species of eel, that the larvae get caught up in Atlantic currents and deposited at their separate destinations, and that if you develop in cold water like a European elver you will have more vertebrae in your back than if you grow up in warm water like an American elver. In the manner of most good, solid, environmentalist solutions, it combined improbable biology with impossible statistics. Wynne-Edwards has since shown that if it were true that the number of vertebrae depended solely on water temperature, then a good many eels would have to come out of it with an in-between count. Yet there are almost none with 111 vertebrae, and very few with 110 or 112. Also, there are physiological differences between the two species.

Schmidt's conclusions still stand today, in giddy glory. And yet, as I have said, there is something about the Eel Story a little too much for human credulity, and had I attended the scientific picnic, I doubt that I should have considered any such nonsense a threat to my afternoon. That is how it was, I presume, when in 1951 an excellent student named Lester Aronson, of the staff of the American Museum of Natural History, could come to no explanation other than landscape memory for the weird antics of gobie fish in the British West Indies. Since it was the last major study of animal navigation before the thunderstorm broke, let me describe it for its historical worth.

The gobie is a tiny tropical fish, about an inch long. Aronson first heard of its odd capacities from colleagues at the Lerner Marine Laboratory at Bimini. On this little island in the Bahamas, gobies frequent tidal pools, a yard or so in diameter, that pock the coral shore. And the rumor that came to Aronson was that the gobie always knows his way home and is never stranded by the ebbing tide. Aronson set up a study.

The problem of gobie navigation, as things turned out, was far more mystifying than just knowing his way back home. The tiny pools left behind by the fall of the tide are separated, many of them, by ridges of rock some inches higher than the level of the pool. The gobie, considering how small he is, is a stupendous jumper. Isolated in one pool, he leaps unerringly into the next. But he cannot from his position in the water have any means of knowing in which direction the next pool lies. How does he do it? Aronson concluded that trial and error was out of the question, since most errors would strand the gobie on fatal sun-baked rocks. Any kind of solar navigation was likewise out of bounds, since the gobie flips his way about with equal certainty on cloudy or sunny days. Nor could it be a matter of having learned, through one means or another, a tested path home. He takes different paths to or from the home pool, and, for that matter, is thoroughly independent of home. From any pool he leaps on any course always to safety.

Aronson concluded that there could be no answer to explain the gobie's navigational sense except that at high tide, when he is free to swim about over all the pools, he somehow comes to learn the topography. It was a reasonable enough answer in 1951. It was, in fact, the last sane, reasonable explanation to be made at the picnic before the storm broke.

W. H. Thorpe, whose work on the relation of learning to instinct I have already mentioned, is one of the world's ranking authorities on animal behavior; he is also the authority least satisfied with a "What elephant?" approach to the homing problem. He has provided at his department at Cambridge University a safe anchorage for restless, roving spirits bent on torpedoing biological calm. The most restless of these was a man named G. V. T. Matthews, who in 1951 began methodical experiments with homing pigeons. He published his first conclusions in December of that year.

Homing pigeons, as used in races, are trained for the course. On release after release the trainer takes his flock farther and farther from the home loft, always in the direction of the ultimate racing release point. From such experiences had grown up the assumption, when Matthews went to work, that pigeons home through learning the landscape. It had occurred almost to no one, at this date, to experiment with untrained pigeons. But it occurred to Matthews. And he came up with the insane conclusion that inexperienced birds, who can have no knowledge of the point where they are released, orientate themselves better than trained birds who presumably know just what they are doing. We may recall the Muries' observation, twenty years earlier, that the sub-adult deer mice were the best homers.

A trained homing pigeon may know the landscape in the vicinity of his loft better than the inexperienced, and may find it more quickly once he has arrived in home precincts. But Matthews divorced from what might be called a finding capacity the capacity to orientate, to set a navigational direction when released. He devised quantitative means for rating his birds. Having been thrown straight up at the release point, the bird would circle once or twice before setting out. Matthews kept his bird records on a basis of the angle of deviation from the true course, and the time it took the bird from the instant of release to reach the vanishing point, usually about two miles. In every department, the inexperienced birds made better records than the experienced.

How could one explain it? Only by assuming that the navigational capacity is innate and in some birds may become confused by experience. The genetic basis for homing was further confirmed by Matthews' observation that some individual birds will be superior navigators from their first trial, others poor; and their capacities will change little with experience. So far as success at returning to the home loft was concerned, it mounted rapidly with training. The bird indeed formed a sharp recollection of the landscape in the area of his home, and developed with training a larger and larger geographical target familiar to him. But there was a clean line between this learned ability and the ability to choose a correct course when released in an unfamiliar countryside. Initial orientation seemed an inborn capacity, varying in individuals, and benefiting not at all from experience.

About the same time that Matthews was conducting his

experiments with homing pigeons at Cambridge, a man on the Continent named Gustav Kramer, of the Max Planck Institute, was conducting comparable experiments with starlings and relating the migratory instinct to the homing capacity. At a station on the East Baltic coast Kramer observed that starlings in an outdoor aviary all attempted in October to escape to the southwest. Southwest is the direction of starling migration at this season. And so Kramer built a round aviary without any view of the horizon or identifiable landmarks. The starlings still tried to escape to the southwest.

Things were beginning to get jittery. To say that the capacity to home, or to fix a migratory direction, is innate is to say approximately nothing. One still must ask, how do animals do it? By demolishing the assumption that animals navigate by memory and experience, Matthews and Kramer upset a scientific applecart. By demonstrating that it must be instinct, they set up a new one. What instinct? How? Kramer disposed of one possibility: that the animal is somehow susceptible to magnetic fields, and harbors within him a biological compass. Near his East Baltic station were deposits of magnetic iron ore that rendered unreliable the reading of manmade compasses. "The compass here," he observed, "behaves drastically. The starlings do not."

At the same time Matthews was perfecting his own disposal system for the same possibility. To the legs of one group of pigeons he attached small magnets, sufficiently strong to confuse the earth's magnetic field. To a control group he attached similar ballast, but of brass. All were released, all returned with equal success. But at this point in Matthews' investigations I suggest that the reader cease to envy the fascinating life of the experimental animal, and in particular the lives of Cambridge homing pigeons.

A hypothesis had popped up that perhaps good homers do have a remarkable memory, after all, concerning the route taken from the loft to the release point. Their capacity is for retracing a route. It was a hypothesis conceived in a sinking position, but Matthews was prepared to torpedo anything. And so he devised a demonic bit of machinery which must in some details have resembled a concrete mixer. He installed the device in a closed truck, and installed his pigeons inside the concrete mixer. The machine turned over four times a minute. And so, while Matthews cheerfully drove his feathered charges the seventy-five miles to the release point, inside the machine pigeons were being dumped on their heads regularly every fifteen seconds. It was not a course that any would be quite likely to remember, let alone choose to retrace. And when released, all flew directly to their loft in profound relief that this newest hypothesis had been disposed of.

Then there was the sun hypothesis. Matthews observed that on cloudy days his pigeons made very poor records. The sun, therefore, at least with pigeons, had something to do with it. (Although we may remember that Aronson's gobie fish did just as well with their leaping on overcast days.) The immediate explanation was that pigeons, normally released about the same time of day, develop a memory for the proper angle of the sun in relation to course. The proposition would not explain why untrained pigeons do so well, but Matthews, as usual, would try anything. He trained two sets of pigeons, both at the same hour of the day. Then he released the control group at the normal hour, the experimental group six hours later, with the sun 90 degrees away from the familiar. All came home, unperturbed.

By now the ghostly outlines of the "What elephant?" question were beginning to develop. Was it possible that a pigeon while it circled once or twice after being released took a moderately accurate sailor's reading of the sun? But this would require not only an inner sextant but an inner chronometer. An animal capacity for sizing up the sun's angle might be granted; but the angle is meaningless unless one knows what time it is. And while there are such organic realities as the biological clock, the demand on the pigeon for accuracy seemed a little exorbitant.

We are beginning to know a little about biological clocks. It is the sort of thing that disturbs you when you fly from Los Angeles to Paris directly and have to take to your bed in consequence. The eight-hour change of time, accomplished in a jet in approximately the same number of hours, puts your biological clock out of order. How primitive is the clock may be judged by Best's observation of his brainless, rectumless planarian worms. There is one species, *Dugesia tigrina,* that preys on another species, *Cura foramani,* but only at night. Best kept his Washington laboratory at a constant temperature of seventy degrees Fahrenheit under constant fluorescent illumination. There was no way to tell night from day. He fasted his predators under these conditions for ninety-eight hours, then put them in a tank with their prey. The planarians knew what time it was. Between six a.m. and six p.m. he recorded only two attacks; but when theoretical night came, there were nineteen.

The biological clock is a reality. But does it keep time sufficiently well to enable a pigeon, circling once or twice after its release, to determine its latitude and longitude? By 1953, growing a little desperate himself, Matthews came to the conclusion that the clock was good enough; that there was no other explanation. Then in 1955 another roof fell in.

Duke University, in North Carolina, has maintained for decades a Parapsychology Laboratory dedicated chiefly to the investigation of that scientific shady lady, extrasensory perception. There a man named J. G. Pratt investigated Matthews' investigations. Basic to Matthews' conclusions had been that the pigeons needed a little time to circle for the purpose of taking solar observations, reading their biological clocks, and putting their computers in order. Pratt suspected that the pigeons circled simply to gain altitude. And so he took his pigeons seventy-five miles from their loft to a town where there was a fire tower one hundred feet tall. Half of his pigeons he released from the base of the tower, half from the top. The half released from the ground circled, and took about five minutes to reach the vanishing point two miles away. The pigeons released from the top of the tower set straight out and reached the vanishing point in three minutes.

The shock waves reached back to Cambridge. R. H. Thouless was sent out to check on the experiment. The United States Navy, probably wondering by now whether all the money being spent on sextants and chronometers was really necessary, put up part of the funds. A new, more complex experiment was set up. The birds were released from forestry towers sixty to one hundred feet tall. Some of the birds were in covered crates which made it impossible to glimpse the sun until the instant of release. And Pratt and Thouless agreed that these averaged ten seconds to set their course.

Since homing pigeons become confused on a cloudy day, there can be no doubt but that the sun, by some means or another, enters into their capacity to navigate. Thorpe himself, however, has published the estimate that for a pigeon to make such a determination of position in ten seconds, his biological clock would require an accuracy of plus or minus two minutes in twenty-four hours. And in fact, by 1955, biology was getting into such an uproar over homing that the prejudice of the pigeon in favor of sunny days was beginning to mark it as a backward, insensitive, relatively unenlightened species.

Somebody looked into Scottish brown trout, which spend their first two years in streams, then migrate to a loch in October when the adults come upstream to spawn. The following spring the maturing trout return. Of 3000 trout marked in five tributaries of a Scottish loch, only one made a mistake in the spring. Somebody showed that black-headed gulls, taken from their nests and put in cages in a windowless shed with no external clues as to direction, will concentrate their escape reactions on the direction of the nest. Somebody wondered about sky polarization, which seems to help bees. Somebody else showed that birds, unlike bees, have the wrong kind of eyes. Somebody wondered about ultra-shortwave radiation. Somebody else showed that birds have no reaction to it. Somebody even wondered about the Coriolis effect, produced by the earth's rotation, which is rumored to make the departing water in your bathtub swirl in one direction in the northern hemisphere and the opposite in the southern. This seemed a most penetrating suggestion, since no one understands it anyway; but somebody else put the Coriolis effect down the drain.

These were trying times. Gustav Kramer, impatient with concerns about the sun, pointed out that barred warblers migrate only at night. What about the moon? An unhelpful professor named R. Drost pointed out that migratory birds have no difficulty whatsoever in finding the minuscule island of Helgoland on moonless nights. A desperate German scientist turned a flock of birds loose in a planetarium; they homed.

Somebody even brought up territory.

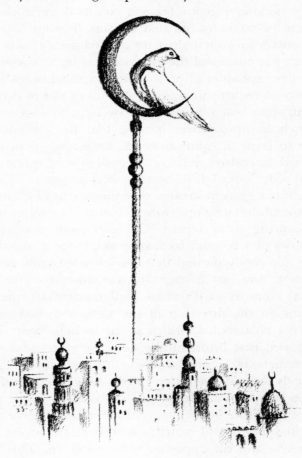

3

Homing and territory are related concepts. For the layman, freshly approaching the materials of the new biology, the relationship must stand forth as clearly as the silhouette of poplar trees standing beside a favorite grandmother's house. Yet in the scientific literature one can find few mentions of it.

When W. C. Allee and his associates in 1949 published their classic textbook *Principles of Animal Ecology,* they seem to have taken the relationship for granted. "Territoriality includes homing or the defense of a given area, or both." As I have already mentioned, however, Allee's great field of authority did not include territory. His judgment was ignored. When some years later J. D. Carthy published *Animal Navigation,* the only book we have presenting a general review of the subject, territory went unmentioned. This was in 1956, probably just a bit early for the more unreasonable dimensions of the problem to have homed to the book's able author. So far as I know, the first clean-cut statement of the relationship had been made only the year before by the English ornithologist James Fisher at a meeting of the International Ornithologists' Union at Basle: "Just as seabirds home to the colony of their birth, so do passerines home to the territory of their birth."

Fisher's statement was a challenge to science. Just what do we deal with when we consider this force called territory? We have seen that it may act against the interests of the individual, that it may restrain his freedom of action and tie him to those responsibilities which he might otherwise avoid. We have seen that in some as yet inexplicable fashion it contributes to his resolution and his energies, even as it inhibits the energy and the confidence of those who would intrude. And we speculate that in fair probability what is true of lower animals is true also of man. What, then, is this force that acts on us? What are its farthest dimensions? Is it possible that, as Fisher implied, territory is the magnet directing the animal compass?

A series of experiments and observations gave strong indication that Fisher might be right. Green sunfish attracted the attention of investigators in the University of Wisconsin's zoology department. It had been determined earlier that the tiny sunfish are intensely territorial, that females are as aggressive as males, and that all defend properties when still so immature that neither sex nor breeding can have anything to do with it. Now the Wisconsin team became attracted by the activity of the little belligerents in country ponds. Tagged fish, trapped in the autumn, were unable to return to their home areas through the four winter months when the pond was frozen. Yet nine out of ten would so return when spring brought its thaw.

Such an attachment to the homeplace seemed worth looking into. How did they find their way back? By random hunting or by true, direct-course homing? To trace the navigation of small fish in large ponds offers a problem, but it was solved by an idea as ingenious as it was inexpensive. Ping-pong ball floats were attached to captured sunfish at the ends of threads. Fish were released in the center of the pond. The ping-pong balls bobbed, then like a fleet of tiny patrol boats under orders from central command headed each on its way home. No random hunting or zigzag uncertainties marred the voyages. Sunfish truly home, and home to territories.

Another observation, this one in the Aleutian Islands, confirmed Fisher's thesis. Karl Kenyon is a biologist, today with the American Wildlife Service, who has done as much as any man to render presently insoluble the problem of animal navigation. The first of his contributions was a study of the Alaska fur seal, which, because of its commercial importance and long-threatened extinction, has been an object of scientific attention for many decades. Tagging has demonstrated that as green turtles converge on their nesting beach, seals return again and again to the same rookery when calving time approaches. The bulls come first, to joust for territories in the island rookery; the cows come later, having completed their long passages from all over the northern Pacific shores. She arrives pregnant, and so chooses not only the birthplace of her present burden but the genetic future of her next-born. What will be the criterion of her choice?

I recorded earlier the results of Bartholomew's brooding about seals: the cow could not be less concerned with which bull will become her lord and master; what attracts her to a territory is the sociability of other cows. But Kenyon, through remarkable luck, found evidence that, whatever bull may

attain mastery over a property, the cow tends to return to the territory where she was born.

Kenyon made his study at Polovina Rookery on St. Paul's Island in 1954. His luck was to find a photograph of the rookery made in 1896. The photograph showed virtually the same distribution of harems, large and small, as almost sixty years later. The distribution was quite unrelated to topography, despite a significant change which had come about. In 1898, out of concern for the welfare and number of baby seals, what might be called a slum-clearance project had been inaugurated. Earth had been filled in and areas leveled to extend the rookery's space. But in 1954 the improvements of 1898 were yet unoccupied by harems. Nothing, evidently, could induce a cow to choose a birthplace for her calf other than that of her ancestors.

The female seal homes to that territory where she was born. But let us look also at salmon, another species long studied because of its commercial importance. There is no more famous or inexplicable animal migration than the upriver spawning run of the salmon. Even by the 1920's it was

135

established that salmon return not just to the general area of their origins but to the same stream and even portion of stream. How do they find it? How, after two to six years at sea, does the salmon find its proper river mouth and then trace its way through perhaps a thousand miles of dividing tributaries on a course that will lead it home?

We do not know. There has been the memory explanation, as in homing pigeons. But, as Thorpe has pointed out, if a salmon is to memorize all the twists and turns and junctions on his way downstream, then he must unreel it all *backwards* on his return perhaps six years later. A. D. Hasler and W. J. Wisby, who gave us the green sunfish and their ping-pong balls, have advanced the taste hypothesis, the reasonable suggestion that if you are a salmon then all streams taste differently. Fish entering the Columbia River mouth, for example, simply keep going whichever way the water tastes more like home until at last they arrive at the unadulterated, undiluted memory of youth. But there is a problem. Evidence indicates that, wherever he is in the broad blue sea when the spawning urge strikes, a salmon lays a direct course for his home river. How can the taste of home waters guide him through the generalized flavor of sea water?

The navigation of salmon remains as closed a secret as does the navigation of homing pigeons. But in 1962 the authoritative Dutch journal *Behavior* published a heavily documented study of the territorial activities of juvenile Atlantic salmon, and the Fisher hypothesis again flashed forth. Are the fish returning to definite territories?

The observations were made in Canada, partly in the field, partly in the laboratory, by M. H. A. Keenleyside and F. T. Yamamoto. The study related not at all to homing, but rather to the previously unknown behavior of immature fish before they set out to sea. Reaching that stage is a tediously long process, a year or two in the warmer streams, as much as seven in the colder. Yet from his earliest, newly hatched, free-swimming moments until at last physiological development makes possible the wider life at sea, each young salmon has his defended territory. Normally he lingers near the bottom of the stream, feeding or chasing intruders; after every chase, however, he will return to his precise station. Even in the fastest river currents he will swim upstream at a rate which maintains without variation his relation to a fixed spot in the stream bed below. And he will do this for the entire period of his immaturity, be it two years or seven.

Why? When asking such a question in biology, of course, what one means is, What is the selective benefit to the species of maintaining territories under such difficult conditions for periods so long? No answer which we have encountered thus far can, I believe, explain it. The investigators favored the food theory—that the division of available space between an appropriate number of young salmon assured food supply for each. This could be true in a still pond, but in a rapidly flowing stream bringing continually fresh supplies, the answer seems dubious. Besides, many fish species travel in dense schools without creating a food shortage. The Canadian observers, however, faced a severe problem, for if it was not division of food giving survival value to such extreme behavior, then what was it? Neither sexual rivalry nor protection of offspring could have anything to do with it. Security from predators seemed unlikely. Why would natural selection demand of a baby fish that from his first swimming days he define a small area of stream bottom, defend it as his alone, and against a rapid current swim without an instant's variation of pace for a term of years, keeping himself in absolute relationship to a few pebbles on the bottom?

To me, of course, there can be no answer but homing. Those who succeed in their youth at playing this natural, infinitely demanding game of territory will return to spawn. Those who fail, on the other hand, will in some fashion lack sufficient motivation to return and so will fail to reproduce. How the sexually mature salmon finds his way back remains as great a mystery as ever, but why he returns, what environmental consummation he seeks before he can reproduce his kind, becomes a bit less obscure. Homing is another extension of the territorial power.

That natural selection should encourage in certain species

such extraordinary capacities could have made no sense to orthodox biology. It is population genetics—the foundation of modern biology and its chief revolutionary agent—that furnishes us with our explanations and makes probable the rightness of James Fisher's thesis. Yet population genetics is a science so new, and so forbidding in its theoretical complexities, that we tend to label it "Unfit for Human Consumption." It would be unwise, certainly, for you and me at this stage of our inquiry to enter its mathematical labyrinth; we might never come out. Nevertheless, if we are to grasp the profound link offered by animal navigation to territory and reproduction, then we should knock around at the doors of population genetics even if we do not go inside.

In the year 1930 the work of three of the world's most eminent geneticists was coming to a conclusive crisis. Two were English, R. A. Fisher and J. B. S. Haldane, and the third was an American, Sewall Wright. All were mathematicians, and all, in the course of two years, published books or papers setting the theory of evolution on a new course. Through their collective mathematical genius they drew on the principles of heredity as discovered by Mendel to establish the precise structure of mutation and selection in relation to evolutionary change. It was something that had always eluded Darwin, and the consequent renovation of Darwinian thought made possible the new biology.

Population genetics, raw food that it is, may be best assimilated in such digested form as is offered by Julian Huxley in *Evolution: The Modern Synthesis* or by George Gaylord Simpson in *Major Features of Evolution*. Its prime principle, however, is simple enough: the basic evolutionary unit is not the individual but the population of which he is a part. I have used the term again and again, and it will be just as well if we now define it. A population, in biology, is a reproductive community. More sharply stated, it is any group of individuals who have a modest probability, within any generation, of meeting and mating. Where high improbability takes over, there lies the border of the population.

We have seen the kob divided invisibly into breeding

populations through the attraction of the stamping ground. We have seen it in ruffs, and in Wyoming's sage grouse. We shall see that in almost all species there are barriers—what biologists call "reproductive isolating mechanisms"—separating individuals into these reproductive communities. While in theory any two members of a species may meet, mate, and produce fertile offspring, in fact it does not happen. Even in the human species such barriers as language and religion, geography, provinces, nations, tribes, classes, occupations divide us into a visible or invisible mosaic of reproductive communities. Our increasingly fluid societies of the twentieth century, our increasing ease of travel and communication and of geographical migration in search of work or education, tend all to break down these barriers and provide wider mating choice. But if we view the human species in terms of its teeming billions, we must see that this widening of choice, as of our day, remains statistically insignificant.

It was Sewall Wright who explored most deeply the relation of the population to evolution, and demonstrated mathematically its necessity as a reproductive unit. Let us say that an animal population is subjected to a change in climate making advantageous any genetic change in the direction of heavier fur, resistance to new diseases, or capacity to live off novel foods. Natural selection will direct that those individuals with superior endowment will be more likely to survive to maturity, reproduce, and so in a given number of generations spread their fortunate endowment through the whole population. What was at first the genetic equipment of a few individuals has become a portion of the population's "gene pool."

Now, let us suppose that the population is fairly small, say a thousand individuals; then it will not take too many generations to spread the advanced genetic equipment through the entire interbreeding community. But what if there were no isolating mechanisms? What if the entire species interbred with equal probability? The local group, facing local environmental demands, would be unable to conserve genetic advantage within its number and would see with every generation the dilution of its environmental answers in the broad sea of species interbreeding. Sooner or later the population would face extinction.

The American geneticist Theodosius Dobzhansky has written, "The biological function of all reproductive isolating mechanisms is essentially the same—inhibition and eventual stoppage of the gene exchange between populations. . . . Without reproductive isolation, species would disappear, submerged in a mass of genetical debris."

We have most of us grown up with the older notion that inbreeding is harmful, and such statements from the population geneticists may bring us unease. It was Sewall Wright, in a triumph of theory, who synthesized the two views. Long before we possessed observations of natural animal populations which might have checked or contributed to his conclusions, Wright through purest mathematics calculated that to attain an ideal evolutionary balance there must always be those two or three males, out of every population of a thousand, who go astray and deposit their genes in the next population's pool. Observation has almost perfectly confirmed it. Buechner found that five males, in two years, reappeared in other populations of Uganda kob. There will always be that odd roebuck who does not return in the autumn but stays on in another forest. Of homing fish there will be always a few that return to the wrong stream yet manage to breed. Accident and adventure, forgetfulness and rebellious disposition all combine to realize a natural design which our genetic necessity imposes.

However complex may be the equations of population genetics, simple words tell their story: the material of the evolutionary process is not the individual but the population; not my genes or yours, but that more enduring, more immortal entity, the pool of genes from which I was conceived and my possibilities determined, and to which I shall contribute through my children and my children's children. Here is the vital entity which must continue, through an infinity of years, to meet the exigencies of daily need and the contingencies which the world sets up on it. You and I are the accidents of a night's union. You and I, in evolutionary terms, are expendable. If you or I fail in our ambitions and our purposes, evolution shrugs. But if you and I and too many others through our failures bring damage to the sum of a population's genetic potential, then that is another matter. It is the population which will be here when you and I are gone; it is the population which holds membership in life's immortal club and must adjust itself to new rules, new regulations; it is the population, as a biological reality in evolutionary space and time, which must meet the full rigor of natural selection.

It is the population, in other words, which is evolution's intermediary between the individual and an unborn posterity. And, viewed from such a perspective, many an observation of the new biology begins to make sense. That an animal may through innate compulsion act against his personal interest; that creatures of the arena may through their losing be subjected to psychological castration; that the male of a pair through his attachment for territory may be held responsible for offspring: all such phenomena, which I call expressions of a biological morality and see enforced by the territorial imperative, exist as commands of the population. It is not enough to seek explanations for behavior in terms of individual interest. If the welfare of the population is the final value of natural selection, then it must be assumed that selection will have favored those innate behavioral patterns and capacities in the individual, however extraordinary, which in turn favor the population's good.

So it is with homing. If the integrity of the reproductive unit is to be preserved, then any animal species which for reasons of food supply or physiological development or getting away from a hard winter must disperse its populations far from their breeding grounds will develop, as a selective necessity, means of finding the way home. Two factors must as a rule exist: a territory or cluster of territories commanding the loyalty of a population and serving to isolate it from all others; and an innate navigational mechanism, whatever it may be, that with unfailing accuracy will direct the return of the population's most far-ranging citizens to their ancestral acres when breeding time draws near.

There are exceptions. I can hear a derisive voice in the back of the hall crying out, "Very good. And how are the eel territories doing these days, down in the Sargasso Sea?" And I can recognize in myself the half-demented posture of science and the impulse to look in all directions and reply, blankly, "What eel?" The preposterous animal most definitely homes to a seagoing swamp southeast off Bermuda where no likelihood at all can exist that he possesses or ever possessed a home of his own. Neither does there seem much likelihood that eels there sort themselves out into populations; they interbreed, we believe, as a species. But we must recall that the eel is a creature even more ancient than the green turtle and may have perfected his ways before innovation took the course of evolution in other directions. If this is the answer, then it is also worth recalling that, despite his antiquity, the eel is no less susceptible to the powers of animal nostalgia which invest his sunset days in some comfortable, brackish, northern European pond and direct him to return across the comfortless Atlantic to breed and die where his life began.

We do not, of course, understand the eel any more than we understand the primitive nostalgia that brings assurance to a brainless planarian worm and permits it to feed more quickly and freely in familiar places. We may speculate that it is this ancient nostalgia which natural selection has organized into the territorial power, the capacity to navigate, and the evolutionary device of the isolated breeding community. But we do not know. And the pity of it is that the sciences have all but surrendered in their efforts to find out. A few hardy souls like Archie Carr may still persist, and may contemplate the fixing of radio transmitters to green-turtle backs and observation from whirling satellites. But biology as a whole, despite the theoretical aid which population genetics has brought to the subject, has been tempted to sweep the homing problem under the rug.

I cannot wonder that biologists tend to shy away from a challenge so mighty. When neither sun, moon, stars, magnetism, polarized light, the flavor of rivers, or the swirl of water around a bathtub drain offers sufficient mechanistic explanation for a form of behavior so observable, so measurable, then anyone must be tempted to change the subject. But as we inspect a few more examples of these farther shores of animal capacity, and we keep in mind its linkage with the territorial power shared even by man, we may ourselves be tempted to hope that science will soon gain its second wind.

4

The man named G. V. T. Matthews, who made everyone so much trouble with his Cambridge homing pigeons, came down with another catastrophic idea. It was to investigate the capacity of sea birds to navigate over land. Having afflicted the peace-loving occupants of his Cambridge lofts with every device from magnetic ballasts to out-voyage concrete mixers, he retired to an island named Skokholm, off the coast of Wales, to make a nuisance of himself with the local shearwaters.

The Manx shearwater is one of some 200 species of sea bird who nest in dense colonies in unlikely places. He is a bird with a belligerently proletarian look, mostly dull gray and white, and a turned-over beak like an old-fashioned socialist determined to stir up an argument. His life experience includes only the sea and the breeding colony where he nests in a burrow with his mate. Matthews subtracted from several hundred burrows one parent each and distributed them to various British release points, all of which demanded a return flight over land. Only a few found the novel navigation a problem. The general success was to be expected at this stage of disintegration of old assumptions concerning homing. But what impelled Matthews to send off two birds to Boston—whether curiosity or simply a sense of mischief—I do not know.

The Boston birds were sent off by transatlantic airliner, and one died of injury. The other, however, with the name tag AX 6587, was released at Harvard University by a group of zoologists all suffering, we may assume, from the suspicion that this was going a bit far with dumb animals. That was on a June 3. On June 16, twelve and one-half days later, AX 6587 was back with his mate in the burrow on Skokholm Island. He had

11 143

covered 3050 miles at an average speed of 244 miles a day.

While AX 6587 was a bad blow to science's prospects, he did not quite finish off the efforts to find a reasonable explanation for homing. There were to be two more major encounters between man's capacity to explain and the animal's capacity to confuse. And these, one voluntary, one involuntary, were enough, it seems, to finish man off.

The voluntary encounter occurred when the International Geophysical Year met the Antarctic skua. There were few bird watchers among the many scientists who adjourned to Antarctica in that year, but there was an abundance of boredom and at most stations no creatures to relieve that boredom but the skua and the penguin. Sympathies were quickly joined, since all adored the penguins and hated the skuas who preyed on the penguin young. And so, as a by-product of the physical sciences' immense project, there came about one of the widest bird studies ever made. Teams from the Soviet Union, the United Kingdom, the United States, and many other countries cooperated to band and keep track of 6000 specimens of the world's most disreputable bird.

The Antarctic skua, like the great-crested grebe, is a bird of old origins, descended probably from the common stock of plovers and gulls and terns and guillemots. He is a giant, with a

wingspread of almost five feet. Like the albatross, he takes a long time to grow up—five years—pairs for life, is monogamous, and returns again and again to the same breeding colony where he was hatched. So far as I know, he has but one charming way. When the polar winter closes down and the breeding season ends, the skuas disperse all about the rim of the Antarctic continent to follow the icepack and live off marine life. Pairs break up, and he may feed in McMurdo Sound, she a continent away. But when October comes, and the Antarctic springtime, both return to the area of the colony. If both have survived, then he finds her or she finds him, and domestic life is resumed just where they left it when the great dark fell.

I can think of nothing further of an attractive nature to record about the skua. They return when they do because the Weddell seals are pupping in October, and he and she have an insatiable appetite for seal placenta. About then the Adélie penguins are beginning their inland march to the breeding grounds. The skuas follow, preying on the weakest. When the penguins settle down and build their nests, the skuas establish their traditional breeding ground on the outskirts of the penguin colony, thus making egg-stealing as convenient an entertainment as possible. Penguin tradition demands that Adélie females, having laid their eggs, return to the sea for a few weeks, leaving the males to guard and incubate them. This is a time of total warfare between skuas and penguins. Then the females return, freeing the males to go off to sea, there to feed and put a little fat onto their emaciated frames. At the colony the eggs are hatched and females now battle to protect the chicks. It is a hard life, in the Antarctic; and it takes a hardhearted scientist, far from wife and children, to resist a passionate alliance with the beleaguered penguins against the diving, devouring skuas. In all fairness to the skua, however, we must keep in mind that the penguin chick does not receive his exclusive attention. He preys on and devours chicks of his own kind with an appetite just as hearty. The Antarctic skua is one of the few cannibals among nonhuman species.

Carl Eklund, who was an ornithologist with Admiral Byrd's

earlier expeditions to the Antarctic as well as with the American team during the International Geophysical Year, believes that the cannibal tendency in the skua may have increased the selective value of a tight territorial defense. His territory is large, about fifty feet in diameter, and he defends it against anything that moves by every means at his disposal. And his means are considerable.

Readers of *African Genesis* will recall the experiences of C. R. Carpenter with the howling monkey in Panama. Tradition had it that the howler would defend his arboreal territory by the lowest of means, even urinating and defecating on intruders below. Carpenter found through many an unpleasant experience that tradition was quite correct. Similar experiences have confronted the scientific observer in the Antarctic since the earliest explorations, for the skua is the howling monkey of the world of birds. And skua tradition is correct as well.

Herbert George Ponting was photographer with Commander Scott's tragic expedition to the South Pole in 1911. Ponting recorded in his notes, concerning the skua: "By outward and visible signs, the skua-gull is a gentleman, and his mate a dainty, well-dressed lady—appearances being thus deceptive, for, except for their looks and cleanliness, there is nothing refined about either male or female; both are scamps and malefactors. . . . They would fly towards us from the rear and, carefully making allowance for speed and distance, discharge a nauseating shower of filth. I was more than once the victim of this revolting habit."

Eklund confirms it. The skua has two noteworthy means of territorial defense. One is to dive from a height and slam the intruder on the head with its claws. Eklund outwitted the birds by wearing a tall feather on his cap; the birds slammed the feather. But a feather is a poor defense against the alternative attack, a shower of well-directed fecal matter let loose with the most careful calculation, as Ponting had recorded, of speed, angle, and distance.

I do not believe that the inspiration to dump a few skuas at the South Pole was motivated by any simple desire to get rid of them. Such justification existed, and I can conceive of no more satisfactory disposal of a few of my own less-loved acquaintances than flying them to the South Pole, extending them a cordial farewell, and leaving them there. It seems, however, that when Robert Wood, of Johns Hopkins University, supervised the arrangements, he did so with higher scientific motives.

It was a most extraordinary test of animal navigation. Wood took six skuas from their nests on Ross Island, near McMurdo Sound on the fringe of the continent, and shipped them by plane the 825 miles to the South Pole. A distance like that may sound like the immediate vicinity as compared with Matthews' Boston shearwater. But we must think things over with care. The Antarctic continent, even in midsummer, is not the North Atlantic. At the South Pole the ice is two miles deep. Not for hundreds upon hundreds of miles will the least landmark puncture the flat white plain. There is even the matter of altitude, over 9000 feet, a considerable thin-air problem for a heavy sea bird who has never known anything but sea level. And there is the problem of north.

As one stands at the South Pole—and may I assure my readers that I have never stood there, I am simply fulfilling my creative commitment—one faces, in every direction, north. There is no choice. To the front, to the back, to the left, to the right, all is north. The sun circles above an expressionless horizon. It does not set. It does not rise. The sun offers no indication. Shall we grope in desperation for the Coriolis effect and the earth's rotation? Twenty feet from the South Pole a fixed point in the ice will move, with the earth's rotation, 62.8 feet in twenty-four hours, and if one can find a bathtub the water will go straight down the drain without swirl or hesitation. What, then, shall we do? Look to the stars? It is summer, friend, and they will not return till fall.

One skua came back. What happened to the others, we do not know. But in a matter of ten days one had returned to his nest and his territory on Ross Island. How did he get home? It is possible that, despite the thin air, despite the lack of landmarks, despite a circling deceptive sun, he flew a dead straight course north—which would be in any direction—until after a thousand miles he arrived at the continent's rim; then, doggedly following it perhaps half the world around, he at last arrived home. It is possible; but in ten days, and in the light of what we know about other homing creatures, it is most improbable.

The encounter with the skua, which began with the International Geophysical Year, was of a voluntary nature and finished off with the accomplishments of a single bird. The encounter between the United States Navy and the Laysan albatross involved 100,000 breeding pairs, was wholly involuntary, and came to a conclusion as statistically convincing as it was embarrassing for both the Navy and science.

Midway Island became famous for the sea battle which took place in its vicinity at a major moment in World War II. It is a lonely atoll 1300 miles west of Honolulu, and until 1903 was nothing but a range of sandspits inhabited by neither man nor albatross. Then a cable station was established there, and its operators planted gardens, trees, shrubs. They were unaware that by making the island more attractive for man they were making it even more attractive for the nesting albatross. A breeding colony established itself. It flourished. And when Pan-American Airways established an airbase on the island in the 1930's, albatross enthusiasm seems to have known no end. Word must have been spread around all the mid-Pacific that Midway was more fun than anywhere; by the end of the pre-war decade there were 10,000 breeding pairs on Sand Island, the only spit large enough to accommodate a flying strip.

The albatross is a bird both unique and unfathomable of nature. He is not only unafraid of man but seems to enjoy our beastly companionship. It was because of this strange character that he became known to all the American fleet as the gooney bird. And it was his fearlessness, along with an uncompromising attachment to his bit of island soil, that was to prove the undoing of the United States Navy.

With the war, Midway emerged as an irreplaceable link in the chain of American air communications between Pearl Harbor and the Pacific's far-flung scenes of battle. The activity was sufficient, one would think, to discourage breeding activity in the hardiest of species. And it did so discourage the black-

footed albatross, who declined in numbers. But the racket of
aircraft and the jostling of men seemed only to stimulate the
Laysan to more formidable nesting activity. By 1945 there were
30,000 nesting pairs sharing the sandspit with the United
States Navy. And ten years later accurate counts placed the
number at 60,000, with 40,000 more on neighboring Eastern
Island. By then jet aircraft had become standard equipment
in the American defense establishment. And we need only
recall, to visualize the problem of the Navy, that the albatross
is a very large bird. It takes just one, sucked into a jet engine
on take-off, to wreck a plane.

The reader, whether callous or thoroughly objective, may
say, "But where's the problem? If it's human life or albatross
life, then slaughter the birds." But this is to ignore the delicate
sentiments of the American taxpayer, who would rise in
outrage if he knew that his Navy was slaughtering innocent
gooney birds in the middle of the Pacific Ocean. It is also to
ignore the annual necessity facing the United States Navy to
pry monumental appropriations out of the American Congress,
an institution which would like nothing better than to take
advantage of any popular outrage to denounce the Navy and

cut its money. If the reader cannot take the situation seriously, he must accept it that the United States Navy did.

By the middle of the 1950's a vast comic plot was taking shape on a stage as large as the Pacific Ocean. In the middle sat the United States Navy, sweating it out. On one side ranged the American people, the American Congress, and the nightmare of a public scandal. And on the other sat the gooney birds, fearless, trusting, immovable, breeding insanely, 100,000 pairs on tiny, irreplaceable Midway. The Navy decided to call in science. Two biologists from the United States Wildlife Service reported for duty. One was Dale Rice, the other Karl Kenyon, whose observations of the fur seal I have already reported. They were given all facilities, all most urgent encouragement. But their consequent study of the behavior of the Laysan albatross could have brought encouragement to none. One wonders how the United States Navy had the stamina to remain in business.

The Laysan albatross pairs for life—a very long life—and is as loyal to his mate as to his territory. In many ways it is a classic example of the pair territory as reinforcement for the pair bond. Pairs who twenty years earlier had been banded in the neighborhood of the old Pan-American hotel, Gooneyville Lodge, were still mated, still breeding. Attachment for the nest site went beyond explanation. Like all sea birds, the colonies disperse at the end of the breeding season to gather again the following year. While the birds are away at sea, as I have already mentioned, storms may erase all landmarks in the breeding area. Yet when Rice and Kenyon mapped the territories of 100 pairs, they found that only five in the succeeding season built their nests more than thirteen feet from the site of the previous season's nests. The average distance was little more than a yard. How did the birds know where last year's site had been?

It is the kind of question which cannot be answered but can at least be approached through the principles of population genetics. It is to the interest of the population that the propinquity of a breeding community be preserved. If we cannot yet understand the mechanics of natural selection's devices, we can at least understand what natural selection is up

to. And just how far evolution is concerned with the population, to what lengths evolution may shrug at the fate of the
individual, finds no more gruesome illustration than in the
behavior of the Laysan albatross. Human sympathies may
recoil, the United States Navy may have shuddered, but Rice
and Kenyon recorded all.

The observers noticed first that if a nest with a chick should
be moved more than six feet from a site, the parents would
attend it for a day or two, then return to the site and leave the
offspring uncared for. Then in February, 1957, the fundamental devotions of albatross life were exposed in grotesque
severity. A new installation at the Navy base was being
constructed. Crews went in to bulldoze the area. Under strict
instructions to go easy on albatrosses, they moved 100 nests
together with chicks distances of up to 100 yards from the site.
The chicks huddled in the nests or dug new little nests of their
own in the sand. The parents ignored them. Day after day they
sat on the sidelines, watched the construction work, and waited
for day to be done. With the five-o'clock whistle the crews
would leave the gouged area and the parents would return to
where their homes had once been. There they would spend the
night until the morning whistle drove them away. All chicks
died.

Shortly after Rice and Kenyon made their ultimate observation concerning albatross site attachment, the United States
Navy made its ultimate decision that, whatever the cost,
Midway Island's gooney birds must be transported so far away
around the world that none would ever return. How far need it
be? Kenyon took charge of the ultimate experiment, and Navy
bombers were assigned to the project. Eighteen birds were
captured, banded, and their plumage marked with distinctive
dyes. They were crated, loaded into the waiting planes, dis-
patched. Four went off to Puget Sound on the northwestern
coast of the continental United States. Others were deposited in
Japan, in the Philippines, in the Marshall and Mariana Islands,
on the island of Oahu in Hawaii.

If there was a sense of finality in the Navy's action, then it
failed to impress Midway's eighteen expatriates. The fate of

four remains unknown. But fourteen returned. It is true that a bird abandoned in the Philippines, far outside the range of the species, took a very long while returning—thirty-two days. But he had 4120 statute miles to cover. The birds sent to Puget Sound, on the other hand, did very well. Two vanished. But the other two returned in ten days and twelve, having traversed 3120 miles of Pacific Ocean lacking a single island or other landmark between the mainland and Hawaii. Weather reports revealed that during the time of the journey a low-pressure area had prevailed. There had probably been adverse winds and, for much of the journey, overcast skies prohibiting solar observation.

Hand in hand, science and the United States Navy surrendered. "We suggest that existing theories of bird navigation do not fully explain their homing behavior," wrote Kenyon and Rice at the end of their report.

5

Our failure to penetrate the wilderness of the homing problem must rest, one suspects, on some larger failure to comprehend the powers of animal perception. We have scored some conspicuous successes along this frontier. It has become common knowledge, for example, that a porpoise "sees" by means of echoes. Otherwise it should be a secret as inscrutable as animal navigation itself how a porpoise, in water so muddy that he cannot see to the end of his own snout, can still find food in your hand and with all delicacy take it from you. It is less than common knowledge, perhaps, that a fish called *Gymnarchus* in an equally muddy African river like the Niger will stake out a territory around his nest and recognize and expel all intruders. How does he "see" them? *Gymnarchus* generates an electric field, swims in the middle of it, and has means of sensing any object intruding on the field. How he discriminates between legitimate enemies and his mate, whom he never attacks, remains a little obscure.

These, of course, are the kinds of sensory powers for which students of animal navigation have made such exhaustive searches to no end but the exhaustion of science. And so one must suspect that the homing power, like other inexplicable territorial powers, may rest on perceptions of a quite different order, and that until science accomplishes some major penetration into areas of perception at present unknown, we shall continue to grope through our own muddy waters. Whether perceptions of an extrasensory order exist, no layman can judge. Hints, not evidence, are all we have. Accidental encounters, not systematic investigations, have characterized the scientific approach to perceptions lying beyond the normal range of explicable senses. A few of those encounters, however, have given us hints of a sort.

In late 1965 the American journal *Science* published a short account of an unexplained relation between certain identical twins. The electroencephalogram is a commonly used device for measuring activity in the brain. A recognizable activity is known as an alpha rhythm, a peculiar wave set up in the absence of visual stimuli, as when one closes one's eyes. The twins tested in a Philadelphia laboratory were separated and placed in different rooms. In most cases nothing happened. But in two out of fifteen sets of twins a remarkable event left its record on the apparatus. Again and again, if one twin closed his eyes, thus setting up the alpha wave, the same wave would instantly appear in the brain of his twin in the next room.

Protest is the normal posture of science when confronted by such observations, and the editors of *Science* received the predictable and perhaps justifiable bagful of protests to the alpha-wave report. But one must recall the strange and thoroughly inexplicable behavior of tilapia made by the Dutch ethologist G.-P. Baerends many years ago. These are the fish among which the intruder must be twice as big as the proprietor if the intruder is to succeed. When tilapia are young, however, they have not yet established territories and live in schools. At this age the fish are gray with dark horizontal stripes. And if a strange fish, no matter how small, is introduced to a tank of young tilapia, there will be the strangest of responses.

All will instantly and simultaneously show vertical bars of marking. Baerends interpreted the response as anxiety, perhaps one of selective value providing camouflage in weedy waters. But all members respond at once, whether or not threatened by the invader, whether or not even within sight of it. How is the anxiety communicated within the school?

Neither the arguable alpha wave nor the inarguable vertical bars of the tilapia tell us anything about the homing of the Laysan albatross or the stimulation of energy in a man defending his hearth and home. But all suggest much about that vast green continent of knowledge, wild and almost untouched, which the new biology today faces. Population genetics informs us as to why natural selection, through a billion or two of developing years, may have encouraged the most subtle powers of alliance between the individual and the evolutionary unit of which he is a part. It now becomes the business of the scientist, in the interest of his species, to discover just what evolution has accomplished, and how it has done it. And let no layman rest content if a scientist here or there gives the great green continent a puzzled frown, and says, "What elephant?"

The territorial imperative shapes your way and mine to patterns larger and more immortal than ourselves. As we move on to explore the social territory, so significant in human life, we shall see that the patterns of value to man are of a different sort than those of value to homing animals. The adaptability of man and protoman has made unnecessary a periodic dispersal of our numbers about the seas or continents, and consigned to selective neglect any mechanism beyond homesickness to aid us on our return. Even so, we may glimpse in our nostalgias a shadow of that force compelling the voyages of animals.

The individual, whoever he may be, is not quite free to mate with whom he pleases. And so the homing creature, wherever he may be when the season comes around, finds nostalgia enfolding him. The seal will abandon her growing pup in warm California waters though she must swim across all the northern Pacific to reach the place where she was born. Gravid salmon, bulging with eggs, must navigate a thousand miles of blue water to reach the mouth of a certain river, must surmount rapids and waterfalls and pass the forks of a hundred streams, and must at last reach that certain stretch of fast-flowing brook, the only place on the watery earth where nature will permit her eggs to be fertilized.

So it is with the skua, treading the air of a stormy continent. So it is with the barred warbler, deserting an African feeding ground to die, perhaps, in some late northern blizzard. So it is with geese as we see them tall in a springtime sky traveling in their imperishable V's toward a faraway, finite tract of marsh, remarkable only to the eyes of a goose, in a featureless Canadian plain. Devotion to homeplace commands the sorting of animate beings, of gulls and shearwaters and returning soldiers, so that species shall not vanish in a chaos of genetical debris.

The portrait of life being painted by the new biology bears small resemblance to that natural world of anarchistic instinct and relentless self-interest which depressed a Tennyson, inspired a Freud, perturbed a Darwin, and confused a century. It is a world of order and ordained self-sacrifice to greater and longer goods; it is an ordered world in which territory, I maintain, exerts a prime moral force; and it is a world—we must remind ourselves again and again—to which we belong. Should all this be so, and should a little piece of sovereign earth or air or water provide indeed such a key to the locks of animate necessity, then I myself can little wonder that evolution has equipped us with not only the key but an almighty urge to defend it.

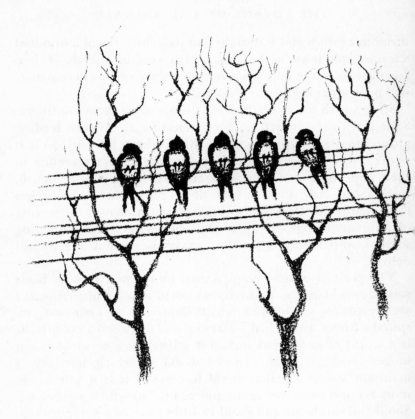

5. The Noyau

Antagonism must have some value to living things: why otherwise would evolution have tolerated so much of it?

In 1925, when the territorial concept was still a young and budding thing, two young and budding scientists went to Holland, pitched their tents on the island of Texel, and went to work on the black-tailed godwit. One was Julian Huxley, then a professor of zoology at King's College in London, who for the next four decades would be a world figure in biology. The other was Ashley Montagu, then a student at Oxford, who would become in the same period a world figure in anthropology. The two published their study the following year, and it is a pity today to find it so forgotten. It was a thing of beauty and insight, touched by intellectual breezes as fresh as a North Sea beach.

Huxley and Montagu in that single paper pioneered several notions. The black-tailed godwit is a wading bird, a handsome creature related to the curlew, the sandpiper, and our friend the ruff who falls on his face when the hen chooses somebody else. Godwits are migratory birds who arrive on the Dutch coast in March, frequently already paired. The pair together seizes a territory in the breeding area and defends it. Their action suggested to the two young scientists that if the two together seize a property, then in the case of the black-tailed godwit territory can have nothing to do with selection of mates.

These were very early years in the development of the territorial concept, and there was still little to go on but the conclusions of Eliot Howard himself. Huxley was a friend of Howard's, but he and Montagu went on to show that control of food supply can have little to do with the territorial animosities of colonial birds. The gull, the tern, the black-tailed godwit will defend a territory as small as two feet in diameter just as vigorously as will a warbler a much larger area. Howard had recognized this, but had felt that, in one way or another, food supply for the family must enter into the territorial function, and that the size of the colony itself must be related to total available food. Huxley and Montagu doubted the interpretation, for many colonies were small and the sea was large. Why then did sea birds nest in colonies at all?

It is a question of importance to this chapter, for we shall be gradually moving from the relation of territory to the individual toward its relation to society and the total population. We have seen enough of such phenomena as homing, the pair territory, and the behavior of the arena to grasp the basic territorial principle in its adjustment of the individual to the demands of the population and the species: what I have described as the innate enforcement of a biological morality. Now, if we are to approach a general application of the territorial principle to the condition of man, we must come also to understand the ways in which territory may be related to the formation and perpetuation of society itself.

Why are there species who insist on nesting or living the year around in colonies so dense that individuals or pairs quarrel constantly over space? Why don't they spread out? Huxley and Montagu brought up a question in 1925 for which there is no agreed answer even today. "It is safe to say," they wrote, "that this disposition to resent intrusion into an area is almost universal and certainly primitive and normal among birds." They accepted the territorial principle as the cause of the quarreling, but they could not explain why the birds came together.

We shall return to this. But another salient point they pioneered we should inspect in passing. Huxley and Montagu recorded a form of behavior that would not receive a name, let alone further observation, for almost another twenty years. Black-headed gulls also nested on Texel Island in large colonies each divided into tiny hostile territories. They noticed that in this species a pair of gulls would resent the approach of a nearby pair even off in the grassfields where no property rights were involved. It was as if an invisible, movable fence encircled each feeding pair at an invariable distance. Let another pair come close and it would be chased away. "An apparent territorial instinct may be seen," they wrote, "even in cases where true territory is not involved."

A German ornithologist, Dieter Burckhardt, is usually credited with at last giving this demand for privacy a name— "individual distance." It was in 1944, and he observed that for any given species the demand for distance is specific. In fact, however, it was Zurich's Heini Hediger who a few years earlier observed the phenomenon and gave it the name. But it was not until well after the war that the term began to gain currency. Then an observer in London noticed that tufted ducks, swimming in the civilized lagoons of St. James's Park, kept two to three body lengths apart. The same observer visited Skokholm Island, that fragment of Wales so beloved by the Boston shearwater, and gave his attention to meadow pipits. It was September, the breeding season long over. There were neither sexual arguments nor quarrels over food, yet the meadow pipits chased each other continually to wind up a minimum of six feet apart.

Batches of species came under observation as if seen for the first time. A covey of partridges, non-territorial, will drive any other covey from wherever it happens to be. European brown trout even in the fry stage demand and receive three inches in all directions. Wildly unrelated species like the lucerne flea and that oysterish bivalve called *Tellina tenuis,* an inhabitant of coastal mud flats, keep neighbors at a tiny, fixed distance. The cliff swallow, flying always in flocks, nesting always in dense colonies, would seem to regard privacy as of small value. Yet no two nests will be built within pecking distance.

To confirm the prevalence of animal privacy one has only to close one's eyes and remember: antelopes, golden and gleaming, spread across a swelling African veld; spaced cattle in an English field; birds resting on a telephone line that we pass in our cars, each separated from his neighbor by a distance so invariable that they resemble beads on a string or markers on a giant ruler. Patterns lie all about us in the arrangements of living beings, and with eye only for the beauty we move through the mathematics of natural dispositions. Perhaps it is enough that we ask solely for beauty; but it will diminish the beauty not at all if we also ask why.

No passage in the literature of animal behavior is lovelier than Niko Tinbergen's description of the first arrival of herring gulls at any of their traditional breeding grounds on the Dutch coast. As a boy he watched the gull communities, year after year, and came to see them not as random collections of birds but as expressions of an intricate social structure, of infinitely complex relations between individuals. To the untrained eye the relationships were invisible, yet slowly they revealed themselves as firm and real. Even the tutored observer, however, could still but guess and hazard why was this, why that. As a mature scientist Tinbergen would return to his Holland shore and be seized by the beauty and the wonder.

"On a warm, sunny day in March we may watch the first revival of the gulls' interest in their traditional breeding haunts. As the tide rises, covering the sandy beach where the herring gulls forage, the hazy blue sky above the dry dunes may suddenly become alive with gulls. Their strong and melodious voices can be heard long before one sees the gulls themselves high up in the air where hundreds of them are soaring and circling. As they come gliding down, we see their wonderful white wings flash up again and again; like huge snowflakes they whirl around, coming down in what seems to be wild disorder."

But the gulls do not alight. For a quarter of an hour they may dip and turn and give every indication that the moment has come, then as if by mysterious command they will vanish, winging away to the west. And that will be all for that day. But as the sunshine strengthens and the days grow longer, the flock will return. Out of the pale blue space of a springtime afternoon, voices will clamor, white wings will flash, snowflakes will tumble in confusion's blizzard as the gulls come swirling and turning, dipping and gliding lower today than yesterday, lower tomorrow than today. Still they will not alight. Perhaps a solitary bird will come down on the top of a dune, there to stretch his long neck, look all about, sample the breeze, inspect the springtime. Then he too will leave and vanish with the flock.

A day will come, nevertheless, and it will be a day like any other day. But the mood will be right. Out of a golden haze will come the flashing wings and the clamorous chorus. There will be no dipping today, however, no whirling, sampling, soaring hesitation. The immense flock will glide in, alight, and in moments will be in possession of its inheritance of grass and dune. And the scientist will stand where the boy once stood, moved by the wonder, while an enchanted moment transmutes perfect chaos into perfect order.

The herring gull is a creature of sufficient ingenuity that if he picks up a mussel with a shell too hard for his beak to break, he will carry it to a height and drop it on a hard road. He is a creature of sufficient loyalty and perception to guarantee that he will never attack his own mate, and will recognize her among dozens flying into the colony at a distance to defy human

binoculars. He is a creature of sufficient social sophistication that, while many arrive in the spring already paired, definite areas in the colony which Tinbergen calls "clubs" will be set aside as meeting places for the unpaired. He is a creature also, as we have seen, of such sensitive social adjustment that the arriving flock will make "decisions" of mood and readiness as if it were one being. So dependent is the herring gull on the community of his citizenship that he would probably be unable to breed were he to return in the spring to the wrong gull town. So powerful and incomprehensible is his attachment for home that, like the albatross, a pair may return year after year to nest in precisely the same spot, although the North Sea's winter storms will have effaced all landmarks to guide his eye.

This is the herring gull, vital, vociferous, numerous, enduring, one of evolution's noisiest successes. And yet the only obvious good that he acquires from his community is the opportunity to quarrel with his neighbors. These are the fellows who will stand at their boundaries in a rage so purple that both will find vent for it by pulling up all the grass in sight. It is a society, in my opinion, formed and maintained by the lure of its inward antagonisms.

If there exists in the world of social animals a biological right of privacy, as expressed through either the private territory or through individual distance, then it is of infinite concern to contemporary man. Natural arrangements confirm that such a right exists, and so it must have biological value, although to my knowledge the value has never been explored. But if the right does exist, then why do we ourselves challenge it? Why do we enter crowds the more advantageously to resent them, gather in cities the more richly to possess neighbors to complain about? If we are a Turk or an African, then why do we leave our secure village or quiet kraal to join the squalor and the unemployment, the uncertainties and physical miseries of city life? Nothing, we may be sure, could keep us away.

Nature may abhor a vacuum, but it has even less use for boredom. In species after species natural selection has encouraged social mechanisms which seem ultimately to exist for no reason other than to provide conditions for antagonism and conflict and excitement. We may comprehend the evolutionary necessity for bringing together a breeding community and through migration and other forms of homing capacity for ensuring its reproductive isolation. But why must it live in a dense, disturbing, challenging, competing, squabbling, argumentative mass? If it is not to avoid boredom, then why must the animal demand for privacy stand cheek-by-jowl with the urge to plunge into the largest available crowd?

Human beings may not all emulate the herring gull in our search for diversion. We may or may not, according to temperament, seek to jostle that we may be jostled back. Of one thing, however, we may be certain: *Homo sapiens* is not one of those rare species that, renouncing both individual distance and the private territory, renounce the right of privacy. Fair evidence that distance matters to us was assembled just a few years ago when my own countrymen, renowned for their production of ingenious gadgets, attempted to foist on the world a chrome-and-plastic design for living called "togetherness." Togetherness sought to resolve the opposing demands of privacy and society by eliminating privacy. A man and his wife were allowed a few moments by themselves in bed, if they would be quick about it. Beyond that, so far as I recall, all private appetites—whether geographical, intellectual, or spiritual, whether in matters of what one reads or what one eats, whether in relations between next-door neighbors or husband and wife or parents and children or employer and employe—were regarded as somehow or other obscene. I foresaw at the time little future for togetherness. It was too boring.

The world may have joked about the American invention; but even as it joked it acknowledged the reality of that vital paradox which many of my countrymen had believed it possible, through self-induced imbecility, to deny. We are antagonistic beings, despite all social necessity. In our arts we demand color and contrast, conflict and surge. Of our news we demand scandal and mayhem, danger and dread. To the eye of man the brawling community of the herring gull is a thing of beauty. Perhaps we identify ourselves with these white-winged beings dumped on a beach like snowflakes from heaven, there to behave like demons with haloes, angels with tails. And if we remain unconvinced that the herring gull is of our sort, then we have only to turn to its antithesis in behavior, a rare beast who seems never to have heard of the rights of privacy and whose diurnal society must be accepted as an ultimate if improbable realization of the fleeting American dream. I refer to the community of the hippopotamus.

I have watched hippo schools in the upper Nile, in the eastern Congo, in Lakes Albert and Edward, in nameless pools scattered here and there across Africa's dry face, and as far south as the broad, shallow rivers of Mozambique's remote

Gorongosa. And in all humility, and without the least desire to scandalize his name, I must propose the hippopotamus as the most unattractive creature that land or water supports. Here is an animal who in his daytime life asks for nothing but togetherness.

In all fairness to the hippo, one must grant that he leads two lives and upholds two psyches. His skin is badly adapted to a tropic sun, and so all day he submerges himself in the neighborhood's dirtiest water, closely accompanied by his friends. At night he emerges to graze, and as you lie on your cot you can hear him roaring and groaning and hiccuping through the meadows. Were it not for one of his more astonishing daytime habits, we might never have learned what a nocturnal individualist he is. Submerged in the water in his friends' close embrace, the daytime hippo when impelled to have a bowel movement always raises his vast rump above the surface, makes the sound of a train going through a tunnel, and with rapidly flipping tail spreads fecal matter for ten yards about.

It must have been centuries ago that the Bushmen began wondering why the hippo behaved so oddly. And so they introduced to their folklore an explanation far more charming than the subject deserved. The hippo, it seems, had been originally a land animal but wanted to live in the water. He went to the Lord of the Animals seeking permission, but permission was denied. The crestfallen hippo asked, "Why?"

"Because!" said the Lord of the Animals, impatiently. "Because you are a monstrous big thing and you will eat up all the fishes."

"No," the hippo protested. "Master, I swear on my honor that I shall never eat a fish."

"Who would ever trust anybody who looked like you?" said the Lord of the Animals. But the hippo was thinking it over.

"Master," said the hippo, "I'll make a bargain with you. If you will let me live in the water, then whenever I have a bowel movement I shall spread it around with my little flipping tail, and you can see for yourself that there are no fishbones."

The Lord of the Animals thought it over and decided that it was a fair enough proposition, so the hippo went to live in the water. Many years later, however, another lord of the animals came along who felt that there must be more to it than that. This was Heini Hediger, and in the Congo he found his answer. The grazing hippo, in the dark of night, is so territorial in his exclusive demands that the pygmy form even has his penis on backward. Nature has lent structural support so that he may urinate and defecate in the same direction, and with his little fanning tail spread a mixed trademark over his grazing land, in well-founded confidence that, dark though the night may be, no one will get confused as to what is his and what isn't.

This is the nighttime hippo, with habits if disreputable then at least his own. The daytime hippo is another thing. His flesh, I must admit, is not too bad to eat; but beyond that I can think of no virtue in all his vast carcass. He is ugly: his eyes are ugly; his mouth can exist for no purpose other than to provide the nightmares of children with appropriate furniture; his body resembles a gigantic bathtub. He is the idealized synthesis of all things ugly, and perhaps the perfection of that synthesis, viewed through a hippo's goggling eyes, is hippo beauty. But I am not a hippo, and I see nothing through his eyes. Neither can I engage myself with his ways or identify myself with his purposes. He is the most graceless of beings, the most fathomless of idiot souls, a kind of prince among morons. I praised evolution for making me a man and not a Uganda kob, but the most moving of my thanksgivings must be reserved for that genetic fortune which did not make me a crocodile who must lie on some sunny sandbank somewhere, day after day, month after month, looking at hippos.

I should not detail at such length the totality of my hippo-rejection were it not for my conviction that the most monstrous of all his dedications is his diurnal acceptance of collective existence. Only through haunting a hippo pool or a hippo shore can one come to realize how rare in nature is the species that makes no demand for privacy, not even three inches. A school of twenty or thirty hippos is a mass burial, half underwater, of living corpses. If a hippo is capable of pleasure—and one must assume that he is—then that pleasure must be derived largely from leaning on somebody else. If a hippo finds joy in hippo togetherness—and why should he indulge in it if he did not?—then it is the joy of pursuing one's daytime hours with one's throat clamped firmly to somebody's neck while one roars in somebody's ear, jostles eternally somebody's ribs, and defecates cheerfully in somebody's face.

It is a way to live, perhaps, reserved for creatures unlikely to be admired by any but their closest friends. But I maintain

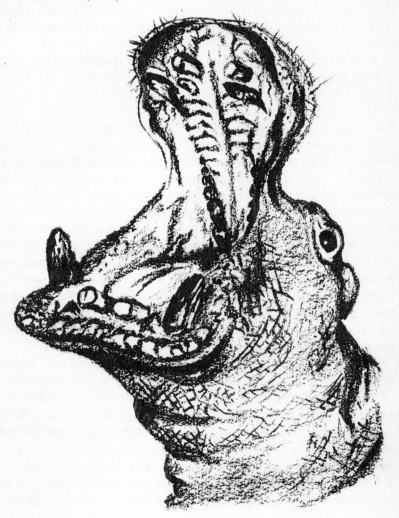

that man is not such a species. We are not hippopotami. And for those advocates of human togetherness, voluntary or involuntary, who maintain that we are, and who see in such pleasures the human solution, I recommend a quick and perhaps one-way journey to Lake Edward's Congo shore.

2

I have taken from the French ethologist Jean-Jacques Petter the term *"noyau"* as a label for the society of inward antagonism. It is awkward—even bad taste, perhaps—to introduce a foreign word to a discussion in which we are afflicted by so many concepts foreign to our normal thinking. It has seemed to me wise, however, to get as far away as possible from all those English words like "community" or "society" which inevitably bear connotations of co-operation. *Noyau*—meaning, roughly, a nucleus—is correct in that it implies a primitive evolutionary step toward societies characterized by mutual aid. But more important to this inquiry than its precision is its lack of connotation for the English-thinking mind, and that is what we shall need if we are to build up an appreciation for those groups of individuals held together by mutual animosity, who could not survive had they no friends to hate.

The *Lepilemur*, or sportive lemur, has furnished us with a type species for the general *noyau*. He is just one of thirty-odd species of pre-monkey primates, the lemurs, still extant on the island of Madagascar. Petter and his wife have studied fifteen of them, and most lead a daytime life and have normal societies of mutual aid and co-operation. But there are nocturnal species whose manner of life corresponds not at all to that of their diurnal cousins.

The sportive lemur is one of these. He resembles an oversized African bush baby, with the pointed snout, huge round eyes, and delicate primate hands typical of all lemuroid species. He sleeps all day in a hole in a tree, but with darkness he comes out to defend a small solitary territory. All night one can hear his cries of warning or threat to the intruder. Direct observation of any nocturnal animal is difficult, as I mentioned in connection with my unfriend, the hippo. But Petter by some means obtained from the United States Army a snooper, one of those infra-red telescopes which we developed during the war for night observation. And so he was enabled to make a rough assessment of the night life of the sportive lemur. And what was remarkable was population distribution.

The solitary *Lepilemur* defends a territory no more than sixty or so yards in diameter. A little society of six or so may crowd itself into an area as small as an acre, where it will live in perfect recrimination. And yet there will be no other *Lepilemur* for miles around. Petter gave the name *noyau* to the angry little group, and found three such *noyaux* in the Ankarafantsika region of Madagascar. No consideration of food supply, of topography, of favored trees could account for either the tightness of the groups or their wide separation. Security from predators could have no bearing, since one reason for the survival of the lemur on Madagascar is lack of predators. Why, if they did not like each other, did they hang out together? It is the same question which the herring gull presented to Huxley and Montagu. And even as we slowly turn our camera from the individual to society and from animals to men, we must begin to include in our biological frame those scenes and shadows which normally we should regard as psychological.

Throughout all his career Frank Fraser Darling has been skeptical of physiological interpretations of territory. Perhaps his early years of following herds of Scottish red deer through wild highland corries gave him ample time to think. These were the same years when David Lack was teaching school and watching robins, and if it is true that an ethologist is nothing but a zoologist who likes to work in the open air, then Darling had the most pressing desires of all. In his haunting volume *A Herd of Red Deer* he recalls those days when he walked thirty or forty miles and managed 8000 or 10,000 feet of climbing as the most pleasant in all his recollection. To preserve the sharpness of his vision, he read little at night. It gave a man, one must assume, time to think things over.

In Darling's view, territory is psychological, not physiological. Innumerable biological benefits may be gained, as we have seen. In the end, however, there are two ways to live: to defy or to defer. With the startling exception of Prior's roebucks, deer defer. Darling's red deer displayed no less attachment to a piece of earth than would lion or lizard or man. One cold winter Darling tested that attachment in a small hind herd by putting out little piles of maize. They were wary at first, but in time became quite skilled at discovering his piles wherever he might hide them. Then one day he put a pile in plain view on the far side of a brook that formed one boundary of their range. The brook was shallow and offered no obstacle. But they would not cross it. Although neither wolves nor wildcats lurked on the farther side, although no peril of any sort might confront the wanderer, still in the course of two whole years of varying weather and varying hungers no single member of the herd would leave her world to sample the alien corn.

Neither, however, would Darling's deer defend their world. Such experiences as these, I believe, led the Scottish biologist to conclude that one cannot look to food supply or the normal physiological explanations for a final distinction between species that will defend their homes and species that will not. Later on Darling had ample experience with such defiant creatures as sea birds and seals in his long period of isolation on an island in the Outer Hebrides, which he recorded in the volume called *A Naturalist on Rona*. The experience deepened his views that territory is in essence a psychological expression.

In 1952 Darling published "Social Behavior and Survival" in the magazine *Auk*. It was a paper of lasting significance. "The animal cannot stand alone," he wrote. One naturally concedes this on a basis of security, but Darling emphasized stimulation. To attain full potential, most animals need the stimulation of others of their kind. Such stimulation may come from the mere presence of other animals, as in a herd or flock. Territorial behavior, however, enhances it. Darling felt that too much attention had been paid to the fighting of neighbors; that in truth the hostility is more of a show than a fight, an act than an action. The tumult of a colony of sea birds is a vast charade, in a sense, in which few will get hurt. And the more the challenges, the tempers, the crowding, the calling, the preening and display, the greater will be the satisfaction and general social welfare.

Now he emphasized what had never been properly suggested by science before: "I would like to put forward the hypothesis that one of the important functions of territory is the provision of *periphery*—periphery being defined as that kind of edge where there is another bird of the same species occupying a territory. By pushing up against each other, rather than spreading themselves out, the birds are giving themselves peripheries. The breeding territory . . . is a place with two focal points, the nest site *and* the periphery."

In other words, it is what I might call the castle-and-border interpretation of territory. There is the castle or nest or heartland or lair to provide security, and, just as important, the border region where the fun goes on. These are basic needs of a psychological order, for security and for stimulation, and under normal circumstances they would conflict. The territorial principle has, however, satisfied both without loss to either. And I believe that if we elaborate Darling's hypothesis with the addition of a third basic need, also satisfied by territory, we shall complete a psychological pattern common to all higher animals, and perhaps to many lower animals as well.

That third need I describe as one for identity. I find it useful to define the three needs in terms of their opposites: to think of security as the opposite of anxiety, of stimulation as the opposite of boredom, of identity as the opposite of anonymity. The bird seeks his invariable branch from which to advertise his presence; it is a portion of his identity. The immature Atlantic salmon seeks his unchanging pattern of pebbles on the bottom of his swift-rushing stream; they make possible his identity. A flock of Canadian geese seeks that tract of marsh which is distinguishable only to the eyes of a goose, but which distinguishes the flock from all others; the lone Uganda kob will be found always near his rock, his tree, the cricket always in his particular niche; a family of viscachas, little non-territorial rodents in the Peruvian highlands, will have an unchanging, undisputed resting place in the midst of the colony; the non-territorial starling will have always its same perching place when the flock, though numbering tens of thousands, settles for the night's rest. Neither a need for stimulation nor a need for security can explain the motivation for such attachments, but I believe that the third need can.

The animal seeks to differentiate himself from all others of his kind. As a member of a herd or flock or school or troop or *noyau*, the social animal belongs to a group differentiated from all other groups; and within that group he acquires a territory or a rank of status or a perching or resting place, acknowledged as his alone, which distinguishes him from all other members of the group. He has achieved identity. Through a fixed and unique relationship with something larger or more lasting than himself—the pebbles in a stream bed, the herd grazing on a slope—he has defeated the pressures of anonymity which myriad life continually brings to bear on the individual's psyche.

To discuss the psyche of the animal is to walk across dangerous ground, as Darling well knew when he proposed his hypothesis of security and stimulation as motivation for territorial behavior. To expand the hypothesis by the addition of a need for identity is to render the ground no less perilous. We cannot know what an animal "thinks," how he "looks at things." And so perhaps it will be just as well if I take my hypothesis of three basic animal needs and put it out in the sun where it may ripen for a while, where we shall find it when we return later. Just now it will do if we return to Darling's excursion into psychological motivation and his pioneer thoughts concerning security and stimulation.

Two years after Darling's statement, James Fisher took the proposition a long step further. Fisher is the imaginative ornithologist who suggested the relationship between territory and animal navigation. Now in 1954 he gave first scientific recognition to what I term the *noyau*. Fisher regarded Darling as the "oracle" in the field of animal sociality. He agreed with the psychological interpretation, and pointed out that the ecological interpretation of territory—the spreading out of a population to make best use of a region's resources—comes up against the thorny barrier of being so often untrue. Robins are not distributed evenly all over England, nor are song sparrows throughout the Ohio River Valley. Populations occur in clusters with wide areas, unpopulated or underpopulated, between. And when migrants enter the area, they will not be attracted to the unsettled regions of space, peace, and plenty; they will head for the metropolitan regions of jostling and pushing, conflict and quarrels.

"The effect," he wrote, "is to create 'neighborhoods' of individuals who while masters of their own definite and limited properties are bound firmly and *socially* to their next-door neighbors by what in human terms would be described as a dear-enemy or rival-friend situation, but which in bird terms should more safely be described as mutual stimulation."

Fisher's stunning perception of an animal relationship so suggestive of human relationships went a little too far, I believe, for most of his colleagues. Like his perception of the relationship between territory and the inexplicable homing faculty, it raised questions for which the sciences have no means as yet of providing answers. Rapid though the advances of the new biology have been, the progress has been uneven. Particularly in that area lying between biology and psychology there still exists a scientific no man's land which most biologists would prefer not to enter. To follow too closely on Fisher's heels into the evolutionary aspects of social psychology is to risk seeing your reputation blown heaven-high by some unanticipated booby trap.

One eminent man of science with a taste for such adventure is the Scottish ecologist V. C. Wynne-Edwards, of the University of Aberdeen. His giant volume *Animal Dispersion in Relation to Social Behavior* was published in 1963, so recently that the land mines have only begun to explode. His reference to society as "a brotherhood of tempered rivalry" recalls James Fisher. And his basic definition of society takes one so far into the future of a presently nonexistent rapport between the natural and social sciences that neither is yet prepared to deal with it: "A society can be defined as a group of individuals competing for conventional prizes by conventional means." Let us leave that one out in the sun, too, to ripen for a while.

The *noyau* is Fisher's neighborhood of territorial proprietors bound together by a dear-enemy relationship. It is Wynne-Edwards' brotherhood of tempered rivalry. It is what happens when Darling's proprietors press together to provide themselves with the stimulation of peripheries. It is Huxley's and Montagu's colony of black-headed gulls who insist on breeding together so that they may argue not only over territory but individual distance. It is a mass of cliff swallows who can have no good reason for building their nests so closely together except to bring their dear enemies within more convenient pecking range. It is what happens when the country boy forsakes a secure, small-town, low-keyed existence in search of city lights. It is the Kikuyu in Kenya's empty yellow hills or the Zulu in Natal's green slumberland leaving the kraal's predictability behind, willingly, joyfully to enlist himself in Nairobi's quarreling mass of unemployed or Johannesburg's crime-ridden, pass-carrying black utopia.

3

The probability is better than fair that among most vertebrate species which do not form overt social groups—herds, flocks, schools, troops—but seem to the eye to spread more or less continuously, more or less evenly through an appropriate environment, *noyaux* form a typical if invisible social organization. Chipmunks and deer mice in our woodlands, jack rabbits and ground squirrels in our deserts, bullhead and pike in our rivers, lizards and toads in our farmyards, rats and house mice in our cities seem none to belong to social groups larger than the pair or the family, and to be most antisocial in all their ways. But if you are a member of a *noyau*, then the degree of your hostility and the depth of your bad manners will in no way provide a proper measure of your social independence. Furiously you may need the group to serve you with members of your kind to be furious with.

A prime difficulty facing the student of the *noyau* is that of identifying it. Margaret Morse Nice, one of America's most notable ornithologists, achieved it in her banding of song sparrows on some lowlands near Columbus, Ohio. On these ample acres the song sparrows bunched their territories, created their peripheries, and argued endlessly. And by banding them she found that they returned season after season from their annual migration to resume their discussions with favorite enemies. Here was a society of inward antagonism. In a world of unfriendly birds and beasts, however, it is not easy to discover whether a creature must have favored fellows to be angry with or is willing to be angry at anybody. The logic of population genetics says that borders most probably exist, and that *noyaux* invisible to man but of social reality to deer mice and toads divide the great population into breeding communities. The difficulty is to identify the group and to define its limits. By the greatest fortune, we have two quite different creatures, Australia's satin bowerbird and South America's callicebus monkey, which have been superbly studied and which reveal each most perfect glimpses of life in a *noyau*.

In Australia, unlike New Guinea, civilization has made possible long-continued research and a fair history of bowerbird observation. Several species inhabit the northern and eastern regions, and the satin may be found even in the suburbs of Sydney. In his comprehensive study of Australian species, A. J. Marshall placed special emphasis on the satin, and his efforts were thoroughly rewarded. The satin bowerbird is not only the citizen of a cleanly defined *noyau;* he is not only the cultural champion of the nonhuman animate world: he is also a habitual criminal, a thief, a vandal, a bully, and all in all one of the most intriguing creatures that evolution has ever turned out. And along with his remarkable qualities of behavior is a remarkable physical characteristic. The male turns blue when he becomes important.

I do not know what there is about the color blue. We speak of bluebloods. A sexually mature vervet monkey has a blue scrotum of considerable fascination to amateur photographers in southern Africa. But C. K. Brain found that if a mature vervet monkey is unwell, or inordinately dominated by fellow members in a troop, his scrotum may pale off to white. The patas monkey likewise has a blue scrotum, and when that of a maturing male turns blue enough, then it is a signal to the patas despot that the time has come to drive him out of the troop. Satin bowerbirds have a glossy plumage somewhat resembling the northern martin. The female's has a greenish tinge, and most males though sexually mature resemble the female. Not until an indeterminate age between four and seven years will his plumage turn blue as a signal to all that he is a boss. The blue males of a satin clan constitute an elite class. They build the bowers. The greens will do no better than to collect a mess of sticks.

The bowers built by blue males in Australian forests cannot rival in complexity of construction such New Guinea cousins as Lauterbach's bowerbird or the crestless gardener. The satin builds a rather ordinary structure of the avenue style with a rectangular floor plan. But by a single feat he places himself in a cultural class quite his own. Beavers may build the most elaborate dams and lodges. Gophers in Kansas and lesser mole rats in Hungary may dig the most complicated burrows equipped even with sanitary chambers—little rooms for defecation which may be walled up when they are filled. But the blue male satin bowerbird builds his bower at right angles to the rising sun.

It is fruitless to attempt to explain everything in the natural world in terms of selective value and survival necessity. There are times when one can only record what is true, and dissolve in wonder. There is a possibility that Peking man made some of his chopping tools of quartz simply because of the material's beauty, but not until human evolution produced fairly recent editions of *Homo sapiens* do we begin to find unarguable evidences of such dedications as that of the blue male satin bowerbird. And as if the orientation of his bower were not enough to establish his cultural championship, he paints it.

For decades the unconfirmed rumor went around Australia that this feathered demon with the house in the woods paints its interior walls dead black. Then a man named R. A. Gannon in

1930 published a careful observation in *Emu,* the journal of
Australian ornithology. Gannon late one afternoon had come
on a bower bearing signs of fresh black paint on its inside
walls. The proprietor was absent. At five o'clock the next
morning Gannon was staked out, waiting. The bird appeared.
He moved about inside his house where the observer could not
see. After a while the proprietor left, and Gannon found on the
inner walls a freshly applied layer of a black sticky substance.
Gannon found bits of charcoal about, but no clue as to how
the bird had converted it into paint or how he had applied it.
The observer waited some more. The blue male at last
returned but, to Gannon's exasperation, got sidetracked by
flower arrangements on his display ground. Dark fell. Having
invested this much time in the mystery, the observer could not
let go. Once again at daylight he was back at his post, and so
was the satin bowerbird at his. The glossy little creature
hopped about, chewing and swabbing, chewing and swabbing.
When at last he flew off, Gannon laid hands on his materials.
Out of charcoal and saliva he had produced his paint. Sponge-
like wads of bark had been his paintbrush. Blackened little
pellets, discarded, lay all about.

In later years other observers and Marshall himself confirmed
the observation. As no parallel exists, short of *Homo sapiens,*
for the orientation of a structure, so likewise in all the subhuman natural world one can find no equivalent for such a
feat of decoration. The satin bowerbird is a cultural genius.
That the blue male is also the animal world's most persistent
thief, its most remorseless vandal, and one of its most towering
bullies is a lamentable footnote which must be appended to
his accomplishments. Perhaps this is what inevitably follows
when you go in for the cultured way. Or perhaps it is simply
the life of the *noyau.*

Black may be the color that the satin applies to his bower,
but blue is the color that dominates his life. It is not only the
color of the elite male, signaling to all lowly greens his position
of privilege; it is also a symbol of worth in the species, just as
gold is a symbol of worth to man. Satin bowerbirds will steal
anything blue. They will raid the countryside for the most

unreasonable items: blue parrot feathers, blue lobelia blossoms, bits of blue crockery, or scraps of blue wrapping paper —all wind up on the display grounds of their bowers. In the vicinity of Sydney the satin is a fairly common bird, to the anguish of any housewife trying to raise delphiniums or cornflowers. But unlike the baboon, the thief of Africa who seems to make a specialty of plundering man, the blue male saves his best energies for raiding other bowers.

Few vertebrate species come quite so close to a caste system as does the satin bowerbird. Green males are less discriminating than blue males and will make off with dead crickets and cigar butts. But they too will steal something blue. Marshall witnessed green males hauling twenty-four-inch spikes of delphinium out of the garden of one harried Australian household, but he could never find the spikes in the greens' rude bowers. All, to the last spike, were stolen by the blues. How sharply the blue males keep an eye on any green-male collection was demonstrated by one of Marshall's experiments. He placed 100 fragments of marked blue glass in eighteen green-male rudimentary bowers. By noon the next day seventy-six were on the display grounds of neighboring blues. There had been no

protest or conflict. The greens had watched the looting in silence.

Vandalism is another form of behavior unknown in the subhuman vertebrate world. Perhaps it is because vandalism demands culture to vandalize. In any case, beavers do not go around smashing each other's dams, robins for all their belligerence do not wreck each other's nests, Lauterbach's bowerbird will not bring to ruin the next Lauterbach's bowerbird's bower, and the lesser mole rat, so far as I know, does not attempt to cave in his neighbor's toilet facility. The satin bowerbird is a horror, an appropriate hero for adolescent gangs in London or Los Angeles. A blue male establishes and defends the territory on which he builds his bower, and to leave it unguarded for long will be to see it despoiled. A rival may come to steal; he will remain to ruin. Marshall writes that "the marauder works swiftly and silently. He tears down beakfuls of the walls and strews them about in disorder. A wrecker rarely completes his task before he is disturbed by the swift swish of wings of the owner. Usually he snatches up a beakful of blue feathers or glass as he flees. He never stays to fight."

Despite all one's prejudices in favor of prostitutes with hearts of gold, of clouds with silver linings, of the shining nobility of natural beings were they only allowed to be natural, can one honestly claim for this many-splendored scamp of the Australian forest one redeeming feature other than his creative genius? His heart is as black as his tastes are blue, and it seems impossible to believe that a being so dastardly would acknowledge rules and regulations of a social nature or accept borderlines limiting his depredations. But he does. What we have been watching is life in a definable *noyau*.

Marshall became curious about blue-male thievery and launched an experiment of colossal proportions. He obtained a supply of glass bottles of a uniform royal-blue color. He smashed them into fragments, numbered each fragment with a diamond stylus, distributed them in conspicuous piles over an area of fifty square miles. So voracious was blue-male appetite for royal-blue fragments that within a month 80 percent of the fragments were on the display grounds of known bowers. By then, of course, the show was on the road. Fragments whistled from this bower to that as honor was demonstrated to exist not at all among blue-male thieves. Since all fragments were numbered, Marshall had the goods on everybody. No Scotland Yard found itself ever possessed of a more enviable dossier of crime. But after two solid years not one blue fragment in the entire area of fifty square miles had traveled a distance greater than 1000 yards.

The blue male steals only from his friends. And the *noyau* of the satin bowerbird is approximately 1000 yards in diameter, with invisible fences as high as the sky.

The fences of the callicebus monkey, by grace of human ambition, are of a far more tangible sort. In a broad area of Colombia east of the Andes is a region known as the *llanos*. Here for the past generation ranchers have been moving east from their Andean villages, cutting down forests to provide grazing space for their cattle. But in river bottoms and on certain steep hillsides not to the liking of cattle, the ranchers have left behind little islands of forest grove surrounded by the sea of grass. And within each little isolated grove is preserved a *noyau* of the callicebus monkey as in a laboratory cage.

William A. Mason is one of a new generation of American primate students, and his work with the callicebus is still in progress. Since his observations are so recent that some have not yet been published, I am personally grateful to him for permission to record conclusions which after further years of study he may choose to revise. Mason is a scientist, however, of a most conservative sort, and I doubt that observations which he has made with such objectivity will be revised sufficiently to change their basic outline.

The callicebus is a tiny monkey, twelve inches tall and weighing about two pounds. The subspecies studied by Mason, *Callicebus moloch ornatus,* is a colorful little beast, as his name implies. He wears a cape of auburn fur over his chest and shoulders, and has a dark face, a bright white line across his forehead, and all is topped by a shock of red hair. A few individuals, indeed, are so gay that they wear white gloves. Sexual dimorphism is entirely absent, and the female is as brightly adorned as her mate. But the callicebus is shy, and for all his bold looks is disturbed by man beneath his trees. Mason

179

found that it was his face that caused most disturbance. Prior had found the same thing true of his roebucks, and he worked out a peculiar cape that went over his head to alter and obscure the relation of head to shoulders. Mason just waited, and kept his head down for a few weeks, and in the end animal boredom provided his camouflage.

Like that small ape, the gibbon, the callicebus operates a family-sized territory which father and mother defend with whole heart. Like the gibbon also, they are treetop creatures who normally descend to the ground only because they have missed their footing; and they are monogamous. Male and female evidently pair for life, but, unlike the gibbon, the exclusiveness of the arrangement, as we shall see, applies to everything except sex. It has been suggested to me that the chief social attribute of the primate has been his willingness to try anything. Nothing could be more true of the callicebus, the Parisian's delight. Or perhaps it is the *noyau* that encourages originality.

The principal area of Mason's study has been a twenty-acre grove containing nine family territories. Every family knows its boundaries to the last inch: a broken branch here, an isolated bush there, a slanted tree trunk across the way. Were the grove not so isolated and the territorial pressure-cooker not so severe, the properties might be larger and the boundaries less sharply defined. The callicebus, however, in the situation in which he finds himself, knows like a peasant every inch of his domain. And its periphery, as Darling suggested, represents his fun in life.

The little red-haired monkey wakes up in the morning with a sigh, a yawn, and a shudder of monkey regret that the night is gone. Mason's forests are so deep, so dark, that almost all of his photographs are failures. One finds in these forests no sudden, splendid tropical dawn. Here the dawn comes along like gentle, insistent fingers scratching cautiously at the nape of one's neck. Slowly the callicebus family wakes. Mother and father sleep side by side, tails frequently intertwined. He, the good husband, does all the lugging about of children, and if they have an infant under four months he will be so burdened. The family shuffles about in its heartland, its castle, its sleeping tree, lapping dew off leaves, snipping a bit of fruit or a berry or two. Then about seven o'clock, suddenly galvanized, the family makes for the periphery.

I find that one of the most touching qualities in the callicebus monkey is its willingness to sacrifice a hearty breakfast for a hearty periphery. Not unless faced by extreme emergency should I make such sacrifice myself. The little family makes no compromise with principle, but bright and early is on duty at the border, only partly fed, hankering for action, waiting for the arrival of neighbors to be angry at. Shoulder to shoulder mother and father wait, tails intertwined, nursing their grudges, feeding on their animosities, impatient for the arrival of their beloved enemies. Not one foot will the family place on the neighbors' domain unless neighbors are present to make intrusion worthwhile. But let the neighbors appear, having had their dew and their scanty snack, and callicebus hell will break loose.

When I was a young man in Chicago we used to say that the secret of acknowledged Chicago vitality was the *Chicago Tribune*. We read it at breakfast, we hit the ceiling in rage either for or against it, we hit the street on a dead run, and we could not survive without it. The callicebus monkey has substituted the periphery for the *Chicago Tribune*. There is a deal of screeching to begin with. Then father intrudes. The opposing father chases him back and intrudes in turn. Now family is after family. Mothers put aside all grace and give themselves over to lifetime grudges. Juveniles learn the way of all flesh. Bedlam and bellicosity rule for half an hour or so, then someone recalls that there is another boundary undefended and unexploited. The family withdraws. The family across the way recalls that it too has another border, another enemy to become enraged at. No cards or apologies are exchanged, for the rules of the game are too well understood. Were the opponents medieval knights, haughtily bowing, spreading their mailed fists in a gesture of you-know-how-it-is, the callicebus monkey could no more perfectly execute the gallant code of chivalry. Here are Wynne-Edwards' conventional prizes competed for by conventional means.

On other boundaries the contestants will oppose other rivals.

Vast must be the satisfactions of such engagements. Blood pressures rise, tissues expand, brains roil with conventional angers. Then just about nine o'clock in the morning, after a couple of hours of emotional daily dozens, it will occur to someone that somebody is hungry. That will be the end of the day's hostilities as all take their ravenous appetites to the breakfast trees.

At a time when we had a most limited knowledge of primate behavior, Darling made his statement about the importance of the periphery as well as the heartland, of stimulation as well as security. And in a South American monkey we find the creation of a social system which provides the two. The environmentalist might argue that a special circumstance, the isolation of the forests, has imposed the pattern on the inhabitants. We have come to know enough about the territorial pattern, however, to recognize that such formal behavior is not produced by an environmental circumstance but fifteen or twenty years old. Mason informs me, furthermore, that his brief contact with the callicebus in larger, continuous forests indicates no departure from the behavior of the groups he studied. We may suspect that in a continuous forest the *noyau* would be larger and would contain more groups, and that the groups might control somewhat larger properties. They would not be so large, however, as to make access to the periphery and morning confrontation with one's dearest enemies inconvenient.

Finally, there is Mason's evidence of the callicebus *noyau* as a most original interbreeding unit. In most vertebrate species which base their social life on the pair territory, the male asserts exclusive rights over not only his space but his female. So broadly is this true of birds that, so long as the territorial concept was an ornithologist's preserve, it was generally accepted that territory was necessarily a sexual expression in the male. Until quite recently, likewise, it has been assumed that in primate species the sexual attraction of male and female has been the bond of primate society. It is a proposition which we shall investigate at greater length in the next chapter. But the callicebus monkey, red-headed and white-gloved, has somehow upset both assumptions at once.

The female callicebus, unlike many primate species, has a

season of heat like the lower mammals and is sexually unresponsive the remainder of the year. Mason's observations have continued long enough to assure us that throughout all of that long portion of the year when sex plays no part in callicebus life, territorial defense is perfect, tolerance of intruders unthinkable, marital loyalty most estimable. Fidelity in the callicebus applies to everything, it seems, but sex. When the season of female heat arrives, carnival takes over. The territorial system breaks down, borders are violated by hungering males, by famished females, and for the duration of the season the ordered animosities of the *noyau* give way to a merry-go-round of affection, a Mardi Gras of sexual adventure in the groves of unforbidden fruit. Then the season ends. Wives forgive husbands, husbands wives. All settle down to raising those inevitable bastards conceived in the *noyau's* genetic popcorn-shaker. Side by side these marital paragons sleep, tails intertwined, on a tall branch in the dark forest. Side by side they report for duty on the periphery every morning, where, tails again intertwined, they will enjoy that more permanent of life's satisfactions, screeching at one's enemies.

4

Italy is a *noyau*. It is not a nation. Shortly before he died, Cavour is reputed to have said, "We have created Italy, now we must create Italians." But a century has passed since the *risorgimento*, and no one has yet succeeded.

Italy was a *noyau* even in the time of the Empire. Rome with firm hand and clear eye ruled provinces at the end of the known world, disposed law, order, stability, and a measure of justice, established memories and purposes to endure the millennia. But it could not thus rule its own peninsula. Italy remained a patchwork of jealousies, feuds, ambitions, rivalries, and headless horsemen. Rome, a small city-state, was lucky to make Italian alliances lasting a generation.

A society founded on family territories, innumerable peripheries, and an unholy complexity of inner antagonisms is a society of remarkable staying power. It is flexible. Lacking

heart or head, it is difficult to kill. It may lose a portion of its body this century and get it back the next; in the meantime the absence of an arm or leg goes virtually unnoticed. It is healthy. I have only one Italian within my acquaintance suffering from ulcers, and he spent too many years in America; although daily life borders on the apoplectic, few die of cerebral hemorrhage.

Noise, naturally, is a prominent characteristic of a *noyau*. You can hear one from a long way off. There is not only the screeching, the yowling, and the hammered insults of the peripheries, but decibels rise like chimney smoke from the heartland too. As a bird must sing from his accustomed twig to announce his propertied existence, so the Italian must turn up his radio or his television set to maximum volume or quarrel with his wife in such tones as to leave no neighbor in doubt that the master is home and in charge of the situation. If an Italian drove his car quietly or failed to rev up his engine at four in the morning, it would be a public humiliation, an announcement that he did not own a car.

Life in a *noyau*, for all its din of battle, is markedly lacking

184

in danger. There are the normal bloody rendezvous, of course, for Italians are not inhuman. But life, despite the corpses floating down the Tiber or Po, is dedicated to stimulation, not assassination. I have lived for five years in a part of Rome famed for its cutthroats; New York's upper East Side is more dangerous. I have windows overlooking one of the rowdiest piazzas in town, and no Elizabethan tavern ever supported discussions more passionate; I have yet to witness a bloodied nose. A successful *noyau*, like any successful gullery, has its rules and regulations which all understand. Should a society of inward antagonism produce nothing but decimation, little could be said for its survival value.

All forces in a true nation work for compromise and inner peace; all forces in a true *noyau* for division and emotional mayhem. If in Britain two drivers lightly touch their bumpers, both will say "So sorry" and drive on. In Italy there is no worse moment than when, late for an appointment, you hear a featherlike touch against your taxi's bumper. You are finished. Your drivers will stop, descend into the street, and explain their woes to heaven, to each other, and to whoever else will listen. Why else touch bumpers? But while you in your back seat explain your own woes to heaven, it will be wise to recall how infrequently you have observed a drunken Italian. It is the courteous American, Briton, Scandinavian who drinks up the world's hard liquor. The members of a *noyau*, for stimulation, need only drive across Rome.

Nations produce heroes, *noyaux* geniuses. The nation is fundamentally anti-genius, since survival rests on uniformity of response; the *noyau* is fundamentally anti-hero, since variation is its life's blood. The *noyau* must look skeptically on the hero and hope that he will not get anybody into too much trouble. The nation must look with suspicion on the genius and pray that common sense will somehow survive him.

I do not wonder that the English and the Americans have always held such affection for Italy. It was never the sun or the song. It was that here, for a while at least, they could put down their heavy suitcases of national necessity. Without loss of identity, without feeling for a moment less the Englishman or the American, they could find in old Italian streets and young Italian crowds more room to be themselves. Here tastes at home unorthodox might be explored without self-consciousness; here values less than fashionable in London or New York might be meditated, weighed with less distracted mind. The Arno, the Tiber, the Po flow past as if you were not there; and that is freedom too. The *noyau,* were it to encourage the obedient, would return to dust.

For the foreigner the *noyau* has other charms. He is accepted. He may even be liked. He will seldom be made to feel that he is a foreigner. It is a comment on the structure of the society of inner antagonism that its members gain nothing from xenophobia. No portion of Italy's enduring quality has ever been forwarded by an assertion of superior identity. The Rome of Nero, of Caligula, welcomed strangers. Italy's one brief flutter, in the years between the wars, with that gown of such normal habit among true nations, manifest destiny, was a catastrophe. The Italian is a model international citizen. He will loot you, naturally, but with the charm of a man who is looting an equal. He will insult you, naturally, but with a diffidence and lack of whole heart which he would never exhibit were he insulting one of his own kind. The member of a *noyau,* if he is to hold his social position, must never spend his anger on any but his fellows. It is the other way around in a true nation.

Best of all from the viewpoint of the foreigner is that he need not commit himself to the *noyau's* hazards, immediate or ultimate. They are real, and he can always go home. The society of inward antagonism, confronted by crisis, contains no innate mechanisms to command the loyalty of its members. It is not for lack of personal courage that the Italian soldier has acquired a reputation of doubtful merit. It is for lack of inward motivation. To die for one's country is a dull way to end one's days if one has no country. The *noyau,* confronted by an aggressive power, must lose or make deals. Confronted by internal crisis, it must choose between disaster and the despot. Either, of course, it will outlive in a century or two.

It is an odd sort of comment, yet I should suspect that an African tribe called the Baganda, a valid nation with a million and a half members on the northern shore of Lake Victoria, has generated in the last three centuries more loyalty, more mutual aid, more self-sacrifice and dedication to the common good, than has Italy as a whole in the last three thousand years. But neither has the Baganda gallery, or the gallery of any other valid nation of greater privilege, mounted the portraits of a Michelangelo or a Machiavelli, a Leonardo da Vinci or a Lorenzo di Medici, a Dante, a Fermi, a Giotto, a Marconi, a Cristoforo Colombo or a Galileo, a Titian, a Raphael or a Modigliani, a Hadrian, a Marcus Aurelius, a Julius or Augustus Caesar, a Vergil, a Verdi, a John or a Gregory or a Thomas Aquinas, a Cicero, a Caruso, or, for that matter when you come down to think about it, an Al Capone or a Cesare Borgia.

The nation has its deficiencies. None can but bow before the legitimate splendor of the Italian *noyau*. The splendor has been bought, however, at heavy cost. There is not only the social vulnerability; there is individual vulnerability as well. Italy is the loneliest place on earth.

You must live in a *noyau*, I suspect, for ten or twenty generations before you find yourself equal to it. The Italian is friendless. The society of inward antagonism, whether of human or bowerbird arrangement, cannot tolerate loyalty, honesty, trust. It forbids that total abandonment known as friendship. The animal cannot stand alone; this is true. And so the Italian has family. He may find his family an abomination, a curse laid on his life, a collective fright wig to horrify an audience of Norway rats, a genetic railway accident; but in the end he will be loyal to his family, responsible, trustworthy, self-sacrificing. He cannot be otherwise, since his family is all he has. Aside from his family, what may seem to be love in his life is merely entertainment; what passes for friendship, mere shifting alliances. It is a sad sort of place, in the end, a *noyau*.

The Italian, most remarkable of men, has demonstrated with his society of inward antagonism that it is possible to survive with a miraculous minimum of social trust, personal honesty, concerted action, and effective sympathy. He has survived a very long time, too, and he has presented all of civilization with individual achievements perhaps unattainable if one is burdened by national necessity. But he has paid a heavy price in vulnerability both social and individual. It is a price that most primates, human or subhuman, have been unwilling or unable to pay. I find it understandable that natural selection in the primate line, even fifty or more millions of years ago, began to turn its attention from the old *noyau* to the experiment known as the biological nation.

6. The Nation

Madagascar is evolution's liveliest museum. It is a chip off
history, an enormous chip 1000 miles long floating in the
Indian Ocean, 250 miles at its closest point from the southeast
African coast. And deep though the sea may lie between them,
Madagascar seems also to be a chip off the African continent
that somehow came loose a very long time ago. Just how it came
loose and wound up where it is—whether it is a piece of flotsam
left behind by the drifting of continents or whether it was a
victim of local geologic grievance—is a matter of some debate.
It is one debate which hopefully we may stay out of.

Something happened to Madagascar; that we know. And it
happened so cleanly, with such surgical purity, that it left
Madagascar's inhabitants of the time all but untouched by

189

subsequent world events. Lions and tigers and leopards and jaguars, wolves and jackals and coyotes have all evolved since the ancient event; on Madagascar there are no large predators at all. Monkeys first appeared in the Oligocene, thirty or forty million years ago; though elsewhere they spread all over the Old and New Worlds, on Madagascar there are none. The most primitive apes that we have so far found laid down their bones in Egyptian fossil beds at an oasis near Cairo, Fayum. That was not too long after the monkey's appearance. Since then one ape or another, at one time or another, reached all of Africa, of temperate Europe and Asia, and penetrated as far as Indonesia where a last sad descendant, the orangutan, today hangs in trees like yesterday's oversized fruit and swings his way slowly, heavily toward extinction. But the ape did not reach the New World of the two Americas, and he did not reach Madagascar.

The green strip of sea was just too broad, like a moat forbidding the world's evolving zoo. Competition is an essential force in evolutionary progress—competition within a species, competition between species, the competition of predator and prey. That effective moat, the strip of green sea called the Mozambique Channel, shielded Madagascar's early inhabitants from lethal competition with the world's evolving fangs and claws and brains and weapons, and from broader competition with all those teeming superior species which mammal vitality would so effectively bring forth. No elephants would ever march in silent single file through a Madagascar forest; no giraffes would peer down from spotted watchtowers, or goats from windy peaks; no zebras or other horses, no elands or other antelopes would ever graze the sunny pastures of the high pink plateaus. There is no sure evidence that man himself came to the enormous island until the time of Christ, and when he came it was not from Africa but from Indonesia, far beyond the Indian Ocean. Man did not arrive from nearby Africa until he came escorted by Arab slavers.

All—men, zebras, elands, elephants, goats, giraffes, monkeys, apes, lions—belonged to evolution's future when Madagascar put out to sea. And so it came about that a portion of the earth's surface was subtracted from the market place of mammalian competition. Here obsolete species could thrive like obsolete industries behind a tariff wall. Here in a lost world ancient creatures could feed and sleep, breed and survive, untroubled by the competition of any but each other. So it was with the true lemurs, dawn creatures of our primate line, who fifty or sixty million years ago were either carried off to sea on Madagascar's broad back or else reached the island when access was still easy. Shielded by the moat, they survive today in thirty-nine species. Elsewhere they are fossils.

It is in this living museum that today's observer is privileged to look through time's long window at the beginnings of our kind. And he will make the astonishing discovery that the small-brained beings of our primate dawn were capable of every known form of territorial social life. There is the *Lepilemur's noyau*, the society held together by its inward antagonisms. There is the sifaka, and probably the indris, with family groups like those of the gibbon or callicebus, all defending pair territories. Almost surely, unless these species are exempt from the processes of population genetics, such hostile family groups are portions of larger *noyaux*, but we do not yet have the observations to confirm it. And finally there is the biological nation of the brown lemur, of the *fulvus* and the ringtail, in which a territorial society is integrated by its outward antagonisms.

The biological nation, as I define it in this work, is a social group containing at least two mature males which holds as an exclusive possession a continuous area of space, which isolates itself from others of its kind through outward antagonism, and which through joint defense of its social territory achieves leadership, co-operation, and a capacity for concerted action. It does not matter too much whether such a nation be composed of twenty-five individuals or two hundred and fifty million. It does not matter too much whether we are considering the true lemur, the howling monkey, the smooth-billed ani, the Bushman band, the Greek city-state, or the United States of America. The social principle remains the same. And Madagascar's stunning truth is that the nation, this most advanced of human societies, one which we have always regarded as of human invention, was realized by creatures who have been elsewhere extinct for fifty million years and who were only beginning to explore the potentialities of the enlarged primate brain.

Let us examine the lemur and his nations. If the lemur was one of the first undoubted primates, he was a last indisputably pretty one. A few monkeys, like the colobus, are not too bad to look at; the gibbon is superb. But I cannot believe that as a zoological group, men and monkeys and apes can regard ourselves as objects of beauty. It must be our consolation, I suppose, that when we were young we still had our looks. *Lemur variegatus,* the ruffed lemur, is one of the world's most beautiful animals. He comes in an assortment of colors, reds, blacks, and whites, and he will lie in the crotch of a tree peering down at you from a foxy face while his luxurious tail, as large as his body, hangs down beneath. *L. catta,* the classic ringtail of northern zoos, is as lively as he is exotic. *Microcebus,* the mouse lemur, is not as large as your hand, yet his huge, liquid, nocturnal eyes are among the most haunting in nature.

When I visited Madagascar I knew little about lemurs. Jean-Jacques Petter's comprehensive monograph *L'Écologie et l'éthologie des lémuriens malgaches* was not published until 1962. Petter and his wife work together, and we met later in Paris. He is with the *Muséum National d'Histoire Naturelle,* she with the *Faculté de Médicine.* His work concerns behavior and environment, his wife's concerns physiology and anatomy. They are young, brilliantly trained. I do not often meet a physiologist with dimples, nor do I often meet a brace of scientists, one with the Christian name Jean-Jacques and the other Rosseau. Since my antipathy for the gentleman who gave us the noble savage must be counted as among my most impassioned possessions, the sound of the Petters' names took a little getting used to.

The significance of the Petters' studies, begun in 1957 and still in progress, rests on the lemur's relation to primate and thus human evolution. When the lemur thrived in Eocene times, fifty or sixty million years ago, he stood as a zoological halfway house between the monkey and ape and hominid to come and the ancestral mouse that we had been before. For tens of millions of years while reptiles still dominated the world's land surfaces, the tiny, developing, primitive mammal had kept himself quietly busy, like some subversive organization, substituting warm blood for cold, hair for scales, babies for eggs, turning out a new kind of teeth, a new arrangement of skeleton, and most definitely a new sort of brain. It was a long job assembling and integrating such unorthodox genetic accouterment. During the period he found it the better part of valor to stay small, to stay out of sight, and preferably to stay home in the daytime. He lived in trees.

Along about eighty-odd million years ago, for reasons best known to themselves, the dominant reptiles died off in droves. It is a widely held misconception that they became too big for their own good; not all of the reptiles were of dinosaur proportions, and the little ones died off too. Also, a few stayed around—crocodiles, lizards, turtles, snakes—and did very well. For the most part, however, the world in all its wonder wore suddenly one huge VACANCY sign to tempt the little fellow in the trees. If by chance the reptile had been tired and old, the mammal was neither.

The shrew is today's creature that most closely resembles this common ancestor of mice and men. He is of a once abundant group called insectivores, a few of which, like the hedgehog and mole, are still with us. Some believe that among the shrews one finds the earliest of primates; others disagree. The tarsier, once a common, nocturnal, arboreal, insect-devouring little creature, is definitely of our line, but only one genus has escaped extinction. In general, all these early mammalian experiments have been replaced by their evolutionary betters, and it is only the lemur, sheltered on Madagascar, that presents us with a full-blown example of our primate beginnings.

We cannot, of course, be sure that the *way* of lemur life as we observe it today—his societies of inward and outward antagonism, and his manners of amity or animosity which he presents to his fellows—have not evolved on his island home since his separation from the wide lemur world. Anatomically, however, he has evolved very little. In Eocene times lemur species were spread throughout all the continents, and there is an extinct variety called *Notharctus*, found in middle Eocene fossil beds in Wyoming, that differs little from some of the more evolved species found today in Madagascar's forests. Our knowledge of the intimate relationship between body and behavior would justify speculation that his behavior has changed as little as his body. Even were this not so, we should still be justified in asserting that a primate which has not yet acquired significant assets of brain and learning capacity has been capable, nevertheless, of attaining a most sophisticated social life.

Bodily, the lemur is still the same zoological halfway house that he was when primate times were young. He has immense nocturnal eyes left over from the reptilian days when you did not go out till dark. He has the round, alert ears, unlike monkey's or ape's, of use when you listen more than you watch. He has a long, pointed snout like a dog or a fox, from a time of dependence on the sense of smell, and he still has scent glands to mark territories and exclusive trees. His brain remains smaller than any monkey's. Fifty or sixty million years of life in Madagascar's noncompetitive museum have left almost no mark on him. So primitive does he remain that one might easily ask, Then why is he a primate? And the answer is: he has hands.

There is no touch more sensitive than that of a black lemur exploring the mysteries of your wife's Sicilian bag or enjoying the soft fascinations of a woolen sweater. He has lost all his claws except the one on his second toe, which he has kept around for scratching himself. His nails—like ours and like those of his Eocene ancestors—are flattened to protect sensitive finger pads. While his hand lacks the flexibility of ours and he is incapable of controlling his fingers individually as do we, it is a hand that in its freedom from distortion resembles more the human hand than does that of the ape.

It was this clawless hand, so well adapted to running and scampering along arboreal paths, that set the primate on a way distinct from the evolutionary roads of our fellow mammals. We acquired sensitivity, but we sacrificed our fighting claws. And so for claws we substituted wits. It was at this ancient crossroad that the lemur stood, deprived of his claws, endowed with primate sensitivity, but lacking the anatomical blessing of brain that would someday take the monkey down the way of wit.

Of the fifteen species of lemur studied by Jean-Jacques Petter on Madagascar, six seem not to have emerged from the time of the monsters when mammals kept out of sight. All are nocturnal, and only one is large. This is the aye-aye, strangest of all primates and among the strangest of all mammals. His scientific name is *Daubentonia* and he is close to extinction's edge. In 1957 Petter was able to find ten small populations in ten small groves on Madagascar's northeastern coast. Now one of the groves is gone, and so nine populations remain. So long as he lasts, however, the aye-aye stands as an example of how close lemurs come to that early moment of evolutionary divergence between the potentials of the primate and the rodent. It is as if the aye-aye never quite made up his mind which way he was going. He lives off larvae found under bark or in the heart of sugarcane. For chiseling through bark he has typical gnawing rodent teeth, like the gopher or prairie dog. But his hand is the normal primate hand in every way but one. Like a weird deformity he has a middle finger very thin, very long. It is for extracting larvae from the hole that his rodent teeth have chiseled.

The other nocturnal species are small. Least of them and perhaps the most primitive is the mouse lemur, and his name recalls our early rodent affinity. He is so small that in the Petters' Paris laboratory several will jam themselves into a tin can to sleep, crowding so closely that nothing appears but eyes. It is not a society, but what Petter calls an *effet de masse;* in the wild they will lead solitary lives. And in one more respect these smallest of lemurs recall the rodent: all bear litters of two or three young after a very short period of gestation.

The nocturnal lemurs were the last primates to lead solitary lives. However it may be explained, of Petter's fifteen species, in the six yet clinging to the nocturnal way individuals are found usually alone. Even *Lepilemur* with his observable *noyau* defends a solitary territory. Yet of the nine more evolved species that have moved out of the dark to accept diurnal life,

all nine form co-operating groups. And while we may ask ourselves, Why did adaptation to the day command the formation of our earliest primate societies? there can be only one answer: that we do not know.

Whatever was the mysterious force of the light of day, it commanded not only the formation of social groups but a powerful attachment to territory. The sifaka is one of the largest and most common of the family, and in the same Ankarafantsika forest where Petter defined the *noyaux* of *Lepilemur* he mapped the adjoining territories of fifteen sifaka groups. All, like the gibbon and callicebus, contain a male, a female, and immature young. They will defend their borders, which are clearly defined but which they seem reluctant to cross. On one occasion Petter was photographing a group on its territory. The sifakas retreated before him, growled, leaped from tree to tree. Then they became hesitant, for they were approaching their frontier. The boundary lay between two mango trees and the space was an easy leap. But none of the group would cross it. When Petter came too close for further toleration, they leaped over his head and vanished in the opposite direction into the territorial heartland.

It is in the group of species that zoologists call true lemurs that we find the first primate biological nations. And of the true lemurs the black, *Lemur macaco,* offers the greatest advantage for accurate observation. He does not live in forests as dense as does the *fulvus,* nor in a portion of Madagascar as difficult of access as does the ringtail. Most important of the black's advantages to the scientist, however, is sexual dimorphism. Only the male is black; females are brown. Even at a distance the make-up of a group can be spotted, and with that make-up its fairly sure identification. On the little island of Nosy-Komba off Madagascar's northwestern coast the Petters were enabled to settle down in unseemly scientific comfort to follow with confidence the relations of ten groups, to map their territories, and to assess activities and individual relationships within each troop.

The black lemur is about the size of a fairly large house cat. Eight, ten, or a dozen adults along with their young form a normal group. As in all lemurs, copulation takes place in a season of sexual heat, on Madagascar between April and June in the southern autumn. Unlike the lower and more primitive nocturnal lemurs, however, the female bears one young at a time in the manner of monkeys and apes, but unlike the young of the higher primates, these offspring grow up fast. By six months of age they are independent; by a year a daughter, though not yet sexually mature, is difficult to tell from her mother as they sit side by side on a branch.

Within the group it is probably this freedom from long-dependent young that makes possible the mother's high social status. Sexual dimorphism revealed to Petter that as a group moves through its exclusive domain it will be more often than not a brown female that leads, with a black male in second position. Sexual dimorphism revealed also that while contact between hostile groups at a border may be made by the black males, it will usually be the brown females who open outright hostilities. In our first primate nations the female, touched lightly by household chores, seems to have been as willing to join the army as to run for president.

Border engagements on Nosy-Komba are run off without the clocklike regularity of Mason's callicebus in Colombia. They seem, however, to be equally stimulating, equally enraged equally lacking in danger for the participants. And in the satisfying volume of noise produced they have of course the enormous advantage of involving so many more animals. It is a matter of interest, although probably not of significance, that whereas the small family parties of the sifaka avoid their boundaries and engage their neighbors only when necessary, the big groups of the black seek the periphery, challenge their neighbors, and precipitate conflict by purposeful intrusion.

Petter watched one border row so absorbing for its combatants that they forgot to take their normal midday siesta. It began late one morning when a male spotted across a boundary a male of a second group. They exchanged cries. They moved about until each had a good view of the other, then settled down to watching with intense mutual curiosity but little show of antagonism. Simply the sight of each other seemed to offer stimulation of sufficient reward. Then about two o'clock in the afternoon—perhaps the first male had failed to answer some roll call—two brown females from his group came leaping, clamoring through the trees. The racket roused two females and a juvenile from the second group, who likewise came on the treetop run. Action broke loose. Females intruded from both sides. The row raised the total population of both clans, ten adults in the first, four in the unusually small second. As we might surmise, though, the disputes of animal nations are like those of pairs or individuals. Being outnumbered means as little as being outweighed.

For an hour the melee proceeded in all magnificence while males chased males or females without discrimination, and females shrieked and pursued females or males with equal belligerence. In the meantime, however, an odd thing had happened. The male of the first group who had started it all, and who had failed to report for roll call, quietly abstracted himself from the conflict, retired into safe territory, and, unmoved by the deafening shenanigans, proceeded to eat his dinner. At last, sometime after three in the afternoon, he was joined by his famished partners. By four o'clock the original troublemaker, refreshed, was off by himself exchanging cries with somebody over another boundary. But this was not the boundary of the small second group, and if it was his intention merely to gawk at a foreigner he was to be disappointed. Within minutes the entire third clan—it consisted of ten adults, as numerous as the first—was answering the alarums from the border by screaming through the treetops, a brown female in the lead, all following in single file about four yards apart. The half-fed first clan rose from its dinner and accepted the challenge. Again females led the charge. And again the male who kept starting things retired in all innocence to the peace of the heartland, there to comb out his fur with his little front teeth.

This was a party that lasted late, almost till dark. Then the exhausted clan made its way to the traditional sleeping place in the heartland, there to raise its blended voice in a customary *cri du soir*. From somewhere in the forest like an echo came the evening cry of the second clan, and from somewhere else the cry of the third. All flags were still there. The clan, one must assume, slept well, one member at least with a full stomach.

So it is that in a Madagascar forest, as in a museum case, the student of man is privileged to watch certain ways of man enacted in a lost little world of fifty million years ago. Here is the exclusive bit of space occupied by a group. Here is the castle—the heartland, the sleeping place—secure in its peace. Here is the border, where life is never dull. Over there—and there and there—are the enemies who from now to eternity may be relied upon to co-operate in our most exciting exercise. And here we are, in our society of outward antagonism, with no choice but to be friends.

It must be admitted, of course, that men have brought a few innovations to the original natural nation. That our nations are larger and far more complex are merely differences of degree. But that we tend to kill each other, and to take each other's land away, is quite something else. A lemur would be aghast at such behavior and would regard it as a violation of natural law. We need not brood at the moment about our human innovations, for we are merely tracing the evolution of a biological institution, speculating as to its selective value, and striving to recognize that it is not something thought up by man. And it is sufficient to give ourselves over to wonder that at the primate dawn the basic outline of modern human society had appeared. Before monkeys were born, before the significant primate brain had more than begun to come into being; before there were leopards to haunt our nights or wolves to beset our days; before year-around sex had given us reason to enjoy and maintain year-around partnerships; before our children had become so slow to grow up that permanent societies were needed to protect them: before any such challenges or demands had entered primate circumstance, the lemur had emerged from the primordial mammalian night to establish that most sophisticated of social inventions, the nation.

We shall return again and again to the incisive studies of Jean-Jacques Petter, even as he and his wife return again and again to the old forests. There is a problem, of course. Lemurs are edible, and unprotected in Madagascar; men eat them. And the forest is vanishing. What the logic of nature had preserved for fifty million years the illogic of man has all but destroyed in less than two thousand. It is as if the two particular human populations who came to this island mingled more thoroughly than their genes their two worst ideas: The Asian brought from his homeland, along with his wheeled carts and gleaming paddy fields, a preoccupation with the next world so intense that he was careless about this one. And the African, far more concerned with the traffic of this world, brought with him from his homeland a conviction that wealth and prestige are expressed by the number of cattle that a man owns, a conviction so intense that for a man to slaughter a beast except as ritual is to reduce his own size. The ideas dovetailed in that no one cared what happened to the land. And so today there are five million people and ten million cattle, and the cattle have eaten up the island. When you look down on Madagascar as you arrive from East Africa, before ever you set foot on the broad red soil, you will see that the forests are gone. It is an old, old, tired, worn land, bare and eroded, gullied and seamed like the face and head of an old, tired man.

It was very good fortune, under the circumstances, that the chip off Africa which put to sea was a chip so large. There are still little pockets of overlooked woodland where the black lemur lingers, and little nations gather with the falling dark to raise their voices in a *cri du soir;* to listen for echoes from distant trees confirming that their enemies are all in good health; to sleep in close comfort. And there are still a few tall stretches of forest inaccessible to cattle where patient men may observe the shy indris, most splendid of lemurs in his black-and-white robes, or may listen to his voice from some hidden place as he sings his sad, siren-like song. And there is the aye-aye, lingering on from the mammalian night, chiseling in the dark with his rodent teeth, feeling for larvae with his middle finger, in a few last groves on the northeast coast; nine, if the Petters are correct.

2

The lemur did not invent the society of outward antagonism. He merely applied an ancient behavioral solution to the new primate problem of life in the light of day. To find its evolutionary origins one must go an astonishingly long way back.

Protozoa, as we all know, are one-celled creatures, and their history must date from the first billion years of emergent life. One kind of protozoa are known as slime molds. They are of the size and general appearance of a white blood cell, and they feed on bacteria such as one finds in moist soil. They divide every three or four hours, and so a population multiplies rapidly. Just about the time, however, when growing numbers have exhausted the food supply in a given area, the single-cell creatures enter the second phase of their life cycle. They begin to form societies. Around a founder cell others will bunch in a growing aggregate, clinging together until they have formed a sausage-shaped slug visible to the naked eye. Now this social slug of individual beings begins to behave as a single organism, and it will even move toward warmth or toward light with precision of direction. At last a portion of the community will differentiate themselves and form a stalk which they stiffen with a secretion. Then others will crawl on top of the stalk and form a sphere of cells each containing a spore, the seed of a new generation.

It sounds like something out of science fiction, but it is not. It is simply a way of life that was worked out a billion-odd years ago and that still works. How it works defies the imagination—or, more accurately, gives some slight evidence as to how little we know about living processes. One aspect, however, of the social behavior of slime molds has yielded to laboratory investigation. It is what I define as a society of outward antagonism founded on the defense of a social territory.

Investigators have been puzzling over the behavior of slime

molds ever since their discovery in 1935. An American scientist began wondering if there could be some form of communication between cells. Placed in a culture dish, they distributed themselves so evenly in their first phase of life that it seemed they repelled each other. (We should call it individual distance.) Then when the time came for aggregation, it was as if a new signal went out and all obeyed. An investigator named Arndt, working in Germany, made the striking observation that the number of fruiting societies in a given area was independent of the number of individuals. In other words, if you had a thousand protozoa in an area, they might form ten groups of a hundred each. But if you had ten thousand. they would still form ten groups. The societies were somehow a function of space, not numbers.

Only recently an American biologist, John Tyler Bonner of Princeton University, has demonstrated that in a given species of slime molds, the size of the social territory is a constant. And he has proved what had been suspected for some time, that the means of social defense is a gas which repels other groups to a given distance and at the same time attracts the clan. Charcoal absorbs gas. By placing charcoal in his culture, Bonner reduced territory size so that four times as many social aggregates crowded the area.

I do not happen to know of an earlier example of the society of outward antagonism, isolated and unified by the defense of a social territory. Ants and termites do something like it. Since early in the century, when the study of social insects was in high fashion, it has been known that every colony has its own peculiar odor, and that a worker, for example, returning to the wrong colony will be smelled by guards, recognized, and instantly attacked. It was thought for a while that the difference in odor might arise from different sources of food supply. Recently, however, a colleague of Wynne-Edwards at Aberdeen, D. I. Wallis, has shown that in ant colonies the familiar, attractive odor of a social partner and the strange, repellent odor of the foreigner must at least in part be genetically determined.

We must be always wary of conclusions drawn from the ways

of the social insect, since their evolutionary track lies so far from ours. But when we find a familiar behavior pattern in a common ancestral type, the protozoa, a creature so remote, so lost in the tides of animate beginnings, then an honest man must take a deep breath and ask of himself, What came first, the cart or the horse? What ultimately preceded which, body or behavior? We know today that it is a behavioral adaptation that as a rule precedes and gives selective value to bodily change. But has natural selection for two billion years chosen among increasingly complex anatomical possibilities to fulfill increasingly complex behavior patterns? Or did these complex patterns exist from the near-beginning in creatures so simple that they lacked any apparent anatomical structures to maintain them?

These are questions of philosophical note which before this inquiry closes we may perhaps be enabled to ask with sharper precision. In the meanwhile we must give our attention to a question of more immediate concern to the human circumstance: Why have students of men failed to gain from students of the animal any notion concerning the biological origins of the nation? When the true lemur, possessing nothing but the anatomical rudiments of our Eocene primate dawn, introduced a social organization which men in their time would so intricately explore, he was merely picking up a ticket written a billion or so years earlier by the brainless, nerveless, sexless, almost formless one-celled protozoa. It passes all logic to believe that if the society integrated by its outward antagonisms has a history so venerable in the transactions of animals, it could have no bearing on the passages of men. But the question, seemingly so innocent, directs an ultimate earthquake at the more inflexible structures of contemporary thought; and in all responsibility we must inform ourselves, as fully as the new biology at present permits us, concerning the implications of the social territory and the consequences which its discovery brought to the development of the territorial concept.

In early chapters I traced the ponderings of science from the days of Aristotle and Zeno down through Altum and Moffat and Howard to David Lack and his curiosity about the private territory as a reinforcement for the pair bond. In those years, however, we find few observations of any but birds. Eagles and falcons, robins and nightingales, moor hens and meadow warblers were the messengers to bring us word that between a living being and the space he occupies there is a mysterious tie beyond habit or mere familiarity. If our observations of territory were limited, it was because insects and birds, until the 1930's, were very nearly the only wild beings that man had ever studied. Territory remained a form of behavior peculiar to the ornithologist's notebook.

There were exceptions, of course. In 1912 a French psychologist published his *La Génèse des instincts*. From studies of laboratory rats Pierre Hachet-Souplet recorded a pessimistic conclusion that neither reason nor justice could ever contravene "la loi de territoire." I have in my notes no earlier speculation concerning territory and the human being. And one must wonder whether the French psychologist retained his pessimism when two years later the taxicabs of Paris headed for the Marne.

There was another remarkable study of a nonbird made so early that its significance was lost. A. S. Pearse of the University of Wisconsin spent years watching that unlikely animal, the fiddler crab, in such unlikely locations as Manila Bay, the Massachusetts coast, and the flooded mangrove swamps of Colombia. He published his observations in 1913, the year after Hachet-Souplet's. Half a century later his fiddler crabs may startle us; then, lacking frame of reference, they earned small attention.

The fiddler crab is a belligerent little animal who lives on the beach and digs burrows in the sand or mud. When high tide flows, he retreats into his burrow and plugs up the opening. Pearse watched thirteen species and found the same behavior in all. Each individual lives his life near his burrow door, cleaning and scraping the sand about it. Seldom will he move more than a yard or two away, and Pearse established twelve yards as the roving limit. It is the smaller area only that he defends, however, and the fiddler will chase or fight off any intruder on his tiny estate. So vicious is his defense that if a

crab is removed experimentally to any distance along a
crowded beach, his return will be a harrowing affair. He must
cross the territories of others, and he will be attacked by every
crab along the way. The chances are better than fair that he
will lose a claw, if not his life.

"Each fiddler's hand is against every man," wrote Pearse, and
it is almost literally true. One claw of the fiddler is overdevel-
oped to huge size, sometimes a third of total body weight. This
claw is called the chela. It is a brilliantly colored display object,
and during the mating season, whenever a female passes, every
male in the colony will stand by his burrow frantically waving
his chela, often adding to the excitement by squatting and
rising as he waves. Throughout the nonbreeding season, however, such diversion is lacking, and then the male fiddler crab
finds other uses for his chela. David Lack concluded that
fighting is what a robin likes best of all. So does the fiddler
crab, but his fighting is highly formalized. Two will meet on a
boundary and lock chelae precisely as two men shake hands.
The object of the action is simplicity itself: by a sudden

wrench, to break the other crab's claw off.

Ornithology was naturally unaware of Pearse's crabs, as it was unaware of the unreasonable rats in a Paris laboratory. Interpretations of territory continued to be based entirely on the behavior of birds. And the interpretations—whether the food theory, or the dispersal of breeding pairs, or the natural selection of superior males, or reinforcement of the pair bond —all referred to the competition of individual males and in one way or another to reproduction. But then, in 1934, the American zoologist G. K. Noble brought in the fence lizard and the upsetting news that the female has a territory of her own which she defends against ali comers, including males. How such behavior promoted successful reproduction was hard to say.

Many years later the way of a female lizard would be explored in sharper detail by the young Rhodesian all-around scientist C. K. Brain. In *African Genesis* I described the anthropological ingenuities which he applied to the australopithecines, the South African man-apes, and today he is curator of anthropology at South Africa's Transvaal Museum. But there was a period in Brain's career when he wearied of ancient dating, of the tools and fossil memories of small-brained protomen, and he turned to the Kalahari desert and the chameleon. I could understand his fascination, in a way. On one of his returns from the Kalahari he showed me among other lively reptile samples a creature as upsetting to a layman as is a female proprietor to birdmen. When you looked into one ear of the deplorable creature you saw daylight coming in the other.

The young Rhodesian's confirmation of Noble's observation concerned the female of a common chameleon species who defends a solitary property against all others, female or male, with such vigor as to raise the question, How does she ever mate? By experiment Brain found the answer. The male displays by puffing out his throat. On that throat is a yellow mark which serves to make the female only worse-tempered than ever. But when the sexual season comes around, the yellow fades. She admits him to her property, and they mate. Then the yellow mark returns and she throws him out.

Brain's detailed observations were unnecessary, thirty years earlier, to lend credibility to the fence lizard. G. Kingsley

15

Noble was curator of experimental biology at the American Museum of Natural History and his authority could not be ignored. Ponderous questions were raised for which ornithology had no answer. The female fence lizard's territorial defense most definitely did *not* reinforce a pair bond, did *not* serve to select worthy from unworthy males, was *not* an expression of male sexual pugnacity, and could by no means be interpreted as protecting the welfare of offspring. Having laid her fertilized eggs, she would from that point on lose all interest in future generations. Then what was the selective value to the species? Brain's later demonstration showed that lizard territory could be definitely anti-sexual, since only by suspension of the behavior could mating take place.

The next non-bird man to complicate ornithology's interpretations was W. H. Burt, whose domain spread through the fields and the woodlands and the brushy river bottoms of southern Michigan, and whose castle was the University of Michigan's zoology department. Burt watched rodents: wood mice, deer mice, pine voles and lemming voles, ground squirrels and flying squirrels, chipmunks. Although he left no book about them, Burt might almost be described as the Eliot Howard of the mouse world.

Rats and mice have always entered the literature of human analogy, and perhaps that is why with Burt's studies one entertains for the first time clear-cut statements of human implication. The bird inhabits the sky, and we do not tend to identify ourselves with a creature so disdainful of human limitation. Eliot Howard may have blurted to a servant girl that territory is everything; but he did not say it in public. The Michigan zoologist, however, did not hesitate to state his conviction that what was true of mice was true of men. Territory for a rodent meant security against the predator. When you live a life of marsh hawks and foxes, then the days will be fairest for those who know their homelands best.

The Muries, we may recall, had a six-week-old deer mouse who homed two miles to the area of her nest. Burt found similar capacities in wood mice. How they got home was as inexplicable as ever, but what they did when they got there was evident. They disappeared. On its own property a small rodent knows every hole, every tunnel, every hiding place. Burt found that a wood mouse released on its own territory would vanish within twenty feet.

Security from the predator is seldom a territorial function in the lives of birds. But in the lives of rodents as in the lives of men its value is universal. One's imagination may spring to the fortified border, the castle, the drawbridge; to the walled town on an Italian hill; to the barrier of living thorns about an African kraal; to the ancestral cave. Or it may spring no farther than to the striving market place and the quiet chair by the fire. No thoughtful observer of the territorial ways of vulnerable man could fail to recognize in them the ways of the vulnerable wood mouse. I have no doubt but that Burt in his time was accused of anthropomorphism by devotees of human uniqueness wielding vocabularies more pretentious than precise. It is an anthropomorphism to attribute to the animal the capacities of man. What Burt was stating was quite the opposite, for he was attributing to man the capacities of the animal.

W. H. Burt was one of the most significant contributors to the concept of territory, and in another field he came into conflict with his contemporaries. A chipmunk, he noted, will vigorously drive away any intruder who comes within fifty yards of her nest. But she will forage for food for a hundred yards or more beyond, ignoring there the same intruder whom she drove away from her nest's vicinity. The defended area, said Burt, is the territory; the foraging area is the home range.

The distinction between territory and range met opposition, since it minimized the economic importance of territory. As we see in instance after instance, there is an allure about the economic principle as there is about the sexual principle, for each provides simple answers: that an answer may be untrue is less formidable than that it be complicated. Fortunately for Burt's distinction, a biologist named Kenneth Gordon was at about the same time watching golden-mantled ground squirrels in the Far West. At two widely separated locations, one in Oregon, one in Colorado, their territorial behavior was identical. A proprietor would chase an intruder for about one hundred feet. But he would forage for nuts and cones to a much greater distance, and there, like the Michigan chipmunks, he would ignore the same individual whom earlier he had pursued. Burt's distinction between range and territory prevailed, and is today accepted widely in science.

While W. H. Burt brought both cleaner definitions and broader horizons to the territorial concept, his rodents and Noble's lizards thoroughly messed up those simpler interpretations drawn only from the life of birds. One principle, however, seemed to remain intact: that whatever the function territory may provide, it remains a competition between individuals and must somehow relate to individual selection. Then the American psychologist C. R. Carpenter returned from Panama with the news that howling monkeys defend as a group a social territory. The last principle was demolished. When five years later, in 1939, Noble at a symposium in Washington casually referred to a territory as "a defended area," biology leaped at the phrase. Problems of function and motivation were relegated to pigeonholes. From that day to this, biology as a whole asks but one question of a territory: is it defended? Defense defines it. Variability became the final description.

Ray Carpenter is a tall, quiet, scholarly man with a touch of

Woodrow Wilson about him. And I should find it as difficult to visualize the late American President up to his armpits in an Asian swamp or ducking fecal matter showered down on him by large black belligerent monkeys in a Central American rain forest as I do this elegant academic gentleman in the bifocal glasses. Carpenter today is professor of psychology at Pennsylvania State University, and he lives in a low-flung modern house in a neighboring woodland alive with civilized squirrels and accustomed birds of soft-spoken manner. For a quarter of a century Carpenter's central preoccupation has been with university administration and the mental acrobatics of contemporary man. Yet for almost ten previous years his normal home was the jungle, his normal circle of acquaintance the jungle's temperamental citizens. A full quarter-century before Petter went to Madagascar, Carpenter went to Panama to initiate the modern study of primates in a state of nature.

At the time—and it was not so very long ago, for I must recall that I myself had already completed my formal education—there existed nowhere on earth a body of information acceptable to science which revealed the behavior of apes or monkeys in the wild. The amateur South African naturalist Eugène Marais had at the turn of the century lived for three years with a troop of baboons in the northern Transvaal, but his observations were regarded as unreliable and besides had not yet been translated from Afrikaans. Another South African, S. L. Zuckerman, had published his *Social Life of Monkeys and Apes,* and it was regarded as definitive. But according to the modern authority of K. R. L. Hall and Irven DeVore, Zuckerman's monumental study had included but a few days of experience in the field, and had otherwise been based entirely on observations in the London zoo. In large part, what science knew about the behavior of primates, that zoological family of which we are a part, had been obtained in zoos and laboratories. Under such conditions, so little did the behavior of apes and monkeys resemble our own that we came to the logical conclusion that the human way was of our own making and owed little to animal inheritance. Schools of psychology were set in motion to explain our nature in terms of the conditioned reflex. Trends in anthropology and the social sciences went their cultural or environmentalist ways. Then in 1934 Carpenter made his first return to civilization bearing under his arm a clap of thunder: our information was false.

For two years the American psychologist had been watching howling monkeys on an island in the Panama Canal's Gatun Lake. Barro Colorado Island is almost 4000 acres in extent, and at the time of Carpenter's study it was divided between twenty-eight clans, each defending a social territory and living in total hostility with its neighbors. Only three clans were so small as to include but a single mature male; in all others the males ranged from two to five and the females from two to ten. Carpenter recorded their sexual relations and the care of their young, their social organization and means of communication, and their remarkable systems of group territorial defense. The sum he published in his classic monograph *Behavior and Social Relations of the Howling Monkey*.

The first of those assumptions which his study demolished was the scientific *idée fixe*—one of such influence on the work of Sigmund Freud—that the primate is obsessed with sex and that it is sexual attraction which holds primate troops together. The assumption of a sexual obsession had offered scientific justification for the romantic tenet that love is all, for the psychological tenet that sexual energy is the fuel of the human mechanism, and for the more everyday conclusion that when you come down to it nothing matters much except fornication. The assumption that sexual attraction is the magnet drawing together the adults of a primate society had consequences even more far-reaching: Since human society is most obviously *not* held together by such a sexual magnet, then our forms of social life must be unique to man, created by man, and subject entirely to human manipulation according to our vision of human good. Anything, in a word, is possible. This is the premise of most contemporary sociology. It is also the premise that left the social sciences without other than sentimental defense against such totalitarian glimpses of the human good as fascism and communism. If anything was possible, then these were too.

The sexual assumption lies today in ruins. Mason's study of the callicebus shows the year-around integrity of the family group *except* during the sexual season. Petter's ancient lemurs, unlike most of the later monkeys and apes, retain the general mammal characteristic of seasonal heat and rut; yet their societies show an all-season solidarity. The same has been shown for the rhesus and the related Japanese monkey. Recent studies of less seasonal primates like the gorilla, the baboon, and the chimpanzee offer not a gleam of evidence to support the obsolete assumption that sex is the central preoccupation of the primate and the central force holding together his society. Yet that obsolete assumption remains today the cornerstone of most psychology, most anthropology, and very nearly all of sociology.

The assumption was, of course, rendered obsolete in 1934 by Carpenter's observations of the howling monkey. But he went further to demonstrate that it is the troop itself which is the focus of primate life. In his howler clans sexual jealousy was nonexistent. No male asserted a sexual monopoly over females, and sexual activity was an amiable entertainment in which all males shared all females. But the troop was another matter. No jealousy, neglect of young, defiance of leadership or failure of communication could exist at the cost of the clan's welfare. Years later S. L. Washburn and Irven DeVore would record that a baboon without its troop is a dead baboon. So it was with Carpenter's howlers. On rare occasions he spotted a solitary male in the forest. But the wandering male was usually one who out of persistent conflict with his fellow males had elected to leave his clan. Someday after further persistent efforts he would join another clan, or failing, he would die alone. Few so failed. A howler without a clan is a man without a country, and what is true of men and howlers is universally true of primate species.

Finally, Carpenter's careful observations showed that the mechanism isolating and integrating the howler clan is its defense of a social territory. The territories of the callicebus, the sifaka, the black lemur are small, the borders cleanly delimited. The territories of howler clans are large, the borders vague. But clans have only to sight each other in this no man's land and total warfare breaks out. Rage shakes the forest. That rage, however, takes none but vocal expression. As I mentioned in the first chapter, the howler is equipped with a voice box of dismaying dimension from which emerge cries of discouraging proportion. Black lemurs raise their voices in unison in their *cri du soir;* howler clans raise their deafening voices both morning and night as a warning against intruders. Should intrusion occur, these voices joined will be the artillery of battle. And strictly in accord with the territorial principle, the home team will always win, the visiting team will always withdraw.

The howler clan is what I should call a society of most perfect outward antagonism which has achieved a most perfect inward amity. So different from the *noyau,* the biological nation spends its aggressive energies on enemies foreign, wastes none on enemies domestic. Within the howler society as within the society of the black lemur there reigns a kind of democratic tranquillity. Leadership is present, but authority is restrained. Differences of opinion are settled with a mumble and a grunt. While the female is never dominant, still her status is remarkably high. And as for offspring, they are the joint responsibility of all adults in the troop. All males, in response to a special cry, will go to the rescue of a young one who falls from a tree; all males with concerted action will defend it against the advance of a predator.

Such observations were impossible so long as we drew our conclusions from the behavior of animals in the zoo. There no natural society is possible. There no fear of the predator, no pressure of hunger, no boundary disputes with neighboring bands, not even the inconveniences of bad weather can absorb primate energy. If he seems absorbed by sex, it is simply because his captive life presents him with no other outlet for his energies. Our conclusions concerning the nature of the primate, from which we came to such dubious conclusions concerning the nature of man, were based on the behavior of bored, deprived, essentially neurotic animals. Carpenter presented a preliminary review of his new findings at a meeting in 1933. "You're wrong," said a dominant figure in the old biology. "I've only reported what I saw," said Carpenter. "Then you've seen wrong," said the dominant biologist.

Carpenter went back to his rain forests. In succeeding years he added major studies of that small, lithe ape, the gibbon, in Thailand, and of the rhesus monkey both in India and in a free-ranging colony which he established on an island off Puerto Rico, together with lesser studies of the red spider monkey in Panama and of that great ape, the orangutan, in Sumatra. Through the mass and variety of his experience he established standardized, objective, quantitative techniques for the difficult task of observing and recording the behavior of animals in a state of nature. In a sense he imposed the mathematics of the laboratory on the confusion of the jungle, and there are few studies made in the wild today that do not in part found their techniques on those established by Carpenter in the 1930's.

The ultimate importance of his work, of course, was less to the natural sciences than to the social sciences, less to the study of the animal than to the study of man. More recent observation might reveal primate species integrated by other than the social territory. More recent studies might reveal species in which social amity is far less perfect than is achieved by the howling monkey or the gibbon. But Carpenter's discoveries bridged the unbridged gap between man and his primate cousins, and made not only possible but compulsory a consideration of all animate life as an evolutionary whole.

What then was the impact of his discoveries on world science and world thought? The impact may be summarized briefly.

The studies were completed about 1940. When I published *African Genesis* in 1961, all were out of print, some could be obtained in specialized libraries such as those of the British Museum, several existed only as single remaining copies in a file at Carpenter's home. All since, it is pleasant to note, have been reprinted in a single volume, *Naturalistic Behavior of Nonhuman Primates,* by the Pennsylvania State University Press.

Among students of animal behavior, W. C. Allee was one who immediately grasped the whole significance of Carpenter's work, and in his article on animal sociology in the *Encyclopaedia Britannica* he discusses it at length. Little other discussion appeared, however, in reference works available to the layman.

Anyone would assume that political scientists, confronted as they are with nations and nationalism, with inspiring dreams of world federation and with the less inspiring agonies of the United Nations, would find among their numbers at least a few crackpot souls for whom the animal's social territory carries significance. If there exists such a political scientist, then I admire him. I happen myself to be unaware that the nation as a biological expression has ever entered our lengthiest debates.

One would assume likewise that anthropology, the science of man, would have been revolutionized by Carpenter's findings. For Sir Arthur Keith, anthropology's most famous figure and one of the founders of the science, such a revolution came about. We shall return to Keith later. It is sufficient here to note that when in 1948, at the age of eighty-two, he published his masterwork, *A New Theory of Human Evolution,* he recorded that Carpenter's social territory had been a catalyst for his thinking. The book exists, however, virtually unread.

There are certain anthropologists who in the past few years

have found new inspiration in ethology's investigations of animal behavior and paleontology's startling illuminations cast on the human emergence. It would be an exaggeration, though, to state that the name of C. R. Carpenter had made deep inroads on the science as a whole. In 1965, for example, the American Association of Physical Anthropologists held its annual meeting at Carpenter's home university. An official report of the conference was written by an anthropologist from the neighboring University of Pennsylvania and published in *Science*, the organ of the American Association for the Advancement of Science. Passing reference was made to the address on primate behavior delivered at the annual dinner by "Clarence S. Carpenter."

Within the specialized, developing field of ethology, of course, Carpenter's name correctly spelled traveled far. But even there something was strangely missing. When in 1960 I was completing field and reference research for my own book, I faced a mystifying absence of further material on wild primates. Niels Bolwig, the previous year, had published observations of chacma baboons drawn to the garbage pails of a camp in South Africa's Kruger Park. The conditions seemed to me artificial. A Japanese group had begun observations of semi-wild macaques frequenting traditional temple areas, but their preliminary reports had not come my way. For lack of further material I made a wrong guess or two: I underrated primate social ingenuity and presumed that he would always found his society on territory; and I overrated the probable importance of the family as his social building block.

While I was finishing my work, the vanguard of a new generation of primate students was already at theirs. Petter was in Madagascar, K. R. L. Hall in the Cape of Good Hope watching baboons, George Schaller was in the high mists of Congo volcanoes with his mountain gorillas, Jane Goodall was beginning her observations of the savannah chimpanzee near Lake Tanganyika, Adriaan Kortlandt his of forest chimpanzees lingering near a Congo plantation. The following year, too late for my book, Washburn and DeVore gave us the first of the new publications, their superb account of the social life of the baboon. But this was simply the opening wave; then came the flood: K. R. L. Hall on the patas monkey as well as the baboon, Schaller on the orangutan as well as the gorilla, Stuart A. Altmann on the rhesus in Puerto Rico, Charles H. Southwick on the rhesus in India, Stephen Gartlan as well as Brain on vervet monkeys, V. Reynolds on the forest chimp, H. Kummer and F. Kurt on the hamadryas baboon, Mason on the callicebus, Phyllis Jay on langurs, Ellefson on the gibbon in Malaya. Today, one suspects, there must be hardly a bush or a clump of vines that does not shelter a scientist, or a monkey or ape who is not busily engaged in making notes on the remarkable behavior of man.

The primate, in a scientific twinkling, became fashionable. And we may hold the legitimate suspicion, I believe, that a turn so world-wide, so spontaneous, so spectacular, has registered like a fever thermometer some change in the public temper. Monkeys and apes are the most controversial of animals, suffering as they do the misfortune of being closely related to man. And when men abruptly embrace them—it is a guess—we are seeing the first step of a rebellion, probably as yet unconscious, some first symptom of a profound dissatisfaction with all the old answers.

We shall be unwise, however, if we forget that twenty years earlier, when Ray Carpenter last emerged from the rain forest, no scientist took his place beneath the trees. He brought drama, but he played to an empty house. To believe that the sciences are rigidly objective and unswayed by the winds of intellectual fashion, of public mood, of political temper, of personal prejudice, is to go forth into the human storm clad only in trust's most innocent winding sheet. To believe that a scientist is unaffected by public disapproval, unaffected by the regard or disregard of professional colleagues, unaffected by the lack or abundance of funds for his work, is to characterize the scientist as an unperson. We, the laymen of the world, provide the milieu from which the scientist must draw his sustaining breath. You and I, we laymen, provide the freedom and the inhibitions, the receptivity and the intolerance, the affluence and the poverty, the honors and the oblivion which direct our sciences toward this goal, dissuade them from that. And it was you and I, whether we knew it or not, who in the critical year of 1940 and the decades thereafter failed to encourage our sciences to investigate further certain possibilities perhaps remote: that man and the monkey have more in common than mere anatomy; that our infant species is not as yet divorced from evolutionary processes; that nations, human as well as animal, obey the laws of the territorial imperative.

It has been an expensive failure.

3

An effective social organization in primate groups will be achieved through territory, or it will be achieved through tyranny. Contemporary research has revealed no third way.

When some years ago I first read Tinbergen's *The Study of Instinct* I regarded as absurd his view that a social instinct does not exist. For generations we have accepted the notion of a gregarious instinct in social beings, and we have referred to the herd and the animal horde with a rough assessment that such groups are simply agglomerations of individuals drawn together by gregariousness. In later decades we have been presented with the alternative thesis that the primate group is drawn together by sexual attraction, but we are seeing that leaky vessel sink. What then could account for the universal primate society but a social instinct?

Happily for me, I faced no need to record publicly my conflict with Tinbergen's view; this is one sin for which I need not seek the confession box. But I was undoubtedly wrong. The mass of information which has come our way since 1961 indicates to me that if a social instinct is a portion of primate endowment, then it is a very small candle on a very dark night. We face a *need* for society. From the true lemur to true man, we have been creatures who combined a generalized body— one lacking armor or significant armament, massive strength or dazzling speed—with a single specialized asset, an increasingly better brain. For a creature as vulnerable as ourselves, there was no evolutionary road other than to join forces and out of an effective union of bodies and wits to make the best of what we had. The animal cannot stand alone: no zoological group has endorsed the statement with a more fervent amen than has the primate. The combination of a generalized, all-purpose, but vulnerable body, a better brain tracked by more open instincts and wider capacity for learning, and a co-operating society which could enhance the powers of both brain and body, has been the holy trinity of primate success. And yet, after sixty-odd million years of evolutionary trial and error, the fellow seems to have developed nothing but the most unholy skepticism concerning the arrangement. For nature to induce a primate to assume any but an anti-social posture he must be tempted, stimulated, cajoled, tricked, threatened, terrified, and if necessary hit over the head.

How then is the essential society to be formed if the primate in his heart of hearts wants no part of it? It was George Schaller who once suggested to me that the only safe generalization to be made about the societies of monkeys and apes is that the primate has tried everything. And it is true. Out of our filling bag of primate observation, swollen so rapidly by the new studies, we may select examples of every conceivable social form: There is the biological nation of the howler, realized in its earliest form by the true lemurs, in which inward amity and co-operation is achieved through outward antagonism and to which strength is lent through the normal channels of territorial possession. Going down the scale in social number we find the patas monkey, living in fairly large groups but containing only a single, large, dominant male and his harem of females. The patas is one of the few known primate species with polygamous households. The wives may number up to a dozen, but the group is intensely territorial, and inward amity and co-operation are as perfect as in the biological nation. Still smaller territorial societies are those of monogamous, one-family units such as the callicebus, the gibbon, and the early sifaka, all of which we have examined. All defend territory, maintain inward amity through outward animosity, and secure co-operation in a voluntary manner. Seldom is it necessary for leadership to use force; relations between male and female are tranquil; conflict occurs occasionally, but usually between adults and maturing juveniles.

At the opposite end of the social spectrum is the society of compulsion, owing no part of its structure to the organizing force of outward antagonism. Of these species, the only one which neither defends territory nor shows attachment to an exclusive range is the wandering, submissive, inoffensive, vanishing gorilla. His bands may be large, containing as many as nine mature males, but the band is ruled with total authority by a single chief. It is a benevolent despotism, in which there is rarely conflict because the will of the leader is never challenged. In the aggressive baboon, on the other hand, we find the harshest of all primate authorities. The large baboon troop with numbers of up to a hundred occupies a huge, permanent range which is exclusive in that none ever intrudes. Lacking challenge, the range is undefended and the resident troop gains no organization from concerted defense and outward antagonism. All co-operation rests on fear of an oligarchy of three, four, or five powerful males among whom there is amity, and whose combined dominance none dares challenge. It is an authoritarian society of compulsion and compliance, threat and punishment. Japanese monkeys form similar unchallengeable oligarchies, as does the African vervet monkey under special conditions. All, whatever the degree of force which dominant animals must exert on the subordinate, are essential tyrannies; and all are non-territorial in that none spend their energies on or gain co-operation from joint defense.

Between the two extremes lie species which maintain distance between groups, in which the effect is the same as that of individual distance. The exclusive area occupied by a group shifts as it gives way to the pressures of stronger groups. Outward antagonism may be extreme, as in the rhesus, or less demonstrated, as in the langur, but the antagonism springs not so much from the defense of an area of space as from defense of society itself. And, significantly, strong dominant orders based more on threat than punishment are necessary to the social organization.

The primate has indeed tried everything. There is even the amiable chimpanzee who seems to found his society on nothing very much but his own good nature. There is an order of dominance, but it is not at all severe. When band meets band in the forest or on the savannah, there is enormous excitement but no antagonism, and all may wind up feeding in the same trees. The chimpanzee has demonstrated, I presume, that we must reckon on some degree of innate amity in the primate potential; but as I have indicated, it is a very small candle on a very dark night. The chimp is the only primate who has achieved that arcadian existence of primal innocence which we once believed was the paradise that man had somehow lost. And the achievement offers small promise for chimpanzee survival. We may deplore baboon tyranny, with its gang of thugs at the top; but the baboon is nevertheless an outrageous evolutionary success from the Sudan to the Cape of Good Hope, and the effectiveness of his society has made him the equal of the leopard and very nearly of man. The chimp, in contrast, despite his intelligence and strength, is confined to a few remote, diminishing African places. The troop is incapable of concerted action. If an individual senses danger, then a forest chimp will hide himself before giving a cry of alarm; the savannah chimp will give none at all, leaving his partners to look out for themselves. The amiable, otherwise admirable animal is an evolutionary failure. Second-most intelligent of all the world's beings, either he has lost the capacity for social effectiveness or he never gained it, and as purple night, black night steals through his forest galleries he makes his nest by a guttering candle.

If the primate has tried everything, there are still two generalizations which I believe one can make: There is not a species defending territory which is in the least danger of extinction. And there is not a species gaining outward antagonism through territorial defense which gains inward co-operation through compulsion. Dominance and subordination characterize all animal societies with the possible exception of certain schooling fish. Ethologists refer to these orders of dominance as hierarchies of low or high gradient. Barnyard hens, for example, have the well-known pecking order in which alpha may peck beta but beta may not peck back and if upset about the altercation must go and find gamma and peck her. This is an order of high gradient, as is the baboons'. But while future primate studies may present us with exceptions, on the basis of our present knowledge I believe it is safe to state that through a wide variety of effective primate societies a clean line falls: territorial societies tend toward the equalitarian, exhibit the lowest gradients of dominance, present the fewest examples of physical conflict or punishment, and while attaining a maximum of social solidarity and co-operation, sacrifice a minimum of what a human being would call personal freedom.

The status of the female offers an excellent contrast of freedom and oppressiveness in primate groups. We have seen that in territorial lemur groups, like the sifaka and the black lemur, a female may even be the leader. But those were the days before melancholy fortune burdened the primate with children who take forever to grow up; the evolutionary advance may have been of intellectual advantage to primate potentiality as a whole, but it reduced the primate mother to the status of a second-rate citizen. In every species of monkey and ape she is subordinate to all mature males, and in most species sexual dimorphism has made her smaller, too, and quite defenseless. How then does she fare in her subordinate role?

There is not, so far as we know today, a territorial species in which the female is abused. Among his howler clans Carpenter never witnessed an instance of male aggression directed at a female, nor did he ever examine the body of a female which bore scars of punishment. Neither do females suffer from quarrels with each other; the amity prevailing within the female group of a clan extends even to that time when one is in estrus and seeking male attention. Ronald Hall, on the other hand, found that in his troops of chacma baboons in the Cape of Good Hope two-thirds of all acts of aggression were committed by females against females, and that over one-half of all acts of punishment delivered by the dominant males fell on the females.

An even cleaner contrast is offered by the patas monkey, studied by Hall in northern Uganda, and the hamadryas baboon, studied by Kurt and Kummer in Ethiopia. The male hamadryas is the big, maned animal, seen frequently in zoos, which once was sacred to the ancient Egyptians. The male patas is a lean, rangy, handsome creature, swiftest-running of all monkeys, whose speed has been clocked at thirty miles an hour. Both species are terrestrial. Both live in the same kind of country, open savannah broken by clumps of trees. Both form polygamous societies in which a large, highly dominant male has a harem of females. But there the similarity ends. The patas is intensely territorial, the hamadryas not at all.

A patas group controls an area as large as a dozen square miles, moving rapidly about its estate. Most of the overlord's energy seems devoted to sentry duty as he watches for predators or other patas monkeys. If it is a predator, his movements will be instant and spectacular to draw attention to himself while his females hide; if it is an intruding patas, then he and his entire harem will join in a dizzy chase. And within this society of outward antagonism, as in the howler clan, peace is unbroken. Though the male have ten or a dozen wives, within the female group all is harmony. He may on rare occasion threaten a female, but there is never physical aggression. Neither are there vocal disputes; the patas is the most silent of monkeys.

The household of the hamadryas, in contrast, is a regime of fear. Whereas the patas male watches always for enemies, the hamadryas male watches always his wives. They sleep at night in a tight group, move in the daytime in a tight group ignoring all others of their species. Seldom will a female stray ten feet from her overlord. Should one stray farther, he will leap at her in instant attack, biting her neck, although this is frequently unnecessary. As a rule he has only to lift his great, maned head and point his dog-like snout at her. She will leap to his side, screaming in terror.

As Darling found two ways to live, to defy or to defer, so the primates have found two ways to attain that organized effort essential to their survival: through tyranny, whether by force or by compliance, and through territory and a voluntary association of partners for whom equal siege brings closer equality of status, and with it something resembling the personal dignity which man so prizes. But man has improved little on the social mechanisms of forest and bush, other than their complexity. We too have our subsidiary network of relationships within our societies: male and female, male and male, female and female, mother and infant, the young and his peers. As in every society of monkey and ape, we suffer our most serious conflicts between adult and adolescent. All these relationships we shall explore someday when, making full use of the treasure of primate information now coming our way, we turn our attention to society as an evolutionary mechanism.

A wonder of nature, mystifying and beyond all easy answer, is that the biological nation immediately appeared when true lemurs emerged from the long mammalian night. Could we only know better the animal psyche, we might find that terror of the day and subconscious remembrance of the monster combined to command the most perfect of primate defensive weapons though real need was lacking in a time before leopards were born. Could such a thesis be a subject for demonstration, we might know ourselves better. In strict truth, however, the vulnerable hominid in his long evolution on the

African savannah faced in shuddering reality the terror of night as well as day; and when true man emerged from the hominid shadow, he had no need for subconscious recollection of monsters. We clung to and perfected further that most effective of defensive weapons to be found in our primate legacy; for the monster was within us.

7. Look Homeward, Angel

On the day of the armistice in 1918 I was ten years old and playing in a gravestone storage yard on East 67th Street in Chicago. In the midst of the war my elementary school, to the delight of all, had burned to its foundations. It had been a wonderful fire, for in those days fire engines were still pulled by horses and were truly fire engines, with power for water pressure furnished by a coal-stoked furnace and boiler. They made a splendid spectacle of spark and smoke as they charged through the dull geometry of Chicago's streets. The disaster by some blessed fortune occurred at night, so that the burning of the school itself provided a further spectacle of such garish grandeur as none of us had ever witnessed. Flames roared high above the cottonwood trees, clouds of sparks assailed the ruddy heavens, and we the assembled children cheered the fall of every rafter. We believed, I suspect, that we should never go to school again. If so, then the hope was false. Within weeks the Chicago school board betrayed us and we were back at our desks in a dozen portable schoolrooms erected on a vacant lot in East 67th Street, across from Oakwoods Cemetery.

This, then, was the school that I was attending when on a November morning every factory whistle in Chicago announced that war was over. We had no schoolyard, but there was a monument works down the street and some of us played in the storage yard, a granite jungle of immense stone blocks, fresh from the quarry and piled every which way, along with fractured crosses and noseless angels which had emerged from the works in a condition less than suitable for paying tribute to the dead. It was not too bad a play yard, for beneath the granite disorder were caves and mysterious recesses and passages, and it was from these that I emerged at the sound of the whistles to mount a pile of gravestones unmade or unworthy and to stand at the top and survey the peace. And I did not believe it.

There had been a false armistice a few days before, when everyone had run around and shouted in useless excitement. Now with the true armistice there was no sensation at all. Within my view a single figure showed agitation, a grown-up man running beside the cemetery wall. I thought that he was making a fool of himself. I felt nothing. I was only ten years old, of course, and World War I had been going on for approximately as long as I could remember. I accepted it as I accepted the thunder of elevated trains on the structure above 63rd Street. Also, being unable to recall anything but war—and a thoroughly dull and unremarkable experience it had been—I possessed no pressing visions of peace. But beyond all that there was something else. I was cynical.

An adult who cannot comprehend the cynicism of children knows little about them. It may be a cynicism as petty as it is uninformed, yet still it contains that sophistication of young beings who have seen more than they will discuss. One night, for example, I had marched in a parade carrying somebody else's air rifle. And I had seen on the crowded sidewalk a young man knock an older man down because the older man had failed to take off his hat as our flag passed. I responded to the incident with the same lack of pleasure with which I recall it today. Yet I rushed to no parent, no teacher, to pour out my rejection of such remarkable adult emotions. I simply stored it away like a squirrel a nut, in a hole in a cynical tree.

Now the war was over and whistles blew and I stood on top of my granite jungle watching a lone man running beside the

cemetery wall, and I was as unstirred by the joys of peace as I
had been unmoved by the rages of war. I disbelieved, in what I
cannot say. And I should hazard today, looking backward, that
I was not alone in disbelieving. The whistles announcing the
end of the First World War were our formal introduction to
the Time of Disbelief, that period of necessary preparation for
the Age of the Alibi.

Since we are about to take a look at war, and to inspect those
forces which direct the human being to defend his country, let
me make a very slow dissolve, as we say in films. Let me go from
the monument yard in Chicago, in 1918, to a hotel room in
New York on a Sunday afternoon in 1941, twenty-three years
later. It was December, but the weather was decent and those
of my friends who could take the opportunity had gone to the
country for the week end. New York streets wore the silent
Sunday look that induces wonder as to whether the inhabitants
have not at last come to their senses and sold the island back to
the Indians. I was enjoying my solitary state, for I was busy
writing a final draft of my fifth play in preparation for
Broadway. Indeed, I was feeling intolerably good about myself,
for my last had developed into an inexplicable success in
Britain, where it had been running all through the blitz before
audiences hugging gas masks on their knees. Also, I had
recently completed my first Hollywood experience, and I was
not only prosperous for the first time in my life but the film
itself had managed to combine a fair degree of art with an
enviable run at the Radio City Music Hall. I was in good
shape. Then my phone at last rang and it was an agent with
some casting assurances which pleased me further, but he
seemed in a hurry and said he had to get back to the bombing.
I asked, what bombing?

"You didn't know?" he said, with the tone one reserves for
the feeble-minded. "The Japanese are bombing Pearl Harbor.
You'd better turn on your radio." And he hung up.

I had no radio. I did not believe him, of course, but even so I
shuttled vaguely about my room not knowing what to do next.
I recalled a friend, an attorney, who was in the city for the week
end. I called his house. I could hear his radio going in the

background. The broadcast was coming from Hawaii and it was all true. I have little recollection of leaving my room or finding a taxi. My brain, I believe, went out of business for a while. I arrived at the apartment in Central Park West and my friend was alone and he said very little when he let me in because he was listening to the radio in the next room. I joined him there. It was afternoon in New York, early morning in Hawaii. The broadcaster there had little to offer but chaotic descriptions of the burning naval base, the sunken fleet—how many ships, who knew?—of hospitals choked with American wounded and dying—how many, who knew?—of the hundreds upon hundreds of Japanese bombers that had flown in from the sea to create a glaring, unguessed dawn.

It is always strange, recalling, to discover the precise and unreasonable moment when the knife strikes deep. I listened too shocked to respond. Then in the midst of it all came a bulletin that Ecuador had declared war on Japan. I choked. I saw my friend looking away in an effort to hold onto himself. It was an absurd thought that Ecuador had come to the rescue of the United States of America, it was like a bad line in a play, and yet what was happening to my emotions had no least connection with either thinking or playwriting. Something within me burst, and I ached with my gratitude to Ecuador, I ached with my love for my country, I ached with horror at the Japanese deception, I ached with sickness for the American loss. I had encountered, slam-bang, for the first time in my experience, the territorial release.

After sufficient passage of time and sufficient exposure to repetitive bulletins, my friend and I collected our wits sufficiently to conclude that what we had just witnessed was the political blunder of the age. Not a significant segment of American opinion had favored our entry into World War II. That we might eventually have entered the war against Nazi Germany was possible but unlikely; that we should ever have gone to war with Japan was virtually unthinkable. So dedicated were we to our isolationist faith—the faith that if you keep your nose clean you yourself will get into no trouble—that our administration was pressing the most meager measures of defense through an unhappy Congress by the slimmest of margins. Only weeks before, an effort to end national conscription and return our army to its small peacetime size had been defeated by about four votes. Yet by a single spectacular stroke Japan had guaranteed that the most powerful country on earth should enter both wings of the war, that it should proceed as an undivided people, and that its resolve would remain undiminished till war's end.

I had most obviously not heard at the time of what a territorial intrusion does to the energies and the resolve of a territorial proprietor; and neither, as obviously, had the Japanese. C. R. Carpenter had made his last return from the rain forest the previous year, but his message had not got around. The Japanese command, we may assume, took the calculated risk that Americans might react at least to a degree as they did. But every rational assessment of the American will to resist, every consideration of human behavior then prevailing, would have tended to confirm that the risk was small, and that a demonstration of Japanese power would further divide us and further discourage us from a course of military adventure. What was not assessed, of course, was the weight of the irrational: the behavior of a robin on a lawn in Devon or of a troop of brown lemurs in a Madagascar forest.

We tend today, with the equanimity of hindsight, to dismiss the Japanese command as a shipload of fools, and to shrug off the events of Pearl Harbor as the simple consequences of a simple if incredible blunder. But let us beware of equanimity. The story of World War II, from beginning to end, was a dizzying sequence of similar blunders. And despite the passage of a quarter of a century, despite the evidence which the new biology has so abundantly accumulated and the evidence which history has so abundantly disposed, we are in our day as innocent as were the Japanese in theirs. We shall discover, I believe, as this inquiry progresses, that our contemporary governments in one fashion or another, on small scale or vast, reiterate the Japanese blunder in faith as full, in folly as real. If the Japanese command was a shipload of fools, then ours is no less. And the equanimity, which for times past provides such becoming costume, may for times to come provide shrouds of even more expressive merit.

I submit, of course, that the continuity of human evolution from the world of the animal to the world of man ensures that a human group in possession of a social territory will behave according to the universal laws of the territorial principle. What we call patriotism, in other words, is a calculable force which, released by a predictable situation, will animate man in a manner no different from other territorial species. I recognize, of course, that no school of thought prevailing today on any continent will inform you that my proposition is correct. And so I must pursue my prey with all the delicacy of a stalking leopard. The American must become for the moment my study species, Pearl Harbor my laboratory experiment, and I myself a convenient specimen to prod, measure, inspect, shock with electricity, inject with chemicals, dispatch, dissect, and if necessary grind up and feed to my friends.

Was my response to Pearl Harbor innate or conditioned? This is the question we must ask. Was it something I had been born with or something I had been taught? Was it truly a command of genetic origin, an inheritance from the experience and natural selection of tens of thousands of generations of my human and hominid ancestors? Or was it a display of a cultural heritage to which I had been conditioned during my lifetime?

We must grant first that my response was instant. I required neither opinion polls to advise me as to how others were responding, nor consultation with my neighbors, nor even discussion with my friend. We made our commitments in silence. Neither was the decision arrived at by inner debate of a rational order. At one moment I was at peace, the next at war.

As the decision was instant, so was it voluntary. No measures of government authority or sanctions of social disapproval or erosions of inhibition through inward guilt gave shape to my response. There was no time.

As my response was instant and voluntary, so was it universal among my social partners. Dissent must have existed, particularly among Americans of German or Japanese extraction: but dissent was so rare as to be statistically nonexistent.

As my response was instant, voluntary, and universal, so was it contrary to personal interest. I know of few Americans who by their inward commitment gained a richer, easier, or more comfortable life. The inconvenience of death was the reward for many.

My own response, then, was not unique, but common to my kind. Were the Americans a species, we should be justified in regarding it as species-specific. And so we must ask, if the remarkable uniformity was not innate, by what processes of social conditioning had Americans been instilled with such love of country as to guarantee that when challenge arose we should act as one?

Since the *milieu* of my growing up on Chicago's South Side was dismally typical of that of many another, let me continue in my role of laboratory animal. I have mentioned that when at the age of ten I stood on a pile of gravestones listening to Chicago's whistles announce the end of the First World War, I entered the Time of Disbelief. From that moment on, when we sang the national anthem at school we forced our voices to break on the high notes and inserted ribald phrases in the lyric. Marching bands and martial music vanished from our streets; if you liked brass bands, you went to football games. The flag, making an occasional appearance, passed unnoticed. George Washington, we discovered, may have been the Father of our Country, but he was a mediocre sort of man blessed with a few bright lieutenants and uniformly dim-witted opponents. It was a bad time for heroes. Napoleon got where he did because he was five feet three. Ulysses was as commonplace as George Washington and infinitely sillier. England's eminent Victorians had been homosexuals, drunkards, and prigs.

Generals, in the time of my growing up, were something to be hidden under history's bed, along with the chamber pots. Anyone who chose the army for a career was a fool or a failure. At my high school there was something called R.O.T.C., a training course for reserve officers. If you wanted to sink out of sight in the estimate of your contemporaries, if you wanted to be checked off as someone whose pimples would prove to be permanent, you had only to appear at school in a khaki uniform. I doubt that among the 3500 students who were my fellows at this giant Chicago high school there was one who chose to be a professional soldier.

Certain words almost vanished from the American vocabulary during the 1920's, the Time of Disbelief. *Honor* was one, *glory* another. A man of honor was a hypocrite. He who achieved glory had undoubtedly a hollow leg, he who desired it a hollow head. Patriotism, naturally, was the last refuge of the scoundrel. It was the time of Watson and his striped muscles and conditioned reflexes. The human being, at bottom, is nothing. Watson's basic claim was that under ideal circumstances he could take any baby born and, by proper conditioning of a few basic reflexes, turn out a butcher or a banker, a soldier, a thief, an artist, a lunatic. Implied was the natural equality of man in the natural equality of zero. Although Watson plied his trade at the University of Chicago, just around the corner, I doubt that many of us in high school ever heard of him. He played a tune of a popular sort, however, and, like "Yes, We Have No Bananas," you could hear it anywhere drifting along on the American breeze.

The Time of Disbelief gave way in the 1930's to the first mighty waves of the Age of the Alibi. Watson vanished from public view, but his doctrine of human nothingness manipulated by conditioning spread out into the broader concepts of environmentalism. We were still nothing, but a touch of nobility had crept into our nothingness. We were naturally good, amiable, gentle. Only social manipulation and pressures of environment made us greedy, antagonistic, brutal. At last we had something to believe in: that whatever happens, it is somebody else's fault.

In my first chapter I conducted a sufficient excursion through America's murky, depression-haunted streets. Out of our joint desperation something that we called the social conscience, as opposed to the older personal conscience, began to take form, and with it the political philosophy that we today call liberalism. But our liberalism was founded on "us" against "them."

The generals and the munition-makers, sharks of the international deep, were among the most horrendously "them." The liberalism of the time was a bastion of pacifism.

We were conditioned, it is true. The generation that was to respond to the last man on Pearl Harbor's dawn had been conditioned to the last man to believe that wars accomplish nothing. Had America been an enormous laboratory and had we all been albino rats, no more elegant experiment could have been devised to test the powers of social conditioning. Perhaps its only equal has been that of the Soviet Union in its total effort half a century long to induce the Russian farmer to put his heart into crops raised on land not his own. Ours was as total in its way, and it lasted for twenty-three years, and it failed in a dawn's bad hour. Yet human gullibility is such that a generation who survived the experiment will instruct another generation that patriotism is something we are taught.

Pearl Harbor was a phenomenon less than unique in the history of peoples. Its significance rests on that period which preceded it, when a people chose its gods from the disenchanted. I may look homeward, search old corridors, old streets, old schoolrooms, hear once again Chicago's tongue, and I shall find in my memories no instant's instruction concerning the virtues of dying for one's country. I may recall New York and the years of protest against man's injustice to man. I may recall California and the growing terror and thunder as war at last extended its heat and its horror across all of Europe, as I may relive our sympathies for Britain and for France. But except in the unpopular anticipations of a far-sighted few, nothing in our sympathies, our fears, or our revulsions persuaded us that war could ever bring human solutions. To the very last moment we preserved like laboratory rats the perfect posture of our perfect conditioning. Then all in an hour evolution took charge.

If life is to go on, then there must be those moments in the history of animate beings when nature will brush aside the most perfect of conditionings, as it will brush aside the most imperfect of philosophies, to put older, more trusted mechanisms to work. Towers of reason, of impeccable design, will topple in a dusty instant. The waters of our most genuine idealism and of our highest moral purposes, which have made green our fields of longing and made seemingly real our gentlest hopes, will be dimly recollected tomorrow as a mirage upon the desert. The intruder will have knocked.

The territorial imperative is as blind as a cave fish, as consuming as a furnace, and it commands beyond logic, opposes all reason, suborns all moralities, strives for no goal more sublime than survival. Today's American may give thanks that on December 7, 1941, this was so. But today's American must also bear in mind that the territorial principle motivates all of the human species. It is not something that the American thought up, like the skyscraper or the Chevrolet. Whether we approve or we disapprove, whether we like it or we do not, it is a power as much an ally of our enemies as it is of ourselves and our friends.

2

The principal cause of modern warfare arises from the failure of an intruding power correctly to estimate the defensive resources of a territorial defender. The enhancement of energy

236

invariably engendered in the defending proprietor; the union of partners welded by the first sound of gunfire; the biological morality demanding individual sacrifice, even of life: all of the innate commands of the territorial imperative act to multiply the apparent resources of a defending nation. We have traced the territorial power back through the ape and the monkey and the lemur; we have weighed it in other mammals—beavers and antelopes, chipmunks, roe deer, squirrels; we have observed it in birds, in reptiles, in fish, even in certain insects like the cricket and a species of wasp; the force has been apparent in slime molds so ancient that we have no knowledge of its evolutionary genesis. Yet the force has been anything but apparent to those who intrude on the territories of their fellow men.

"It is high time that social and group psychology began to occupy itself with the physiological side of behavior and more especially with the innate processes," Konrad Lorenz once told a symposium. "Hitherto it is only the demagogues who seem to have a certain working knowledge of these matters." In a way, Lorenz was right, for it is the demagogue's intuitive knowledge of what men are—as opposed to what they think they are or are told they are—that manufactures his principal stock in trade and perhaps makes possible his success. But for once Lorenz was in part wrong: while the master politician seems acutely aware of how far the forces of outward antagonism will go toward unifying his own people in support of his rule, history offers few evidences that he is equally aware of what the same forces will accomplish with his enemies.

In 1940, when Carpenter completed his investigations of the primate social territory, history was arranging an exhibition of incomparable gore and variety to demonstrate, one might conclude, the human validity of his findings. In the space of a few years the laboratory of war provided almost every possible combination of territorial intrusion and territorial defense. Shock and immediately applied overwhelming power might crush the defenses of a nation: it was the essence of the blitzkrieg. Poland, Norway, and the Netherlands fell, for the multiplication of territorial resources, as we have seen, cannot be extended indefinitely. Or a major population which the world had come traditionally to regard as a nation might turn out to be a *noyau*.

The fall of France shocked the world far more, I suspect, because of the collapse of the French will to resist than because of the failure of French arms. In the most profound recesses of our animal-subconscious minds—of our visceral brain, as someone once described it—we take for granted the territorial imperative (in our friends; in our enemies it is known as fanaticism) though we have no name for it and we live in a culture that would deny its existence. The French collapse seemed a kind of cry against nature, an evolutionary sin for which the French have been demonstrating guilt and neurosis ever since. And yet, one must suggest, the fall of France was an event less dramatic in territorial terms than evidence would warrant. France in the years between the wars had slipped, like Italy, to the status of a *noyau*, the society of inward antagonism which it yet, in all probability, remains.

Whatever may account for the French territorial collapse—the vulnerability of the *noyau*, the shock of the blitzkrieg still redolent of terror, the emasculation of a people by World War I—it was the last territorial collapse of World War II. The succession of events to follow—in which Pearl Harbor, shattering though the blunder may have been, was still just an incident—gives us the classic demonstration of the intruder's inability to assess properly the multiplied powers he confronts. While the intruder faces always the temptation to estimate an opponent nation as indeed a defenseless *noyau*—and he may very well be right—still the record indicates that the intruder who counts on a fall of France with every territorial invasion lives dangerously indeed.

One is apt to forget about Finland's Winter War, while at once hoping that the Russians will not. When in modern times has an insignificant nation met the intrusion of a great power with such resolve? The free world thrilled, as it will and must always to the spectacle of any David facing any Goliath. One lacks the imagination, however, to apprehend the consternation which must have gripped the Kremlin when, out to accomplish a bit of minor larceny, it had to witness its divisions being slaughtered in the snow-gripped Finnish woodlands. Why did Finland fight? No explanation less than ten million years old can provide a significant answer.

I mentioned in passing the Battle of Britain. If one asks, why did Finland fight? there is a shadow of an answer in the truth that the Finns had nothing to lose: it was fight, and at the worst be destroyed; or surrender, and at the best be devoured. No shadow of an answer greets the question, why did Britain fight? With Hitler in control of the Continent, the British for all their power were as isolated, as helpless, as hopeless on their islands as the Finns in their forests. It is this quality of inspired lunacy that so distinguishes the defense of a social territory. The British had every sane reason to accept an accommodation with the Germans which Hitler, many believe, was eager to offer. Hitler, on the other hand, had every sane reason to anticipate acceptance. If nothing else, German devotion to the principle of economic determinism, which had so limited the mind of Karl Marx, would direct an Adolf Hitler to regard the British as a nation of shopkeepers, and nothing more. That they should turn out to be a nation of madmen was beyond calculation. One can only reflect that what human reason must regard as madness, relative to our living to a ripe old age, evolution—careless concerning the fate of individuals—may regard as utter logic relative to the survival of populations. Britain fought. A world survived.

In our terrifying laboratory, the Second World War, we watch the repeated spectacle of predatory powers, directing the most sophisticated war machines which the mind had yet devised, colliding blindly again and again with energies galvanized and organized by an animal instinct the existence of which would have been denied by the most learned minds of the time. I have said enough about the Japanese and Pearl Harbor. A less-remembered episode in southern Europe is equally revealing.

Benito Mussolini was one of the century's more imposing cynics. His prestige was created in equal parts by world credulity, fineness of Italian calculation, and magnificence of lung power. I live in Italy, and I have acquired the most humble respect for that superb Italian capacity to discriminate between the demonstrative and the dangerous, to pursue the *bella figura* with minimum risk of its decorating a *bello cadavere*. And I find it impossible to believe that a man like Mussolini would have invaded Greece had he not regarded the invasion as an in-the-bag, one-hundred-percent, falling-off-a-log sure thing. The little Greek army, undoubtedly recalling Marathon and Thermopylae, stopped the Italians at the first mountain ridge. It was the most embarrassing moment of World War II. A furious Hitler, preparing for his invasion of the Soviet Union, had to rescue his partner. From that moment on, Mussolini ceased to exist as a figment of anyone's imagination other than his own.

Greece was crushed by German arms, as Poland had been crushed, as Norway had been crushed, as the Netherlands had been crushed. The social territory commands its partners to join against an intruder though chance of success be nonexistent. If the inexplicable multiplication of power which territory vests in the proprietor is insufficient, the defense of course will fail. Territory cannot of itself provide miracles, but it can provide inconveniences of a superb order. Hitler encountered such an inconvenience in Greece at a most inconvenient hour. Greek unreason, combined with a Yugoslav passion for nonsense, combined to put Hitler's invasion of Russia five weeks behind schedule.

In the logical elaborations of hindsight it is easy to lose one's focus on the uncertainties of the past. That the Soviet Union with all its might and immensity survived the German on-slaught may seem inevitable today. It seemed impossible at the time. I was working with the overseas division of our Office of War Information through the period, and while there must have been those who had their hunches, I can recall no reputable authority who expected of Russia anything but total collapse. Within a few weeks after the invasion, a prominent American magazine published an analysis, *in the past tense,* of how Hitler had conquered Russia. The issue of that magazine is a treasured object for collectors today. And while American inability properly to assess the Russian will to resist may have been influenced by our antipathy for the Soviet political system, still this cannot explain the world's underestimation of the Finnish will to resist, or of the British will to resist, or of the Greek will to resist, or of the Yugoslav will to resist, or, for that matter, of our own will to resist.

Our side's failure to comprehend the force which in the end would save us had no effect on the course of the war. We acted by instinctual command. Whether we were enlightened or ignorant, self-aware or self-deluded, whether we acted in the light or we acted in the dark, we should have in any case acted the same. But the same cannot be said of the intruder.

I suggest that had the leaders of the predatory powers in World War II known what in the end they would be up against, the war might not have taken place. I recognize that human capacity for folly has a splendor all its own. I recognize that no human gift carries quite such unimpeachable authority as that of self-inflation, and that Adolf Hitler, Benito Musso-lini, and the Japanese military clique were all so singularly gifted. None, however, were true fools. All were men of war who made a business of war: who laid their plans with care, totted up their machines and their manpower, their resources and their deficiencies, made estimates of their potential enemies as they made estimates of themselves, and concluded from balance sheets, however wishful, just what they could get away with. But it seems to me a pity that the compounding powers of territorial defense could not have been included in their statistics of aggression.

The record of the Second World War suggests total ignorance on the part of intruders as to how defenders were likely to behave. The record likewise suggests that were men fashioned from those designs which we so fashionably suppose, then the balance sheets of aggression would have been neither wishful nor inflated but precisely correct. Were we creatures of the conditioned reflex; were we products solely of our environments; were we beings revolving like slow solar systems about this sun or that, this sexual organ, that material interest, or yonder parental circumstance: were we any of these things, then the design of man would have fitted nicely the designs of aggression, and a world that was ours would today be somebody else's. But we were more than these things; and in aggression's miscalculation of man lay the margin of aggression's failure.

Any species is a contemporary expression of the total of its evolutionary potentiality. The complexity of the human past is rivaled only by the complexity of the human present; and so man must be regarded as incalculable. From an inquiry into a single innate pattern of human behavior we shall gain few precise formulas to feed into the computer of the human future. We shall be unable to guess, for example, what would have happened in 1940 if France had possessed an alpha fish of the order of a Churchill, a De Gaulle, or even a Joffre. The incisively different responses of the Belgians in the two wars, in the first led by Albert I, in the second by a nonentity, would point to the importance of an alpha fish in the territorial tank. About such matters as these we cannot speculate without valid knowledge of the social mechanism. But this we may say with definition: the presence of a single, dominant, even magical individual in a society would be meaningless were there not in his social partners a territorial imperative awaiting release.

Man may be incalculable. But within his potentiality are knowable ingredients which may combine. They were unknown to the intruders of the 1940's, as they are unknown to the intruders of the 1960's. Twenty-two years after Dr. Carpenter's last return from the rain forest to the century's intellectual wilderness, it was still possible for a military adventurer to approach catastrophe lacking the roughest estimate of the territorial imperative's lunatic dimensions.

We need not stir about among buried recollections to recall that in the autumn of 1962 an irreproachably innocent Kremlin directed the secret mounting of nuclear missiles in certain shy Cuban preserves. Since the missiles were directed at various American capitals, they constituted a territorial intrusion of magnitude. The Americans, however, were believed to be fat, they were rich, they were preoccupied with the material things of life, they were politically divided at home and diplomatically irresolute abroad. That they were all of these things is indisputable, yet such indulgences did not add up to a *noyau,* for American society was not held together by inner antagonisms and we remained a biological nation. The threat was revealed. And while a helpless, watching world suffered a succession of cold sweats and heart attacks, the American put his Cadillac in the garage, returned his two-inch steak to the frigidaire, turned off the television set and the air-conditioning, kissed his wife and his children and the stock market goodbye and marched as one man to the confrontation. The Soviets withdrew. And the world in a dead faint was carried out of the ball park.

None can fail to be grateful to a Kremlin willing to admit its error, and with its withdrawal publicly to accept a humiliation from which Soviet prestige has not yet recovered. No man alive, however, has the right to expect that the next intruder will have the willingness or the capacity to accept a comparable humiliation. And so we face a choice of clear order: we may provide ourselves and all aggressors among us with more reliable information on which to base our estimates of man; or, when the moment of truth arrives, we shall be permitted to take our seats in the last grandstand and to put our hands over our ears. We shall have had it coming. We shall have been selected out.

243

3

Territory is not the cause of war. It is the cause of war only in the sense that it takes two to make an argument. What territory promises is the high probability that if intrusion takes place, war will follow.

In his *Essays on Human Evolution,* published soon after the last world war, Sir Arthur Keith expressed his view that to discover the causes of war one need look no further than to territory. His final great work a few years later, *A New Theory of Human Evolution,* incorporated the territorial principle into a general hypothesis regarding the emergence of man from his subhuman primate ancestry. It is the only major work in which the modern concept, denied Darwin when he wrote *The Descent of Man,* is fully explored as a force playing on our origins and on the development of modern and ancient societies. Much of it is cluttered; much of it leaps to conclusions which we know today are unjustified; much of it records the thoughts of a very old man who, knowing that he is committing to print his last words, commits too many: yet among modern studies in anthropology it stands as a masterwork, a memory of the time of the giants. But the final great work by the greatest of anthropologists was published in 1948 when the dogmas of environmentalism had begun to establish their cartels in the traffic of learning, and so the masterwork remains all but unread.

Much of Keith I agree with, but I do not accept and have not accepted his conclusion that territory is the cause of war. I have been frequently misinterpreted, although I wrote clearly in *African Genesis:*

> I should suggest today that Sir Arthur . . . spoke too soon. The more recent revelations of our African beginnings have contributed factors more starkly terrifying than simple territoriality to the animal instincts directing our behavior. In contrast, the drive to gain and defend a territory, even to live in undying hostility with one's

neighbors, must be interpreted . . . as a conservative force in the broad panorama of species.

Later in the book I added:

But the drive to maintain and defend a territory can be regarded not as a cause but only as a condition of human war. One can recognize its workings in the fury of a Finland attacked by a monstrous large enemy; in the madness of Hungarians attempting to reassert their land's integrity; or in the lonely, irrational heroism of the Battle of Britain, when never did so many owe so much to so few. These were defensive social actions taken in strict accordance with territorial law and deriving from profound instinct the unbelievable magnitude of their energy. But in every case territory was the *condition* of war, not its cause.

Since I wrote these lines, our new knowledge of monkeys and apes has underlined the conservatism of the territorial principle. The biological nation we have seen emerge as at once the maximum guardian of a population's integrity and the maximum source of social amity as a product of outward antagonism. But in primate societies the biological nation as guardian of security has perhaps been too perfect, for it has sacrificed stimulation, the second of territory's psychological functions. The fun, one might say, has gone out of the border. The concerted defense of a border by forty, fifty, or a hundred animals leaves the intruder in a condition less stimulated than stupefied. And so the more sophisticated and highly evolved among primate species—the great apes, the baboons, the langurs, the vervet, rhesus, and Japanese monkeys—no longer intrude but maintain each other's exclusive space by avoidance.

If this be so—and I am speculating, since we possess no fossil record of ancient behavior to confirm this evolutionary progress from defense to avoidance—then a great red question mark must overhang the human species: Why has man, with all his intellectual resources, been incapable either through intuition or instruction of absorbing a lesson so obvious to monkeys and apes? Why do we still intrude when the consequences are apt to be more painful than paying?

Primate example is not quite so speculative as lack of a fossil history might indicate. Washburn has estimated that in two years we shall have doubled the material we now possess, whereas two years ago, for lack of observations, it was difficult to teach a class in primate behavior. It is a time, today, of chilling risk to make sweeping generalizations concerning not only the behavior of primates but the evolution of that behavior. Nevertheless, strong hints have already accumulated. Pairs like the gibbon and callicebus intrude and defend with all the enthusiasm of gulls or moor hens. The noisy, belligerent biological nations are confined to species forming groups of moderate number, whereas with the exception of the rhesus the more potentially powerful societies—larger and stronger as individual animals, or larger and stronger in numbers—have substituted avoidance for defense, outward indifference for outward antagonism.

The student of man, perturbed by the future of human warfare, by the apparently inviolate laws of territorial conflict, and by human reluctance to abandon the intruding way, may find the baboon the most instructive of species. Among primates his aggressiveness is second only to man's. He is a born bully, a born criminal, a born candidate for the hangman's noose. As compared with the gorilla—that gentle, inoffensive, submissive creature for whom a minimum of tyranny yields a maximum of results—the baboon represents nature's most lasting challenge to the police state. He is as submissive as a truck, as inoffensive as a bulldozer, as gentle as a power-driven lawnmower. He is ugly. He has the yellow-to-amber eyes that one associates with the riverboat gambler. He has predatory inclinations, and in certain seasons he enjoys nothing better than killing and devouring the newborn fawns of the delicate gazelle. And he will steal anything. The thief of Africa harbors an insatiable appetite for everything a farm can provide, from maize to orchard fruit. Men and baboons have been at war since the farmer black or white first planted a crop. But the creature has cunning. Raiding an orchard, a troop shows little

fear of women. Should, however, an outraged farmer appear disguised in a woman's dress, the troop will spot him at hundreds of yards and go over the hill.

It is this animal—this oversized terrestrial monkey whose ways are so uncomfortably reminiscent of man's—who has proved just how brilliantly the primate alliance of body, brain, and highly organized society can be made to pay off. It is this animal—with his gang of implacable thugs at the top, also so unpleasantly reminiscent of man—who has proved how effectively tyranny and fear may socialize the most incorrigible of rogues. Yet K. R. L. Hall, S. L. Washburn, and Irven DeVore, in a combined 2000 hours of published observations of the most aggressive of subhuman primates, never witnessed a single demonstration of territorial conflict. Exclusive ranges are large, so large that there may be overlap around the edges. But troops maintain exclusiveness by avoidance. Even at water-holes they ignore each other.

Has the baboon learned, as man might learn, that intrusion on a social territory defended by fifty or a hundred members is an experience so unrewarding as to be best not attempted? Should this be so, then the experience must have come about so long ago that avoidance has become a segment of the baboon's innate behavioral equipment; the observers witnessed no example of juveniles learning through the punishment of experience. Or, on the other hand, is the baboon simply the way he is because it is the way he always has been, thus offering no evolutionary hope for intruding man? A single observation points to the optimistic conclusion that the baboon is as territorial in his responses as the most belligerent of proprietors, and that it is experience, probably ancient, that has brought peace to his kind.

Some time after Hall had completed and published his study of the chacma baboon in the Cape of Good Hope, he shifted his attention to the patas monkey in northwestern Uganda. Ronald Hall was widely regarded as the world's foremost student of primates in the wild; perhaps it was because of his energy, perhaps because of his attitude toward science, which combined formidable imagination with the formidable objectivity of a hard-nosed Chicago cop. It was in the superheated bush-and-savannah country lying at the bottom of the Rift Valley that we met and, for reasons unclear to either of us, became instant friends. Later, in the spring of 1964 on his return through Rome, he described the incident which for him had been of such highly dramatic order.

Since baboons and patas monkeys in this area frequent the same regions, Hall had been keeping an eye on his old loves as well as his new. The patas troop moves so rapidly, it takes an energetic observer to keep up with them. Nevertheless, Hall had become familiar with all the baboon troops in the area, knew their ranges and approximate populations. Then one morning, pursuing his patas group, he came on a troop of baboons feeding peacefully in the heartland of another troop's range. He knew that the resident troop was small, numbering no more than twenty-five. The intruding troop was large, over twice the size. He had never witnessed such a deep intrusion, nor to his knowledge had Washburn or DeVore. The residents were away somewhere on their range, far out of sight. What would happen when and if they returned? The potential drama was too much for Hall. He let his patas go their way, and settled down to wait.

The morning slipped past into the stunned, low-altitude African noon. The baboons before him, all up in a clump of trees gathering fruit, continued to feed peacefully. Then it happened. Over a distant yellow rise came a few young males, the normal vanguard of a baboon troop in movement. They sighted the intruders, started barking and advancing. And that was all that was necessary. The feeding trees rained baboons like palm trees their coconuts in a sudden tropical storm. Within minutes the intruders were a mile away.

In Hall's opinion it had been territorial behavior in the strictest sense: the attack of the defenders despite all odds; the instant recognition on the part of the intruder of the proprietor's rights; the panic flight. The intrusion, so rare in baboons, may have come about by accident, by oversight of leadership. But the incident had demonstrated that baboon peace is maintained not by unwillingness to defend, not by lack of that innate territorial command dominating the lives of roebuck and gibbon, three-spined stickleback and great-crested grebe, but simply by unwillingness to intrude.

An innate compulsion to defend one's property lies, of course, at the heart of the territorial principle; but just as close to its heart lies recognition of the rights of the next animal. And this too must command the attention of the political scientist, the statesman, or any student, amateur or professional, whose thoughts turn to the human future. Stephen Gartlan, until Hall's death one of his students at the University of Bristol, spent almost two years in the midst of Lake Victoria on an island inhabited only by himself and 1500 vervet monkeys. It is thirty miles to the nearest landfall on the Kenya shore; when and how the ancestors of the present vervet population became isolated on Lolui Island we do not know. Natural increase, however, has brought about conditions verging on overcrowding, for the island is but eleven square miles in extent and only its margins offer vervet comfort. The troops have divided this margin into territory-ranges little over an acre in size, and Gartlan has told me that the borders are so clean and so permanent that they could be marked with whitewash. Every economic pressure would seem to impel intrusion. Yet Gartlan never observed territorial conflict or defense. A troop on infrequent occasion might intrude along the edges of the next troop's property but it would flee at the sight of the residents.

Jean-Jacques Petter on Madagascar watched black lemur groups, regularly leaving their territories to seek water, skirting the borders of other groups' properties though it meant taking the long way around. Durward Allen and his students from Purdue University have watched for season after season two packs of timber wolves on a huge island in Lake Superior. The wolves have divided the island into hunting territories, one approximately double the size of the other. The large one is occupied by a pack of fifteen or sixteen animals, the smaller by a group no larger than three or four. Yet the large pack is never to be found on the smaller pack's domain, despite the minimum resistance which the small pack could offer. Farley Mowat found the same recognition of rights among Arctic wolves on Canada's forsaken Barren Lands of the Keewatin Peninsula. In one of the most hilarious yet penetrating books on animal behavior ever published, *Never Cry Wolf,* he records the arrival of visiting wolves at the local pack's borders. Sniffing, nose rubbing, and tail wagging denoting friendly intentions are dutifully, even ceremoniously, exchanged. And the visitors in all hospitality are issued their visas.

A comparable ceremonial gathering was witnessed by P. O. Swanberg in his remarkable observations of a remarkably specialized bird, the thick-billed nutcracker. The bird lives in Swedish pine forests, nesting in holes in the trees, but gains its living from adjoining hazel woods. For thirteen years Swanberg kept track of his pairs on their exclusive domains and never witnessed intrusion except just before nesting time. Then all the local proprietors would gather on the homestead of an amiable host in what Swanberg could only interpret as a ceremonial festival.

With or without ceremonial exception, we witness the observation of property rights in species after species. Baumgartner watched great horned owls in Kansas. Never so far as he could observe did they leave their hunting territories. Loye Miller watched the same great predatory birds in California's San Bernardino Mountains. He learned to imitate their calls, and to coax them to follow him; but he could never coax them to cross the neutral strips into the next pair's hunting territory. Bushmen may wound an animal in the Kalahari desert; but, famished though they may be, they will not follow it if the animal crosses the neutral zone into the next band's territory.

We have seen in all our collected observations of arena, pair, and social animals the inhibition that saps the confidence of the intruder: it is recognition of the proprietor's rights. And almost from the beginning of territorial observation students have jotted in their notebooks the evidences of a sense of wrongdoing on the part of the lawbreaker. Long ago Kenneth Gordon reported the behavior of a thief on a territory adjoining his camp in Oregon. This was one of the Douglas squirrels that frequent

the towering stands of Douglas fir. The proprietor of this territory was 200 feet overhead, busily occupied with scaling cones in the crown of a fir, quite unable to see what was happening on his borders below. Scales fluttering down testified to his location and to his preoccupation. Yet when the thief intruded to steal a cone on the ground, his movements were furtive, hesitant, nervous, "guilty."

Even longer ago Stevenson-Hamilton, founder of South Africa's renowned Kruger game reserve, reported on the obvious "guilt" of a blue wildebeest intruding on the exclusive pastures of another herd. And that hard-nosed observer of the callicebus monkey William Mason has recorded the same behavior on the part of the thief in a *noyau*. Normal intrusion, we may recall, is formal, takes place at an appointed hour, and will never occur unless the neighboring proprietors are present to contribute their share to an elegant row. But after hours and for other purposes intrusion takes a far different form. The callicebus *may* be tempted to steal a bit of fruit from his neighbor's estate. He will accomplish the larceny alone, when no one from either his own side or the other can observe him. And "guilt" again becomes the only word to describe his actions. Furtive, alert, nerves a-popping, he will consummate his theft and leap back to the portion of the earth's surface where his presence violates no rights.

The austere Niko Tinbergen, in his *The Study of Instinct,* condemns subjective interpretations of animal actions: "Because subjective phenomena cannot be observed objectively in animals, it is idle either to claim or deny their existence." And yet so objectively demonstrated is this universal recognition of territorial rights that in a later book he was moved to write: "Trespassers are personifications of bad conscience; territory owners those of righteous indignation."

I have said that at the heart of the territorial principle lies the command to defend one's property, but as close to the heart lies recognition of the next animal's rights. But we may state it in another way, from the viewpoint of the intruder. Fundamental to the territorial principle are two opposing impulses: there is the urge to intrude on the property of one's neighbor, and the urge to avoid it. Out of the basic psychological need for stimulation or the alluring temptation of loot, the balance will be swung in favor of intrusion. But if the life of a species keeps the animal too busy gathering hazelnuts in far-off thickets or provides him with such hazards and natural excitements as abundantly to fill his daily quota of thrills, or if some defensive asset of the proprietor—shocking fangs, appalling claws, a murderous disposition, or the concerted ranks of a biological nation—renders loot unlikely and excitement suicidal, then the balance of innate command will be swung toward avoidance. Animal treaties will be signed. Rights will be not only recognized but honored. Uninvited guests will be few.

There is nothing in the territorial principle to deny peace among nations. The student of man's evolutionary nature may ask his great-aunt to embroider the statement on fine linen, that it may be framed and hung on the wall where once hung the testament HOME SWEET HOME. Nothing in animal example or primate precedent offers any but the conclusion that territory is conservative, that it is invariably defensive, that the biological nation is the supreme natural mechanism for the security of a social group, and that when intrusion becomes maladaptive and no longer of selective value to a species, the territorial imperative will itself command its abandonment.

The question, then, must again arise: Why do men intrude? And once more we must remind ourselves that we are not the descendants of these monkeys and apes which today we so assiduously observe. We are distant, distant cousins with our own ancient line of evolutionary experience and selection. And once more we must remind ourselves, too, that as man is not all sex, and not all economics, and not all cultural tradition, and not all a pot rounded on environment's wheel, so he is not all territory. We are also predators.

4

The Miocene was an epoch of world-wide benevolence. Rain was abundant; lakes brimmed. Forests were richly disposed, lending comfort of leaf and fruit to their arboreal inhabitants.

Modern grasses took root as never before. Broad were the prairies, green the pastures, fat the grazing creatures who dined thereon. And in this fortunate time the ape that would someday be man spoke his evolutionary farewell to the ape that would someday be chimp or gorilla.

It was a.long time ago. The Miocene ended as best we can reckon about twelve million years ago, to give way to the deepening despairs of the drought-ridden Pliocene. Good times had lasted long, however—almost twenty million years. For the human mind to comprehend such spacious vistas of ensuing seasons is a challenge as formidable as the counting of milestones lying between stars. Time and space may yield to our mathematics, but they become as one in their defiance of our perceptions. And yet, with a reality as true as tomorrow or the fall of next autumn's bright leaves, the Miocene passed like infinity's procession through twenty long millions of years. Animals bred, died. Generations of horses and mice and monkeys joined the ancient democracy of death. The advancing shore of life formed new coves, new sea cliffs, or clung to old broad seemly beaches facing out on posterity's unknowable sea.

We went our way. We left our bones on this old mountainside or beside that lake. More and more we lived beneath the open sky, less and less beneath the forest canopy. We were the adventurers, the seekers after farther fields, whereas our cousins of the forest remained the conservators of the arboreal primate traditions. Luck and circumstance combined, here and there, to preserve our bones for a fossil eternity. Rarely in the depths of the forest, amid the rot and disintegration of broken bough and fallen leaf, could the arboreal ape anticipate such immortality. Fragmentary though knowledge of our own history may be, our knowledge of his is less.

Even from these bits and pieces, however, that have come to us from most ancient of days, we may demonstrate or deduce a few fair certainties. When in the midst of the Miocene, twenty or twenty-five million years ago, our hominid line renounced the arboreal way to embrace a life on the ground, we accepted hazards and opportunities, stimulations and social necessities of an order quite different from life in the trees. The ruthless commands of natural selection would press us one way, press the ape of the forest another. We retained the vulnerable primate body, but any mutation favoring survival on the hostile earth would spread through the generations to whole populations, through the ages to entire species. Our feet flattened, our backs straightened, our buttocks strengthened their muscular arrangements to permit us to run. And as more and more we became specialized earthlings, so more and more it became anatomically impossible for us to return to the arboreal life. Such trends take place in an evolving world. A minor alteration of behavior and body, a change of equivocal value, may command that further genetic alteration be of increased specific value until a course is determined, and horses are set upon their way, men upon theirs. Now evolution becomes irreversible.

As important as our anatomical adjustments to the terrestrial life were the psychological changes which such life commanded. Shyness is a luxury permitted the mountain gorilla in his high, remote, cloud-softened bamboo thickets. The modesty once demanded of the tiny, primitive mammal in his monster-dominated times retained a value in the lives of jungle primates with profound green tangles of vine and leaf in which they might vanish. But for the ape of the field in those long-gone Miocene times, hiding places might be far from hand. Not unlike the baboon today, the aggressive spirit became a survival asset. Time and again we had no alternative but to stand and fight. And the social necessity, since the time of the true lemur a primate compulsion, doubled and redoubled its survival value.

So we, the developing hominid, found ourselves committed to a course quite unlike our ever more distant forest cousins. We scratched for a living. Like the baboon we became omnivorous. Apes and monkeys in their forest home might retain their dependence on fruits and shoots. We came to eat anything. In all likelihood, long before the Pliocene presented all primates with a climatic crisis, we developed a certain taste for meat. The savannah chimpanzee, Jane Goodall has learned, will kill a young bushbuck or monkey and devour it with utmost relish. The baboon when fortune presents him with a victim will do the same, and when the season is right will become a systematic predator. Neither, however, is dependent on meat, and neither, probably, were we—not so long, at least, as the mellow Miocene brought to our table a copious larder.

Millennia passed upon millennia. And something new came into our lives—new in the history of primates—and the new thing was freedom. Our growing adaptation to life on the ground gave us the freedom to move anywhere; our growing independence from any single source of food made us free to adapt to this environment or that; our growingly aggressive spirit gave us the freedom to dare, to explore. It is a quality in animals which ten years ago we should have dismissed with raised scientific eyebrows. But now we know that in countless species there is an innate compulsion to explore, lacking either the pressure of deprivation or the seeking of economic reward. Adventure—there is no other word for it—satisfies the basic need for stimulation. Whether we sought adventure in the old lost golden days, we cannot know. But we were free to. And then came the Pliocene.

The prime time of a good, ripe earth slowly vanished. Seasonal rains on the high African plateaus became shorter and more irregular. Old lakes shrank; rivers became less dependable. Forests diminished, and with them the primate populations imprisoned by forest necessity. Grasslands spread, and impenetrable deserts like the Sahara and the Kalahari made of certain African areas impassable seas of sand. Perhaps these were the days when the ancestral baboon took to the field, and certain monkeys like the patas and vervet found marginal accommodation to terrestrial life. But we do not know anything for sure. So dry became the Pliocene that the fossil record vanished. There was not enough water to provide the lime to turn bone into stone.

We who complain of a drought lasting four or five years, what shall we say of a drought that lasted, with deepening ferocity, for ten or twelve million? And yet it was the time that saw the making of man as we know him. He became a carnivore. The grasslands still teemed with those edible grazing creatures prepared by evolutionary fortune to survive on the Pliocene's scant offerings. Perhaps at first we scavenged the kills of the lion and cheetah and leopard, and we competed with hyena and jackal and vulture for the crumbs of the kills. We retained our omnivorous way, our taste for roots and tubers, when we could find them, and for berries and edible greens; even the chimpanzee when he is consuming a monkey will after each bite eat a leaf, just as man, today, will eat salad. But we became dependent on meat as our main source of sustenance, and sooner or later we became systematic hunters.

When exactly did it happen? Again, we do not know. It was Raymond A. Dart who discovered man's predecessor in the hominid line, southern Africa's small-brained australopithecines, and it was Dart who formulated the theory of the predatory transition from ape to man. And in the past five years —in the same period when, as with a burst of stage lighting, science has illuminated the lives and the dramas of monkeys and apes—science has likewise gone far to illuminate the hominid stage on which the human drama was prepared. The spectacular discoveries of Louis S. B. Leakey and his family in East African fossil beds have confirmed the theories of Raymond Dart. But they have not informed us as to just when proto-man became a predator, dependent on his hunting life for survival.

I have regretted in these pages that we must confine our thoughts to the subject of territory and cannot stray far into the evolution of society and the influence of animal dominance on the ways of modern man. But I have little regret that for another five years I may postpone an inquiry into the relation of predator and prey and its significance to our evolutionary behavior. In *African Genesis* I predicted that Tanganyika's Olduvai Gorge would prove to be the Grand Canyon of Human Evolution. Then it was all but unknown; five years later it is besieged by tourists. What will happen in the next five years to our knowledge of human evolution, no one can say. Discoveries pile on discoveries. For lack of time, adequate scientific descriptions are lacking. Authorities disagree as to interpretation; contradictory statements appear in the scientific press. It is a poor time indeed for lasting conclusions.

In our concern for territory one deduction, however, will probably prove unshakable: with the coming of the hunting life to the emerging hominid came the dedication to territory which we regard as human. S. L. Washburn and V. Avis, just before the rush of discoveries, stated admirably the effects of the hunting life:

Hunting as an important activity had three important effects on human behavior and human nature: psychological, social, and territorial. Man takes pleasure in hunting other animals. Unless careful training has hidden the natural drives, men enjoy the chase and the kill. In most cultures torture and suffering are made public spectacles for the enjoyment of all. The victims may be either animal or human. This behavior is strikingly similar to that of many carnivores, and no parallel behavior has been observed in wild primates. . . . Hunting not only necessitated new activities and new kinds of cooperation but changed the role of the adult male in the group. Among the vegetarian primates, adult males do not share food. They take the best places for feeding and may even take food from less dominant animals. However, since sharing the kill is normal behavior for many carnivores, economic responsibility of adult males and the practice of sharing food in the group probably result from being carnivorous. The very same actions which caused man to be feared by other animals led to more cooperation, food sharing, and interdependence of the group. . . . The acquisition of hunting habits must have been accompanied by a great enlargement of territory since the source of food was now more erratic and mobile.

They conclude:

The world view of the early human carnivore must have been very different from that of his vegetarian cousins. The interests of the latter could be satisfied in a small area, and other animals were of little moment, except for the few that threatened attack. But the desire for meat leads animals to know a wider range and to learn the habits of many animals. Human territorial habits and psychology are fundamentally different from those of apes and monkeys. For at least 300,000 years (perhaps twice that) carnivorous curiosity and aggression have been added to the inquisitiveness and dominance striving of the ape. This carnivorous psychology was fully formed by the middle Pleistocene and it may have had its beginnings in the depredations of the australopithecines.

I have quoted Washburn at length because of his broad knowledge of man's place in the natural world. He published these thoughts in 1958, just before Leakey's discovery of the australopithecine *Zinjanthropus* in the Olduvai Gorge. That discovery led to the uncovering of *Homo habilis* in the oldest sediments of the gorge and publication in 1964. Whether *habilis* is in fact man or an advanced australopithecine is a matter of scientific dispute, and largely one of semantics. But neither his antiquity nor his manner of life is disputable. He lived about two million years ago, an age corroborated by two independent means of radiogenic dating, fission-track and potassium-argon. And he was a hunter.

The predatory life, and with it the human commitment to territory, was pushed back a few ages with the discovery of

Homo habilis. A small, agile, toolmaking being with a brain half the size of modern man's had flourished in East Africa a million and a half years before the demonstrated presence on earth of those developed beings which we might call true men. And he had lived at least in large part by killing, as the litter of bones on his living site bears testimony. But how much earlier had the way of the killer been the way of man's ancestors?

It is at this point that we encounter just one of those confusions and ambiguities so characteristic of the new discoveries. In his early announcements and at two lectures which I attended in London, Leakey emphasized that the fossil bones of creatures found at the early living sites were of small animals, giving indication that *Homo habilis* was an awkward and inexperienced hunter, and that the predatory way was new. But in 1965 the Cambridge University Press published the first of a series of definitive volumes on Olduvai Gorge, its geology, its climates, and its fossil remains. And in this Dr. Leakey refers to the presence of *Bovidae,* that zoological family which in Africa includes all manner of buffalo and antelope. And he writes:

> Fossil remains of *Bovidae* are exceedingly plentiful in the Olduvai deposits. There are two reasons for this. In the first place *Bovidae* normally represent a high proportion of the total animal population of most African habitats other than dense forest. Consequently it is only to be expected that fossil remains of this group should outnumber those of any other. Secondly, the vast majority of the fossils which we find in the excavations come from living-floors or camp-sites of prehistoric man and represent the remains of his meals. Man apparently preferred the flesh of *Bovidae* to that of many other groups, as he does throughout the world today.

At the end of his long and exquisitely detailed examination of the extinct genera and species of *Bovidae* which have been found and so far described, he writes:

> Perhaps the most remarkable fact that emerges so far is the scarcity of fossils representing the smaller members of

the *Bovidae,* for example the duikers, the dik-dik, the oribi, the steinbok and the klipspringer. This cannot be due to the bones of these species being small and possibly escaping notice since thousands of bones of much smaller size are in the collections. There must therefore be some other and at present unexplained reason for the scarcity of small antelope remains on the living-floors of the early hominids.

Despite our most clinging antipathies concerning the antiquity of man's predatory ways, or our most personal prejudices against acceptance of Raymond Dart's thesis, so long held, so long rejected, that the selective necessities placed on ancient killers accomplished the transmutation of ape to man, there must seem to the layman no unfathomable mystery about the scarcity of small antelope remains on the living-floors of early hominids. *Homo habilis* killed ancestral buffalo, eland, kudu, and wildebeest because they had more meat on them than the ancestral duiker, dik-dik, oribi, and steinbok. And far from being a beginner at the killing game, far from being as first described an awkward pursuer of dassies and rabbits, this pygmy-sized predator of the high savannah, two million years ago, was a skilled and successful hunter of what man today would still call big game. One must surmise that he had been practicing his trade, even then, for quite some time.

We killed animals ten or twenty times our size. Did we kill each other, or was this some later and more manlike innovation? When Leakey first announced his sensational discovery but had not yet concluded that his find deserved the title of *Homo,* he told a Washington press conference that the child— *Homo habilis* was perhaps twelve years old—had been murdered. The headlines glared; so did his colleagues. Leakey had offered science no evidence to support his claim. Nor did he ever to my knowledge repeat the claim in public or provide appropriate evidence. The sensation died away. Few realized that the murdered child, called by Leakey "pre-Zinj" in 1961, was 1964's *Homo habilis.* But I have examined the fossil, and the once-living being died of a radiating fracture of the skull.

Did the youngster run into a tree on a dark night? The fracture is centered on top of his head, an awkward situation for such an injury. Did a stone roll down the steep slopes of the gorge to score a direct, unlucky hit on his crown? There was no gorge two million years ago; the site was then a flat plain beside a lake.

Leakey was correct, I believe, when he issued his original statement, and until convincing evidence is offered to the contrary, the supposition must remain that the earliest known specimen of our probable ancestry died from a blow by a probable weapon in the hands of another of our probable ancestors. But why this most significant attribute of the world's most famous and significant fossil should be consigned along with other skeletons to the concealing darkness of the human closet remains any man's guess.

Back in 1910 William James anticipated the new anthropology when he wrote, "Our ancestors have bred pugnacity into our bone and marrow, and thousands of years of peace won't breed it out of us." Man is a predator of long predatory origins, whose predatory nature has shaped much that we are. We cannot in this brief digression inquire into the nuances of our predatory past, nor do our rapidly accumulating, hastily interpreted evidences yet permit such inquiry. But we may be permitted, nevertheless, certain broad conclusions:

The dependence of our small-brained hominid ancestors on the hunting life may date back perhaps millions of years into the demanding, desiccated Pliocene. So long have we been hunters that a specific instinct has become part of our evolutionary equipment. Even Tinbergen grants, "The human male is a hunting animal."

Unarmed and unarmored because of our primate legacy, we were pitifully equipped for offense or defense on the hostile savannah. In the mid-Miocene we still retained, like today's baboon, formidable canines, our fighting teeth. But the adoption of the weapon in the hand reduced such teeth as redundant. The canines of *Homo habilis* are as small as modern man's. And a startling fossil from Kenya's late Miocene, fourteen and a half million years ago, shows the same reduced canines. Were we armed, perhaps defensively, even at that date?

We were small, we were vulnerable. We could have hunted large game successfully only in bands with certain, reliable leadership and certain, reliable co-operation of individuals willing to risk death for the success of the band. The way of the chimpanzee was not for us.

As we were predators, we were also prey. While we hunted the grazing creatures of the savannah, so the carnivorous creatures hunted us, for we were edible. There is little reason to believe that in those far-off years before the development of sophisticated weapons the lion regarded emerging man with fear, or as anything other than a proper luncheon.

That we preyed on each other is probable, and rests on evidence broader than the fractured skull of some forgotten youth. Cannibalism has been a prevalent pastime throughout all of the human record. Half a million years ago Peking man left the first real assemblage of true man's remains in the caves of Chou Kou Tien. The skulls had been opened to extract the brains.

Faced by equivalent necessities for successful aggression and successful defense, the hominid band faced ultimate necessities for social amity and co-operation and maximum exercise of primate wit. Are we to wonder that emerging man turned to the biological nation, the defense of a social territory, and a society of outward antagonism to weld his numbers into one?

From his beginnings in Miocene days through the deprivations of the desperate Pliocene and on into the vagaries, the glaciers, the pluvials of a Pleistocene blowing now hot, now cold, now wet, now dry, the evolution of man has brought him to his present estate: he is the world's most successful predator, and the richest of all the world's prey.

Are we to wonder that man intrudes?

5

The île Rousseau is not much over a hundred yards in diameter and it is covered by poplar trees that in midsummer drop a deep clear shade on the island and furnish intense contrast to the shining lake. Whether one should say that the island rises in the middle of the Lake of Geneva or in the middle of the River Rhône is a matter of taste; the lake at this point is narrowing so rapidly into its outlet, the Rhône, that one cannot be sure. A long flat bridge with a bend in the middle—the shape is that of a dog-leg fairway on a golf course—connects the two halves of the city of Geneva and makes of the island a leisurely moment of stock-taking at the point of the bend.

When I first moved to Europe I lived for two years at one end of the bridge in a venerable hotel which, mourned by many, was later torn down. On my occasional visits since then, I have found it rewarding to stop at a hotel at the other end of the bridge. Despite not infrequent times of despair and disillusionment which I associate with Geneva and share with the world, I love the city. And despite those cherished animosities which I lavish on the man for whom the island was named, I love the Île Rousseau. It provides for the traveler as it provides for the bridge a rare moment of stock-taking, a contemplative opportunity to watch nothing but swans go by.

It was in this lovable Geneva that, on a recent trip back to Rome from somewhere, an airline strike grounded me for a day or two. There are joys that one never seeks but must have forced upon one. I read my newspaper under the plane trees of a favorite riverside *place;* I consumed slices of that orange cake which only the Genevoise seem to know how to make; I drank *renversé,* the local concoction of hot milk and coffee which is not *café au lait* and is not *cappuccino.* I walked in the *Jardin des Anglais* and recalled with something like affection the summit conference of 1955 when Eisenhower met here with Bulganin and Khrushchev to settle some territorial disputes; their affable accord—it was called the Spirit of Geneva—lasted, as I remember, for about six weeks. And I recalled with greater melancholy a night when the city of peace and reason lost its self-possession. Hungarian dreams had been blasted in Budapest by 4000 Russian tanks. Every light in the city was turned off. I had never seen the Swiss weep before, nor have I since. But the Genevoise, that night, dressed themselves in black and marched in silence through their darkened streets. There was no sound but the shuffle of feet, and the slow, grave tolling of the great deep bell in the cathedral up on the hill. Men wept that night, and old walls too.

You sit in the shade of the poplars on the Île Rousseau, or take a table in the islet's little restaurant. You order a *Punt e Mes* or a second-rate omelet. A swan slides past in state. You take stock, look back with nostalgia on a city that ever so briefly was once your home. It was never reason that failed in this city of failure so world-renowned; it was unreason. Sentimentality, ignorance, hypocrisy, illusion—these have been the legions that marched and countermarched on the fields above the shining lake. On the parade grounds before the *Palais des Nations,* savagery could pass in the gowns of civilization, brutality in the disguise of man's nobility, greed and relentless self-seeking on the stilts of high purpose. Here on this neutral ground spies of all nations could meet to sell each other secrets, and diplomats to exchange human rationalizations of animal demands. Self-delusion, the final lie, has been amply tried here and amply found wanting. Truth and reason, on the other hand, have seldom been tested.

It is a paradox of sorts that one who defends the primacy of instinct in the transactions of man finds himself defending the primacy of mind as well. In the course of meditation I have found it necessary, now and again, to invent new terms or give new meanings to old ones. So broad is the no man's land between the natural and the social sciences, between reality and romance, that there does not exist even a common vocabulary. I have kidnapped from ethology certain terms like alpha fish, pecking order, displacement activity, territory itself, and in their human application I have adhered to strictest biological definition. I have never, for example, extended the concept of territory beyond its biological meaning, defense of an area of space. But in other situations there exists no vocabulary at all. And so I have introduced such terms as the *noyau* and the biological nation, and the societies of inward and outward antagonism. I have spoken of a biological morality to describe that conduct dictated by innate command which sacrifices individual interest for a larger or longer good, and soon I must turn to the amity-enmity complex.

So it has been that I have introduced the terms closed and open instincts, more sharply to define those innate patterns of behavior common to all higher animals which to complete their patterns must gain information from individual experience, from home and school and the street. A Frenchman must learn that he is French: the passion for territory is inborn, its borders learned. The German must learn to speak German: his capacity to speak and his necessity to communicate with his kind are innate, but the words he must learn. And so it is that one who defends the primacy of human instincts defends the quality of human mind that in the end will complete the innate patterns.

The failure of Geneva has been symbolic of a world-wide failure of mind: the failure to recognize those inborn patterns which human experience must fill. We have led our children to believe that babies are born good, and that if subsequent behavior leads them straight to the jailhouse the fault must be somebody else's; we have not spoken of that Intruding Man lying within every human heart, and for which every human being must assume responsibility. We have many of us encouraged our children to believe that Territorial Man is a disgrace, a creature of greed and cruelty. We have not mentioned that Intruding Man and Territorial Man are fraternal twins, born on the old, dry African savannah, the Cain and Abel of the inmost human psyche.

Geneva is a symbol: here we enshrined our fallacies, entombed our futures. Truth was never explored, never displayed, never tested. Why not? Because, I believe, we could afford the luxury of lies. The fate of nations might be always at stake, but never the fate of man. Such times are gone. You and I know that we live in years of strange grace. It is a time of peace enforced by terror, an era without precedent since those terrestrial apes who someday would be man first emerged from the forest galleries of the African Miocene. It is an interlude which mathematical probability dictates must end at some unpredictable date in ten or a hundred years—or even tomorrow—when the wheel stops and the ball falls on double zero, when the house wins and all customers lose, and total accident or total cynicism at last finds us out. We face, in other words, Judgment Day. And when the day comes, natural selection must make a grave decision. For all of its show and all of its splendor, just how much has the natural experiment with the big brain been worth?

The great apes have failed. The orangutan, the gorilla, the chimpanzee proceed at varying pace toward an extinction hastened but not caused by man. No remote destiny, no orthogenetic favor reaching down through the billennia from the time of original animation dictates that man's fate will be unlike the gorilla's. Every species comes equipped with its own Judgment Day when changing environments demand a balance sheet of total assets and total liabilities. Man's uniqueness among species rests on his capacity to perfect the arrangements for his own Judgment Day, instead of waiting for nature to do it for him.

In this interval of the second chance, how shall we conduct ourselves? Shall we continue on the course of falsehood, accomplishing with remarkable consistency the precise opposite of our best intentions? Or shall we with all resolve and courage look into our most secret hearts and, allying the wisdom of old natural forces with that intelligence which has made us men, trust that a hand will reach into the game and·stay the wheel as the ball nears double zero? If we dispose such trust, then we must know, of course, that the game will continue. *Homo sapiens* must learn not only to live with a final fear, but to use it. He must recognize that from Hiroshima to eternity he will live and behave in full knowledge that the Judgment Day of his own invention awaits his error and will demand an inventory any beclouded morning.

One cannot be neutral in the conflict of falsehood and truth. One cannot sit out these years of grace on an islet however refreshing in the middle of Geneva's failing waters. Beside us the lake's intense blue shades off into river green. Across the way on the left bank's quai stately buildings sit shoulder to shoulder like dowagers at a New Orleans carnival ball; they watch the dance but take no part. Beyond and above lies the Old Town with its cathedral and its memories of Calvin. But you and I must go: you and I must dance.

8. The Amity-Enmity Complex

Plutonium is a substance which does not normally occur in nature. You can make it, though, out of uranium, a widely spread ingredient in the earth's crust. If you make enough you can even ask in your friends, make sure that the children are sleeping soundly, sing a few sad songs, and blow up the world.

Concrete is another substance which cannot be obtained from nature. But since it is put together from some of the commonest stuff that we have about us, if you have the right formula—not a complicated one at all—you can make enough concrete to build a new world.

Amity is still another substance which if it exists in nature occurs in quantities insufficient to be useful. It too must be made. For fifty or sixty million years our primate family has been experimenting with techniques for manufacturing the stuff. Those species which survive have been uniformly successful. Those species which failed to survive have left us no exact information. Perhaps some were so clever that they became romantics and, believing that amity grew on trees, saw no need to manufacture it: so they died of social starvation.

The process for the manufacture of amity is simple enough, requiring almost no brains at all, as the lemurs have demonstrated. Its formula a child can grasp, and to emphasize its simplicity my wife has inscribed the equation of the amity-enmity complex on children's blocks:

$$A = E + h$$

The amity, in other words, which an animal expresses for others of its kind will be equal to the sum of the forces of enmity and hazard which are arrayed against it. By enmity I refer to those forces of antagonism and hostility originating in members of one's own species. By hazard I mean those threats which do not originate in one's own species. They may be natural or they may be supernatural. There is the threat of the predator, for example. In the life of the baboon, leopards and men and pythons may be regarded as natural hazards. In the life of the bird, snakes and hawks may dominate his natural fears. In the life of the emerging hominid, to such predatory hazards as lions and wild dogs and cheetahs and leopards was added the powerful defensive equipment of his prey, the horns of the buffalo and kudu, the fangs of the hippo and baboon, the trampling feet of elephant and rhino. For the emerging hominid there were also hazards commonly afflicting all animals: drought and the vanishing of old accustomed water holes, floods and the raging of rivers, cold and blizzards that paralyzed all life. And as man rose higher along his evolving way, he encountered hazards uncommon to his fellow animal: pests that denuded his fields, predators like wolves and foxes whose victims were his livestock rather than himself and his kin. Storms at sea afflicted his journeyings, fire attacked his home and his forests, drought and flood raised new hazards to existence. As higher and higher rose his technology, accident arrived as a major threat, natural in its random meanderings. Wrecks of cars, trains, and aircraft dotted his new experience with hazard. All for the moment or for the month brought forth amity among men.

And we must not forget the supernatural hazard, as real as the natural so long as men believed. Witchcraft and hexes, omens and portents, the thunder of Jehovah and the slyness of Satan, sulphur and brimstone and the afflictions of the hereafter, all powerfully affected the way of man. Whether our hominid ancestors had the capacity to dread the hazards of the supernatural, we cannot yet know. In the history of human affairs, however, they made an honorable contribution to social amity, and the fact that they lose force in our enlightened times is no reason to demean their memory.

Such are the varieties of hazard that may be summed up as *h* in the amity-enmity equation. But it is *E*—enmity, hostility, antagonism, aggression, however you may care to express it—that is the major ingredient in amity's making, for *E* grows truly on trees. Hazard is fluctuating in supply, unreliable in quality, temporary in effect. Enmity is the gold of amity's market, the magical fiber in amity's thread. Without enmity we should be nightingales and no air to tread on, three-spined sticklebacks and no water to fin through, the larvae of Capricorn beetles and no tree trunks to bore into. Without enmity we primates should be lost and forgotten along with the pterodactyl, for workable amity is our strand of life weaving ineffective bodies and limited brains into a multipatterned fabric of lasting strength, cohesive in its functions, legitimate in its grandeurs. Primates, fortunate creatures that we are, have the privilege of spinning this artificial stuff from an ingredient omnipresent in nature, a commodity that grows on every bush and tree, that flourishes in every glen, on every highland pasture, along the water meadows of every seeking stream, in this black forest nook, on that bright rocky height, in the blindness of moles and the seeing of eagles, in the butting of cows and the coughing of leopards, in the challenges of mice and the defiance of lizards: hostility for others of one's kind.

I do not deny that amity exists in nature, as there is a trace of gold in all sea water. We have even seen one social group, that of the chimpanzee, where amity seems the dominating force, drawing individuals together through nothing much but good nature. And there may very well exist in species some residual force of amity which through long association presides on its own. If so, then we may speculate that such innate or residual amity multiplies to slight degree that amity which is a product of enmity, and to a greater degree that amity which occurs in the face of hazard. And letting *k* stand for such natural amity, we may rewrite the equation more accurately and in a fashion comprehensible only to mathematicians:

$$A = k(E) + k_2(h)$$

And we may promptly forget it. I am speaking of workable amity, of effective social amity that enhances the survival prospects of the individual and the population. (We must not forget that in the face of danger the amiable chimpanzee hides himself without warning his partners.) The factor of innate or residual amity, k, whether we use it to multiply simply or by its square, will affect our equation too little to be of significance And besides, let us when dealing with fine points keep in mind that the equation has been introduced by means of children's blocks. I am reminded of my oldtime friend and adviser in such matters as these, William Fielding Ogburn. He was a superb sociologist and chairman of the social sciences at the University of Chicago. And Ogburn's friendly advice was homely indeed: "Never take a trend out a window." We may remind ourselves that since the human being is an incalculable stew of evolutionary endowment, individual genetic variation, and personal experience never common even to identical twins, so man lies beyond all mathematics. $A = E + h$ is presented for purposes of illumination, not definition. As an equation it is an expression of probability, not determination. If we are to pursue this particular trend out the window, then it would be better by far that we left it undisturbed on the floor of the kindergarten. So let us get back to the amity-enmity complex in its most general terms.

Enmity is the biological condition of cross-purposes. It is the innate response of an organism to any and all members of its own species, and enmity will be suspended, totally or partially, only for such period of time as two or more individuals are embraced by a single, more powerful purpose which inhibits all or part of their mutual animosities and channels the inhibited energy into a joint drive to achieve the joint purpose. Since amity persists no longer than mutual purpose, then when the purpose is either achieved or permanently frustrated, amity will end. Unless a new joint purpose arises to channel joint energies, individuals will return to a normal condition of mutual animosity.

I am sure that in a generalization so broad, the ethologist, with an eye on species lacking any discernible capacity for foresight, would prefer that I speak of appetite and consummation rather than purpose and achievement. And in truth, if we think of our own sexual behavior, it becomes a little grand to speak of sexual purpose to describe what occurs in the eyes of a man and a woman when they look at each other in a wondering way. It is a little pompous to speak of achievement when hostilities have been suspended and energies channeled, and a wondering look has been converted into a mutual orgasm. Yet the pattern has been followed. With consummation, amity will vanish and hostilities and suspicions will be resumed unless rewards have been such as to arouse further mutual desire. It then becomes an affair. But sooner or later the affair will end; he will go his way, she hers, rarely with residual amity. New mutual conditions, of course, may have come to dominate their lives: children, marriage, home, the pair territory. Only when defense of what is mutually theirs turns their antagonisms jointly outward may we properly speak of effective social amity.

While I grant the real distinction between appetite and purpose, I do not believe that it significantly affects this discussion. Neither do I believe that the human psychologist, with an eye on learning and the conditioned reflex, may raise significant objections. He may ask: Does not the habit of association and the habit of acting in concerted fashion contribute a measure of permanence to amicable arrangements? Granted that enmity is the root of all goodness—a concession which he is unlikely to make—will there not be some conditioned residue of affection, loyalty, trust that will continue to motivate the pair, family, or larger social group even when common defense no longer unites them? Must there always be enmity? What about love, for God's sake?

I hasten to confess that I have nothing against love and indeed should lack the courage—a most salient point—to contemplate existence without it. But I do not believe that long association in amity or long conditioning of individuals to a habitual way contributes measurably to the human outcome.

The mother-infant relationship prevails in exquisite amity—

for a season. Shall we inquire of a jury of mothers what normally happens when the season of dependence fades? Or for the value of long association in amity we may glance at two well-told tales. Amity may have prevailed in a family for a lifetime, in a marriage for decades. Yet when death strikes the one or divorce the other, the innocent bystander watches in dismay. One would have had no clue that anything but affection, loyalty, trust, and civilized understanding dominated relationships. Yet all in a dirty twinkling such sentiments vanish. Property is king. Bitterly, resentfully, contestants face each other while each tries to jerk from the hands of another this old table, that old tray of silver spoons.

Roe deer, not unlike certain wise observers of human nature, take the outcome for granted. As the doe with her fawns drifts down through the forest toward the winter browse, and the buck returns from his autumn's wanderings, they well may meet on some dusky afternoon when nights grow long. He will not know her, or she him. No tears will dampen the fallen leaves nor recriminations soil the woodland's stillness. As nature permits these summertime lovers no recognition in the fall, so she endows them with an animal wisdom: where goes real estate, there goes love.

The amity-enmity complex need not be the product of the territorial principle, for we must not forget the factor h in our equation. Simple arithmetic will demonstrate that to produce a given quantity of amity in a social group, every increase in hazard which the group faces reduces the need for enmity. As h goes up, so E comes down. A human community facing extraordinary hazard may well have no need of enemies at all to attain the most perfect social amity and concerted action. This, however, has not been the common human circumstance. The amity-enmity complex has been the behavioral mechanism innately commanding the defenders of a social territory threatened by Intruding Man. With every addition to the value of E, there has been produced an additional value of A. Our propensity for preying on our own kind has commanded the identity of territory and the amity-enmity complex.

The territorial imperative may have fashioned one biological morality for this species, another morality for that. But the territorial principle has perfected the amity-enmity complex as the supreme morality for ours.

2

Three examples will sufficiently show, I believe, that the amity-enmity complex works in other than primates as smoothly as in higher animals. The first of these was carefully observed in Chicago's Jackson Park, a locale intimately familiar to me in those younger years when I had graduated from the monument works but had not yet obtained a ticket for more distant rock piles. The park faces Lake Michigan and there was the shore with a veritable surf, there were curving paths between tall oaks and elms, there were green dells leaping with veritable squirrels, and there were the broad winding peaceful lagoons. It was a good green sort of place when all else you had was the South Side's bleak geometry. I can only wish that in my time, as in Dale Jenkins' later time, the lagoons and the islands had been set aside as a bird sanctuary.

Jenkins must have been another student of Allee's at the nearby University of Chicago. By the 1940's the lagoons were attracting geese and ducks as permanent residents. There were Canada geese, lesser snow geese, blue geese; there were mallard and wood ducks. All species of geese and ducks belong to a family called *Anatidae,* and they row with each other as freely as if indeed they were members of a single family. Through an autumn and winter of observation Dale Jenkins' chief attention was on a family of blue geese—a father and mother and two almost fully grown juveniles—and its relation with neighbors whatever the species. The blue-goose family held a lagoon territory about thirty-five feet in diameter, surrounded by six territories held by twenty-six larger Canada geese. The blue-goose family could not abide Canada geese and would tolerate no least intrusion. If the Canada geese were away feeding, the family might on occasion allow snow geese or even a pair of their own species on its paddling territory. But if the Canadas returned, the blues would chase everyone away. What irritated them most, in traditional territorial style, was the neighbor whoever he might be.

The record of the terrible-tempered blue-goose family was unassailable. They dominated the much larger, much stronger Canada geese in every instance, even twice when the family of four faced simultaneous invasion by all twenty-six neighbors. The family finished the season with what we call in American baseball a shut-out: they had pecked the Canadas 259 times and had never been pecked back. Their less violent response to other species had paid off approximately as well. They had shut out mallard ducks 44–0, and all other ducks 13–0. They had taken a few pecks from their fellow blue geese, but had still won, 99–6. The snow geese they blanketed, 185–13. Their record for concerted action was as impeccable. The four attacked as a group, and when faced by challenge on two borders, at once divided forces as occasion demanded.

One may admire such handsomely successful outward antagonism, but it was the consequent inward amity that deserves the silver cup. While in the course of the autumn and winter the family dealt out some 600 pecks to its enemies, the members delivered two to each other; and even these, between the family's young folks, Jenkins records as doubtful. And while the skeptic may protest that no relationship of cause and consequence has been established, and what we have observed may well have been the natural action of a naturally loving, amiable, co-operating family, my answer must be of the gentlest sort. Never since animal records have been kept, never certainly since Noah ushered his passengers aboard the ark, has history recalled the hatching of a naturally loving, amiable, co-operative goose.

Another unreasonable bird, with an unreasonable name as well, is the smooth-billed ani, an aberrant member of the cuckoo family. D. E. Davis, today a colleague of Carpenter's at Pennsylvania State University, spent 1300 hours in the field studying the bird's most exotic behavior. The smooth-billed ani lives in groups containing from seven to two dozen adults jointly defending a social territory, it forms a true biological nation complete with amity-enmity complex, and the females lay all their eggs in one nest which the whole group builds co-operatively. Hens take turns brooding and when the young are hatched, all or most join the feeding.

The primate may have achieved triumphs of social amity in the defense of the young, but no monkey or ape ever faced the problem of putting all its eggs into one basket. For the smooth-billed ani there is amity or there is extinction. And so there is amity. Never in his long observations in Cuba did Davis witness discord. Everybody preens everybody. If one should be injured, all crowd about in intense excitement. The group has a large social territory, perhaps ten acres, but it sleeps together in a single tree or bamboo clump. Territorial defense is total, including all adults and all juveniles.

And that defense is ferocious. An intruding individual will

be chased by a member of the group, by a relay of members, or by the group as a whole. As a robin will attack a stuffed decoy, so the smooth-billed ani will destroy and tear to fragments a decoy placed on the property. A live decoy will be killed by the group even though at the same time a man threatens the collective nest. Hierarchy of instinct determines that territorial defense and outward antagonism come first; inward amity will follow. If a brood must be sacrificed in the process, then social integrity will have been preserved and another brood may be raised. It is a hierarchy of instinct with which warring man is not unfamiliar.

Another kind of community in which the amity-enmity complex has been exploited for all its worth is the prairie-dog town. It is a social organization resembling that of modern man more acutely than does that of any primate. John A. King, in the early 1950's, made one of the lasting American contributions to ethology with his study of a town in Custer County, South Dakota. His town spread out over seventy-five acres with a population of about 800, a number so common to the reproductive communities of population genetics. But what is unique and perhaps ideal about the prairie-dog town is that it manages to apply the pattern of the *noyau* to the competition of biological nations, while at the same time achieving defensive co-operation.

Each nation—each coterie, to use King's terms—has a territory up to an acre in size, with forty or fifty burrows. All members are free to use any burrow. King divided his town into "wards," and in Ward A, his study area, there was a population of about sixty divided into four major coteries. In each coterie one male will be dominant and will spend much of his time patrolling boundaries. He will lead all actions of defense and be the first up in the morning and the last in the burrow at night. If a social partner gets into a border row, he may drive the partner away and carry on the fight himself. Not even in the baboon troop does the gang at the top assume greater responsibility.

Defense as a rule, however, is a joint affair enlisting all males, all females, and all maturing young. It is aroused by a special cry which draws response *only* from the members of the coterie. It is a cry quite distinct from a series of short barks warning of the approach of a hawk, a golden eagle, a coyote, or a man. This the whole town responds to, standing alertly on their mounds if the predator is ground-borne, diving into their burrows if airborne. Here is one *noyau* which has managed to eat its cake and have it too. Since the alertness of but one pair of eyes is sufficient to warn the entire community, the *noyau* is well-nigh invulnerable. But since its organization is that of a society of inward antagonism, security is achieved at no loss of stimulation.

That stimulation is intense. Within the town, the intrusion of one nation on another is normally accidental, or at the most experimental. But conquest occurs. In the prairie-dog town we encounter the only equivalent of human conquest that has ever come to my attention. Two male lions once entered the Nairobi game reserve, drove out all other lions, and took the place over for themselves. They were extraordinary lions. When C. R. Carpenter first established his colony of rhesus monkeys on an island in the West Indies, groups established territories, and one, led by an alpha male of enormous dominance, continually intruded with success on neighboring preserves. When the male was experimentally removed, the group no longer trespassed. Restored, he again led it on the path of conquest. Carpenter's experiment has impressive significance for man but later research has revealed that in rhesus life the conditions were artificial, that territorial defense is abnormal, and that defense was probably inadequate. Also, Garibaldi was a remarkable monkey.

Among all my notes on territorial behavior, these are the only exceptions to the rule that territory is a mechanism entirely defensive. The lions and the monkeys involved special circumstance; prairie dogs involve none. As in the history of Intruding Man, the threat of conquest is normal, continual, and resting on ingredients neither exceptional nor artificial. Every leader seems aware of the quality of defense put up by neighboring coteries. There is constant probing. Any symptom of illness, disability, or social instability will be rewarded by invasion. Just as defense unites all members young and old, so invasion will be the work of a coterie's entire ensemble. And it may succeed. A portion of a neighboring property may be added to the domain of the successful.

Such enhancement of territorial animosities through the threat of conquest has had a consequence in achievement of amity comparable to few animal societies. If $A = E + h$, then the enhancement of E has produced an enhancement of A. The vigilance of defenders is constant. The responsibility placed on the leader is never neglected; neither need he exert the least threat to obtain discipline. As in the smooth-billed ani, there is much general nibbling and grooming among members. They play together. And there is the famous prairie-dog kiss. The kiss came about, I should assume, as a means of identification in the dark recesses of one's burrow to make sure by proper flavor that no stranger has sneaked in. Whatever its origin or selective value may be, when two members of a coterie meet, they exchange what is very nearly a human kiss, open-mouthed, and they seem to enjoy it. But the value of extraordinary amity to prairie-dog society may be measured in terms more quantitative than the arguable pleasures of kissing. In King's Ward A, fifty-eight pups were born the first season, and only one failed to survive. I know of no animal parallel.

A prairie-dog town is like some realistically idealized human society, some entire civilization. Within the civilization, nations compete even to the ultimate inimical threat of conquest. As in a giant *noyau,* ultimate stimulation is achieved through ultimate competition. And since the competition is among biological nations, the amity-enmity complex generates within the groups those social imperatives of co-operation and individual sacrifice essential for security and identification. Yet enclosing the entire community of competing nations, as certain rules and regulations and tacit understandings might ideally unite a civilization against threats from without, are the barks and innate responses understandable to all. The hawk is anticipated, the coyote foiled. Hazard is rightly if innately comprehended, and enmity is suspended.

The prairie-dog town is a wonder of nature, in its rodent

fulfillment perhaps impossible of attainment by that most afflicted of primates. man.

3

The amity-enmity complex is the resolution of a paradox posed by Darwin, solved by Wallace, explored by Spencer and Sumner, revived and extended by Keith, and for the last twenty years cast aside under the pretense that it does not exist.

The paradox may be simply stated: If the evolutionary process is a merciless struggle among individuals to survive, with natural selection determining the fittest, then how could such human qualities as altruism, loyalty, charity, and mercy have ever come into existence? If Darwinian evolution presents a picture of dog eat dog, then how did dogs ever get together?

The newcomer to the history of evolutionary thought may with difficulty apprehend the stress that this single question has placed on philosophy. How can man's ethical values be a product of the evolutionary process? How can there exist, for example, such a human factor as conscience if natural selection demands of the individual self-dedication that he may survive?

I shall not belabor the question, since the perceptive reader of these pages is probably by now far ahead of the answer. But there is a danger that this same perceptive reader will take the answer for granted. Philosophy does not. To account for man's undoubted moral nature, a variety of suppositions have been advanced: that man is at constant war with the evolutionary process; that his mind has delivered him exemption from evolutionary law, and that natural selection takes place now only in the field of ideas; that intervention, divine or cultural, has created a gap between man and other animals. All or some of these suppositions, to a degree which you cannot guess, combine to provide your children with their education and to provide you, in your daily life, with dubious solutions to the problems which surround you.

All, of course, are false. What seems to have occurred to no one, excepting possibly Keith, is that the animal is a moral being, and that human morality is a simple evolutionary extension of a form of conduct which has existed in nature for many hundreds of millions of years. But unless we inspect both the history of the falsehood and the history of the truth, we shall not in least part grasp our contemporary predicament. Let us look at the history of the truth first, since it is simpler and lamentably brief.

Alfred Russel Wallace was Darwin's great but neglected contemporary, co-originator of the theory of natural selection. And it was he who gave preliminary resolution to the paradox just a century ago. The answer lay not in selection between individuals, but in selection between groups.

When Charles Darwin published *The Origin of Species,* almost undoubtedly he saw evolution as a dog-eat-dog proposition. At the end of his chapter on instinct he wrote:

> No instinct can be shown to have been produced for the good of other animals, though animals take advantage of the instincts of others. . . . [There is] one general law leading to the advancement of all organic beings,— namely, multiply, vary, let the strongest live and the weakest die.

These were not sentences buried in a prolix tome. Modern biologists may explain that the Darwinian view was of a milder order, that it was a gentler conflict in which the more successful left to succeeding generations a more numerous offspring. All is true. But I am a playwright, and for what a play is all about I look to what is said when a curtain falls. Darwin let a curtain fall on an inflammatory definition. And I can understand why his apostle T. H. Huxley interpreted Darwinian evolution as jungle law. I can understand too the pessimism that Darwin inspired in many a Victorian mind, and why Tennyson wrote his famous line, "Nature, red in tooth and claw."

The Origin of Species was published in 1859, *The Descent of Man* in 1871. Between these dates something happened to Darwin's thinking. Group selection entered his appraisal of possibilities. Wallace had bowed to Darwin as the legitimate father of the theory of natural selection; now Darwin bowed to Wallace as the author of the theory of group selection. The bow was clear, obvious, self-effacing. But by 1871 few cared. The melodrama of nature, red in tooth and claw, had become the television serial of the time. An audience accustomed to the gorier interpretations of evolution wanted more gore, not less. Intellectuals growing accustomed to the pangs of pessimism wanted more pangs, not fewer. But I, a century after Darwin, live in a world wherein gore and disaster have become human commonplaces. Pessimism, under the rule of a *Pax Britannica,* was a dirty little luxury which any could afford; under a *pax atomica* it carries small selective value.

Chasing down the original statement of Wallace's thoughts is a chore recommended only for those with a free week in London. He had presented his paper to a meeting of London's Anthropological Society, then only three years old, on the evening of March 1, 1864. It was printed in the young society's *Journal,* and I at last found a copy extant in the guarded library of today's Royal Anthropological Society in Bedford Square.

One must brush through a deal of topical slag to reach the Wallace iron. But it is there. The great but forgotten naturalist, who described for us the beauty of New Guinea's bird of paradise, describes for us the significance of evolution's group selection:

> In proportion as physical characteristics become of less importance, mental and moral qualities will have increasing importance to the well-being of a race. Capacity for acting in concert, for protection of food and shelter; sympathy, which leads all in turn to assist each other; the sense of right, which checks depredation upon our fellows . . . are all qualities that from earliest appearance must have been for the benefit of each community, and would therefore have become objects of natural selection.

Wallace's thought failed to impress those members of the society present on the evening in 1864. The president, a Dr. Hunt, commented that "some members of this society are accused of bringing forward speculations, but none have yet brought forth anything a thousandth part as speculative as this." The thought nonetheless impressed Darwin. In *The Descent of Man* he wrote:

> When of two adjoining tribes one becomes less numerous or powerful than the other, the contest is soon settled by war, slaughter, cannibalism, slavery and absorption. . . . [But:] When two tribes of primeval man, living in the same country, came into competition, the tribe including the greater number of courageous, sympathetic and faithful members would succeed better and would conquer the other.

Neither Wallace nor Darwin conceived of the principle as applicable to the prairie dog, the howling monkey, the true lemur, the blue goose, the smooth-billed ani. They saw it as a characteristic of human evolution once man became approximately man. Even so, the principle was laid down that in group competition, amity will have a selective value comparable to that of enmity. The profound abyss between biological evolution and human ethics was provided with a bridge. Yet the bridge was ignored. T. H. Huxley failed to consider it when he presented his Romanes lecture, "Evolution and Ethics," in 1893. He could do no better than to conclude that civilization must be eternally at war with the evolutionary process.

One thinker who did not ignore the bridge was Herbert Spencer, Darwin's contemporary and the philosopher most influenced by evolutionary thought. Since his name is associated with the concept of social evolution, modern sociology holds him in low esteem. We may remind ourselves, however, that he was the man who thought that there could be no infidelity to compare with the fear that the truth will be bad. Spencer gave us the phrases "the code of amity" and "the code of enmity."

The dual nature of man has puzzled philosophers since philosophy began. In the same individual we find infinite capacity for tenderness, sympathy, charity, love, and infinite capacity for cruelty, callousness, destruction, hate. Herbert Spencer saw it as the natural consequence of the life of social man, who must obey two codes: there is the code of amity, which he must honor in his relations with his social partners, and the code of enmity, which he must honor in his relations with the outside world. He follows them unthinkingly, since he has no alternative. Let enough members of a society disobey the code of amity, and the society will fragment; let enough disobey the code of enmity and the society will be crushed.

Another nineteenth-century thinker whose views on the human paradox resemble those of Spencer, but whose reputation has survived somewhat better, was Yale's William Graham Sumner, economist, anthropologist, sociologist. At the turn of the century he gave us the terms "in-group" and "out-group," and neither has vanished from circulation. Sumner came very close to a formulation of the amity-enmity complex:

> The relation of comradeship and peace in the we-group and that of hostility and war towards the others-group are correlative to each other. The exigencies of war with outsiders are what make peace inside, lest internal discord should weaken the we-group. These exigencies also make government and law in the in-group, in order to prevent quarrels and enforce discipline. Thus war and peace have

reacted on each other and developed each other, one within the group, the other in the inter-group relation.

Profound though their insights were, the weakness of both Spencer's and Sumner's thought lay in the assumption that they were dealing with qualities peculiarly human. Sumner seems to have felt that education, travel, and growing human sophistication would finally make impossible the primitive, parochial in-group mentality. Oddly enough, it is Spencer, the evolutionist, who seems by some quirk to have clung to a belief in man's original good nature. He saw the code of enmity as something laid onto man, something that history must one day wash away. Neither was around, of course, to witness the major entertainments of the twentieth century.

Sir Arthur Keith was the last of the line. Even by the 1940's he had become an obsolete man, a living fossil, a poignant leftover reminding us of a day when honesty, courage, and intellectual ruthlessness were qualities generally admired. "Human evolution is based on injustice, and man's mentality has been biased to make him the willing subject of the dual code." We do not say such things today—or not out loud. "We are ready to believe all that is good about our friends, all that is bad about our enemies. Our minds are enslaved to our prejudices to a far greater degree than is usually thought." His devotion to evolution was without reservation: "A living group is but a link between a dead ancestry and an unborn progeny."

As the last of his line, Keith was the first to see that the territorial concept lends biological unity to Spencer's dual code, to Sumner's in-group and out-group. Keith immediately perceived the implications of Carpenter's work on gibbons and howlers. "Every territory is an evolutionary cradle," he wrote. He had small patience with anthropology's growing vogue of studying kinship relations as a demonstration of the social organization of primal man. "Man must have reached a considerable degree of mental capacity before he could become a genealogist." His allegiance to Carpenter's concept of the social territory led him inevitably to a unified view of duality:

There is no more opposition between the ethical and cosmical codes than there is between the Home Office and the Foreign Office of a Government; the one reacts on the other. The effect of their combined activity determines a nation's evolutionary path and destiny.

Sumner, I believe, would have agreed to this. But Keith's understanding that territory provides the unifying principle led him just as inevitably to a biological interpretation of duality, to rejection of the dual code as something peculiarly human, and to an acceptance of its evolutionary origin. Neither Sumner nor Spencer, unaided by modern studies of animal behavior, could have reached such a conclusion except by sheerest speculation. Keith writes:

> Spencer regarded our mental subservience to the dual code as of recent origin; the code had been practiced and ultimately grafted into our inherited nature. He was confident that the cosmical code [of enmity] would die out and the ethical code would be left in sole control of our actions. I, on the other hand, look on the brain-mechanism which subserves the dual code as of extreme antiquity, for it is obeyed instinctively by social animals low in the animal scale; it is deeply entrenched in human nature.

In his last two books, *Essays on Human Evolution* in 1946 and *A New Theory of Human Evolution* in 1948, Keith took the final, remorseless step which his thinking had made inevitable. Conscience, he affirmed, is simply that human mechanism dictating allegiance to the dual code. Those who assert that conscience is inborn are therefore correct. But just how far does conscience *compel* our actions in such an ultimate direction as that of the brotherhood of man? Not far. Conscience is the instrument of the group.

> Human nature has a dual constitution; to hate as well as to love are parts of it; and conscience may enforce hate as a duty just as it enforces the duty of love. Conscience has a two-fold role in the soldier: it is his duty to save and protect his own people and equally his duty to destroy

their enemies. . . . Thus conscience serves both codes of group behavior; it gives sanction to practices of the code of enmity as well as of the code of amity.

These were Keith's last words on the subject. If the grand old man had any noteworthy capacities for self-delusion, they escape the eye. And when he died a few years later, at the age of ninety, with him ended truth's brief history. His thoughts by then were overwhelmed by the new romanticism, when falsehood came to flower; his sentiments were condemned by that academic monopoly which substituted high-mindedness for the higher learning. And as for almost twenty years no one followed C. R. Carpenter into the rain forest, so for almost twenty years none has followed Sir Arthur Keith into the jungle of noble intentions.

4

In his *Essays* David Hume wrote, "Should a traveler give an account of men who were entirely divested of avarice, ambition, and revenge; who knew no pleasure but friendship, generosity, and public spirit, we should immediately detect the falsehood and prove him a liar with the same certitude as if he had stuffed his narration with centaurs and dragons." That was in 1772. When almost two centuries later Ashley Montagu expressed the conviction, which I quoted in my opening chapter, that aggressiveness is not inherent in human nature but like all forms of human violence is learned, one shudders to think of what Hume's comments might have been. But Montagu, one of the most distinguished of contemporary anthropologists, goes to more specific lengths in another work, in the course of which he criticizes Freud:

> The evidence concerning the biosocial nature of man, as we know it today, does not support the notion of an aggressive, death, or destructive instinct in man. In fact, the whole notion of predetermined forms of behavior in man is outmoded, for man's uniqueness, among other things, lies in the fact that he is free of all those predeterminants which condition the behavior of nonhuman organisms. . . . The evidence indicates quite clearly that everything human beings do *as human beings* they have had to learn from other human beings. . . . So far as the development, by evolutionary means, of aggressive tendencies in man is concerned, the idea can be thoroughly dismissed.

The spiritual roots of such contemporary sentiments go back, of course, to Jean-Jacques Rousseau, Hume's fellow and friend in the eighteenth-century Enlightenment but scarcely his philosophical comrade. There is today no influential mode of fashionable thought which does not, however much it may be disclaimed, go back to Rousseau's original goodness. But the original goodness is modestly attired in a "scientific vocabulary. Montagu discusses the origins of human aggression:

> The evidence is today overwhelming that in order to become an adequate, healthy, cooperative, loving human being it is necessary to be loved. No child is born hostile or aggressive. It becomes so only when its desires to be loved and to love are frustrated, that is, when its expected satisfactions are thwarted—and the thwarting of an ex-

pected satisfaction is the definition of frustration. This is what Freud failed to perceive. What he took to be inborn hostility is, in fact, an acquired form of behavior following upon the frustration of the organism's satisfactions.

I have quoted Professor Montagu at length not because his conclusions differ measurably from those of a majority of his colleagues, but because he expresses them so much more eloquently and concisely. And if he is correct, then amity does indeed grow on trees, and my amity-enmity equation is utterly false. It is enmity which must be manufactured, not amity, and frustration is the machinery of its assembly. In all fairness we must investigate in some detail this competitive interpretation of why men are the way they are.

The frustration-aggression hypothesis is a relatively new interpretation of man. It was conceived by a group of psychologists headed by John Dollard, and born with the publication of their revolutionary book, *Frustration and Aggression.* I quote two sentences from the book's first page, including the authors' italics:

> This study takes as its point of departure the assumption that *aggression is always a consequence of frustration.* More specifically the proposition is that the occurrence of aggressive behavior always presupposes the existence of frustration and, contrariwise, that the existence of frustration always leads to some form of aggression.

Entirely by coincidence, the book was published in 1939, at just about the moment when Adolf Hitler was blowing up his first city, Warsaw. The coincidence failed to dampen the enthusiasm of American psychologists for the book's thesis. The Dollard group must today take immense satisfaction in having exerted a greater influence on psychology, on the social sciences, and on informed lay thought than did Sigmund Freud with his entire life's work. Yet Dollard's name remains relatively unknown, and since the book is available today as an inexpensive paperback, this is one reason why I urge every reader to possess it. No citizen, bewildered by mass violence, by government by demonstration, by soaring rates of crime and delinquency in a time of affluence, by evidences of social irresponsibility on the part of groups both old and young, even by certain trends in the arts, should in his inquiry into first and collateral causes fail to read *Frustration and Aggression,* by John Dollard, Neal E. Miller, Leonard W. Doob, O. H. Mowrer, and Robert R. Sears.

A remarkable quality in this omnipotent classic—almost as remarkable as its treatment of evidence—is its treatment of Freud. As I have quoted, Montagu courageously flayed Freud alive for his refusal to accept frustration as aggression's cause. But in their acknowledgments the Dollard group's first sentence reads:

> Among the many investigators who have struggled with the problem of frustration and aggression special acknowledgment must be made to Sigmund Freud who more than any other scientist has influenced the formulation of our basic hypothesis.

The implication is clear that Freud endorsed the thesis. Did he or did he not? In the labyrinthine bowels of the Dollard book one will discover, if one looks hard enough, that "in recent years" Freud's other concerns turned him toward other explanations for aggression; their gratitude is for his earlier work. That by as early as 1913 Freud had abandoned frustration as the cause of aggression, and that in his final works his opposition to such an interpretation is adamant, rests lightly, it seems, on the Dollard group's premise. What Freud thought about aggression cannot rest lightly on ours.

I am not, as is fairly well known, an apologist for Sigmund Freud. But he brought to human attention three endurable verities—the role of the unconscious mind in human behavior, the role of instinct as the prime energy source in the workings of the unconscious, and the role of evolution in the development of the unconscious mind itself. What more can be demanded of one man, in one career, I do not know. There is a problem, however. Freud's personal preoccupation with a single facet of instinct, sex, had such a sensational reception in a post-Victorian world that the innocent passerby must be on constant guard against it, as against rocks in a riot. But such a natural defensive posture must not blind one to his genius. His perceptions never failed him. Only his explanations, limited by the conceptions of evolution prevailing in his time, ever went awry.

It was in *Totem and Taboo*—a work that in general leaves me with the dark-brown taste of overindulgence the night before—that Freud in 1913 abandoned frustration as a cause for aggression. The sons, frustrated in their sexual desire for the mother, become aggressive and turn against their father in consequence. But why was the father hostile in the first place? That the conflict between generations does not add up to an Oedipus complex is another day's issue. What Freud anticipated was the chicken-yard question: Beta hen pecks gamma hen because beta got pecked by alpha. This may be interpreted as frustration-aggression. But why did alpha peck beta to begin with? Freud was an honest man. He never again went back to frustration as a cause for aggression.

Sigmund Freud's problem was that while frustration came to seem to him naïve as an explanation for aggressiveness, he could find no other ready answer. He resorted to the death instinct turned outward, but it seems never to have quite satisfied him. One looks to his final statements in *Civilization and Its Discontents,* published in 1930, and in his last essays published posthumously as *An Outline of Psychoanalysis.* Is there a clear, independent aggressive instinct or is there not? He writes, in his relaxed way:

> I once interested myself in the peculiar fact that peoples whose territories are adjacent and are otherwise closely related are always at feud with and ridiculing each other, as for instance the Spaniards and the Portuguese, the North and South Germans, the English and the Scots, and so on. I gave it the name of "narcissism in respect of minor differences," which does not do much to explain it.

There is no indication in his writings that Freud had ever heard of the social territory in animal life, yet on the private territory his intuitions are equally clear. He writes, concerning communism:

I have no concern with any economic criticisms of the communistic system; I cannot inquire into whether the abolition of private property is advantageous and expedient. But I am able to recognize that psychologically it is founded on an untenable illusion. By abolishing private property one deprives the human love of aggression of one of its instruments. . . . This instinct did not arise as the result of property; it reigned almost supreme in primitive times when possessions were still extremely scanty.

He turns to more general forms of hostility, and writes of the injunction to love one's neighbor, and the dilemma of strangers:

Not merely is this stranger on the whole not worthy of my love, but to be honest I must confess he has more claim to my hostility, even to my hatred. He does not seem to have the least trace of love for me, does not show me the slightest consideration. If it will do him any good, he has no hesitation in injuring me. . . . What is more, he does not even need to get an advantage from it; if he can merely get a little pleasure out of it, he thinks nothing of jeering at me, insulting me, slandering me, showing his power over me; and the more secure he feels himself, or the more helpless I am, with so much more certainty can I expect this behavior towards me. . . . The bit of truth behind all this—one so eagerly denied—is that men are not gentle, friendly creatures wishing for love, who simply defend themselves if they are attacked, but that a powerful measure of desire for aggression has to be reckoned as part of their instinctual endowment. . . . Anyone who calls to mind the atrocities of the early migrations, of the invasion by the Huns or by the so-called Mongols under Jenghiz Khan and Tamurlane, of the sack of Jerusalem by the pious Crusaders, even indeed the horrors of the last world war, will have to bow his head humbly before the truth of this view of man.

I find myself bowing my head humbly before this view of Sigmund Freud, who did not live to witness the horrors of the Second World War, yet needed no Belsen to confirm his perceptions of eternal truth. And yet, before he is finished, self-contradiction creeps in:

> Never before in any of my previous writings have I had the feeling so strongly as I have now, that what I am describing is common knowledge, that I am requisitioning paper and ink, and in due course the labor of compositors and printers, in order to expound these things that in themselves are obvious. For this reason, if it should appear that the recognition of a special independent instinct of aggression would entail a modification of the psychoanalytical theory of instincts, I should be glad enough to seize upon the idea. We shall see that this is not so, that it is merely a matter of coming to closer quarters with a conclusion to which we long ago committed ourselves and following it out to its logical consequences.

In *Beyond the Pleasure Principle* Freud had come up with the idea of a death instinct constantly working toward an organism's disintegration in opposition to the forces of life, and which when turned against the outside world shows itself as aggression and destructiveness. He now reviews his development of the theory and the controversy which it aroused, and he reaffirms his position. But there is the ambivalence:

> In all that follows I take up the standpoint that the tendency to aggression is an innate, independent, instinctual disposition in man. . . . The natural instinct of aggressiveness in man, the hostility of each one against all and of all against one, opposes the program of civilization. This instinct of aggression is the derivative and main representative of the death instinct we have found alongside of Eros, sharing his rule over the earth.

Freud lived and worked too soon. He wrote most of these words in 1930, just as population genetics and the new biology were coming into being. He died in 1939, in the same social season in which the Dollard group introduced their bastard debutante with the claim that she was sired by the master. The Age of the Alibi applauded; Freud, no man for alibis, would have hissed from the wings. Were he alive and active today, applying his genius, his honesty, his humility, and his courage to the materials of the new biology and the problems of contemporary life, we should witness some wonders. I cannot conceive of the existence of a no man's land between the social and biological sciences were a man of Freud's audacity poking about in its thickets. Nor can I conceive of his greeting the works of Lorenz and Tinbergen, of Howard and Carpenter, of Allee, Hediger, Wynne-Edwards with anything but the vastest cry: "Well, why didn't somebody tell me before?"

Biology presented Freud in his time with nothing but sex, family, and older views of evolution. From this restricted patch he had to dig up answers as to why people behave as they do. Some of those answers were indigestible. If he explained friendship in terms of aim-inhibited eroticism, or the desire to possess in terms of a child's undying attachment to his feces, we must remember that he had no ethology to present him with wider fields of evolutionary choice.

Despite those limitations which the old biology and his own preoccupations with sex combined to place on his work, Freud's was the last fresh breeze of common sense to reach that dank, many-chambered nautilus, modern psychology. Certain revisions and modifications of the original Dollard thesis were proposed, and some generally accepted. Miller, one of the original group, had immediate second thoughts and showed that frustration might, under certain conditions, lead to consequences other than aggression. P. McKellar showed that aggression grows greater if it does not draw retaliation, a vital point to which no one paid much attention. Another of the Dollard group, R. R. Sears, got together a new batch of colleagues and showed quite the opposite, that the more aggression is punished or frustrated, the greater is the incentive to aggress. With still another colleague he demonstrated that the rise and fall of lynchings in the American South has always been correlated with the fall and rise of the price of cotton. One cannot but recall Raymond Pearl's famous correlation between the rate of survival in cockroaches and in motor cars. Pearl, of course, made his demonstration before science lost its sense of humor.

The compelling literature of frustration-aggression, known in the trade as F-A, while retaining America as its chief print shop, spread to include most of the English-speaking world. Beyond the reaches of the English language there remained a few firm citadels of high barbarism where enlightened minds still clung to the outdated notion that your actions might just possibly be no one's fault but your own. The Anglo-Saxon spirit, however, with all that charming exuberance reserved normally for the discovery of a new religion, threw itself into the ecstasy of F-A, clapped hands to alibi's insistent drum, rolled its delirious body in irresponsibility's resourceful dust, and as the Etruscans once consulted only the livers of sheep to discover the future's auguries, consulted only environment's frustrations to divine the future's peace.

It was a dangerous orgy, of course, and dangerously timed. An understanding of aggression had become central to the general problem of human survival. With the sudden rise of American power the role of the American scientist became one of aching responsibility. John Paul Scott, world authority on dogs and perhaps our most quoted student of animal behavior, published his *Aggression* in 1958. His publisher was the respected University of Chicago Press, and on the dust jacket one reads: "All research findings point to the fact that there is no physiological evidence of any internal need or spontaneous driving force for fighting; that all stimulation for aggression eventually comes from forces present.in the external environment."

The phrase "all research findings" recalls Montagu's "the evidence is today overwhelming." Is it? The participant in our inquiry must find himself just a bit stunned, and moved to inquire, *"Certain* research findings, maybe, but *all research findings?* Is this science?"* Charitably we must recall that Scott's book was published in 1958, a date in the rapidly moving new biology of virtual Neanderthal antiquity; and a man can change his mind. Three years later our most widely read authoritative journal, *The Scientific American,* published a piece by Irenäus Eibl-Eibesfeldt called "Fighting Behavior of Animals." The author is one of Europe's most respected ethologists, a colleague of Konrad Lorenz at Germany's Max Planck Institute for Animal Behavior. He pointed out that Scott's conclusion had been largely based on an experiment with mice, back in 1951, which seemed to indicate that aggressiveness had its cause in early unhappy experiences with nest mates. But Eibl-Eibesfeldt had raised rats in isolation, without any possible benefits of youthful frustration, and on their first contact with another rat they had gone through the entire repertory of species-specific aggressive behavior—the high cries, the arching of the back, the gnashing of teeth. His experience had been extended to many species in a state of nature—the iguana, the lava lizard, the rattlesnake. He recorded the observations of aggressiveness in the oryx antelope, fallow deer, cichlid fish. And he concluded:

> A growing body of evidence from observations in the field and experiments in the laboratory points to the conclusion that this vital mode of behavior is not learned by the individual but is innate in the species, like the organs specially evolved for such combat in many animals.

In March of the following year *The Scientific American* published another paper by the late Erich von Holst. It was called "Electrically Controlled Behavior." Two decades earlier, a Swiss investigator, W. R. Hess, had succeeded in producing predictable behavior through the discharge of a low-voltage current through an electrode planted in the brain of a cat. Now von Holst and a colleague had completed a series of experiments with chickens. An electrode planted in a particular area of the hypothalamus would produce aggressive action against a stuffed hen, theoretically a rival in the pecking order, and planted in another area would produce attack of a different sort against a stuffed weasel, in theory a threatening predator. Yet in the same year, in his contribution to a volume called *Roots of*

Behavior, Scott calmly recorded:

> All our present data indicate that fighting behavior among the higher mammals, including man, originates in external stimulation and that there is no evidence of spontaneous internal stimulation.

Now, it is true that a chicken is not a mammal and that external stimulation was present. But since the chickens exhibited only indifference to the stuffed objects until receiving the electrical charge, the statement that there is no evidence for spontaneous internal stimulation skirts the thinnest of technicalities. And to conclude the same volume, David E. Davis, who gave us the smooth-billed ani, wrote a superb paper called "The Phylogeny of Gangs." It is an analysis of the biological motivation of street gangs, and it will concern us in detail at some future date. Davis points out that rank and territory are the objects of aggression in the human gang, as they are likewise the goals of most animal fighting. He concludes:

> A wide variety of observations suggests that fighting for rank or territory has innate features. . . . Thus contrary to the conclusions of some authors, it seems that aggression is heavily dependent on genetics. Probably only the means of fighting and the object of attack are learned.

John Paul Scott was undismayed. In his review of a book in *Science,* on a date as recent as May 7, 1965, he wrote:

> All that we know (and this comprises a considerable body of information in certain species) indicates that . . . there is no known physiological mechanism by which internal stimulation for fighting arises. Rather, the physiological mechanisms for fighting are triggered by immediate external stimuli.

"All that we know". . ."all our present data". . ."the evidence is overwhelming". . ."all research findings". . . What must be described as a party line has appeared in the American sciences, protected by its most respected adherents through the use of such iron-curtain phrases as "all that we know." The phrases are false. Is the falsehood successful? Write to your children at university. Ask them, as a favor, to get down their College Outline Series and look into the volume with the title *Psychology*. What does it say about instinct? Page 51: "Though all the explanations are not worked out, it appears clear that there is no instinctive behavior in man, and probably not in animals."

I suggested on an earlier page that unless we could grasp the extent to which falsehood has triumphed over truth in contemporary thought, we should have difficulty in comprehending our contemporary predicament. In America we appropriate tens of billions of dollars each year for the education of our children: do we ask, as we pay our tax bill, what does that education consist of? Will an education captured in large areas by the forces of scientific romanticism produce citizens less or more able to deal with the dubious future? We do not ask. And yet it is a future of the spinning wheel, of the ball ever poised above double zero.

Still, however, we have not come to a final grip with the contemporary predicament. The problem of aggression could be consigned to the future if it affected merely the education of our children. But it concerns ourselves, as it is part of today. And if you and I fail to understand it, then whether or not our children receive any education at all may be of peripheral significance. Let us take a look at a symposium held in London in October, 1963.

The scientific meeting was called by Britain's Institute of Biology. The symposium's arresting title, *The Natural History of Aggression,* was drawn from a book by Konrad Lorenz not yet published in English. Five years earlier, I suspect, such a meeting could not have taken place, and certainly not under auspices so respectable. In an academic world of psychological certainty, of instincts as rare as the griffin, a title like *The Natural History of Aggression* smacks of science fiction. That the Institute of Biology could dare to enter the no man's land between the social and biological sciences carrying such a banner, to invite representatives of both disciplines to present their views, and as a final heroic gesture to invite a small audience of the scientific elite to witness the mayhem and take part in the reassembly of mutilated corpses, was one of those acts of courage recalling the Spanish Armada and the Battle of Britain which so frequently grace the history of the English people.

James Fisher, D. I. Wallis, Harrison Matthews, K. R. L. Hall, and Konrad Lorenz gave the main case for the universality of innate aggressive behavior in the animal world and the all-but-universal means which evolution has perfected whereby the impact of aggression is ritualized, subjected to rules and regulations, and otherwise diverted to harmless consequence. Stanislav Andreski, John Burton, Denis Hill, and Cecily de Monchaux presented the central arguments for interpreting aggressiveness in uniquely human terms. Derek Freeman, the Australian psychologist, made a spectacular break with his trade, joined the ethologists, presented an interpretation of Dart's theory of the predatory transition from ape to man, and along with it a nightmare record of that human consequence which has failed to acknowledge animal rules and regulations. Another student of man, the London psychiatrist Anthony Storr, likewise accepted ethology's view, and made the stunning suggestion that the space race, which so consumes our imaginations as well as an inordinate portion of American and Soviet budgets, is in truth a ritualization of the cold war.

Otherwise, nothing happened. The students of men remained right where they were. I was in Africa at the time of the symposium. I returned to London a few weeks after its close and heard gossip's bemused comment that for many of the eminent minds who attended, the meeting seemed not to exist; that one would have supposed that the theory of evolution had never been successfully demonstrated and that we lived again in the days of Bishop Wilberforce. No historic row had developed; no mutilated corpses had been removed by night from the South Kensington Museum's Gothic pile. It had been as if some defect in the meeting room's acoustics had prevented one side of the house from hearing what the other side was saying.

Gossip was unfair. A confrontation had at least been arranged, a confrontation between the two points of view: that aggression is innate in man, and a fraction of his evolutionary heritage; and that human aggression is acquired, a product of frustration. To achieve such a confrontation was, if only for a day or two, to raise the iron curtain with which environmentalism shields itself, and to reveal if nothing else the breadth of the no man's land between the two wings of our science. It will be enough if I summarize here the conclusions of the men who might be regarded as team captains, Konrad Lorenz for ethology, and John Burton, the historian of London's University College, whose paper closed the meeting.

Lorenz' basic position, in his paper as well as in his forthcoming book, is that few animals can survive without aggressiveness, such is its selective value to the welfare of individuals, populations, and species. Among its obvious values are the spacing of individuals over an available habitat, the selection for breeding of better-qualified males through competition, and in social animals, the formation of a dominant order providing leadership and discipline through which the superior wisdom, experience, and courage of the leaders are disposed with greatest advantage to the entire community. Out of his immensely broad experience with animals Lorenz gives case upon case to demonstrate the natural history of aggression, and to make evident the means by which nature ritualizes and inhibits actual fighting so that the individual may benefit by aggression's values while the species is saved from aggression's toll. He told the meeting:

> There cannot be any doubt, in the opinion of any biologically-minded scientist, that intraspecific fighting is, in Man, just as much of a spontaneous instinctive drive as in most other higher vertebrates. The beginning synthesis between the findings of ethology and psychoanalysis does not leave any doubt, either, that what Sigmund Freud called the "death drive" is nothing else but the miscarrying of this instinct which, in itself, is as indispensable for survival as any other.

In other words, which is the father, which the child? Freud saw the death instinct as fundamental, and aggression as the death instinct turned outward. Lorenz sees aggression as the normal, natural, fundamental instinct, and any death wish as its neurotic, frustrated consequence, aggression turned inward. The Lorenz approach to human aggression is, first, that we must recognize that it is healthy, that it is necessary, that it is innate, that it is ineradicable; second, that the solution to the human problem is to be sought in the direction of imitation of nature, in other words by the enlargement of all those less-than-lethal competitions, ritualizations and displays, whether between individuals or groups, which absorb our hostile energies and turn them to ends either harmless or constructive; and, finally, that to deny innateness of human aggression is to approach its possible control from an inevitably impossible quarter, that to accept its cause as lying in frustration is to lend hostility moral sanction, and to turn its most virulent, violent, antisocial, antisurvival forces loose on a defenseless world.

If, when Konrad Lorenz' book appears in Britain and

America, it does not take its place among the landmarks of our thought, then for all my congenital optimism I shall begin to believe that, whatever happens to Lorenz' geese, the human goose is cooked. He even expressed at the symposium what for me is the essence of the amity-enmity complex: "It is a fact worthy of deep meditation," said Lorenz, "that for all we know the bond of personal friendship was evolved by the necessity for certain individuals to cease from fighting each other in order more effectively to combat other fellow-members of the species."

My optimism concerning the capacities of fellow members of my species to come at last to grips with themselves survives, at times, out of processes which must be physiological; it receives small intellectual nourishment. The historian Burton closed the conference with a summation in itself historic: "The notion of aggressiveness in animals may finally be shown to be valid," he began; "however, it should not escape attention that in the present state of our knowledge we have no conclusive evidence of this."

The funds spent on organizing the symposium would seem to have been totally wasted. The lifetime observations of such biologists as Lorenz and Hall and Fisher are dismissed by the historian who wields not the minimum of authority within their discipline. Burton goes on to grant that if such innate hostility is ever finally demonstrated in lower animals, it will have in any case no significance concerning man. He falls back on that wheels-within-wheels academic defense of quoting sympathetic authority unexposed to present, contrary information, in this case a statement by the psychologist F. H. Stanford that "there is no direct physiological evidence for aggression, although the blocked, frustrated or deprived organism can be counted on to show the physiological changes accompanying emotion." In a single sentence we return to 1939, to Dollard, and to F-A.

If we regard the cost of the conference as money wasted, however, we are wrong. For Burton proceeds in all innocence, with all noblest of intentions, to expose in most precise if unself-conscious terms the perilous path of applied F-A:

[The] academic conception of aggression as a secondary or derived motivation does not prevent aggressiveness being treated by law, and by society generally, as a primary one for which the individual himself is responsible. We still endeavor to control and suppress aggression by the individual without regard to environmental causation. Just as vagabonds were once hounded as lazy people, and not considered to be the product of a system which included unemployment, so aggressive people are still an object of social condemnation, and subject to laws designed to suppress them.

This gap between academic theory and social practice, which exists within a society, is very small when compared with the gap existing between the same theory and practice within the international community. We did not stop to consider the degree to which Western nations were responsible for Italian, German, and Japanese aggressions, and all the atrocities associated with them.

Dr. Burton proceeds to bring us up to date with reference to the Korean conflict and the Indian-Chinese border disputes, and to suggest that the "facts" now available give no support to any notion of unprovoked aggressiveness or expansionism on the part of China (a conclusion of great interest, we may assume, to the Soviet Union).

In both cases domestic political considerations of a most pressing nature in the countries confronting China—the United States and India—were relevant to the policies which preceded tense relations with China.

And he concludes his paper and the symposium:

The extension of the findings of biology and psychology into the international relationship is probably false; but as an analogy it could be useful to point out that in animals and in man, aggressiveness is a non-passive response to the perception of a threat, or to the experience of frustration. Political leaders of states who accuse other states of being aggressive, would then know where the responsibility for aggression finally lies.

I have digressed sufficiently from our basic inquiry, I believe, to acquaint the reader with the development of two opposite points of view within the sciences, with the no man's land existing between them, with the general effects on our educational system and the influences on our daily affairs, and with the degree of suspense which such conflict of academic authority must bring to normal hopes for human survival as we place our faith in "science says." For the reader who wishes to inquire at more detailed length into the present disagreement, the entire proceedings of this remarkable London symposium have been published by the Academic Press in London and New York. But since observations and conclusions fundamental to our present investigations relate not to the aggressive ingredients of man so much as to the defensive mechanisms with which nature has equipped him, it is time, I believe, that we return to the territorial imperative.

I do not agree, quite obviously, with Dr. Burton's suggestion that any extension of the findings of biology into the field of international relations is false. As I believe is easily demonstrable, it has been our failure to comprehend the innate mechanisms of the amity-enmity complex which leads us consistently in our international relations to accomplish the precise opposite of our intentions.

5

If you program the territorial computer with the amity-enmity equation, and you feed into the machine the State of Israel and the Jewish people, then the monster will cough twice and give out the lunatic answer that there never was any such thing as a Jew, and that if it were not for the Arab League there would probably be no State of Israel, either. And no matter how many repairmen you call in, or how viciously you accuse the computer of drinking too much or how many cold cloths you wrap about its head, the computer will still grind out the same answer.

According to the computer, the story goes like this: For a very long time human nature has been playing a grotesque joke on Jew and Gentile alike. He and we have joined in regarding him as a race. And yet he has less racial distinctiveness than the southern Italian or the Swede. He is a descendant of a mixed bag of Middle Eastern tribes, as I am a descendant of a mixed bag of Scottish clans, and he has no more genetic distinction than you or I or the next man. But nevertheless there has existed a profound difference between us. We have had territories, he has had none. Among modern, civilized peoples he has been unique. And what we have described as a Jew has been nothing other than a de-territorialized man.

Jewish difficulties with territory, it seems, began a very long time ago, when God promised Abraham, leader of some wandering pastoral tribes, title to a most unremarkable piece of real estate on the Mediterranean littoral. No people ever took a promise harder. They managed to gain it, and to settle down, but they were such a quarrelsome, rebellious lot that somebody was always carting them off into slavery. First it was Egypt, where they made out very well but still dreamed of nothing but the Promised Land. After some hair-raising experiences they managed to regain their territory, but then it was the Chaldeans. Nebuchadnezzar hauled most of them away to Babylon. Later it was the Roman Empire that found itself unequal to Jewish argument and so dispersed them by force to a variety of Western destinations. For almost 2000 years the Jew of the West and the Jew of the East had one thing in common: they never saw their Promised Land again.

By the waters of Babylon the Jew sang his song: "If I forget thee, O Jerusalem . . ." And he never did.

Jews call it the Diaspora—the dispersal of the people. As a

population they were denied a social territory; as individuals in most times and places they were denied even the right to own land, to possess private territories. Despite all indignities heaped upon him, the Jew of the East had the easier life, since Mohammed out of respect for Jewish and Christian religions decreed him a "People of the Book." It was not the Moslem but the Christian, we may remember, who drove the Jew out of Spain. Through all Christian lands his fate was a harsh one; perhaps Christian amity demanded an enemy to complete its own complex. Should this be so, then secular society was not one to abjure the Christian creation of an omega fish.

The suspicion must exist that if anti-Semitism had pleasant conveniences for Christians it had certain unpleasant conveniences for Jews as well. The Jew faced a genetic problem confronting no other Western people: How, without the reproductive isolation of territory, could he maintain his genetic integrity? He owned nothing but memories. Anti-Semitism helped. He accepted the grim ghetto. He forbade marriage or intercourse with Gentiles. His rabbis and scholars maintained the memories. The Jewish family became the impregnable equivalent of a Greek phalanx. Spectacularly, the Jew refused to conform, cultivated outlandish costume, beard, headgear, cultivated outlandish dietary customs. He pursued the arts while we pursued each other; he reveled in education while we still reveled in illiteracy. He overlooked nothing, forgot nothing. As century passed into century, millennium into millennium, like some ancient magician the Jew made memories from the dust of the years.

The Jew was different, let there be no doubt. And he maintained that difference with unflagging resolution. We regarded him as a race apart; it was to Jewish interest to agree. We derided the "Jewish personality"; he exaggerated the personality. None of us guessed, of course, he or we, that the "Jewish personality" was nothing but a bundle of mannerisms preserving the identity of a de-territorialized man. And then came Zionism.

Let us pause for a warning: My sympathies have been always with Zionism. But neither my sympathies nor those of the computer at my elbow have the smallest effect on the workings of the amity-enmity equation. We shall see, in due course, what happens when sympathies are reversed.

Zionism, in any event, enlisted my imagination as the next man's dream or the next man's adventure might enlist one's imagination in the reading of a good novel. As the great day of British withdrawal from Palestine approached, my Washington friends panicked. They foresaw an Arab massacre of defenseless Jews beyond anything in the history of pogroms. I was skeptical. I knew nothing about territory in those days, of course, but a playwright tends to give weight to the irrational. It seemed to me that the history of pogroms cast little light on what would happen when a people homeless for two thousand years had again the opportunity to defend its Promised Land.

What happened to the Arabs, then, did not surprise me. But many, many years later, when I had still not visited Israel but my computer and I were beginning to wonder about man and territory, I made a little list. If a territorial interpretation of the Jew carried validity, then certain theoretical consequences should have come about in reality.

First, a territory is a defended area. To defend it one must have hostile neighbors. The Arab League, happily for the Jew, presented him not only with a wealth of hostile neighbors but with the opportunity to make legitimate his territory in the strictest biological sense.

Second, if civilized man is to respect someone else's title to a territory, he needs evidence other than a questionable, long-ago deal with God. He needs, in other words, to see the proprietors in defense of their land slaughter a maximum number of their fellow human beings. Here again the Arab League co-operated splendidly with Jewish purposes. They bared their bodies, they died in piles.

Third, such an astonishing reversal of what we had always regarded as the "Jewish personality" should have shaken the West. It did. From that date in 1948 anti-Semitism may have retained a nostalgia or two, but it ceased to be a workable institution. We flatter ourselves that the Hitler outrages awakened the conscience of mankind. They did nothing of the sort. I recall that in America immediately after World War II anti-Semitism reached peaks never before attained, despite all Nazi contributions to our universal conscience; and the literature of the period will bear me out. It was the photographs of dead Arabs, not of cremated Jews, that awakened our famed conscience. It was in 1948 that a stunned world realized that Jews could behave just like anyone else.

Fourth, acquisition and defense of a territory should have brought the usual enhancement of energy to the Israeli. It did. The Promised Land was as unpromising a collection of rocks, gravel, malarial swamps, and out-and-out desert as the Mediterranean littoral can provide, and had I been Abraham I should have demanded a better deal. Yet a people who for 2000 years had been denied ownership of land, had lived almost entirely in towns, and lacked both farming tradition and experience, have made themselves very nearly self-sufficient in food supply and are capturing one European market after another with their agricultural exports. I have mentioned the kibbutz. One understands why the collective farm has succeeded here and nowhere else in the Western World. You may visit a kibbutz called Sha'ar Hagolan, near the Sea of Galilee and within gunshot of the Jordan border. You may inspect the Neolithic antiquities which in their spare time the members have dug from their fields and which they display in a convenient bomb shelter; and you will have no need to examine the beaver to confirm the enhancement of energy in a territorial defender.

Fifth, a most important point. If the Jew never existed but was simply a de-territorialized man, then in theory he should cease to be a Jew when he becomes re-territorialized. When you visit Israel you will discover that it is the new nation's favorite joke. There is the story of the visiting French-Jewish doctor met on the dock at Haifa by a friend. The doctor looked in puzzlement at the barrel-chested porters throwing luggage around. "Who are they?" he asked. "Jews," said his host.

It is not just physique. It is posture, a manner of walking, a manner of speaking, a manner of thought. The "Jewish personality" has vanished, replaced by that of the Israeli, a being as confident, as resolute, and as willing to do battle as a roebuck on his wooded acres. You go to a party in Tel-Aviv and someone asks the inevitable question, "How do you like Israel?" and you answer, "Fine. But where are the Jews?" And the party goes off into the greatest laughter, for it is the nation's joke.

Sixth, if territory has transmuted the Jew, physically and psychically, into another being called the Israeli, then in theory there should be a widening breach between the Israeli and the Jew of the Diaspora. The breach is far from theoretical; it is regarded by many in Israel as the second most severe problem that the new nation suffers. Many a thoughtful British or American or Continental Jew reproaches the Israeli as a chauvinist, as a man who has lost his world view and no longer acts according to his conscience, as one who has somehow betrayed the most profound ideals of a people. To the Israeli, his fellow of the Diaspora is a moralizer whose sermons if put into practice would mean death to Israel. Since it has been the financial generosity of world Jewry which has made Zion possible, there is anguish on both sides. What neither understands is that natural law has intervened; that they are no longer the same people sharing the same conscience and the same amity-enmity complex. Life would be easier for both if they understood.

The same division between Jew and Israeli witnessed a heart-rending demonstration during the Eichmann trial. I had not anticipated it with my theoretical list, but the Israeli elders with their intuitions had, for they dreaded what would happen when the inevitable documentation of Nazi atrocities unfolded. The dread was well founded. As the trial progressed, the bewildered young people—the sabras, the Israeli-born—confronted their parents in household after household. "Why didn't you do something?" "You don't understand," said the parents, "there was nothing to do." "But if you were going to die—if somebody knew he was going to die anyway—why didn't he die fighting?" "You don't understand," said the parents. And it is true that the sabra will never understand, for unlike the Jew of the gas chamber, he is a territorial animal.

The final point I did not anticipate, the Israeli did not

anticipate, none but the computer could have anticipated. It is the first of all Israeli problems, and it will be solved or it will destroy the nation. The Arab, of course—as he well knows—scarcely constitutes a problem at all beyond the military expense that he adds to the nation's budget. Israel's problem is race.

Had I been a Jew and a pioneer Zionist, I too should have had no inkling as to the horror that would raise its ugly head someday. The Zionist in his innocence accepted the Jew as a Jew, even as did the Gentile. He anticipated difficulties in the welding together of peoples from a hundred different lands speaking a hundred different tongues. He recognized his people as an opinionated lot, and foresaw quarrels. But he foresaw no transcendent problems once all were together in the Promised Land, once all spoke Hebrew as a common language, and once all children grew up in common schools. That the racial reality of the Jew did not exist did not enter his calculation, nor that out of the conglomeration of background would come two entirely different peoples, the Jew of the East and the Jew of the West.

The Zionist fallacy was at first not revealed. Of the 650,000 Israeli who in 1948 fought the War of Independence, almost all were of the West. For eighty or so generations they had survived the hard conditions of environmental selection imposed by Christian lands: they were tough, resourceful, educated, and none paled at confrontation with a hard day's work. The Arab League, with its generous gift of blood to sanctify their legitimate union, launched successfully the Israeli ship. Then and only then arrived the other Jew in his massive migration. Israel braced itself, embraced the brother who had sung by the rivers of Babylon. It occurred to no one that the Oriental Jew, after one hundred generations of survival and natural selection in environments from Casablanca to Baghdad so different from those of the West, in societies for example where work if possible is left to women and study if possible left to scribes, might bear a genetic scar or two which no classroom could immediately erase.

Today at Hebrew University, Oriental Jewish students are so

few that they are outnumbered by Arabs. Abba Eban, until recently Minister of Education, has stated that 30 percent of Oriental children who have reached the age of fourteen and have had eight years of Israeli schooling are unable to write a simple Hebrew text or a legible letter, or to perform the four basic calculations of arithmetic. The attitude toward education differs as does the eagerness to work. While the Western Jew, renouncing the ghetto, has accomplished the agricultural miracle, the Eastern Jew, creating a new ghetto, has crowded over half of his numbers into the Tel-Aviv area. There is little intermarriage. Less than 5 percent of Western women marry Eastern men. The comment of a girl at Hebrew University that the Oriental Jew is "not of our sort" sounds like discrimination; but the Eastern male, of course, is even more unlikely to tolerate a wife with education than he is to seek it himself.

The Oriental Jew is today in a 55-percent majority. He makes bitter charges of racial discrimination. Israeli leadership recoils at a phrase that for any Jew is a blow to memory's solar plexus. Yet discrimination exists. Michael Selzer, writing in London's *Jewish Observer,* describes a housing development in Jerusalem which excludes *schwarzim,* the blacks. Epithets like *Cushim* and *Frankim* are common; they correspond to the British *kaffir.* Zionist leadership in its innocence failed to reckon that when the Jew became an Israeli he would take on his newly straightened shoulders all the common burdens of mankind.

Yet despite all: despite disillusionment in the immediate efficacy of education, despite the failure of social conditioning, despite the entrenchments of "racial" animosities, despite deepening pessimism in many informed Israeli circles: despite all, Israel thrives and will achieve integration long before its pessimists believe. Why? Because of the amity-enmity complex; because the Arab League, persistent to the end in its animosities, will further accomplish the opposite of its purposes and in the end succeed in creating what no Israeli resource can produce, a truly permanent and united nation.

As the knowledgeable Israeli must dread the day when the Arab League appears on the Promised Land's doorstep, in its hands an olive branch, so the South African must dread the day when like the apocalypse itself there appears below the Limpopo the unheralded cordiality of nations. He could, just possibly, be destroyed.

For a good many years now I have been a commuter in Africa, pursuing my animals and my fossils, and watching out of the corners of my eyes the arrangements of *Homo sapiens* with an incredulity which my computer does not share. When I began my travels, Ghana was still the Gold Coast and the Mau-Mau still the preoccupation of both Kenya and the world press. As my understanding of territory grew, I came to recognize that the independence movement included two serious flaws: First, the black nations were accepting those arbitrary borders which had been drawn by the colonial powers in their splitting up of the world's spoils. In the Congo, for example, a major tribe like the Bakongo was divided among European-derived entities known as Angola, the Belgian Congo, and the French Congo; whereas, on the other hand, Katanga, a separate entity ethnologically, traditionally, and geographically, had for conveniences of Belgian administration been placed within that area which all but the Congolese regarded as the Congo. And the second serious flaw, of course, was that none of the new states remotely resembled biological nations. Allegiances were tribal and local.

Linear social evolution—scorned by many a social anthropologist as an affront to human dignity—has in most peoples proceeded through coalition of primitive hunting bands, differing little in size or organization from animal societies, into larger clans holding merged territories, through the coalition of clans into enlarging tribes perhaps grouped into confederations still recognizing with varying strictness the older boundaries, and finally the evolution of such loose confederations into modern nation-states in which through various political or historical mechanisms a single unified territory commands the allegiance, the sacrifice, and the effective amity of all social partners. The normal condition of coalition comes about when adjoining groups face an outward enemy too strong for any singly to resist, so that alliance becomes voluntary and if the combined amity-enmity complex persists long enough, true coalition will follow. The conquest of a weaker group by a stronger may produce coalition of a temporary nature, but as a rule any permanent, reliable arrangement must be sealed by voluntary allegiance in the face of common threat.

It is difficult to explain why the history of African peoples below the Sahara offers so few examples of coalition beyond the tribal level, while the most ancient monument we have to such social evolution is to be found on the African continent itself. Not an hour's drive from Cairo is the oldest masonry building in the world, the famous step pyramid built for King Zoser of the Third Dynasty almost 5000 years ago. Zoser's predecessors had succeeded, to begin with undoubtedly by conquest, in uniting all those tribes of Upper and Lower Egypt with territories facing the Nile. These districts were called nomes. By the time Zoser came along, the national union must have reached an effective level. In the midst of the hot high glaring desert standing above the Nile's green valley there still remains that ancient community of the dead, the necropolis called Saqqara. Here history's first architect, Imhotep, constructed the pyramid that was to be his king's monument, and reproduced in superbly carved stone for the king's eternal entertainment the living court over which in life he had ruled at Memphis. Politics must have been King Zoser's chief amusement. One explores the great walled compound, the structures built for ceremonies now forgotten, and like boxes in an opera house the flanking niches occupied once by representatives of Egypt's federated nomes. And wandering about among these crumbling niches I discovered to my lasting astonishment symbolic but emphatic fences separating niche from niche. Our first nation had recognized the territorial integrity of each nome in the federated whole, and in civilization's first building of stone had accepted symbolically the territorial boundary as of immortality's stuff.

The date was approximately 2750 B.C. Tribal allegiances while retaining territorial identity as in my own United States deferred to central, national authority. Nearly 5000 years later no comparable condition had been yet achieved in the new

African states. Tribal loyalties were uniformly paramount Black nationalism held meaning only to northern whites, usually painfully ignorant of the man in the bush, or in the ambitions for power of that handful of white-educated blacks who came to be known as black Europeans. The talk in northern circles was of "viable nations" as if economics constituted a significant force in the establishment of national identities. The independence movement was real enough, but its emotional basis was a tribal demand first for freedom from the rule of the white man, but second, and finally, from the centralized rule of the black man as well.

Such was the background, as I saw it, for the chaotic future of the new black states. And yet strangely enough, everything that could be said of the black state could be said of that white pariah South Africa as well. Ten years ago little difference met the eye. Tribal animosities were more immediately apparent, in truth, than in most black states. There were two white tribes, Boer and British. The Afrikaner, an amalgam of Dutch and French, had been in possession of its land for so many centuries that its solidarity and political power was the greater. The British tribe, however, was the richer; and the two held each other in mutual contempt. Of comparable size were two black tribes, the Zulu and the Xhosa, among the most able of all tribal groups on the African continent. Their mutual animosities, however, might be compared to that of Boer and Britain, and the Zulu possessed, moreover, a chilling history of warlike ferocity known the world around. And then there was another sizable group known as Cape Colored, more an agglomeration than a tribe, and bearing little relation to modern Africa. Descendants of the pre-Negro Hottentot, of Malay slaves brought in the seventeenth century to the old Dutch colony, and of the whites themselves, the Cape Colored held common bond with almost no one. And besides all these, there was the Indian, and there were minor black tribes to complete the "national" mosaic.

There was one striking difference, however. Whereas the new black states commanded the sympathy of the entire world, South Africa because of its social policy commanded as universal an antipathy. My computer, grinding away at its equations, presumably knew all the answers. I did not, or did not, at least, until the sums lay glaringly before me.

Today there is not a black African state which for all the world's good will and economic aid does not stagger along on one side or the other of the narrow line between order and chaos, solvency and bankruptcy, peace and blood. Whereas the pariah state South Africa is attaining peaks of affluence, order, security, and internal solidarity rivaled by few long-established nations. A degree of tyranny has contributed to the change, but that degree is far smaller than world failure is yet willing to grant. What since 1960 has transmuted a divided, unstable, near-bankrupt state on the verge of racial explosion into a stable, united, incredibly prospering nation in which the threat of racial explosion is almost nonexistent has been natural alchemy: the forced withdrawal of South Africa from the British Commonwealth, the boycotts and embargoes stemming from a world conscience more declared than real, the meaningless threats of war on the part of powerless black African states, the unenforceable resolutions passed unanimously by United Nations, the establishment of training camps in Africa for saboteurs and guerrilla fighters and the raising of funds in Europe for a revolution which will never occur, have in a world holding sacred the sovereign rights of nations been all territorial intrusions. Every law of the territorial principle has been set in motion: the proprietor's innate defense, enhancement of energy, co-operation and acceptance of leadership, and the final $A = E + h$.

Had the world conspired to make apartheid a permanent South African institution, it could have done no better job. As the Arab League has accomplished in Israel the precise opposite of its intentions, so better than a hundred nations voting in New York have accomplished the precise opposite of theirs. In recent months the most incredible of predictions has come to me from South African sources all of which I trust: were South Africa physically invaded by white forces, 80 percent of South African blacks would join in the country's defense; were the invasion to be mounted by black forces, the defense would be total. One cannot know the accuracy of the prediction, but since it falls within the probability of the amity-enmity equation and since history, one day, may put it to the test, the suggestion for all its seeming lunacy is worth recording.

The intruder's motives may be superior morally, politically, ideologically; the defender's motives may be parochial, contemptible, justifiably intolerable on the part of world opinion; or relative merits may be reversed: it is all one, since our sympathies are meaningless. Unless the intruder, lacking the biologically compounding forces of the defensive territorial principle, is both willing and capable of making such sacrifices as to overcome the proprietor's inherent advantages, intrusion will not only fail but will accomplish, in all probability, the opposite of its objectives.

Another excellent contemporary example was the American adventure in Vietnam. My sympathies lay frankly on the side of intrusion. I do not share with Dr. Burton his judgment of Chinese aggressiveness as a simple product of F-A. The odors arising from Peking carry to my nostrils a pungency which I cannot ascribe to the springtime blooming of a hundred flowers. My sensibilities remain quite unoffended by actions offering permanent damage to what I regard as the Chinese dream. Furthermore, if containment of Chinese expansionism was our motive, then our adventure in its earliest stages was a grand success. That China failed to come to the rescue of its small ally had immediate consequences in the world's most likely and unlikely capitals. Heads labeled "Made in Peking" rolled in Algeria, in the new black states, in Cuba, in Indonesia, in almost every quarter wherein Chinese expansionism had to that date made substantial progress. The Soviet Union, it is true, busied itself picking up most of the loose Chinese change, and in a way we presented the Russians with their most massive political victory since Yalta. Whether such a consequence was to American interest may be arguable, but fortunately is not the subject of argument here. What lies beyond argument, and what is most definitely a facet of the subject before us, was that policy called escalation, the gradual and almost imperceptible increase of the intruder's exhibited might.

At the very word *escalation,* my computer groans and wanders off to the bathroom in search of aspirin. If there is a policy of aggression more doomed to failure, then the dreamy Americans, we must assume, will someday invent it. Escalation has several virtues, it is true, but all are clouded: It is a means of getting into a big war in such a small way that your allies will not desert you—at least not until you need them most. Also, like an economic policy of good money after bad, you will at first gain the support of your own people, who though unmotivated by territorial defense will accept what seems at the moment aggression on the cheap; not until your investment has become so great as to preclude any course but further investment will your troubles at home begin, for the digging into economic and emotional pockets will be made in a spirit notably lacking that enthusiasm so essential to war. Another virtue, more apparent in day-to-day routine than in consummation of victory, is that escalation makes quite unnecessary knowing what you are doing. And a final virtue, of fundamental appeal to a people as virtuous as the Americans, is that after a while it becomes difficult to discern just who is escalating whom, so you can more easily blame the bloody state of affairs on the other fellow; the drawback, of course, being that by then you are truly a victim of circumstance, you have lost all military initiative, and as you have forgotten who started the war, you will probably have forgotten why, too.

Whatever escalation's debatable assets may be for the intruder, it is a ladder to heaven for the defender. Since $A = E + h,$ and E by its slow increase loses all shock value, A will be generated at a rate amply to exploit the defender's resources, however slim. The most minute advantage, the most subtle, marginal multiplication of territorial power, will be placed in the hands of your enemy. And even though in the end you may seem to win—a probable outcome if you are the world's greatest power and your adversary has been chosen as the smallest and poorest contestant in sight—then two grave consequences may be anticipated: The long, painful, grinding of attrition which has brought you victory at maximum cost may have reduced your enemy's land to ashes, but as there will always be embers there will always be memories, and someday out of the charred old ruin will emerge the unforgetting phoenix, and you must begin all over again. The other consequence, perhaps indeed more ludicrous than grave, will be that while David has never looked braver, Goliath has never looked sillier.

The amity-enmity complex, put to full use by the modern development of the ancient biological nation, has presented to the intruder's path something less pleasing than roses, roses all the way. Since the eighteenth century I can recall only two cases of permanently successful conquest, and neither is clear-cut. My own country successfully stole Texas and California from Mexico; but Mexico was not then a true nation. And the Soviet Union after World War II made off with Eastern Europe; but whether even that conquest will be made to stick seems ever more doubtful. Conquest, whether for causes noble or causes base, ceased to be a profitable enterprise when broadly organized, thoroughly integrated territorial societies became the bastions of the freedom of peoples. This biological fact of life is what the potential intruder must learn. As smooth-billed anis will defend their territory though their collective nest be meanwhile robbed, evolutionary processes of such eternal value must shrug at temporal loss. Human sympathies, moral convictions, political absolutes, philosophical certainties— none, whatever the discomfort their frustration may cause us, will suborn or suppress the territorial imperative, that biological morality which will still contain the behavior of beings when *Homo sapiens* is an evolutionary memory.

9. Three Faces of Janus

Once upon a time, when things were just getting started in my neighborhood, there was a king named Janus who had a stronghold just a mile or so from my house, up on the hill which we call the Janiculum. This was long before the days of Romulus and Remus, when Rome was just a trading village at a bend in the Tiber. Over in the Aegean the Greeks of the time were having troubles with the Trojans, and since Janus had no Homer, we have no palpable or poetic evidence that he existed at all. I like to think of him, nevertheless, in his citadel up on the hill, for Janus was to become a most remarkable man once he became a god.

The Romans were great ones for cults, and the cult dedicated to Janus must have lasted for better than a thousand years, down at least to the time of Hadrian and the later Empire. His jurisdiction was of an odd sort: he was the god of doorways. This is why we see him as a rule with two faces, for this is how they arranged him over the door, with one face looking into the house, the other out. But beyond this matter of doorways Janus had a larger and more splendid jurisdiction, for he was the god of the beginnings. He was the god of the beginning of the day, and of the beginning of the month, and of the beginning of the year. January was named after him. Janus ruled over the beginning of almost anything, like the laying of an aqueduct's first stone, or the birth of a family's first baby, or the sowing of seed in the first early springtime fields. Romans trusted him, and regularly they climbed the Janiculum's slopes to refresh themselves with his memory. I have a sneaking admiration for a people who cared that much about beginnings, just as I have a sneaking admiration for an old god sitting up on a hill and giving his undiverted attention to the matter.

We live in years of strange grace, as I have said, a time of the second chance when a sword hangs heavily over every head. I do not believe that we are too afraid; perhaps we should be more so. But there is a wisdom in confronting today's problems today —so long as we confront them—and leaving tomorrow's until we have all had a good night's sleep. Otherwise we run that risk, so evident in contemporary literature, of sinking back into inertia's despairing pool from which nothing can emerge but low whimpers, sad whines, and finally from somewhere in its dankest depths a few last unremarkable bubbles. In general, however, we seem to remain that youthful species which indeed we are, perhaps overconfident, perhaps a bit insensitive, but certainly unconvinced that one so youthful can die so young. And perhaps it is just as well.

Whatever our fears or our confidences, and however properly or wrongly they may be disposed, I feel a restiveness in men. It is a dissatisfaction of a universal sort, the special character of no special people. Its outlets are frequently senseless; its displays lack definition. It is unease unaware, demand undeclared, the hunger of a man at midnight who opens the refrigerator door, finds nothing that he really wants, and closing the door goes back to bed. There is a darkening, inward, indefinite mood that retains an outward poise, like that of a box of nitroglycerine at rest.

Perhaps such moods pressed the ancient Romans to climb the Janiculum and there beneath the tall cool pines to seek of an old god young refreshment. And perhaps I can lend to my feeling greater clarity if I recall an incident which occurred in Rome—and throughout all the world—just a year or two ago. I refer to the death of John.

Italians have a special attitude toward Popes which they do

not extend to the Catholic Church itself. Most of them cannot abide the Church, though they attend it. I live in a part of Rome called Trastevere, which means across the Tiber and was once that trading village at the foot of the old king's hill. The Trasteverini are very poor, very proud, look on all other Romans as immigrants, and so loathe the Church that they vote Communist almost to a man. Yet even they have a special attitude toward Popes ranging from tolerance to love. John in his lifetime they did not take too seriously: he genuinely amused them, and they responded with genuine affection; since he had once been poor they felt, I believe, a genuine bond with him. Yet nothing can quite explain what happened to the Trasteverini, or for that matter what happened to most of the world's peoples, when the old man was almost gone.

On the night before John died I went over to St. Peter's, which is just around the corner of the Janiculum from my own belligerent neighborhood. Many Trasteverini were there too, as were a good share of all those natives and strangers who happened to be in Rome at the time. We stood together in the immense Piazza di San Pietro enclosed by the curving wings of Bernini's columns. It was not an experience to take lightly, or later to lay aside with ease. The Piazza was almost dark, lighted only by a few street lamps. The Vatican Palace is a square building rising beyond the curve of the columns. It was dark. One light burned. It was in a room with an open window on the top floor next to the room where John lay dying.

Contrary to those reports published widely abroad, it was not a religious experience. Few knelt. I have since suspected that those photographs of kneeling little boys which appeared in the world press were in fact of little boys hired by photographers to provide suitable models for the occasion. But there was a silence quite unbelievable in Italy. It was as if the *noyau* had gone out of business for the time being. Nobody smoked. Despite the tens of thousands gathered in the Piazza, nobody jostled anyone. If somebody brushed against you by accident, he apologized in a low voice. The throng stood in shadowed, tight little knots, watching the lighted window, all with heads slightly tilted. What they were doing was listening to muted transistor radios, in the hands of others, relaying the most recent reports coming from the dying Pope's doctors.

I lingered, I lingered. I could not go home. I found myself gripped by an absurd emotion, one as pure as any I had ever known, and I believe that it differed little from that experienced by Catholics, even the most devout: I could not bring myself to go away and leave the old man to die by himself. If it was a religious experience that united us, that quelled even the *noyau,* then it was an experience of pagan order. We were citizens of most ancient days who had climbed the Janiculum. John, that dying king, had in his long, last, agonizing hours become consecrated throughout almost all the world as our god of the beginnings.

The death of a Pope or even of a president may unite the world in grief or shock. The union may last for but hours or days, yet brief though its stay may be, we cannot ignore it. The union transcends all boundaries, all seas, all ranges of mountains however high. The union ignores religious convictions and religious denials, the parochial sentiments of territory, the mathematics of amity-enmity, all social and racial antagonisms, the aspirations or frustration of status. One might suggest that the final hazard of death becomes real to all men and makes them, if only for the moment, one. Yet while this may be a portion of the answer, it does not satisfy me, for we tend to discover our hunger for these men only after they are gone.

And what is that hunger? What is this visceral need so desperate that it unites even enemies? I do not know. But as we finish this inquiry which for so long has absorbed us, let us ask three questions which have no answers, and all of which relate to beginnings.

2

Someday, I predict, a symposium will be convened somewhere, and to it will be invited not only men of all the sciences, but men of the cloth and of philosophy as well, and perhaps even an artist or two. The conference may well not occur within our lifetimes, but occur someday it must. And its subject will be First Causes.

Two recent events, one in the physical sciences and the other in the biological, have raised signposts painted in particularly brilliant colors, and both point toward a someday convention of minds. The most recent occurred on the evening of September 6, 1965, when at Cambridge in an address to the British Association for the Advancement of Science the great astronomer Fred Hoyle abandoned his steady-state theory of the universe. As so often happens when lightning bolts split the scientific sky, the thunder takes a long time coming. It has not yet truly begun to roll.

Some twenty years ago Hoyle and several associates put forward the entirely rational proposal that the universe has always existed and will always exist more or less as it is today. It continually expands. Galaxies of stars like our own, which we call the Milky Way, move ever farther apart from their neighbors. But as voids open, new stars, new galaxies condense from far-spread clouds of gas to enter the spaces between. Time and matter as we know them are truly infinite. And the world of which our earth is a fraction so small has been a world without beginning, as it is a world without end.

The steady-state theory, then with evidence in plenty, was one of comfort as infinite to the rational mind. The inexplicable bowed before the ineradicable. Laws of science might be modified, amended, even repealed in favor of new laws. Science itself, however, rested on that most absolute of foundations, absolute infinity. But then came radio astronomy, a new technique through which giant antennae discover and explore distant stellar objects by means of the radio waves which they give forth. And with radio astronomy came Martin Ryle, and the big bang.

Ryle proposed that, far from our world's being one with neither beginning nor end, the universe as we know it had originated little over ten billion years ago (a little longer ago, in other words, than twice the age of the earth itself) with an enormous explosion. Before that date, all existing matter had been packed into a solid mass of a density which we need not discuss since we cannot conceive of it. Then an explosion had occurred of a magnitude which likewise we need not discuss since we cannot conceive of it, either. But as you and I step out on a roof or a grassy hill, and we allow our imaginations to wander freely among those starry reaches of perpetual wonderment, then if Ryle is correct we wander among fragments of that ancient cataclysm which created all things that are.

The names of Ryle and Hoyle were reminiscent of some oldtime team of vaudeville hoofers, and Big-Bang vs. Steady-State added small solemnity to the famous controversy. The implications were sobering indeed, for the layman almost as incalculable as the astronomers' equations. Should Ryle be proved right, and the Creation placed at a finite position in the continuum of space and time, then all the fading arguments of metaphysical tradition would receive as from some unexpected oxygen tent new breath; and the otherwise impenetrable laws of science, founded on the eternal dimensions of infinity itself, would like a maze of man-made dikes and levees broached at a point of singular flaw, vanish in the omnipotent flood of ancient, imponderable waters. But you could no more take Ryle seriously than you could accept as literal argument the opening statements of a scriptural Genesis.

Then came 1960. In that year the techniques of visual and radio astronomy were combined to reveal a queer object in our skies: so distant it was that billions of years had elapsed since the light we observed had actually been brought forth; we observed the past. Yet as its light was dim its energy was enormous, and its energy was that of an object in precipitous flight. It was not a star; it was not a galaxy: we spoke of it as a quasi-stellar object, a phrase which quickly became contracted to quasar. And as more and more quasars were discovered in the space beyond ultimate space, fleeing at speeds approaching the ultimate speed of light itself, a terrifying possibility presented itself like a ragged stranger at the doors of our cosmologists: Ryle could be right. The quasars behaved in accordance with his equations: here were the farthest projectiles cast out by the original explosion, the primal objects of a primal moment, sifted and softened by that laggard, time. So far were the farthest, so long had their light taken to reach us, that what we were looking at, closer and ever more closely, was the Creation itself.

The heavens enclose us, yet beckon. As we stand on our hill, the stars imprison yet free us. As *Homo sapiens* is an incident in the history of organic being, so organic being becomes an accident, perhaps a prevalent accident, in the history of matter, time, and energy. We exist; we are here. Let probability defy or support us, it but enhances our role; let the accident of stars deny us, yet as stars remain, so likewise do we; let First Cause, imperturbable, neglect our statistical presence: still we are here, in triumph or in tribulation, in divine accordance or desperate anomaly, asserting our existence in that fugitive cosmos of which we are a part.

It was against such a philosophical backdrop that there had emerged those vaudevillean hoofers Ryle & Hoyle in an act called Big-Bang vs. Steady-State. Things move rapidly these days. Observations of quasars multiplied, and five years in our observatories was enough. Fred Hoyle appeared at Cambridge to give his audience a summary of evidences for his own version of a logical, rational, self-perpetuating cosmos and for Ryle's illogical, irrational, inexplicable condition of things. And with an integrity that one expects of science yet too infrequently encounters, he surrendered: "From the data that I have presented here it seems likely that the idea will now have to be discarded, at any rate in the form that has become widely known—the steady-state universe."

Various alternatives are today emerging which attempt to preserve some kind of order—an oscillating universe, for example, which explodes, expands, and in enormous cycle falls in on itself to explode and expand again. But the alternatives are little more than scientific rationalizations, thumbs in the bursting cosmic dike. With the triumph of Martin Ryle has reappeared—not from the altar or the cloistered cell but from the observatories and laboratories of science itself—the problem of First Causes. And it cannot be banished from future thought.

Into biology too, simultaneously and independently, has

emerged that old ghost of human preoccupation. I have twice in these pages referred to American experiments with the planarian worm: to its sense of assurance in a familiar place, and to its capacity to know what time it is. Although the evidence mounts that this simple being stores its memories in molecular lockers which may be transferred from one creature to another, I shall still avoid that most controversial of laboratory conclusions both because I believe it incompletely demonstrated and because it is inappropriate to our present reflections. The planarian's capacity to learn, however, is neither. It has been demonstrated, and demonstrated brilliantly; and with the demonstration the ghost of First Causes walks again within our walls.

Let us remind ourselves: the planarian worm is an aquatic creature so primitive in the evolutionary scale that it lacks a true central nervous system, possesses a brain consisting of nothing but two enlarged ganglia connecting its two lateral nerves, lacks a stomach or rectum or anything resembling a modern digestive system, and while capable of laying an egg is equally capable of dividing itself in two and growing a new head on the front of its old rear section. Since it can grow that head in six days, we may safely assume that the planarian's brain is an organ of no great planarian concern. And we may also assume that had the planarian worm been a creature of natural invention at any time in the last half billion years, it would have incorporated into its old-fashioned architecture a modern gadget or two. It therefore seems likely that the creature is a leftover from those hazy pre-Cambrian days of evolving life about which we know so little. But when we say that, we talk of ages belonging to the same time scale as that which absorbs the cosmologist. When we look at the planarian we are looking back into the history of life, just as when we observe a quasar we are looking back into the history of all things.

Jay Boyd Best and his colleague Irvin Rubinstein began their Washington experiments with the planarian in 1958. Their initial interest was to discover just how much such an all-but-brainless being could be taught. Most learning-and-memory experiments with the planarian have had a weakness, that the learning has been a matter of inducing a conditioned reflex, the all-purpose tool in the kit of most American psychologists. But this kind of learning, called "classical conditioning," is losing ground among our more advanced observers of behavior. What intrigued Best was that higher accommodation called "instrumental learning" by which, in pursuit of a desirable goal involving choice of actions, one learns to choose the right path and reject the wrong. A creature as simple as the planarian worm might conceivably be "taught" by electric shock a reflex to avoid this and accept that. But could this primitive being lacking sex, rectum, circulatory system, a modern nervous hook-up, a brain that could not be regrown in a few days, learn to choose between the rewarding and the unrewarding? And if so, what was he choosing with?

It took little effort for Best and Rubinstein to demonstrate that the worm could not only learn to choose, but could learn with dismaying aptitude. They constructed a plastic maze, a simple device with a Y-shaped channel connecting three wells. A worm would be placed in one well of the flooded maze, then the water would be drained out. Since the planarian cannot long survive in a dry condition, he would crawl out of the well into his tunnel in search of water. But the Y-shaped tunnel forked. The worm faced two choices. Now the observers would brightly light the well at the end of one branch of the fork and leave the other in darkness. If the worm chose the lighted well, the maze would be instantly flooded as a reward.

A training session for a worm consisted of ten or fifteen trials, and sessions were held every other day. To take account of any innate preference for light or dark, half of the worms were trained to seek the bright well for water, half the darkened. To eliminate any directional prejudices based on right and left, which well to be illuminated was determined by chance. At the first day's session all worms chose by chance; success or failure was fifty-fifty. But even at the second session preferences developed; those being trained to move toward light did so more often than toward dark; those being trained to move toward dark did so more often than toward light. By the third session—a speed of learning difficult to believe—most worms hit their peaks and chose correctly four times out of five. Then came out of nowhere the incredible collapse.

It is at this moment that we, like the observers, enter the haunted house of psychological beginnings. Almost without exception every planarian worm, once he attained a success of about 80 percent, began choosing the wrong road in preference to the right. That he "knew" what he was doing was inarguable. Had he simply forgotten his lessons, he would have relapsed to the fifty-fifty original score, determined by chance. But he did not. He dropped to one out of three. He was discriminating *against* the right choice.

Best describes himself and his colleague as being appalled. They must have been. It is a great enough mystery that such a creature could learn anything. It is an accomplishment defying one's understanding that he could learn so rapidly. But that on the verge of total success the planarian worms should uniformly embrace perversity lies entirely beyond explanation. And to make matters worse, further trials brought rejection not only of the right answer, but of the experiment itself. When the maze went dry the worms curled up, refused to go anywhere, and in arrant rebellion opted for inevitable death in preference to further learning.

The harried investigators, faced by the organic equivalent of apples falling upward and straight lines turning corners, bumbled about trying to find means of appeasing their tiny rebels, who by now had taken charge of the experiment. Perhaps there was something about the kind of plastic used in molding the maze that made worms unhappy. They found other materials. The worms remained unmoved. Perhaps the mere threat of death in a drought was not enough and the worms were on strike for inexpressible fringe benefits. The scientists added that supreme planarian delicacy, finely chopped liver, to the water in the wells which they were supposed to crawl to. The worms remained adamant, muttering some planarian equivalent of "The hell with it." By this point in the experiment it was not the mentality of worms being tested but the sanity of scientists, and hysteria hovered close by. When somebody wondered if the worms might be suffering from claustrophobia, hysteria seemed, in truth, to have closed in. Another maze was built. It offered not merely water-filled wells to save worm life but a new spaciousness at worm's end, a sense of freedom and elbow room where a worm could feel like a worm. And lo! it worked. It had been claustrophobia. The worms co-operated.

Any scientist in his right mind would with this climax assume that he had seen everything. But by now both Best and Rubinstein had long since lost touch with their right minds. They became infatuated with the possibility that worms who could suffer from claustrophobia might also have suffered boredom from a lesson so easily mastered. Fortunately for the future of psychology there was no one present to point out to the two mad scientists that a creature lacking proper brain, proper nervous system, proper belly, proper sex life, and even proper rectum has nothing under the sun to get bored with. Since no one was looking, they constructed another maze, an exact duplicate of the original, but made of rough plastic instead of smooth.

Now they started the experiment all over again. They used the smooth maze as before. They trained their worms to head for brightened or darkened wells, each as loaded with claustrophobia as the wells had been in the first place. Predictably, when the worms hit a level of 80 percent success they promptly went into a decline and started choosing wrong answers. But now the scientists clapped them in the maze that would feel rough on their undersides as they crawled along. From that day on, half of the trials were conducted in the smooth maze, half in the rough. A worm had to learn that if he felt smooth plastic against his undersides he must head for the light to reach water, but if he found himself crawling over rough plastic then to gain water he must head for the dark. In the testing of monkeys and children this is known as a double-ambiguity problem.

One out of every three planarian worms mastered the double-ambiguity problem. Sometimes when they reached the fork they would hesitate, pointing their heads first one way then the other, as if trying to make up their "minds." In animal study this is known as "vicarious trial-and-error behavior." Sometimes, unable to make up their "minds," they would go back to the starting point and begin again. But of the one out of every three who succeeded in mastering the whole problem, none ever grew bored again. None ever showed perversity, none ever rebelled, none ever curled up in tight defiance or muttered, grimly, the hell with it.

Where are we? What forces do we behold when we inspect the mind of worm or man? What is this everlasting scenery that graces our stages? What are these staircases that life has always climbed? What are these beds that life has always slept in, these antique furnishings that seem forever to have been life's own?

We do not know. Our ignorance of the human being is as massive and as measurable as our ignorance of the planarian worm. We are equivalent mysteries, and the man who says otherwise is the supreme ignoramus among us. Best wrote:

> If one finds that planarian behavior resembles behavior that in higher animals one calls boredom, interest, conflict, decision, frustration, rebellion, anxiety, learning and cognitive awareness, is it permissible to say that planarians also display these attributes? . . . Suppose the apparent similarity between the protopsychological patterns of planarians and the psychological patterns of rats and men turns out to be more than superficial. This would indicate that psychological characteristics are more ancient and widespread than the neurophysiological structures from which they are thought to have arisen. . . . Two possibilities suggest themselves. Such patterns may stem from some primordial properties of living matter, arising from some cellular or subcellular level of organization rather than nerve circuitry. . . . An alternative possibility is that the behavioral programs may have arisen independently in various species by a kind of convergent evolution. In other words, the psychology of animals may evolve in response to compelling considerations of optimal design in the same way that whales and other cetacean mammals have evolved

a fishlike shape. Both possibilities seem likely and do not exclude each other.

Whether we gaze upon worms or we gaze upon stars, the most informed of our scientists press on our wonderment the old, old problem of First Causes. We are all of a piece, of this we may be sure, the most distant, fugitive quasar, the most ancient lingering worm. But what of our beginnings? It is the first of the questions for which we have no answers, and for this one I doubt that we ever shall. What is good is the prospect that out of knowledge rather than ignorance men may someday again ask the question together; that one day we shall meet on the Janiculum, and wonder as one beneath the tall cool pines.

3

There is another question concerning beginnings of more immediate, practical, day-to-day importance to our lives; and perhaps it is just as unanswerable. Behavior is a cart, not a horse; it is a consequence, not a cause; it is an end, not a beginning. Behavior is what we do, not why we do it. We may speculate reasonably about selective value and survival necessity, and since the evolutionary process will inform us someday as to how things came out, we speculate properly. But such information will come to us as hindsight, when perhaps we are all nicely extinct, and so offers us today the most debatable compass. If means of prediction are to lie within our grasp, then we must speak of beginnings, not ends.

Why do men and other animals act as we do? Why do individuals of a given species favor this behavior pattern, reject that? Why does a howling monkey defend a social territory while the langur does not? We may trace the evolutionary history of a species, granted that materials for study are available, and come to reasonable conclusions. But they are still conclusions concerning consequence of behavior, not cause. And if ethological study is to supply us with a guidepost or two along our way, then we must come to some clearer

conception of motive, of beginnings. Why do men act as they do?

The question is unanswerable in whole, and perhaps even in part. But I shall dare to make a suggestion which must be taken for precisely what it is, a hypothesis, not an answer. And to begin with let me return to certain thoughts inspired by Frank Fraser Darling's remarks on territory and recorded in an earlier chapter.

It was Darling's conclusion, we may recall, that motivation for territory is psychological, not physiological, that it arises from twin needs in the animal for security and stimulation, and that it is satisfied by the territorial heartland and the territorial periphery. I added to that my own speculation that identity is another animal need which territory satisfies, identification with a unique fragment of something larger and more permanent than the animal itself, a place, whether social or geographical, his and his alone. But we were speaking exclusively of animals other than man. Now let me extend the thought.

I suggest that there are three beginnings—three faces of Janus—psychologically motivating the behavior of all higher animals including man. They are these same needs for identity, for stimulation, and for security. How low and how ancient they may be evidenced in the evolutionary scale we have no means as yet to guess. For all we know, they may be the primordial psychological necessities of life itself. Let us restrain ourselves now to the suggestion that they are the inward and frequently conflicting impulses lending both unity to the behavior of higher beings and continuity to the higher evolutionary processes. They provide the final refutation of human uniqueness.

I am grateful to the American psychologist Abraham Maslow for the concept which he first presented to describe needs universal to a species. He used the phrase "instinctoid needs." I find difficulty with the word "instinctoid," which for some reason or other presents me with the immediate need for either a surgeon or a bottle of Worcestershire sauce. It is an entirely personal affliction, and both Dr. Maslow and the reader must forgive me if I use the term no further. Maslow's thesis stemmed from his radical approach to psychology, the analysis of healthy people. To find out what was wrong with us, his was the heretical impulse to find out what was right with us. He assumed that just as the lack of a needed vitamin will spread disorder through the body, so the starvation of a basic psychological need will spread disorder through mind and emotion. Only through the study of healthy personalities, who through a variety of means have found satisfaction for basic needs, can one discover what the needs consist of.

As a psychologist, Maslow confined his observations to the human being and so came up with answers different from mine. He regarded love, for example, as an instinct-like human need. I should regard it not as a human need but a human answer, satisfying demands of an older and wider order. As specific patterns originating in the evolutionary past characterize the behavior of four-dimensional man, so the more general psychological needs which they serve have seen their beginnings in the time before man was born.

Identity, stimulation, security: if again you will think of them in terms of their opposites their images will be sharpened. Identity is the opposite of anonymity. Stimulation is the opposite of boredom. Security is the opposite of anxiety. We shun anonymity, dread boredom, seek to dispel anxiety. We grasp at identification, yearn for stimulation, conserve or gain security. And brood though I may over Janus' three faces, I have yet to discover a fourth.

The extent of a given need, of course, will vary from species to species, population to population, group to group, individual to individual. The need for security must be greater in prey animals than in predators, in the female than in the male, in the ill than in the well, in the unpropertied than in the propertied, in the omega fish than in the alpha, in the unstable society than in the stable. It is characteristic of an innate need, however, that it is never absent, and never more than temporarily satisfied. Like a vitamin, there must be a daily dose.

Also, there is a definite hierarchy of value among the three needs. Some needs are more pressing than others, and these too must vary from species to species, individual to individual. But curiously enough there is not the variation that one might expect. There are few exceptions to the rule that the need for identity is the most powerful and the most pervasive among all species. The need for stimulation is not far behind. And security, normally, will be sacrificed for either of the other two.

A behavior pattern or a cultural tradition is successful if it satisfies a maximum of innate need. Human war, for example, has been the most successful of all our cultural traditions because it satisfies all three basic needs. Our struggle for identity is the endless quest to achieve recognition of oneself as an individual in one's own eyes and the eyes of one's kind. War provides glory for some, the ultimate identity in the eyes of a maximum number. But the dread of anonymity does not imply a necessary tussle for fame; it is a tussle for recognition, even self-recognition, for knowing who one is. Rank satisfies identity. In a subtle fashion, war provides identity for all, from commanding general to private, through squads and companies, regiments and divisions, functional association with air or infantry or naval disposal, artillery, communications, supply, a thousand satisfying pigeonholes. All are identifications which the anonymity of civilian life can less successfully provide.

The stimulation of warfare is the most powerful produced

ever in the history of species. The flight from boredom has never been presented with such maximum satisfactions for maximum numbers. No philosopher, viewing the horrors of war through the astigmatic lenses of the pain-pleasure principle, can grasp the attraction which war presents to civilized men. It is the ultimate release from the boredom of normal existence. This was what William James so well understood when he wrote that a permanent peace economy can never be based on a pleasure economy. Pain may be far more stimulating than pleasure; death and disaster may present hypodermic charges more potent than life at its fullest, success at its most resounding. In all the rich catalogue of human hypocrisy it is difficult to find anything to compare with that dainty of dainties, that sugared delicacy, the belief that people do not like war.

Finally, there is the need for security. The rewards are equivalent. The predator fights for a net gain in security, whether in loot, land, slaves, or the confusion of enemies. The defender, on the other hand, fights to conserve security, and to destroy those forces that threaten it. A certain local anxiety may be generated, the anxiety of mothers and wives. But it is a small force as compared to the anxiety of losing the war itself.

War has suffered few sacrifices of appeal in this century. As it has gained in size and techniques of terror, it has gained in stimulation. As it has gained in participating numbers, it has gained in identification. The only real loss has been to the security of the predator through the rise of the organized territorial nation, and to the suicidal consequences of nuclear argument. While general warfare has in our time become something too fissionably hot to handle, the result has been not so much to reduce war's basic appeal as to introduce frustration into our lives; we are denied what we want. Under a *pax atomica*, a program for peace which does not include substitute satisfactions for those basic, innate needs satisfied in past times by our most popular diversion is a program of controversial validity.

As we may understand the popularity of human war, we may understand the popularity of territory. There are few institutions, animal or human, that satisfy all three needs at once.

Besides the security and the stimulation of border quarrels which it provides with equivalent largesse among species, it provides identity. "This place is mine; I am of this place," says the albatross, the patas monkey, the green sunfish, the Spaniard, the great horned owl, the wolf, the Venetian, the prairie dog, the three-spined stickleback, the Scotsman, the skua, the man from La Crosse, Wisconsin, the Alsatian, the little-ringed plover, the Argentine, the lungfish, the lion, the Chinook salmon, the Parisian. I am of this place which is different from and superior to all other places on earth and I partake of its identity so that I too am both different and superior, and it is something that you cannot take away from me despite all afflictions which I may suffer or where I may go or where I may die. I shall remain always and uniquely of this place.

I can discover no argument of objective worth which can effectively counter the claim that the psychological relationship of a lungfish to a piece of muddy water differs in any degree from the psychological relationship of the San Franciscan to the hills and the bay that he loves so well. Several hundred million years of biological evolution have altered not at all the psychological tie between proprietor and property. Neither have those unimaginable epochs of evolutionary time altered the psychological stimulation which enhances the physiological energies of the challenged proprietor. Nor have we reason to believe that the sense of security spreading ease through a troop of black lemurs in their heartland has changed a least whit throughout all of primate history in its effect on the sailor, home from the sea, or the businessman, home from the office.

War may be the most permanent, the most changeless, the most prevalent, and thus the most successful of our cultural innovations, but the reasons differ not at all from the prevalent success of territory. Both satisfy all three basic needs. And we have few other institutions to rival them.

Let us glance at love. In its ideal form, love also satisfies all three needs. It provides identity, that intense recognition in the eyes of a loved one that there is no one quite like oneself. It provides stimulation, in the love of adults, through the slam of the heart, the tensions of desire, the consummations of the bed.

337

And it provides security to varying degrees in the varying probabilities that the satisfactions of today will be the satisfactions of tomorrow. Yet the tales of the poets confirm the tragic contradictions of our innate needs. The structure of security is the birthplace of boredom. It is love's aching vulnerability. Sexual stimulation in the hands of a resourceful couple may make of love a device animated by perpetual motion; but it does not happen often. As the history of war is in large part the story of peoples who will risk all for release from boredom, so the history of adultery is in large part the story of individuals who will risk everything of apparent worth for a brief exploration of distant coasts, however paltry.

The tragic tales of the poets confirm more than the vulnerability of love; they confirm the vulnerability of security itself. That it ranks so low in the hierarchy of need is of little wonder, since the more it is satisfied the more it goads our flight from boredom, our dread of anonymity. There is some minimum need for security, without doubt, since lacking sufficient satisfaction we are consumed and immobilized by anxiety. Yet unlike the need for identity and the need for stimulation, both of which are insatiable, the need for security quickly comes to self-defeat and provides nothing but increased hunger for those demands which in the end may leave security again a bankrupt.

Perhaps it is all a part of some vital dynamics. Perhaps the contradictions of innate needs offer guarantee that life will not stand still. Perhaps in the grand psychology of being the quest for identity is nothing more than an individual realization of the demand for variation placed by evolution on animate life. Perhaps the demand for stimulation is the compulsion to compete, without which natural selection could not exist. Perhaps the limitation placed on our need for security rests on the role of the population as an evolutionary unit, in which the fate of individuals has limited significance. All is speculation, but should the relation of our innate needs to evolution be demonstrable, then one might understand why from animate beginnings they have been bound up with the processes of life itself.

338

What is evident without too great speculation is how few are the behavioral outlets which satisfy all three needs. War has been one, territory is another, and there is sometimes love. There is another, I believe, which, since we have not yet investigated it, we cannot enlarge upon: The social invention, which supplies identity on two levels through one's membership in a society and one's rank within it; which supplies stimulation on two levels through the competitions of societies as groups and the competitions of individuals for dominant positions within the group; and which provides security on two levels, the stability of the group and the stability of one's rank within the hierarchy. But few are the behavioral patterns or cultural traditions which satisfy more than a fraction of our needs. Alcohol, that time-tested nourishment, may provide stimulation and heroic identification in our own eyes; in the eyes of others, however, we are a drunk, and security is threatened besides. Crime is likewise an old institution offering immense reward for our needs of identity and stimulation and, granted sufficient social tolerance or indifference, may even gain a measure of security as well.

In general, however, our means of satisfying innate needs are precious few, and the sacrifice of any must mean replacement by another. We may agree, for example, that the smoking of cigarettes is dangerous to health; yet unless we provide alternative stimulation, we shall have little luck stamping out the addiction through appeal to security, weakest of all needs. We may agree, for example, that our societies must provide greater security for the individual; yet if all we succeed in producing is a social structure providing increased anonymity and ever increasing boredom, then we should not wonder if ingenious man turns to such amusements as drugs, housebreaking, vandalism, mayhem, riots, or, at the most harmless, strange haircuts, costumes, standards of cleanliness, and sexual experiments. He is achieving identity otherwise denied him, discovering excitements socially unavailable.

We face in the elimination of war this most fundamental of psychological problems. For almost as long as civilization has been with us, war has represented our most satisfactory means of at once escaping anonymity and boredom while preserving or gaining a measure of security. It has been the all-purpose answer to our innate needs. Now advancing technology may force us to abandon the diversions of warfare; but we cannot discard from human expression an institution so outrageously satisfying without discovering and encouraging substitute outlets. However we choose to state the challenge: as a necessity to nourish our needs so that we shall not fight; or, since we cannot fight, to discover other satisfactions so that we shall not starve: whatever may be our approach, the challenge to human ingenuity remains the same.

That challenge is being met by ethology on two different fronts which are probably one and the same. There is the approach of Konrad Lorenz, with its emphasis on the individual and on the practicality as well as the necessity for the ritualization of aggression. I discussed this briefly in the last chapter as evolution's normal mode of accepting aggressiveness as healthy and essential to animate beings, but providing for it a host of means whereby anatomical or behavioral mechanisms discourage lethal outcome. The vervet monkey has a tiny white line just over its eyelids, invisible except when he lifts his eyebrows in a gesture of threat; the sight of the white line discourages further hostilities. The dog wags its tail as a signal of friendly intentions, and dogs understand; the cat wags her tail as a gesture of unfriendly intentions, and cats understand. The baboon has canine teeth like Florentine daggers, deadly to leopards and fellow baboons alike; but for his fellows he need only throw back his head to exhibit his dental wonders, and it is usually enough.

The pressure of natural selection, we might say, rides with human survival and not against it. We may well complain, "But man is a hunter, and what of that killing propensity within us?" The wolf, however, is a hunter and a killer with an inheritance older than our own; and when wolves indulge in final debate, the loser rolls over on his back, exposing his belly to the victor; the winner, incapable of attacking him further, walks away. It is a behavioral gesture in no wise different from the human gesture of raising one's hands in surrender.

We cannot proceed too far into the ordered parklands of animal example, or we shall be guilty of taking trends out of windows, and of placing human faith in human potentialities which do not exist. But since evolutionary command proceeds on an unconscious, not conscious, level, it is an appropriate moment to recall Anthony Storr's suggestion to the London symposium that the space race has been a ritualization of the cold war. Should this be true—and I accept it intuitively as true—then a phenomenon lacking any possible practical explanation finds its motivation in the secret recesses of evolutionary motivation. Frustrated in our warlike rivalries for power, the Soviet Union and the United States of America have joined in a ritual as expensive as war itself. Identity with one side or the other and stimulations of the most imaginative of competitions receive infinite satisfaction. Yet the security of the species is subjected to no threat beyond the expendability of a hero or two. That the human populations involved have borne with cheer the most improvident of costs for the most implausible of economic returns testifies to the validity of the human demands rewarded. That the ritualization has been unconscious—that, in other words, we have not had a rational clue as to what we were doing—is confirmed by the general astonishment at Storr's explanation. And that the human being, for all his rational uniqueness, could surrender himself to a procedure so rooted in the unthinking evaluations of natural selection is the most hopeful omen for the human future which modern history has so far produced.

Lorenz' preoccupation with ritualization which, while accepting the virtues of aggression, looks for means to contain its vices has approached the challenge largely from the viewpoint of the individual. V. C. Wynne-Edwards, on the other hand, has tended to accept the perspective of society. I have suggested that we put his definition of society out into the sun to ripen for a while; let us bring it in: "A society can be defined as a group of individuals competing for conventional prizes by conventional means."

Wynne-Edwards' definition may be interpreted in Lorenz' terms, as a means of ritualizing the natural and necessary rivalries of man; or it may be interpreted in my own terms, as an institution providing for its members identity and stimulation without undue sacrifice of security. A properly constituted society is therefore a natural society—a society in accord with evolutionary principles—which provides for all its members the stimulation of rivalry for the prizes of identity by means of fair competition governed by accepted rules and regulations. The more open be the rivalry, the more worthy the prizes, the more fair and accepted the rules of competition, the more successful will be the society and the more satisfied the innate needs of its members.

Human history offers few examples of such openness of rivalry, such worthiness of prize, or such fairness of competition. The definition might be dismissed as Utopian were it not for a single exception. For all our efforts to enclose competition within such boundaries as caste, for all our successful ambitions to load the dice of fair competition, for all our sentimental education of recent decades which has attempted to demean competition itself, one human activity has resisted our best efforts, that of the athlete. Never have we regarded him as anything but a natural animal. None has pretended that his aggressiveness is learned. No one has offered him less than the most profuse of conventional prizes. And in no field of human activity have the rules of the game been more strictly enforced, or more willingly accepted.

Since the time of the first Olympic games, twenty-seven centuries ago, ethics and aggression have been the heads and tails of sport. The respectability of rivalry has in a sense generated and compelled the morality—the ritualization—of rivalry's rules and regulations. The cheat occurs, of course, and is the immediate subject of headlines. Lapse of ethics may overcome an entire sport; it will cause the prompt dismissal of that sport as unworthy of popular attention. So rare indeed is the cry of counterfeit in sports of international attention that it becomes overnight the scandal of nations. But the morality of sport has little to do with the pressure of public opinion; it is the innate demand of that innate aggressor, the athlete.

Storr's interpretation of the space race as being unconsciously motivated is hopeful; so likewise is the athlete's willingness—no, far more, innate capacity—for accepting and learning the rules of the game. Russians and Americans without propaganda or doctoral degrees in the theory and practice of ritualization have accepted the cost of the space race with enthusiasm; and so the athlete, that respectable aggressor, accepts and absorbs the rules and regulations of his sport without, in many cases, benefit of a registerable IQ. The open human aggressive instinct, unfrustrated by social disapproval, sucks up like a vacuum cleaner the most minute particles of learning to complete its pattern. Whether the athlete has mental capacities to rattle about in the interior of a thimble or to strain the capacities of a ten-gallon hat, he will learn with equal facility complexities of plays, subtleties of movement, intricacies of rules and regulations to baffle an Einstein. There is no mind within the normal range of *Homo sapiens* which cannot grasp the most complex rules of an athletic competition, as there are few spirits unwilling to abide by the conventions so long as society guarantees that the conventions will be observed by all.

Here in the world of the athlete is Wynne-Edwards' group of individuals competing for conventional prizes by conventional means. As in the world of the animal, aggression is recognized, encouraged, channeled, and by innate acceptance restrained within the bounds of danger. It is then possible to believe that human energies can be so satisfied only on the baseball diamond, the hockey rink, the football field, the runner's track? Were we to reverse our attitudes toward competition and aggression, to recognize and encourage them in all paths of life, to accept as a prime social obligation the guarantee that competition will be open to all social partners and that the conventions will be defied by none, is it impossible to believe that our innate needs for identity, stimulation, and a degree of security lie within human fulfillment?

Civilization already presents us with our putting greens and our stamping grounds, our offices and our factories, our mines and plowed fields, our artists' studios, our scholars' studies, our green recesses of nature where men may meditate, our high stairways of oratory where men may act, our dark alleyways where aggression uncontained asserts its most ferocious practicalities, the sunniness of our campuses where the most impractical of visions may be pursued in full play, our stations of the cross where some may explore one devotion, our carpeted mosques where some follow another, our halls for performance, our markets for trading, our accepted haunts for the opposition of beaks, our traditional grounds for the confrontation of noses. Civilization lacks nothing in its imitation of nature; what it lacks, and lacks only, is its recognition of man as an animal.

What shall we do? How shall we proceed? Shall we make a man to fit the world, or a world to fit the man? It is an open question, probably unanswerable.

4

One more unanswerable question arises from my amity-enmity equation, and involves unpredictables beyond contemporary imagination. It too rests on beginnings, an appropriate subject for meditation beneath the Janiculum's pines. But these are beginnings peculiar to man, without animal precedent since the time of life's origin in the primal slimes. They are beginnings beginning now.

When I conceived of the amity-enmity equation, I did it in the mood of a private joke on those psychologists who must reduce all human qualities to mathematical statements. I recognized and enjoyed its weaknesses, its failure to include minor symptoms of original or residual amity which exist though insufficiently to effect social organization; its failure to recognize the infinite ranges of human variability; its failure, in other words, to accept the incalculability of complex man. As I emphasized in the last chapter, I introduced it not for purposes of predictability but of illumination. And in its conception my engrossment with the relation between amity and enmity was such that I quite failed to consider the harshness of that illumination which the introduction of hazard brought to the equation.

$$A = E + h$$

The simplest of arithmetic will demonstrate that as h rises, then to produce an effective amity, E may fall. But let us forgo the dismal swamp of even the simplest arithmetic and recall those experiences of fire and flood and sudden storm, of natural emergencies which as if by spontaneous combustion produce instant mutual aid, unthinking sacrifice, smiles on the faces of strangers, intimacies exchanged which have never changed hands before, a gladness and trust that leave us sorry when the emergency has passed. And this reduction in animosities through increase of natural hazard is no quality uniquely human. Let us take one last excursion into the animal world.

Penguins are among the most ancient of birds. Fossils from the Eocene as old as the oldest lemurs show them little different in anatomy or distribution from the way they are today. All species, in their chilly devotions, lead lives of a certain hazard. But if you compare species with species, you will discover that as hazard goes up, mechanisms for enmity come down.

All penguins have traditional breeding grounds. Carbon dating applied to the frozen mummies of Adélie penguins at McMurdo Sound—where Wood captured his Antarctic skuas for temporary exile to the South Pole—indicates that the breeding ground there has been in operation for at least 600 years. But while we may regard the raising of children in that part of the world as an occupation of such inconceivable hazard as to be uniform in its dimension, it is not so. The Adélie builds a normal nest of stones on rocky ground, must fight off the raiding skua, suffers it is true the misfortune of being buried in snowstorms now and again, but still has sufficient unspent energy to seek the stimulation of territorial defense, quarreling with neighbors, and raiding nearby nests for stones. So it goes with the gentoo species in milder Grahamsland, where the male defending his four-foot territory will fight anybody including his mate, unless she makes the proper bow at the border. So it is with the chin-strap, also in Grahamsland, who like the albatross returns season after season to the same site and will evict all comers who seek to dispute him. So it is with the jackass penguin of South African islands, who has gained his name from the braying qualities of his imperishably quarrelsome *noyau*. But let us look at the emperor.

No natural hazard which this planet offers can rival those circumstances assaulting the life expectancy of the emperor penguin's young. The emperor breeds only on the ice of the Antarctic continent. And he breeds in winter. When March comes, and the southern autumn darkens, the emperor and his

346

wife and his friends conduct their grave march inland across the
ice to that place where tradition dictates that they must breed.
There will be no nest of stones. She will lay her single egg on
ice of fathomless depth, and he will pick the egg up on his foot.
Then she will go away, back to the sea and their only source of
food. He will remain with the egg on his foot. The perpetual
night will enclose him. The Antarctic winter will blow,
shudder, sigh, snap, crush, torment the present as it has
tormented all ages. He will stand with the egg on his foot. He
will stand very close among his friends as shoulder to shoulder
they preserve their heat. There will be no argument, disputes
over property, dominance, borders, prerogatives. On rare occasion the night will clear to reveal the Southern Cross in cruel
arrangement. The southern aurora will in ironic delicacy
display its gentle, faraway veils, shifting, impalpable, tantaliz-
ing, rewardless. More often the storm will close down. All will
vanish. There will be the wind and the cold beyond calculation. There will be the horror of nature's racket, and the
horror of nature's silence. There will be the terror of nature's
incredible blackness. There will be the terror of nature's soft
illumination. And all the time the emperor penguin and his
friends will be standing in a dense, unarguing mass, each with
an egg on his foot, while slowly they revolve, presenting to this
one the periphery of Antarctic hostility, presenting to that one
a respite, a moment of comfort and warmth in the heartland of
the social body.

For two months, this will be their dispensation. Then their
wives, fat and hearty, will return from the sea. The males will
surrender their eggs, themselves seek the succor of wide-open
waters, the freedom, the succulence of life. When they return,
the chicks will have hatched. Springtime will be on its way, and
the sunshine, and that most favorable season for the survival of
young. This, after all, was the whole evolutionary point, the
reason for the time of winter trial.

Brooks too broad for leaping divide us from animal agony.
Walls too tall for weeping contain our sympathies. We cannot,
with prescience human or divine, apprehend the living moment in a mass of male emperor penguins revolving each with

an egg on his foot in a dark, frozen, endless Antarctic night beneath frigid, withdrawn, uncaring stars. You do not know, nor will you ever. I shall not know, nor shall I ever. We may simply record that when h reaches infinity, E reaches zero.

And that is how it may be when natural hazard unmade or unsupported by man approaches the zenith of its value; but what happens to us when it approaches its nadir? What happens when it is h that approaches zero? What must happen to E?

The story of civilization has been the reduction of hazard both natural and supernatural in its total effect on human existence. And the story of that facet of civilization called war has been one of consolidation and intensification of enmity. Is the one the consequence of the other? Or is all coincidence?

I take nothing away, of course, from the accomplishments of antiquity when it comes to massacre, slaughter of innocents, and designs for decimation. *Homo habilis* boasts a fractured skull; violence seems to have been always with us. The cultured Greek, between exercises in philosophy, oratory, and the allied arts, annihilated whole populations whose opinions differed from his own. By then, of course, hazard was sinking, or art would have been impossible. Neither do I wish to detract from experiments with systematic cruelty practiced in oldtime days. Byzantium, a thousand years ago, was ruled by an able emperor named Basil II who suffered ceaseless inconveniences from the unruly Bulgarians. And so, having captured 15,000 of them in battle, he put out their eyes. One man in every hundred, however, was left with one eye, enough to lead his fellows home to their tsar.

We must accept the possibility that throughout history the ameliorating benefits of conscience, which handfuls of thinkers here and there regard as universal, have saved more men than they have killed. The statistics, however, are not convincing. Elastic application of the universal conscience has merely enforced the parochial commands of the amity-enmity complex, so that God fights always on our side. We must accept also the possibility that the growth of enlightenment, the spread of education, and the lengthening attributes of foresight have introduced some measurable inhibitions to the art of murder. But Derek

348

Freeman has presented figures indicating that between 1825 and 1945, a period in which such growth was notable, fifty-nine million people fell victim of "deadly quarrels." The figure, as Freeman grants, is conservative. And even though we acknowledge that population growth has introduced more ducks to the human shooting gallery, still the statistics remain disturbing. In a period in which technological advance was rapidly pressing natural hazard toward a historic minimum, and in which such supernatural hazards as witches and witch-doctors, spells and charms, and hellfire and damnation were rapidly losing ground to unencumbered intelligence, we pressed lethal animosities to their maximum.

The suspicion must exist that the inverse relationship between the fall of hazard and the rise of enmity which the equation would indicate has had at least something to do with it. Perhaps it has merely been that with growing control over our physical environment we have been left with more free time for killing each other. Without doubt our superb technological achievements have presented us with superb opportunities for wholesale murder denied the ancient world. But even making proper allowance for the manifold inducements, temptations, and opportunities more grandly expanding our natural satisfactions derived from mutual massacre, I cannot eliminate from my estimates the necessity for enemies which falling hazard compels.

And so we must face the unanswerable question: What will happen if the control which we exert over our physical environment ever totally eliminates natural hazard? Will man become the temperamental opposite of the emperor penguin? When hazard appraches zero, will enmity approach infinity?

The human predicament contains two forces: On the one hand that balance of terror, the *pax atomica,* compels a general peace, or at the least insists that a general peace be observed until accident or cynicism end it. In any event, war as we have known it has become both an impractical outlet for our innate psychological needs and an impractical external pressure enforcing our social amity. But on the other hand man's cultural achievements have long since pressed him beyond a point of

349

possible return, and if he is to survive on his irreversible course of technological mastery, specialized skill, and consequent interdependence, then he becomes with every passing year, every passing day, more at the mercy of social amity and mutual co-operation.

And so we must ask: Have our cultural achievements in peacetime, eliminating the reality of natural hazard, matched our cultural achievements in wartime, eliminating the reality of enemies, so that in final sum we must face that primate impossibility, exaggerated by human achievement, reduction to zero of effective amity?

It is the darkest of questions for all those who have placed their faith in cultural evolution as a means for accomplishing the pacification of man. It is a dark enough question for anybody. And unless nature saves us by an unexpected surfeit of earthquakes, volcanic upheavals, tidal waves, and swarms of locusts, we are caught in the most encompassing of traps. I have no suggestion of shaking penetration to offer beyond that most obvious of comments: that we must know ourselves better in the future than we have in the past.

We must know that man, while the alpha fish among species, is unique only in his capacity for getting himself into troubles that for other species nature would be compelled to provide.

We must know that as body and behavior evolve as a collective enterprise, so human behavior like the human body is governed by evolutionary laws comparable to those of any other species.

We must know that while the human brain exceeds by far the potentialities of that possessed by any other animal species, its psychological processes probably differ not at all from those of other higher animals, and from those of lower animals perhaps as well.

While granting that the varying cultural achievements of human populations set man apart from other animals, still we must know that such cultures, however complex, simply serve to fill out behavioral patterns, some as ancient as recorded life.

We must know, and strive with all our might to accept, that while our evolutionary inheritance seems to place a limitation on human freedom, an eternity of natural selection has presented us as its legacy with the foundation of human strength.

We must recall, and recall again, as by choice of subjects I have attempted to emphasize in this final chapter, that man no different from any other animal is a complex of expressions, frequently conflicting, in which no single determinant—territory, society, dominance, sex, economic necessity, or single innate need for identity, stimulation, or security—holds exclusive or permanent domain. Man, as does any other animal, lives the life of a whole being.

And finally we must know that the territorial imperative—just one, it is true, of the evolutionary forces playing upon our lives—is the biological law on which we have founded our edifices of human morality. Our capacities for sacrifice, for altruism, for sympathy, for trust, for responsibilities to other than self-interest, for honesty, for charity, for friendship and love, for social amity and mutual interdependence have evolved just as surely as the flatness of our feet, the muscularity of our buttocks, and the enlargement of our brains, out of the encounter on ancient African savannahs between the primate potential and the hominid circumstance. Whether morality without territory is possible in man must remain as our final, unanswerable question.

5

When Eliot Howard in his country clothes sat quietly by an English pond watching his moor hens in their goings and their comings, their unions and their animosities, their patterned wars and their patterned peace, he opened the covers of a book that no man had more than glimpsed before, and he read and comprehended the first chapter. It was all he had time for in the course of one lifetime. The first chapter was enough, however, to give him, as it should give us, a fair inkling as to what the book is about. While he never had time to get past the first chapter, he was undoubtedly curious about the last one. So shall we be curious, and curiosity will grow as we turn further

pages. But we, like Howard, will never have time to finish reading the book, and our consolation must be that a last chapter, in all probability, does not exist.

What has been good—or so I believe—about an opening inquiry into the role of territory in animal and human affairs is that it gives us in the future some place to stand. The night may be no less dark, the stars no less distant, the human outcome no less uncertain, the voices that advise us in forgotten tongues no less incomprehensible. But we have made a little place in the forest that we may regard as our own. We have sniffed about, recognized a few of its potential resources, found a hiding place or two that seem secure. We have marked out as well as we could the boundaries of our new domain and deposited scent on this tree trunk, that bush, to inform intruders that someone is home. We are predators, of course, and from time to time we shall go out looting and raping and raising general havoc in the surrounding countryside. There will be reprisals, naturally. And that is another reason why it will be so good to have some place to stand, some place to regard as ours.

It is a matter of surpassing remark, when you come down to think about it, what a change in the landscape occurs when you have made a place of your own: how the shape of an oak tree emerges in the darkness to take on that definition which can only be oak; how stars shine brighter, and those of fifth or even sixth magnitude become apparent; how the sound of some running brook—it must be a long way off—chants its quiet cadence; how smells rush at you, the smell of mint—could it be from the brook? impossible—the smell of leaves, green leaves dampened by dew, but of other leaves also, old leaves, last year's fallen leaves, that sweet, soft odor of death's decomposition. And then there is that muskiness. There is an animal somewhere.

BIBLIOGRAPHICAL KEY
AND
BIBLIOGRAPHY

Bibliographical Key and Bibliography

THE NUMBERED REFERENCES are those to which the BIBLIOGRAPHICAL KEY is a guide. If the reference is a book, the title is italicized. If the reference is a paper appearing in a professional journal, the name of the journal is italicized, and volume, page, and date are indicated. If the reference is a paper appearing in a book edited by another author, then the editor's name may be indicated, with the reference number in parentheses.

Bibliographical Key

1. OF MEN AND MOCKINGBIRDS *pp. 3–41*

SECTION 1: pp. 3–7. Steward 217. General territorial background: 44, 104, 106, 108, 177.

SECTION 2: pp. 7–17. College Outline Series 1, 2. Wolf 173. Howler 39 or 45. Ring-tail lemur 104, 184. Night heron 144, 225. Mayr first quote 162, second 163. Piltdown 239. Smith quote 213. Ardrey 9. Dart 54, 55. Present African discoveries 139, 140, 226. Proconsul 137. General background reading in contemporary evolutionary theory 113, 163, 209, and in application to special fields 13, 194.

SECTION 3: pp. 17–28. Maslow 152. Butterfly, Capricorn beetle 76. Behaviorism 238. Whitman, Heinroth *145*. Lorenz 144. Tinbergen 223. Kortlandt 130. Weaver bird 149. Poulsen 185. Herring gull 224. Eskimo dogs 223. Digger wasp 223. Burt quote 76. Bullock quote 34. General background, learning and instinct 76, 146, 194, 221, 223.

SECTION 4: pp. 29–38. Quotes: Mead 166, Montagu first 171, second 172, Hallowell 98, McRae 165.

SECTION 5: pp. 39–41. Quotes: Simpson 209, Spencer *125*.

2. ARENA BEHAVIOR *pp. 42–80*

SECTION 1: pp. 42–51. Uganda kob 32, 33. Seal 14.

SECTION 2: pp. 51–62. Kob 32, 33. Buechner quote, personal communication. Howard 108. Aristotle, Pliny *114*. Zeno, Olina *135*. White *114*. De Buffon *135*. Altum 161. Moffat 169. Darwin 57. Wynne-Edwards 242. Brewster, Herrick *44*. *Ibis* quote *114*. Moor hen, warbler, etc. 108. Albatross 190.

SECTION 3: pp. 62–71. Simpson 210. Wasp species 70. Cicada-killer wasp 142. Ruff 87, 242. Turner quote 229. Blackcock lek 242. Mayr's arena definition 87. Sage grouse 203.

SECTION 4: pp. 71–80. Gilliard quote 87. Wallace quote *85*. Austin Rand *87*. Bowerbird varieties 87, except satin 150.

357

3. *TO HAVE AND TO HOLD* pp. 81–117

SECTION 1: pp. 81–92. Great crested grebe 111. Willock 240. Red deer 51. Indian deer, G. B. Schaller personal communication. Herring gull 224. Three-spined stickleback, fighting cock, etc. 223. Huxley 112.

SECTION 2: pp. 92–100. Gilliard 87. Jackdaw 146. Bou-bou shrike 222. Gibbon 41 or 45, 68. Robin 135. Lack's early doubts, 134. Three-spined stickleback, 225. Wren, mockingbird 135. Altum 161. Howard 108.

SECTION 3: pp. 101–117. Quotes: Hediger 104, Matthews in discussion 160. Burt 36. Heape 102. Beaver 28. Lack quote 135. Carpenter 39 or 45. Platy 27. Swordtails 180. Cichlid fish 12. Cricket 3. Planarian 18, 19. Soviet and American farming 195, 233.

4. *THE VOYAGE OF THE ANIMALS* pp. 118–155

SECTION 1: pp. 118–120. Green turtle 46.

SECTION 2: pp. 121–132. Deer mouse 174. Frog 31. Dog *221*. Trout *221*. Eel 199. Environmentalist interpretation 228, refuted 242. Gobie 10. Cambridge pigeons 155, 156, 157, 158. Starling 132. Planarian clock 17. American pigeons 186, 187. Thorpe on clocks 221. Brown trout *86*. Black-headed gull *221*. Polarized light, ultra-shortwave, Cariolis experiments *221*. Barred warblers, Heligoland 132. Planetarium *221*.

SECTION 3: pp. 132–143. Allee quote 4. Carthy 47. J. Fisher quote 72. Green sunfish 101. Seal 128. Thorpe on salmon 221. Taste hypothesis 100. Juvenile Atlantic salmon 123. Population genetics: R. A. Fisher 74, Haldane 92, Wright 241, Huxley 113, Simpson 209. Dobzhansky quote 63.

SECTION 4: pp. 143–152. Manx shearwater 159. Skua 67. Albatross 127, 189, 190.

SECTION 5: pp. 152–155. Porpoise 126. Gymnarchus 143. Alpha wave 65. Tilapia 12.

5. *THE NOYAU* pp. 156–188

SECTION 1: pp. 156–167. Godwit, blackheaded gull 115. Individual distance 50, 103. Tufted duck, meadow pipit 50. Partridge, brown trout, flea, bivalve 242. Cliff swallow 69. Herring gull 224. Hediger's pygmy hippo 26.

SECTION 2: pp. 167–173. Lepilemur 184. Darling 51, 52, quote 53. Lorenz quote 145. Viscachas 183. Starling 242. Quotes: Fisher 71, Wynne-Edwards 242.

SECTION 3: pp. 173–183. Song sparrow 176. Satin bowerbird 150. Vervet 30. Patas 97 and personal communications. Gopher 212. Lesser mole rat 16. Nest painting 84. Callicebus monkey 154.

SECTION 4: pp. 184–188. No reference.

6. THE NATION pp. 189–226

SECTION 1: pp. 189–201. Lemurs 184. Access to Madagascar 207. Lemur hand 20. General background, primate history 141, 208.

SECTION 2: pp. 202–219. Slime molds 25. Ant colonies 232. Hachet-Souplet 62. Fiddler crab 182. Lizards 178, 179. Chameleon 29. Rodent species 35, 36, 37. Burt's opposition e.g. 22. Golden-mantled ground squirrel 91. Noble territory definition 180. Older studies, baboons 148, 245. 245 criticized 95. Howling monkey 39 or 45. Primate society not based on sex 7, 136, 153, 154, 184, 236, 237. Carpenter's studies 39–45. His name misspelled 122. Japanese monkey 82. Bolwig 24. Schaller 197, 198. Hall 93, 94. Goodall 88, 89, 90. Kortlandt 131. Petter 184. Washburn and DeVore 236.

SECTION 3: pp. 219–226. Tinbergen 223. Howler 39 or 45. Patas 97. Callicebus 154. Gibbon 41 or 45, 68. Sifaka 184. Gorilla 197, 198. Baboon 93, 94, 95, 236. Japanese monkey 117, 118. Rhesus monkey 7, 214, 215. Vervet 30, Gartlan unpublished. Langur 120. Chimpanzee 88, 89, 90, 131, 188. Black lemur 184. Hamadryas baboon 133.

7. LOOK HOMEWARD ANGEL pp. 227–268

SECTION 1: pp. 227–236. No reference.

SECTION 2: pp. 236–243. Lorenz quote 145.

SECTION 3: pp. 244–253. Keith 124. Ardrey quote 9. Washburn 237. Baboon 93, 94, 95, 236. Baboon and vervet territory: Hall and Gartlan personal communications. Lemur 184. Wolf 5, 173. Thick-billed nutcracker 220. Great horned owl 15, 167. Bushman 206, personal communication. Squirrels 91. Callicebus 154. Tinbergen first quote 223, second 225.

SECTION 4: pp. 253–263. General background, human evolution: 9, 21, 49, 54, 55, 99, 125, 137, 141, 175, 181, 192, 235. Washburn quote 235. Chimpanzee 88. *Homo habilis* date 75; controversy 140, 193, 226, present state 227. Leakey quote 138. James quote 119. Tinbergen 224.

SECTION 5: pp. 264–268. No reference.

8. *THE AMITY-ENMITY COMPLEX* *pp. 269–319*

SECTION 1: pp. 269–275. No reference.
SECTION 2: pp. 275–281. Geese 121. Smooth-billed ani 58. Prairie dog 129.
SECTION 3: pp. 281–288. Darwin 56, 57. Wallace 231. T. H. Huxley 116. Spencer 216. Sumner 219. Keith 124, 125.
SECTION 4: pp. 288–305. Montagu 170. Dollard 64. Freud 78, 79, 80, 81. Miller 168. McKellar 164. Sears 204. Lynching 107. First Scott quote 200. Eibl-Eibesfeldt 66. Von Holst 230. Second Scott quote 201. Davis 58. Third Scott quote 202. College Outline Series 83. Aggression symposium 48. Fisher 73. Wallis 232. Matthews 160. Hall 96. Lorenz 147. Storr 218. Freeman 77. Andreski 8. De Monchaux 60. Hill 105. Burton 38.
SECTION 5: pp. 305–319. Selzer 205.

9. *THREE FACES OF JANUS* *pp. 320–353*

SECTION 1: pp. 320–323. No reference.
SECTION 2: pp. 323–332. Hoyle 110. Planaria 18.
SECTION 3: pp. 332–344. Darling 53. Maslow 151, 152. James 119. Ritualization 147, also 66. Storr 218. Wynne-Edwards 242, also 243 and 244 for brief available summaries of his work.
SECTION 4: pp. 344–351. Penguins 11, 191, 211. Freeman 77.
SECTION 5: pp. 351–353. No reference.

Bibliography

1. ALEXANDER, GORDON. *Biology*. College Outline Series. New York, Barnes and Noble, 1962.
2. ALEXANDER, GORDON. *General Zoology*. College Outline Series. New York, Barnes and Noble, 1962.
3. ALEXANDER, RICHARD D. Aggressiveness, territorial and sexual behavior in field crickets. *Behavior* 17:130–220, 1961.
4. ALLEE, W. C., ET AL. *Principles of Animal Ecology*. Philadelphia, W. B. Saunders, 1950; reprinted 1963.
5. ALLEN, D. L., and L. D. MECH. Wolves vs moose on Isle Royale. *National Geographic* Feb. 1963.
6. ALTMANN, STUART A. Social behavior of anthropoid primates. In Bliss (23).
7. ALTMANN, STUART A. Field study of the sociobiology of rhesus monkeys. *Annals N.Y. Acad. Science* 102:338–435, 1962.
8. ANDRESKI, STANISLAV. Origins of war. In Carthy and Ebling (48).
9. ARDREY, ROBERT. *African Genesis*. New York, Atheneum, 1961.
10. ARONSON, LESTER R. Orientation and jumping behavior of gobiid fish. *American Museum Novitates* No. 1486, Jan. 17, 1951.
11. AUSTIN, OLIVER L., JR. *The Birds of the World*. New York, Golden Press, 1961.
12. BAERENDS, G. P., and J. M. BAERENDS-VAN ROON. Ethology of cichlid fishes. *Behavior Supplement* 1:1–241, 1950.
13. BARNETT, S. A., editor. *A Century of Darwin*. Cambridge, Mass., Harvard Univ. Press, 1958.
14. BARTHOLOMEW, G. A., and P. G. HOEL. Reproductive behavior of the Alaska fur seal. *Journal of Mammalogy* 34:417–36, 1953.
15. BAUMGARTNER, F. M. Territory and population in the great horned owl. *Auk* 56:274–282, 1939.
16. BELA, BODNER. Le spalax de Hongrie. *La Terre et La Vie* 4:323–333, 1934.
17. BEST, JAY BOYD. Diurnal cycles and cannibalism in planaria. *Science* 131:1884–5, 1960.

18. BEST, JAY BOYD. Protopsychology. *Scientific American* Feb. 1963.

19. BEST, J. B., and I. RUBINSTEIN. Environmental familiarity and feeding in the planarian. *Science* 135:916–18, 1962.

20. BISHOP, ALISON. Control of the hand in lower primates. *Annals N.Y. Acad. Science* 102:316–337, 1962.

21. BISHOP, W. W. Later Tertiary and Pleistocene in equatorial Eastern Africa. In Howell and Bourlière (109).

22. BLAIR, W. F. Home range of deermouse and chipmunk. *Jour. Mammalogy* 23:27–36, 1942.

23. BLISS, E. L., editor. *Roots of Behavior.* New York, Harper & Row, 1962.

24. BOLWIG, NIELS. Study of the behavior of the chacma baboon. *Behavior* 14:136–163, 1959.

25. BONNER, JOHN TYLER. How slime molds communicate. *Scientific American* Aug. 1963.

26. BOURLIÈRE, FRANÇOIS. *The Natural History of Mammals.* New York, Knopf, 1954; 2nd edition 1956.

27. BRADDOCK, J. C. Effect of prior residence on dominance in the fish Platypoecilus maculatus. *Physiological Zoology* 22: 161–9, 1949.

28. BRADT, GLENN W. Study of beaver colonies in Michigan. *Jour. Mammalogy* 19:139–162, 1938.

29. BRAIN, C. K. Chameleo dilepsis: a study of its biology and behavior. *Jour. Herpetological Assn. Rhodesia* 15:15–20, 1961.

30. BRAIN, C. K. Adaptations to forest and savannah. *Wenner-Gren Symposium No. 31,* 1965.

31. BREDER, C. M., JR., ET AL. Frog-tagging. *Zoologica* 9:201–29, 1927.

32. BUECHNER, HELMUT K. Territorial behavior in the Uganda kob. *Science* 133:698–9, 1961.

33. BUECHNER, HELMUT K. Territoriality as a behavioral adaptation to environment in the Uganda kob. *Proc. XVI Int. Congress of Zoology* 3:59–62, Aug. 1963.

34. BULLOCK, THEODORE H. Evolution of neurophysiological mechanisms. In Roe and Simpson (194).

35. BURT, W. H. Territorial behavior and populations of some small animals in Southern Michigan. *Miscellaneous Publications* Museum of Zoology, Univ. of Michigan 45:1–58, 1940.

36. BURT, W. H. Territoriality and home range concepts as applied to mammals. *Jour. Mammalogy* 24:346–52, 1943.

37. BURT, W. H. Territoriality. *Jour. Mammalogy* 30:25–7, 1949.

38. BURTON, JOHN. Nature of aggression in the atomic age. In Carthy and Ebling (48).

39. CARPENTER, C. R. Behavior and social relations of the howling monkey. *Comparative Psychology Monographs,* May 1934.

40. CARPENTER, C. R. Behavior of red spider monkeys in Panama. *Jour. Mammalogy* 16:171–180, 1935.

41. CARPENTER, C. R. A field study in Siam of the behavior and social relations of the gibbon. *Comparative Psychology Monographs* Dec. 1940.

42. CARPENTER, C. R. Sexual behavior of free-ranging rhesus monkeys. *Jour. Comparative Psychology* 33:113–142, 1942.

43. CARPENTER, C. R. Societies of monkeys and apes. *Biological Symposia* 8:177–204, 1942.

44. CARPENTER, C. R. Territoriality. In Roe and Simpson (194).

45. CARPENTER, C. R. *Naturalistic Behavior of Nonhuman Primates.* University Park, Pa., Pennsylvania State Univ. Press, 1964.

46. CARR, ARCHIE. Navigation of the green turtle. *Scientific American* May 1965.

47. CARTHY, J. D. *Animal Navigation.* London, Allen & Unwin, 1956.

48. CARTHY, J. D., and F. J. EBLING, JR., editors. *The Natural History of Aggression.* New York and London, Academic Press, 1964.

49. COLE, SONIA. *The Prehistory of East Africa.* New York, Macmillan, 1963.

50. CONDER, P. J. Individual distance. *Ibis* 91:649–55, 1949.

51. DARLING, FRANK FRASER. *A Herd of Red Deer.* London and New York, Oxford Univ. Press, 1937.

52. DARLING, FRANK FRASER. *A Naturalist on Rona.* Oxford and New York, Clarendon Press, 1939.

53. DARLING, FRANK FRASER. Social behavior and survival. *Auk* 69:183–191, 1952.

54. DART, RAYMOND A. The predatory transition from ape to man. *International Anthropological and Linguistic Review* 1, 4, 1953.

55. DART, RAYMOND A., and DENNIS CRAIG. *Adventures with the Missing Link.* New York, Harper & Row, 1959.

56. DARWIN, CHARLES. *On the Origin of Species.* 1859. Reprinted Everyman's Library, London, Dent & Sons, 1956.

57. DARWIN, CHARLES. *The Descent of Man.* 1871. Revised edition London, Merrill and Baker, 1874.

58. DAVIS, D. E. Social nesting habits of the smooth-billed ani. *Auk* 57:179–218, 1940.

59. DAVIS, D. E. The phylogeny of gangs. In Bliss (23).

60. DE MONCHAUX, CECILY. Hostility in small groups. In Carthy and Ebling (48).

61. DE VORE, IRVEN, editor. *Primate Behavior.* New York, Holt, Rinehart and Winston, 1965.

62. DE WAR, J. M. Law of Territory. *British Birds* 14:89–90, 1920.

63. DOBZHANSKY, TH. Species after Darwin. In Barnett (13).

64. DOLLARD, JOHN, ET AL. *Frustration and Aggression.* New Haven, Conn., Yale Univ. Press, 1939. Reprinted 1961.

65. DUANE, T. D., and T. BEHRENDT. Extrasensory electroencephalographic induction between identical twins. *Science* 150:367 Oct. 15, 1965. Also Letters to the Editor, *Science* 150:1242–4, Dec. 3, 1965.

66. EIBL-EIBESFELDT, IRENÄUS. Fighting behavior in animals. *Scientific American* Dec. 1961.

67. EKLUND, CARL R. The Antarctic skua. *Scientific American* Feb. 1964.

68. ELLEFSON, JOHN O. Territorial behavior in the common white-handed gibbon. *Wenner-Gren Primate Social Behavior Symposium* 1965.

69. EMLEN, JOHN T., JR. Territories, nest-building and pair formation in the cliff swallow. *Auk* 71:16–35, 1954.

70. EVANS, HOWARD E. Predatory wasps. *Scientific American* Apr. 1963.

71. FISHER, JAMES. Evolution and bird sociality. In *Evolution as a Process,* ed. J. Huxley et al. London, Allen & Unwin, 1954.

72. FISHER, JAMES. Dispersal mechanisms in some birds. *Int. Ornithological Congress 1955,* 11:437–42.

73. FISHER, JAMES. Interspecific aggression. In Carthy and Ebling (48).

74. FISHER, R. A. *The Genetical Theory of Natural Selection.* Oxford, Clarendon Press, 1930. Reprinted New York, Dover, 1958.

75. FLEISCHER, R. L., ET AL. Fission-track dating of Bed One, Olduvai Gorge. *Science* 148:72–4, 1965.

76. FLETCHER, RONALD. *Instinct in Man.* New York, International Univ. Press, 1957.

77. FREEMAN, DEREK. Human aggression in anthropological perspective. In Carthy and Ebling (48).

78. FREUD, SIGMUND. *Totem and Taboo.* 1913. Reprinted London, Routledge & Kegan Paul, 1960.

79. FREUD, SIGMUND. *Beyond the Pleasure Principle.* 1920. Reprinted International Psychoanalytical Library. London, Hogarth Press, 1961.

80. FREUD, SIGMUND. *Civilization and Its Discontents.* 1930. Reprinted London, Hogarth Press, 1957.

81. FREUD, SIGMUND. *Outline of Psycho-Analysis.* 1940. Reprinted London, Hogarth Press, 1949.

82. FRISCH, J. E. Research on primate behavior in Japan. *American Anthropologist* 61:584–96, 1959.

83. FRYER, DOUGLAS H., ET AL. *General Psychology.* College Outline Series. New York, Barnes and Noble, 1963.

84. GANNON, R. A. The satin bowerbird. *Emu* 30:39–42, 1930.

85. GEORGE, WILMA. *Biologist Philosopher: A Study of the Life and Writings of Alfred Russel Wallace.* New York and London, Abelard-Schuman, 1964.

86. GERKING, SHELBY D. Restricted movement of fish populations. *Biological Rev.* 34:221–242, 1959.

87. GILLIARD, E. THOMAS. Evolution of bowerbirds. *Scientific American* Aug. 1963.

88. GOODALL, JANE. Feeding behavior of wild chimpanzees. *Symposium Zool. Soc. London,* 10:39–47, Aug. 1963.

89. GOODALL, JANE. My life among wild chimpanzees. *National Geographic* 124:272–308, Aug. 1963.

90. GOODALL, JANE. New discoveries among wild chimpanzees. *National Geographic* 128:802–31, Dec. 1965.

91. GORDON, KENNETH. Territory, behavior, and social dominance among Securidae. *Jour. Mammalogy* 17:171–2, 1936.

92. HALDANE, J. B. S. *The Causes of Evolution.* New York, Harper & Row, 1932.

93. HALL, K. R. L. Numerical data, maintenance activities, and locomotion of wild chacma baboon. *Proc. Zoological Soc. London* 139:181–220, 1962.

94. HALL, K. R. L. Sexual, agonistic and derived social behavior patterns of wild chacma baboon. *Proc. Zoological Soc. London* 139:283–327, 1962.

95. HALL, K. R. L., and I. DE VORE. Baboon social behavior. In DeVore (61).

96. HALL, K. R. L., Aggression in monkey and ape societies. In Carthy and Ebling (48).

97. HALL, K. R. L. Behavior of patas monkeys. *Folia Primatologica* 3:22–49, 1965.

98. HALLOWELL, A. IRVING. The structural and functional dimensions of human existence. *Quarterly Review Biol.* 31:88–101, 1956.

99. HALLOWELL, A. IRVING. Protocultural foundations of human adaptation. In Washburn (234).

100. HASLER, A. D., and W. J. WISBY. Discrimination by stream odor by fishes. . . . *American Naturalist* 85:223–238, 1951.

101. HASLER, A. D., and W. J. WISBY. Return of displaced large-mouthed bass and green sunfish to a home area. *Ecology* 39:289–293, 1958.

102. HEAPE, WALTER. *Emigration, Migration and Nomadism.* Cambridge, Heffer, 1931.

103. HEDIGER, H. *Studies of the Psychology and Behavior of Captive Animals in Zoos and Circuses.* London, Butterworth, 1955.

104. HEDIGER, H. Evolution of territorial behavior. In Washburn (234).

105. HILL, DENIS. Aggression and mental illness. In Carthy and Ebling (48).

106. HINDE, R. A. Biological significance of territories in birds (1956 symposium on territory in bird species). *Ibis* 98:340–69.

107. HOVLAND, C. I., and R. R. SEARS. Correlation of lynchings and economic indices. *Jour. Psychology* 9:301–10, 1940.

108. HOWARD, ELIOT. *Territory in Bird Life.* 1920. Reprinted New York, Atheneum, 1964.

109. HOWELL, F. C., and F. BOURLIÈRE, editors. *African Ecology and Human Evolution.* Chicago, Aldine, 1963.

110. HOYLE, F. Recent developments in cosmology. *Nature* 208:111–4, Oct. 9, 1965.

111. HUXLEY, JULIAN S. Courtship of the great-crested grebe. *Proc. Zoological Soc. London* 1914:491–562.

112. HUXLEY, JULIAN S. A natural experiment with the territorial instinct. *British Birds* 27:270–7, 1934.

113. HUXLEY, JULIAN S. *Evolution: The Modern Synthesis.* New York, Harper and Row, 1942.

114. HUXLEY, J. S., and J. FISHER. Introduction to Howard (108).

115. HUXLEY, J. S., and M. F. A. MONTAGU. Courtship and sexual life of birds. *Ibis* 1926:1–25.

116. HUXLEY, T. H., and J. S. HUXLEY. *Evolution and Ethics 1893–1943.* London, Pilot Press, 1947. Published in the United States as *Touchstone for Ethics.* New York, Harper & Row, 1947.

117. IMANISHI, K. Social behavior in Japanese monkeys. *Psychologia* 1:47–54, 1957.

118. IMANISHI, K. Social organization of subhuman primates. *Current Anthropology* 1:393–407, 1960.

119. JAMES, WILLIAM. The moral equivalent of war. 1910. In *Essays*

on Faith and Morals. Reprinted New York, Meridian, 1962.

120. JAY, PHYLLIS. Common langur of north India. In DeVore (61).

121. JENKINS, DALE W. Territory, despotism and social organization in geese. *Auk* 61:31–47, 1944.

122. JOHNSTON, F. E. Report on 34th annual meeting, American Assn of Physical Anthropologists. *Science* 149:1526, Sept. 24, 1965.

123. KEENLEYSIDE, M. H. A., and F. T. YAMAMOTO. Territorial behavior of juvenile Atlantic salmon. *Behavior* 19:139–168, 1962.

124. KEITH, ARTHUR. *Essays on Human Evolution.* London, Watts, 1946.

125. KEITH, ARTHUR. *A New Theory of Human Evolution.* New York, Philosophical Library, 1949.

126. KELLOGG, W. N. *Porpoises and Sonar.* Chicago, Univ. of Chicago Press, 1961.

127. KENYON, KARL W. Homing of the Laysan albatross. *Condor* 60:3–6, 1958.

128. KENYON, KARL W. Territorial behavior and homing in the Alaska fur seal. *Extrait de Mammalia* 24, 3, Sept. 1960.

129. KING, JOHN A. Social behavior . . . and population dynamics in a black-tailed prairie-dog town. *Contributions from the Laboratory of Vertebrate Biology,* Univ. Michigan 67:1–123, 1955.

130. KORTLANDT, ADRIAAN. *Aspects and Prospects of the Concept of Instinct.* Leyden, E. J. Brill, 1955.

131. KORTLANDT, ADRIAAN. Chimpanzees in the wild. *Scientific American,* May 1962.

132. KRAMER, GUSTAV. Bird orientation. *Ibis* 94:265–85, 1952.

133. KUMMER, H., and F. KURT. Social units of a free-living population of hamadryas baboons. *Folia Primatologica* 1:4–19, 1963.

134. LACK, DAVID L. Territory reviewed. *British Birds* 27:179–199, 1933.

135. LACK, DAVID L. *The Life of the Robin.* 1944. Reprinted Pelican Books, 1953.

136. LANCASTER, J. B., and R. B. LEE. Annual reproductive cycles in monkeys and apes. In DeVore (61).

137. LEAKEY, L. S. B. *Adam's Ancestors.* 4th ed., completely rewritten. London, Methuen, 1953.

138. LEAKEY, L. S. B. *Olduvai Gorge 1951–61.* Cambridge, Cambridge Univ. Press, 1965.

139. LEAKEY, L. S. B., and M. LEAKEY. Recent discoveries in Tanganyika. *Nature* 202:5–7, 1964.
140. LEAKEY, L. S. B., P. V. TOBIAS, and J. R. NAPIER. A new species of genus Homo from Olduvai Gorge. *Nature* 202:7–9, 1964.
141. LE GROS CLARK, W. E. *History of the Primates.* Chicago, Univ. of Chicago Press, 1957.
142. LIN, NORMAN. Territorial behavior in the cicada-killer wasp. *Behavior* 20:115–33, 1963.
143. LISSMAN, H. W. Function and evolution of electric organs in fish. *Jour. Experimental Biology* 35:156–191, 1958.
144. LORENZ, KONRAD Z. The companion in the bird's world. *Auk* 54:245–73, 1937.
145. LORENZ, KONRAD Z. The comparative method in studying innate behavior patterns. *Symposia Society Exp. Biology* 4:221–268, 1950.
146. LORENZ, KONRAD Z. *King Solomon's Ring.* New York, Crowell, 1952.
147. LORENZ, KONRAD Z. Ritualized fighting. In Carthy and Ebling (48).
148. MARAIS, EUGÈNE. *My Friends the Baboons.* London, Methuen, 1939.
149. MARAIS, EUGÈNE. *The Soul of the White Ant.* London, Methuen, 1939.
150. MARSHALL, A. J. *Bower-birds.* Oxford, Clarendon Press, 1954.
151. MASLOW, A. H. Instinctoid nature of basic needs. *Jour. Personality* 22:326–47, 1954.
152. MASLOW, A. H. Criteria for judging needs to be instinctoid. In *International Motivation Symposium,* ed. A. M. Jones, Univ. of Nebraska Press, 1964.
153. MASON, WILLIAM A. Sociability and social organization in monkeys and apes. In *Advances in Experimental Social Psychology,* vol. 1. London and New York, Academic Press, 1964.
154. MASON, WILLIAM A. Social organization of Callicebus moloch. *Tulane University Studies in Zoology* March 1966.
155. MATTHEWS, G. V. T. Experimental investigation of navigation in homing pigeons. *Jour. Exp. Biology* 28:508–36, 1951.
156. MATTHEWS, G. V. T. Relation of learning and memory to orientation of homing pigeons. *Behavior* 4:202–21, 1952.
157. MATTHEWS, G. V. T. Orientation of untrained pigeons. *Jour. Exp. Biology* 30:268–76, 1953.
158. MATTHEWS, G. V. T. Sun navigation in homing pigeons. *Jour. Exp. Biology* 30:243–267, 1953.
159. MATTHEWS, G. V. T. Navigation in the Manx shearwater. *Jour. Exp. Biology* 30:370–396, 1953.

160. MATTHEWS, HARRISON. Overt fighting in mammals. In Carthy and Ebling (48).

161. MAYR, ERNST. Bernard Altum and the territory theory. *Proc. Linnaean Society N.Y.* Nos. 45–46, 1933–4. Volume date Apr. 1935.

162. MAYR, ERNST, Behavior and systematics. In Roe & Simpson (194).

163. MAYR, ERNST. *Animal Species and Evolution.* Cambridge, Mass., Harvard Univ. Press (Belknap), 1963.

164. MC KELLAR, P. The emotion of anger and human aggressiveness. *British Jour. Psychology* 39:148–55, 1949.

165. MC RAE, DONALD G. Darwinism and the social sciences. In Barnett (13).

166. MEAD, MARGARET, and RUTH L. BUNZELL, eds. *The Golden Age of American Anthropology* New York, Braziller, 1960.

167. MILLER, LOYE. Territorial concept in the horned owl. *Condor* 32:290–1, 1930.

168. MILLER, N. E. The frustration-aggression hypothesis. *Psych. Review* 48:337–42, 1941.

169. MOFFAT, C. B. Spring rivalry of birds. *Irish Naturalist* 12:152–166, 1903.

170. MONTAGU, M. F. ASHLEY. *The Biosocial Nature of Man.* New York, Grove Press, 1956.

171. MONTAGU, M. F. ASHLEY. *Culture and the Evolution of Man.* New York, Oxford Univ. Press, 1962.

172. MONTAGU, M. F. ASHLEY. *The Humanization of Man.* Cleveland and New York, World, 1962.

173. MOWAT, FARLEY. *Never Cry Wolf.* Boston, Little Brown, 1963.

174. MURIE, O. J., and A. MURIE. Travels of Peromyscus. *Jour. Mammalogy* 12:200–9, 1931.

175. NAPIER, JOHN. Five steps to Man. *Discovery,* June 1964.

176. NICE, MARGARET MORSE. Studies in the life history of the song sparrow. *Trans. Linnaean Society N.Y.* 4:1–247, 1937.

177. NICE, MARGARET MORSE. Role of territoriality in bird-life. *American Midland Naturalist* 26:441–87, 1941.

178. NOBLE, G. K., ET AL. Mating behavior of lizards. *Annals N.Y. Acad. of Science* 35:25–100, 1933.

179. NOBLE, G. K. Experimenting with the courtship of lizards. *Natural History* 34:1–16, 1934.

180. NOBLE, G. K. Dominance in the life of birds. *Auk* 56:263–73, 1939.

181. OAKLEY, KENNETH P. Of man's use of fire, with comments on tool-making and hunting. In Washburn (234).

182. PEARSE, A. S. Habits of fiddler crabs. *Annual Report Smithsonian Inst.* 1913:415–28.

183. PEARSON, OLIVER P. Life history of mountain viscachas. *Jour. Mammalogy* 29:345–74, 1948.

184. PETTER, J.-J. *L'Écologie et L'Éthologie des Lémuriens Malgaches.* Mémoires du Muséum National d'Histoire Naturelle, Tome XXVII, Fascicule 1. Paris, 1962.

185. POULSEN, HOLGER. Inheritance and learning in the chaffinch. *Behavior* 3:216–227, 1951.

186. PRATT, J. G. Investigation of homing ability in pigeons without previous homing experience. *Jour. Experimental Biology* 32:70–83, 1955.

187. PRATT, J. G., and R. H. THOULESS. Homing orientation in pigeons in relation to opportunity to observe the sun. *Jour. Experimental Biology* 32:140–57, 1955.

188. REYNOLDS, V. Behavior and social organization of forest-living chimpanzees. *Folia Primatologica* 1:95–102, 1963.

189. RICE, D. W., and K. W. KENYON. Breeding distribution, history and populations of North Pacific albatrosses. *Auk* 79:365–86, 1962.

190. RICE, D. W., and K. W. KENYON. Breeding cycles and behavior of Laysan and black-footed albatrosses. *Auk* 79:517–567, 1962.

191. ROBERTS, BRIAN. Breeding behavior of penguins. *1940 British Grahamsland Exp. Scientific Report* 1:195–254.

192. ROBINSON, J. T. Adaptive radiation of australopithecines and the origin of man. In Howell and Bourlière (109).

193. ROBINSON, J. T. Homo habilis and the australopithecines. *Nature* 205:121–4, Jan. 9, 1965.

194. ROE, ANNE, and G. G. SIMPSON, editors. *Behavior and Evolution.* New Haven, Conn., Yale Univ. Press, 1958.

195. SAKOFF, A. N. *The Private Sector in Soviet Agriculture.* Monthly Bulletin of Agricultural Economics, FAO, Rome. 11, 9, 1962.

196. SCHALLER, GEORGE B. The orang-utan in Sarawak. *Zoologica* 46:73–82, 1961.

197. SCHALLER, GEORGE B. *The Mountain Gorilla; Ecology and Behavior.* Chicago, Univ. of Chicago Press, 1963.

198. SCHALLER, GEORGE B. *The Year of the Gorilla.* Chicago, Univ. of Chicago Press, 1964.

199. SCHMIDT, J. The breeding places of the eel. *Phil. Transactions Royal Soc. London* 211:179–208, 1922.

200. SCOTT, JOHN PAUL. *Aggression.* Chicago, Univ. of Chicago Press, 1958.

201. SCOTT, JOHN PAUL. Hostility and aggression in animals. In Bliss (23).

202. SCOTT, JOHN PAUL. On the evolution of fighting behavior: a review of Carthy and Ebling (48). *Science* 148:820–1, May 7, 1965.

203. SCOTT, JOHN W. Mating behavior of the sage grouse. *Auk* 59:477–98, 1942.

204. SEARS, R. R., ET AL. Some child-rearing antecedents of aggression. *Genet. Psych. Monographs* 47:135–234, 1953.

205. SELZER, MICHAEL. The other Israel. London, *Jewish Observer*, Dec. 13, 1963.

206. SILBERBAUER, GEORGE. *Bushman Survey First and Second Interim Reports.* Bechuanaland Secretariat, Mafeking, 1960, 1961.

207. SIMPSON, GEORGE GAYLORD. Mammals and land bridges. *Jour. Washington Acad. Science* 30:137–63, 1940.

208. SIMPSON, GEORGE GAYLORD. *Life of the Past.* New Haven, Conn., Yale Univ. Press, 1953. Reprinted 1961.

209. SIMPSON, GEORGE GAYLORD. *The Major Features of Evolution.* New York, Columbia Univ. Press, 1953.

210. SIMPSON, GEORGE GAYLORD. Behavior and evolution. In Roe and Simpson (194).

211. SLADEN, W. J. L. Behavior of Adélie and chin-strap penguins. *Int. Ornithological Congress* 11:241–7, 1955.

212. SMITH, C. F. A burrow of a pocket gopher. *Transactions Kansas Acad. Science* 51:313–5, 1947.

213. SMITH, G. ELLIOT. *The Evolution of Man.* London and New York, Oxford Univ. Press, 1924.

214. SOUTHWICK, CHARLES H. Patterns of intergroup social behavior in primates. *Annals N.Y. Acad. Science* 102:436–54, 1962.

215. SOUTHWICK, C. H., M. A. BEG, and M. R. SIDDIQI. Rhesus monkeys in north India. In DeVore (61).

216. SPENCER, HERBERT. *The Principles of Ethics,* vol. 1. 1892. London, Williams & Norgate, 1904.

217. STEWARD, JULIAN H. Economic and social basis of primitive bands. In *Essays in Anthropology Presented to A. L. Kroeber,* Berkeley, Univ. of California Press, 1936.

218. STORR, ANTHONY. Possible substitutes for war. In Carthy and Ebling (48).

219. SUMNER, WILLIAM GRAHAM. *Folkways.* 1906. Boston, Ginn, 1940.

220. SWANBERG, P. O. Territory in the thick-billed nutcracker. *Ibis* 98:412–9, 1956.

221. THORPE, W. H. *Learning and Instinct in Animals.* Cambridge, Mass., Harvard Univ. Press, 1956; revised and enlarged, 1963.

222. THORPE, W. H., and MYLES NORTH. Origin of the power of vocal imitation. *Nature* 208:219–222, 1965.

223. TINBERGEN, N. *The Study of Instinct.* Oxford: Clarendon Press, 1951.

224. TINBERGEN, N. *The Herring Gull's World.* London, Collins, 1953; revised ed., New York, Basic Books, 1961.

225. TINBERGEN, N. *Social Behaviour in Animals.* New York, Wiley, 1953.

226. TOBIAS, P. V. Early man in Africa. *Science:* 149:22–33, 1965.

227. TOBIAS, P. V., and J. T. ROBINSON The distinctiveness of Homo habilis. *Nature* 209:953–60, March 5, 1966.

228. TUCKER, D. W. A new solution to the Atlantic eel problem. *Nature* 183:495–501, 1959.

229. TURNER, E. L. Some notes on the ruff. *British Birds* 14:146–53, 1920.

230. VON HOLST, ERICH, and URSULA VON SAINT PAUL. Electrically controlled behavior. *Scientific American,* March 1962.

231. WALLACE, ALFRED RUSSEL. Origin of human races and the antiquity of man. . . . *Journal of the Anthropological Soc. London,* 1864:clviii.

232. WALLIS, D. I. Aggression in social insects. In Carthy and Ebling (48).

233. WALTERS, HARRY E. *Agriculture in the US and Soviet Union.* US Dept. of Agriculture (Econ. Research Service), Aug. 1963.

234. WASHBURN, S. L., editor. *The Social Life of Early Man.* New York, Wenner-Gren Foundation for Anthropological Research, 1961.

235. WASHBURN, S. L., and V. AVIS. Evolution of human behavior. In Roe and Simpson (194).

236. WASHBURN, S. L., and IRVEN DE VORE. Social life of baboons. *Scientific American,* June 1961.

237. WASHBURN, S. L., PHYLLIS JAY, and JANE LANCASTER. Field studies of Old World monkeys and apes. *Science* 150:1541–7, Dec. 17, 1965.

238. WATSON, J. B. Behaviorism. New York, Norton, 1924.

239. WEINER, J. S., ET AL. *Solution of the Piltdown Problem.* London, Bulletin, British Museum (Natural History), 1953.

240. WILLOCK, COLIN. Deer's friend with a gun. London *Observer,* Apr. 19, 1964.

241. WRIGHT, SEWALL. Evolution in Mendelian populations. *Genetics* 16:97–159, 1931.

242. WYNNE-EDWARDS, V. C. *Animal Dispersion in Relation to Social Behavior.* New York, Hafner, 1962.

BIBLIOGRAPHY

243. WYNNE-EDWARDS, V. C. Population control in animals. *Scientific American,* 211:68–74, Aug. 1964.
244. WYNNE-EDWARDS, V. C. Self-regulatory systems in populations of animals. *Science* 147:1543–48, 1965.
245. ZUCKERMAN, S. *The Social Life of Monkeys and Apes.* London, Routledge and Kegan Paul, 1932.

INDEX

Index